Travis L. Crosby is Professor Emeritus of History at Wheaton College, Massachusetts.

JOSEPH CHAMBERLAIN

A Most Radical Imperialist

Travis L. Crosby

I.B. TAURIS

LONDON · NEW YORK

New paperback edition published in 2018 by
I.B.Tauris & Co. Ltd
Reprinted by Bloomsbury Academic 2019
London • New York
www.ibtauris.com

First published in hardback in 2011 by I.B.Tauris & Co. Ltd

ISBN: 978 1 78831 393 3
eISBN: 978 1 78672 948 4
ePDF: 978 0 85771 950 8

A full CIP record for this book is available from the British Library
A full CIP record is available from the Library of Congress

Library of Congress Catalog Card Number: available

Printed and bound by CPI Group (UK) Ltd, Croydon, CR0 4YY

For Susan
Matt, Yuki, and Max
Tim, Molly, and Mira
Ian
Dan, Emily, Carter, and Katy

CONTENTS

ILLUSTRATIONS

Images are from the Chamberlain Collection at the Cadbury Research Library, University of Birmingham. They appear between pages 100 and 101.

ACKNOWLEDGEMENTS

The Chamberlain Papers at the University of Birmingham have been the most valuable source for this work. Containing both private and official correspondence, these papers reveal Chamberlain as family man, municipal politician, radical spokesman, parliamentary intriguer, ministerial aspirant, and ultimately an imperial leader on a global scale. Other useful archival sources include the Balfour, Bright, Dilke, Escott, Gladstone, and Hamilton papers in the British Library, and the Harcourt, Monk Bretton, Sanders, and Selborne papers at the New Bodleian Library in Oxford. The papers of W. C. Endicott (the father of Chamberlain's third wife) at the Massachusetts Historical Society in Boston were also consulted.

In addition to these primary sources, the following libraries hold important memoirs, biographies, autobiographies, monographs, scholarly articles, theses, and newspapers: the library of the University of Birmingham and the Central Library of the City of Birmingham in the United Kingdom; and the libraries of Amherst College, Smith College, the University of Massachusetts at Amherst, and Wheaton College (Massachusetts) in the United States. To the librarians and archivists at these institutions I am profoundly grateful, especially to Christine Penney and her staff in Special Collections at the University of Birmingham. I also offer a particular note of thanks to Wheaton College, not only to the staff of the Wallace Library but also to numerous faculty and administrators who have encouraged this project. I am especially grateful to Wheaton's conferral of the first Jane E. Ruby Professorship of Humanities and Social Science, which has allowed me time for research and writing. Thanks, too, for the work of Martin Killeen, Senior Librarian, Special Collections, Cadbury Research Library, University of Birmingham for granting permission to publish quotations from the Chamberlain Archives.

Friends and colleagues who have contributed directly to the improvement of the book by reading the manuscript in its entirety include Paul Helmreich, David Vogler, Gerald Zuriff, Hayden A. J. Bellenoit, and Chris Wickham. Conversations over several years in the most convivial atmosphere with Peter Marsh in Birmingham have clarified for me important issues in Chamberlain's life. Leslie Brubaker and Chris Wickham, whose hospitality and good cheer are boundless, also made me feel at home in Birmingham. Many thanks too, for the work of my editors at I.B.Tauris, Lester Crook and Joanna Godfrey. And not to be forgotten is the eagle-eyed Matthew Brown, copy-editor and project manager extraordinaire.

1

THE PURSUIT OF POWER

Joseph Chamberlain's personal life and political career have long fascinated historians and biographers. The most dynamic politician of late Victorian and early Edwardian Britain, he was the 'strong man' of every cabinet, commission, or committee in which he served. He built a political career based upon his indefatigable energy and forceful personality. As mayor of Birmingham, Member of Parliament, and cabinet minister in both Liberal and Conservative governments, Chamberlain pursued his policies relentlessly and often independently. As a public spokesman, he was rivalled only by William Gladstone in his prime. Rallying support in the countryside for his national political campaigns, he was a spirited and incisive platform speaker. In parliament, few could match his coolly dismissive and formidably logical debating style. His administrative and organizational skills in devising extra-parliamentary pressure groups were without parallel.

Chamberlain was also a man of striking contradictions and notable failures. Born into a striving middle-class family in metropolitan London, he made his name and fortune in provincial Birmingham. Lacking an extensive formal education, unschooled in the social graces, and widely condemned as a bully and a parvenu, Chamberlain was nonetheless an avid reader of French novels and a breeder of rare orchids. From the roistering ward politics of an industrial city, he rose to frequent the country houses and drawing rooms of the aristocratic elite. A bare-knuckled brawler and back-room intriguer in political life, he could be sentimental and romantic to a young woman whom he wooed as his third wife.

Dramatic changes of mind and opinion characterized his career. An outspoken organizer of progressive domestic programmes and political movements, Chamberlain eventually became the most eloquent defender of imperial Britain. Entering Gladstone's second cabinet in 1880 as a radical, he played an important role in breaking the Liberal government by opposing Irish Home Rule. Allied later with the Conservative ministries of both Salisbury and Balfour, he advocated a thoroughgoing tariff reform which split the Conservative and Unionist Party, ending its twenty years' parliamentary dominance.

It would be easy enough to write off Chamberlain as simply an opportunistic politician, a man without principles or loyalty who would shift and tack with the

prevailing winds. Indeed, his opponents so charged him. In addition to his reputation as a mutable politician, Chamberlain's personality seemed repellent to many. He
was determined to control events, to manage affairs, and to dominate others to the
extent of excluding the possibility of developing – at crucial times in his life – the
necessary political support to carry out his larger political schemes. Even his friends
noticed that Chamberlain's personality and behaviour seemed at odds with his own
stated goals. His matchless organizational skills were often offset by his arrogance
and demand for complete loyalty. His capacity for unstinting work and his brilliant
parliamentary performances were sometimes vitiated by an overstated aggression
directed toward his opponents in the House of Commons or in speeches in the countryside at large. His demands upon himself and others for accelerated performance
could be successful in the short run, but at the cost of flagging energy on the part of
his subordinates. Chamberlain's hard-driving, aggressive, and competitive behaviour
was summed up by the nickname given him – 'Pushful Joe'.

When Chamberlain could not control or manage successfully the circumstances of
his life, he was not one to retreat: he cut his losses, turned away from friends, and sought
more expansive outlets for his political ideas. Above all, he sought successively wider
opportunities to grasp and maintain power. As his one-time friend and political ally
John Morley put it: 'He loved power, the exercise of his will, having his own way.'[1] A
local Birmingham newspaper, in publishing a favourable sketch of Chamberlain shortly
after his appointment as Colonial Secretary in 1895, could not avoid mentioning a
widely held opinion: 'They say he thinks of nothing but personal power and is forever
seeking it.'[2] Even his more ardent supporters could not avoid noticing his 'aggressive
and daemonic energy' radiating 'an almost electric concentration of striking power'.[3]
Chamberlain himself was not unaware of his need for power. He once confessed that
he 'did not care a straw for office or position', but that he ultimately 'cared for power'.[4]

The need for power and control is, of course, not uncommon. Human beings
struggle for agency. To be master of one's fate, to manage and plan and ultimately to
succeed – if necessary over others – is probably a universal trait. The search for and
utilization of power is certainly characteristic of most political leaders. This is not
necessarily undesirable. Power can be understood as a kind of shared responsibility
between those who wield it and those over whom it is exercised in order to obtain
agreed-upon ends.

The most successful power brokers understand its limitations. A sensible recognition of the appropriate use of power is indispensable in the pursuit of political ends:
compromise and accommodation are essential. Chamberlain, however, was rarely
able to negotiate with others on issues both large and small. His determination to
push forward under full steam on public matters was legendary. In the intricate and
sensitive world of parliamentary deal-making, Chamberlain revealed a reluctance
to participate in the necessary give and take. His inflexible persistence occasionally
caused him to escalate his support for a policy on which he was consistently outvoted. Obdurate at crucial moments, he would baulk or obstruct. Any interference
with his intended and strongly stated aims could lead to anger and a disposition to
punish the offender as a means of restoring his sense of power.

Chamberlain's maladaptive behaviour has not gone unnoticed by historians. Indeed, many historians have characterized his public career as a failure. His legislative output has been described as 'almost pitiful'. His manner – 'cold and chilling' – and personality – 'difficult to unravel' – made him a prickly colleague and 'an implacable opponent'. One historian has called him 'ruthless' and 'authoritarian'.[5] The most recent biographer has noted the 'discontinuities' of Chamberlain's life, his 'destructive' approach to politics, and the 'succession of lost causes' which characterized his political crusades.[6] Although historians have thus sensed the importance of power to Chamberlain, this has often been noted as an incidental characteristic. The aim of this book is to place power at the centre of Chamberlain's private life and public behaviour.

The origins of Chamberlain's quest for power will never be known for a certainty. There are, however, some clues in his background and early life that are suggestive. He was deeply influenced by the nonconformist religion of his parents, by the entrepreneurial ideal of his father's business precepts, and to a lesser degree, by a prideful sense of his own masculinity.

Nonconformity shaped his earliest days. Nonconformist sects had been on the margins of society since the denial of their full civil and religious liberties in the seventeenth century. Marginality had not only radicalized nonconformists; it had also reinforced their determination to redress intolerable grievances. To keep their religion alive and vital, nonconformists created separate educational and religious networks in opposition to the established Church of England. Establishing bible study groups, religious book clubs, and Sunday Schools, nonconformists taught reading, writing, and some arithmetic.[7] Equally important, they taught discipline and a rigorous approach to the mastery of educational material.

Among nonconformists, the Unitarians were the most cohesive and outspoken. This was the chosen sect of the Chamberlain family. With its denial of the Trinity and the consequent rejection of the divinity of Christ, Unitarianism's no-nonsense body of beliefs was the religion of the rationalist. Unitarian families (and by extension Unitarian chapels) were close-knit, reformist-minded, and dedicated to propagating the virtues of acquisitiveness, self-help and independence. As John Seed has reminded us, a church is as real as a factory: religious institutions can have important secular consequences. Chapel meetings were not only religious in intent: they also operated as a nexus of power relations. When families, municipal officials, and business interests came together on Sundays to worship in their spare Unitarian creed, they also met to reaffirm their local preeminence in secular matters.[8] It was not surprising, therefore, that Chamberlain – influenced by his nonconformist background – would have been opposed to the established Anglican elite and to have been predisposed as well to fight against privileged social and political circles.

Even more important as an influence upon the development of Chamberlain's character was his family's business. As the first industrialist to gain notable parliamentary prominence and high political office, Chamberlain carried the 'cinder and soot' of the industrial workplace with him all his days.[9] He followed the tradition of his forebears, who had been small businessmen: maltsters, confectioners, clockmakers, brewers, and provisions merchants among them. From these humble beginnings, Chamberlain's grandfather by the nineteenth century had become the manager of a prosperous cordwaining (shoe manufacturing) company. This firm laid the foundation of Chamberlain's own enterprise and wealth.

The Chamberlains were not unlike thousands of other successful entrepreneurs who made their way during the Industrial Revolution. Entrepreneurs, as dynamic business leaders, had encouraged innovation, organized the resources of production, spurred the marketing and sales of business organizations, and borne the necessary risks. Through their energetic efforts they were significant engines for economic development.[10] Such intensive and competitive work – requiring self-reliance, long working hours, and delayed marriages – not only required but also could shape a distinctive personality type. Theodore Koditschek reveals the importance of an 'entrepreneurial personality-structure' in industrializing Bradford (eventually to become a centre of the worsted trade).[11] To survive in a restless and unstructured economic environment, young men who poured into Bradford hoping to make their mark in the thriving textile mills needed not only a high tolerance for risk, but also an unceasing commitment to 'disciplined labor and rigid self control'.[12] Indeed, failure could be avoided only 'by husbanding all one's material and psychological resources'.[13] Other historians have discovered a distinctive personality type emerging among the businessmen of the Industrial Revolution. Crouzet speaks of 'the complete businessman', who embodied a number of roles: capitalist, works manager, and merchant. At every point during the production process, the new businessman intervened, including the recruitment, training, and disciplining of his labour force. Someone of this sort would likely be, as Coleman has pointed out, a man of boundless energy and dictatorial in his management. W. J. Reader adds another dimension to the new businessman – his search for power to develop his businesses along any route he chose.[14] Chamberlain was a fair representative of the businessman that these historians have portrayed.

But it is unlikely that Chamberlain was moved merely by the accumulation of wealth in the pursuit of a business career. Non-economic reasons can motivate entrepreneurs as much as, or more than, money-making. The British economist, Alfred Marshall, put it thus: 'business work' offers a broad scope 'for the exercise of men's faculties, and for their instincts of emulation and power'. Such men may be stimulated 'much more by a hope of victory over … rivals than by the desire to add' to their fortunes.[15] The influential economic thinker Joseph Shumpeter agreed. He postulated an atavistic will to power as the dominant motive among entrepreneurs. As he describes it, entrepreneurial activity is defined by 'the will to found a private kingdom' and 'the will to conquer: the impulse to fight, to prove oneself superior to others, to succeed for the sake, not of the fruits of success, but of success itself'. What may seem to be economic behaviour only 'becomes akin to sport', not unlike a race or a boxing match.[16]

Thus, it can be argued that Chamberlain acted as an entrepreneur only in part because he sought wealth and a measure of success. He also had a felt need for dominance and power. Chamberlain's compelling personal traits were evident not only in the business world, but also in his private life and in his public career as a politician. For in politics, too, Chamberlain acted 'entrepreneurially' – that is, he was concerned with issues of control and power. As in the business world, the power motive among politicians includes such attributes as dominance, control, influence, or aggression.

At its simplest, the power motive is related to a person's need, capacity, and determination to affect or influence the behaviour or feelings of others.[17] Characteristic actions of individuals with a need for power include a concern for visibility and a strong desire to secure public attention. Building organizations to elevate oneself into positions of power; instigating followers to unusual levels of personal service; and manipulating and controlling one's personal and public environments are examples.[18] There is also some evidence that individuals whose dominant motive and incentive is the drive for power tend to manifest risk-taking behaviour.[19]

To Chamberlain's aggressive personality and his drive for power, there is an additional characteristic that was often expressed in both his public and private lives – his belief in the efficacy of 'manliness'. The importance of manliness in Victorian culture has been thoroughly examined by historians. Davidoff and Hall observe that the 'masculine persona' was widely acknowledged as at the heart of Victorian middle-class culture. Women, portrayed by contrast as relatively frail and helpless in the face of a masculine productive potency, would further enhance a notion of manliness. Thus, a man's determination and skill in shaping the economic environment gave him pride of place in the middle-class home as well as at work. The manipulation of power and opinion were the sole province of men in both family and factory.[20] John Tosh confirms Davidoff and Hall's notion that there were no necessary 'separate spheres' dividing men and women into domestic and workplace areas of activity and responsibility. Indeed, Tosh maintains that the Victorian home was central to the concept of masculinity. In the domestic sphere, men governed as they did outside it: ruling it, protecting it, providing for it, and controlling it.[21] As we shall see, Chamberlain governed his own household as he attempted to govern in public life.

Like the men of his time, Chamberlain revelled in his masculinity. He valued hardiness and courage. Lithe and sinewy throughout his life, Chamberlain radiated a palpable resilience and vigour. His strenuous holidays, prideful demeanour, and aggressive behaviour all contributed to a sense of himself as strong and vigorous. His bravado and often exaggerated sense of his own masculinity peppered his social and informal discourse, and occasionally crept into his official remarks as well. Even such sensitive documents as diplomatic dispatches became in Chamberlain's hands weapons against a potential foe – as though he intended to challenge an enemy in hand-to-hand combat. Chamberlain never shrank from a fight and often enough tried to provoke one.

If Chamberlain did not leave behind a lengthy list of legislative achievements, he nevertheless made substantial contributions to late nineteenth-century and early twentieth-century British politics. After all, such a personality was not without its strengths. Never doubting, supremely confident, and wholly committed to a life in politics, he made his mark. As a municipal activist, he led Birmingham to the forefront of Victorian cities in his social and educational reforms. He was a pragmatic man of action and has been called the first professional politician. He revelled in the democratic process and was an undoubted pioneer of modern electioneering. His popularity and influence outside the halls of Westminster made him a household name. Endowed with a strong social conscience, he had above all a passion for the well-being of working people. Indeed, his ego, his personality, his oratorical skills and his love and craving for mass adulation, coupled with his understanding of the needs of the working classes, were consistent themes in a contradictory life. The result was a man who became in truth the recognizable prototype of the modern political populist – someone who understood how to create and manipulate the newly democratic electorate for both personal and public ends.

2

AN ENTREPRENEURIAL HERITAGE

The lives of Joseph Chamberlain's ancestors are stories of upward mobility. His great-grandfather, William, established a shoemaking business in the City of London in the mid-eighteenth century.[1] In time, William became Master of the Company of Cordwainers, setting a precedent for successive generations of the family who followed the trade and served as officers in the Company. Joseph Chamberlain's grandfather (Joseph the elder) extended the family's industrial heritage by marrying in turn two daughters of the Strutt family. Their uncle, Jedediah Strutt, was partner to Richard Arkwright: both men were giants of the Industrial Revolution.

Joseph the elder brought his two sons, Richard and Joseph (Joseph senior, our subject's father), into the family firm in the 1820s. Demonstrating an admirable aptitude for business, Joseph senior in time became the dominant partner. In 1834, Joseph senior married Caroline Harben, whose family background was also rooted in the solid and respectable business class of London: her father had been a brewer at Mile End, and later a cheesemonger in Whitechapel. As a sign of his modest prosperity and the strength of the family business, Joseph bought in the year of his marriage a solidly built three-story late Georgian house near the top of a hill in Camberwell. At that time Camberwell was a pleasant village south of the Thames, only four miles from St Paul's Cathedral, whose great dome was within sight. On clear days, the heights of Hampstead could be seen in the distance. Coach and omnibus connections between Camberwell and the City gave the Chamberlain home an added advantage of a convenient route to the business.

In this house, Joseph Chamberlain was born on 8 July 1836. The first of eight children, he received his early schooling and religious training in Camberwell. In 1845 the growing family moved north of the Thames into larger accommodations at 25 Highbury Place in Islington. Also sited on a hill, the new house was in a substantial Regency row with rural views to the north and toward the City in the south. Spacious rooms, an enclosed garden, and added attractions such as built-in bookcases and a china closet made a significant impression upon the young Joseph. When he built his own grand house in Birmingham decades later, he named it Highbury.[2]

Joseph's formal learning began when he was eight years old at a dame school near the Chamberlain house in Camberwell. After the move to Islington, he enrolled in a school managed by the Rev. Arthur Johnson, an Anglican clergyman. Here Joseph remained from the age of 10 to 14. He then attended the Benthamite University College School in Gower Street, a leading public school for dissenters. The school was one of the first in England to include natural science in its curriculum. Its headmaster, Thomas Hewit Key, well versed in medicine, was also an eminent Latinist and an accomplished mathematician. Key's progressive tendencies were revealed in his support for both the Reform Bill of 1832 and the abolition of the Corn Laws in 1846. At Gower Street, Joseph excelled, winning prizes in mathematics, French, Latin, and hydrostatics. During school vacations he made use of the cultural attractions of London, especially scientific exhibitions and lectures on chemistry and electricity. After two years at Gower Street, Chamberlain began work in the family firm at Milk Street. From the ages of 16 to 18, Joseph not only learned shoe-making by working alongside his father's employees, he was also apprenticed to the accounting office.

Joseph's apprenticeship in his father's firm was not unusual for the time. It was common among the middle class to train eldest sons for the eventual ownership of family firms.[3] Keeping the management of the firm within the family was a self-conscious entrepreneurial strategy and offered several distinct advantages. In an era of largely unregulated business practices, the loyalty and trust inherent in family-owned firms could reduce transaction costs and smooth the way for more efficient management. Costs could also be minimized by employing family members. In addition, family financial support could provide needed capital in times of expansion or crisis.

This amalgamation of family and business more than likely also had a psychological impact. The continual contractual negotiations between father and son within the framework of the family firm gave an affective charge to their relationship absent in non-familial business settings. Sons in training from their fathers learned not only economic lessons. Fathers also monitored personal behaviour within a business setting. The notions of controlling outcomes, managing variable markets, and exerting the requisite competitive power became inextricably mixed with family values. It is not too much to suggest that such parents (primarily fathers) would continuously place high expectations on their children (primarily sons), and reward aggressive and competitive behaviour. The entrepreneurial ideal was thus stamped indelibly upon rising sons.

That Joseph had earned his father's trust through diligence and discipline was clearly in evidence when he was sent at the age of 18 to his uncle, John Sutton Nettlefold, in Birmingham. For some years Nettlefold had operated an old-fashioned factory producing handmade blunt-ended wood screws. Nettlefold had convinced his brother-in-law, Joseph senior, to share in a recapitalization project that would enable the Birmingham firm to mass-produce a new type of screw with a pointed end which entered wood directly without the need of a pre-bored hole. Joseph senior's loan of £10,000 made possible the construction of a large factory with the capacity for making the most advanced wood screws in Britain. Strategically placed alongside a canal that ran westward toward the London and Northwestern Railway, the new firm of Nettlefold and Chamberlain shrewdly integrated marketing and distribution as well as production in its siting and construction.

When Joseph left London for the West Midlands by train in the autumn of 1854, however, he faced an uncertain future. His father's new venture was an entrepreneurial risk. Apart from the substantial capital outlay, maintenance of the new machines would be costly and the market unpredictable at the outset. Chamberlain's arrival in Birmingham was fortuitously timed however – just prior to the great mid-Victorian economic boom, which launched a vigorous period of economic growth and prosperity.

Birmingham's place in the economic development of the nineteenth century has been well chronicled. By the time of Joseph's arrival, Birmingham was already the third largest English borough after Liverpool and Manchester. Neither a one-industry town nor a centre of heavy manufacturing, Birmingham in the early nineteenth century teemed with smaller enterprises: jewellery making; goldsmithing; and the manufacturing of buttons, coins, medals, and products of brass and wire such as pins and nails. Even the production of larger goods was often contracted out to artisan-managed small workshops. The Galtons, a Quaker gun-making family firm, for example, traditionally employed specialists at every stage of production and assembly. Small boys acted as the conveyor belts between the various shops as each gun took shape.[4] By the 1860s, however, the introduction from America of interchangeable parts manufactured on automatic machines revolutionized gun-making in Birmingham: other businesses followed suit. The story of Joseph Gillott's firm is typical. From the attic of his modest home, Gillott began hand-pressing steel pen nibs in the 1820s. In the next three decades, his business throve, as did other Birmingham pen manufacturers. By the early 1870s, Gillott's, with a labour force of 450, turned out upwards of five tons of pens weekly.[5] These two firms were emblematic of broader changes in Birmingham and the West Midlands as the consolidation of production into factories began to displace the small workshop system.[6]

That Nettlefold and Chamberlain prospered in the new economic environment was not merely a product of market forces. The vitality of the firm over the years also owed much to Joseph's orderly, disciplined, and occasionally ruthless business practices. Over time, he and his cousin Joseph Nettlefold drew into their own hands the day-to-day conduct of the business. The younger Nettlefold, a mechanical engineer, supervised the production end while Chamberlain managed the commercial and marketing side. As the firm prospered, it expanded. In 1864, on Chamberlain's initiative, the firm purchased a wire-making factory adjacent to its own works. Lower production costs led to a price war, ultimately forcing its two main rivals to sell out. By the late 1860s, Nettlefold and Chamberlain had established a virtual monopoly in wood screw production in Birmingham. Chamberlain was also instrumental in designing new products. Nuts and bolts, hooks and eyes, and such specialty items as revolving centres for chairs and piano stools were added to the production schedule. With the growth in diversity of products, Chamberlain initiated a detailed price list, illustrated with accurate drawings and revised month by month. Responsibility for pricing new products made Chamberlain the firm's de facto accountant as well as its commercial head.

As the firm continued to grow, so too did Chamberlain's talent for extending his influence for the benefit of the firm. He became a leading member of the board of directors of Lloyd's Bank of Birmingham, increasing the visibility of Nettlefold and Chamberlain in the eyes of the financial community. He was adept at negotiating favourable contracts with domestic haulers, winning special rates for the shipment of goods from railway companies. Watchful of every opportunity to increase sales, he took along his order book even on holiday. In fact, foreign travel taught him market differences: French customers preferred blue wrapping paper along with their wood screws; the Scots opted for green.[7] Determined to expand sales abroad, Chamberlain time and again demonstrated his persistent negotiating strategies. In spite of strict tariff policies implemented by the United States, for example, he was often able to conclude a substantial sales transaction. And when German troops laid siege to Paris during the Franco-Prussian War, interrupting trade between the large screw manufacturer Jappy Freres and its customers, the firm increased production as Chamberlain himself worked to add customers in France. As Marsh notes without exaggeration, Chamberlain and his partner tackled their business with 'unceasing enterprise'.[8] By the 1870s, Nettlefold and Chamberlain employed more than 2,500 workers and was one of the largest businesses in the city.

By his mid-30s, Chamberlain's energy, sense of practical innovation, appetite for risk, and flair for organization had marked him as a successful entrepreneur in the business world. Yet his behaviour was clearly motivated not only by profit: he was also determined to crush his competitors and to sustain and expand the emerging sense of personal power that his business career had begun to engender. No better example can be cited than his decision in 1870 to beat a potential competitor into the dust. During that year, Chamberlain learned of the formation of a new firm, the Birmingham Screw Company, which planned to construct its mill directly across the canal from Nettlefold and Chamberlain. This was, for Chamberlain, a flagrant challenge. 'We have to smash the new Company', he wrote to his partner. As Chamberlain admitted, money was not the issue. Should the new company succeed, Nettlefold and Chamberlain would no longer be the 'Screw Kings'. It was, therefore, necessary to play 'the bold game'. Plunging deeply into every detail about the proposed new company, he devised a variety of diabolical[9] tactics to torpedo the project. He bought out a local patent file factory to prevent its purchase by the new firm; threatened his own workmen to prevent their leaving for the new company; and let it be known publicly that Nettlefold and Chamberlain would slash prices at the very moment when the new factory would be financially vulnerable. It was clearly a strategy, as Marsh has noted, based upon considerations of power rather than wealth.[10]

During the years when he was building the firm, Chamberlain was also establishing himself in Birmingham society and political circles. As a Unitarian, he joined the Church of the Messiah, a congregation consisting largely of businessmen and their families, including the Nettlefolds. The Church provided an ideal network in

Birmingham, whose large Unitarian population was influential in the city.[11] As one might expect, Chamberlain was no passive church member. He took an active role in teaching Sunday school: his subjects were literature, history, French, and arithmetic. He served as the first president of the Church's Sunday School Mutual Improvement Society. On Tuesday evenings, he taught history to teenage boys in classes organized by the Church. Chamberlain was also active in a number of other organizations unrelated to his Church. Among these was the Edgbaston Debating Society, made up of young professionals and businessmen who regularly discussed topics of historical and political interest at their frequent meetings. The Debating Society saw itself as a 'training school' in which 'the intellectual athlete' prepared himself for the vigorous and difficult 'conflicts of later life'.[12] Chamberlain eventually served in all offices of the Society. He was also active in organizing workers' clubs for his employees. He began their Working Men's Institute, established a debating club, founded their Benefit Club, and once even took charge of their Rifle Club.

In each of these endeavours, Chamberlain brought a characteristic restless energy.[13] But it was neither a frenetic nor a disorganized energy. Chamberlain was, as Garvin has noted, the soul of meticulous method. As a member of the Debating Society, he compiled, numbered, and indexed a collection of anecdotes that could be used by contending debaters. In teaching literature at Sunday School, he devised an abstract of great literary figures of the past, Chaucer and Milton among them. For his history class, he made a complete synopsis of events from Caesar to King George II.

In spite of his capacity for hard work and his aggressively competitive disposition, Chamberlain could on occasion enjoy extended holidays and lengthy intervals of relaxation. Throughout his life, he was an avid continental traveller. In one of his earliest surviving letters, he wrote his mother about the diversions of mountaineering while in Switzerland in August 1857. Walking nine strenuous hours for six days and crossing three 'rather slippery' glaciers, he felt 'not the least tired'.[14] His only problem was a blister on one foot which he treated with a corn plaster. Three summers later, he had an altogether different holiday in Switzerland. Insisting on climbing the Breithorn in spite of bad weather, he had to be taken down by guides. During the trek, he suffered frostbite. Describing his swollen face and lips – 'my lips' 10 times (probably 20) their usual size and covered with breakings out' – Chamberlain tried to make light of his misadventure. He reported that the skin of his face and neck was peeling off 'like a very thin brown paper' and that the new skin was 'very red and tender'. But in a more jocular vein, he noted that the new skin seemed to be favoured 'as a delightful recreation ground by juvenile flies'.[15]

In that same summer of 1860, Chamberlain had more engaging news for his mother. After his recovery from the mountaineering holiday, he proposed marriage to Harriet Kenrick, a young woman whom he had first met at the Church of the Messiah. Her father, Archibald Kenrick, was a prominent businessman and her brother, William, a member of the Debating Society. Harriet's ready acceptance, however, seems to have caught him by surprise. In a curiously muted letter, Chamberlain begged his mother not to disclose the news because he found it 'impossible to say what I feel and think'.[16]

Chamberlain's hesitancy was in time to pass, as he gradually warmed to 'Harrie'. But it is difficult to avoid the impression that Chamberlain may have regarded his proposed marriage to Harriet, at least initially, as a convenient arrangement to ease the way for a merger of two family enterprises. The Kenricks, nevertheless, were clearly pleased with the match. Harriet's father settled on her a £4,000 mortgage and £800 in railway stock at the time of their marriage in July 1861. After a honeymoon in Cornwall, the couple moved into a house on Harborne Road. In less than a year, their first child, Beatrice, was born. Meanwhile the Chamberlain–Kenrick family alliance was consolidated with the marriage of Chamberlain's sister, Mary, to Harriet's brother, William. Joseph the elder, Chamberlain's father, added to the family presence by selling out his London enterprises and moving to Birmingham to take a more active role in the wood screw business. In these years Chamberlain's stature in the community continued to rise: he was elected president of the Debating Society; placed in charge of the accounts of the Church of the Messiah; and elected to the council of the Birmingham Chamber of Commerce. Within a relatively short time, the young entrepreneur had rapidly scaled the heights of wealth, respectability, and connection thus assuring him of a significant role in the life of the city.

In October, 1863, however, disaster struck the family. After giving birth to their son, Austen, Harriet contracted what was then called puerperal fever and within five days was dead. Almost immediately after Harriet's death, Chamberlain and his two children moved into the home of Harriet's parents where Beatrice and Austen could be cared for. For years afterward 'that great and terrible loss' was constantly on Chamberlain's mind. Harriet's death left him with 'a sense of insecurity and ... dread' about himself and his young children.[17] His initial tendency was to withdraw: he resigned from the Chamber of Commerce and became irregular in his attendance at the Debating Society. His most effective coping strategy, however, was to apply himself even more vigorously to his business. As he wrote to a close friend in 1867: 'I work at a lot of things without much serious interest in any.'[18]

Perhaps it was this paradoxical mood of both detachment and intensity that made him receptive to an initiative in early 1867 brought forward by George Dixon, the newly elected mayor of Birmingham and a future member of parliament. Dixon, a senior partner in a merchant firm, was concerned with the poor state of elementary education in Birmingham. Inadequate schooling would, he believed, create an uneducated and illiterate workforce, ultimately affecting productivity and profits.[19] Dixon's reflections were part of a national discourse begun in 1866 during parliamentary debates on a proposed franchise reform bill to expand the working-class vote in urban areas. Critics of the bill questioned the fitness of workers to vote. Even after Benjamin Disraeli's Conservative ministry passed the bill in 1867, doubts remained among middle-class citizens about the qualifications of an uneducated electorate.

In a series of meetings throughout 1867 and 1868 Birmingham civic leaders debated the state of national education. By early 1869 sentiment had crystallized. Following up on a suggestion by Jesse Collings,[20] Chamberlain drafted a memorandum that became the foundation of the National Education League. In a direct challenge to the Church of England's traditional responsibility for the education (and indoctrination) of elementary school children, the League became a national non-conformist crusade, determined to establish free, compulsory, non-sectarian, locally managed schools throughout the country.

Although national in scope, the League was led by Birmingham businessmen. Initially funded by J. H. Nettlefold in partnership with the Kenrick and Chamberlain families, the League's officers included Dixon as president, Collings as Secretary, and Chamberlain as chair of the executive committee in charge of management. The League quickly struck a popular chord in the nation at large. Within three months, the League had received pledges of £60,000; enrolled 5,000 members (including 40 MPs and several hundred ministers of religion); and established a hundred branches throughout the country.

The formation of the League was timely. William Gladstone's reforming first ministry, which replaced Disraeli's short-lived government in December 1868, had begun a review of education under the supervision of W. E. Forster.[21] Seizing its opportunity, the League attempted by direct action to persuade the government to adopt its programme. After many months of consideration and consultation, including a meeting between Gladstone and a deputation of the League – with Chamberlain in attendance – Forster's Education Act of 1870 was passed. Although the Act can now be seen as an important step in the direction of state responsibility for educating children, it also subverted the aim and function of the National Education League. Rather than providing for a unified, national, and non-sectarian system, the Act allowed the continuation of denominational schools teaching their own religious doctrines. The Act also provided for financial assistance to build more denominational (primarily Anglican) schools. In addition, the Act authorized local governing bodies to create School Boards with the power to establish schools financed by the municipal rates. In heavily Anglican communities, this proviso tended to increase the opportunities for a more extensive dissemination of Church of England doctrines among school children. What began as a campaign for improving the productivity of the workforce and instructing the working class in good citizenship had become a conflict over religion in the schools, a conflict which the League had apparently lost.

Chamberlain was not discouraged, however. In his first encounter with the cross-currents of national politics, he displayed the personal qualities that were so much in evidence in his later public life. Breathing aggressiveness (in Garvin's words), he energetically fought back.[22] Even before the bill had reached its final reading in the Commons, Chamberlain had threatened his opponents, especially Forster.[23] Once the bill became law, Chamberlain, from his position on the executive council of the League, organized a strenuous campaign against the Education Act. Not only were additional funds raised: at the instigation of Chamberlain the League decided to take direct action at both parliamentary and municipal elections. Liberal candidates were asked to pledge themselves to the League's goals. To implement his electoral strategy, Chamberlain instructed the salaried agents of the League as they travelled throughout the country to gather political intelligence. Within short order, he had amassed sufficient urban constituency information to rival that of both the Liberal and Conservative Party whips.[24]

To complement his national campaign against the Education Act, Chamberlain launched a scheme to encourage the creation of local school boards throughout the country. The boards would then use their authority to implement the aims of the National Education League. The plan, however, encountered difficulty when the League's Liberal candidates unexpectedly lost the majority to conservative Anglicans in the first Birmingham school board elections. Chamberlain reacted characteristically: he redoubled his efforts. As one of the successful board candidates, he took an active role in the debates as they raged during the early 1870s.[25]

Chamberlain soon broadened his platform beyond educational issues. Using the League's *Monthly Paper* as a mouthpiece, he began to publish criticisms of social and political privileges enjoyed by the governing elite. He spoke of the need to bridge the gap between rich and poor. He welcomed the formation of Joseph Arch's Agricultural Labourer's Union. He supported the aims of organized labour. He applauded the newly formed French Republic and its advanced republican ideals. His most important early statement of an evolving radicalism was given in his speech at Birmingham's Temperance Hall in February 1872. Here, he advocated a tripartite programme. First, he argued for free schools, essentially the agenda of the National Education League. Second, he spoke for a free church – the disestablishment and disendowment of the Church of England. Third, and most radical of all, was his call for free land to ease the transfer of small properties, especially in rural England.[26]

With this speech, Chamberlain's radicalism assumed a coherent programmatic form. He could now be classed as one of a growing number of middle-class radicals who had begun to achieve political visibility. Advocating a practical reformist agenda, middle-class radicals tackled the so-called 'land monopoly' by supporting free trade, both abroad and at home; promoting the disestablishment of the state churches within the kingdom; and favouring nationalist movements in Europe. Middle-class radicals drew their strength largely from nonconformists led by manufacturers such as Richard Cobden and John Bright; and from the philosophic radicals such as John Stuart Mill. These middle-class radicals were distinct from the working-class popular radical movement, which historically had advocated the egalitarian and anti-establishment views of Tom Paine's *Rights of Man*. Popular radicalism's most substantial success had been the Chartist movement of the 1840s. Although Chartism had receded after 1848, popular radical traditions remained active in the countryside.[27]

Chamberlain was not unaware of the potential political strength of both middle-class and popular radicalism: only organization was needed to bring together its diverse strands. From the time of his Temperance Hall speech, Chamberlain's cultivation of the newspaper press and leading public journals was designed to provide the means for such a task. Among his earliest supporters was his friend and former Debating Society companion, J. T. Bunce, who was now editor of the *Birmingham Post*. Bunce not only used his editorial position to further Chamberlain's ideas in his newspaper: he also served from time to time as personal editor to Chamberlain.[28] Chamberlain also courted John Morley, editor of the *Fortnightly Review* and a philosophic radical who had been much influenced by Mill.[29]

As Chamberlain confided to Morley in mid-1873, a radical approach to politics must extend beyond the education question, which was too narrow 'to make it the sole fighting issue'. 'Education for the ignorant', he wrote, 'cannot have the meaning that belonged to Bread for the starving'. A new organization 'on a wider basis' would be the best avenue to capturing broad support for the emerging radical agenda.[30] Chamberlain's strategy seems to have been two-fold. First, he would build up a substantial grass roots radical movement in the countryside. Second, he would establish an efficient political machine to translate the movement into an active and involved electorate who would eventually guarantee a majority in parliament. In September, 1873, Chamberlain outlined in the *Fortnightly Review* his most comprehensive plan of action to date. Attacking the record of Gladstone's Liberal government, he charged it with a lack of sympathy for the poor. The government, he claimed, had become the ally of wealthy landowners and millionaire manufacturers whose sole purpose was to keep things as they were. Something must be done for that 'vast population, whose homes would disgrace a barbarous country, whose lack of culture and education leaves them a prey to merely animal instincts, and who find it difficult ... to procure the barest necessaries of life'.[31] Building on his Temperance Hall speech of the previous year, he now offered a fourth plank to the emerging radical platform – free labour, a reference to the 1871 Criminal Law Amendment Act which restricted the right to picket. The working class ought to have, Chamberlain declared, full liberty of association and organization. The 'Four Freedoms' became Chamberlain's catchy slogan.

Apart from his articulation of the radical platform during the early 1870s, Chamberlain was also beginning to build his local power base. He became a member of the Birmingham school board, the town council (to which he had been elected in 1869), and in 1873 he served the first of his three terms as mayor of Birmingham. He had begun to demonstrate his capacity to initiate and manage complex organizations for political purposes. In so doing, he showed an authoritarian management style, most particularly in evidence during the operation of the National Education League.[32] In addition, Chamberlain was beginning to master the art of public speaking at both large and small gatherings. It was time for him to make a decisive political move that would propel him onto the national political stage.

The opportunity came during the Sheffield election campaign of 1873–4. Invited by a reform association to stand for parliament at the next general election, Chamberlain made several trips to that city. Seeking common ground among the working class and nonconformists, he was especially vigorous in upholding the rights of trade unions. While campaigning for the anticipated vacant seat in Sheffield, however, Chamberlain made an apparent tactical error: he also decided to stand once again for both the Birmingham School Board and the town council elections in the autumn of 1873. Successful in the Birmingham elections, he simultaneously became chair of the school board and mayor of the city.

Fully engaged in the work of Birmingham local government and unable to find the time to grapple effectively with the crosscurrents of the Sheffield electorate, he could not conduct a thorough campaign. His radical platform may also have told against him, as a nationwide conservative backlash in response to the failures of Gladstone's ministry brought in Disraeli's government at the general election of February 1874. Chamberlain finished third in field of four for Sheffield's two parliamentary seats. Confiding to Collings afterwards, he admitted that he was 'vexed' by the result and did not like 'being beaten'.[33] Failure to gain this parliamentary seat dashed Chamberlain's rising political ambitions for the time being. Or so it seemed. In fact, Chamberlain soon entered perhaps the most productive phase of his political career.

3

THE RADICAL POLITICIAN

Chamberlain's defeat in Sheffield had an immediate impact upon his partnership at Nettlefold and Chamberlain. It brought him to a crossroads as his increasing interest and participation in politics began to overshadow his business concerns. The game of business, which he had effectively won, seemed tame when compared to the stimulating challenges and struggles of political life. The surge of power that Chamberlain had experienced during electoral contests whetted his appetite for more. Capitalizing on the profitability and sound management of the firm, Chamberlain and his family sold their half to the Nettlefolds in June 1874 for £600,000, leaving Chamberlain approximately £100,000 – a sizeable nest egg. He could now turn his attention fully to Birmingham public life and, if the winds blew favourably, to parliament.[1]

Chamberlain's most immediate task was to govern the city as its chief municipal officer. It has been said that he was influenced in his memorable tenure as mayor of Birmingham by a new 'civic gospel' preached by George Dawson, minister of the Unitarian Church of the Saviour.[2] Dawson's views differed from the older radical vision which had espoused the reduction of governmental power as the best means of reducing corruption. As a new-style radical, Dawson believed the opposite – that governments had a responsibility to exert their power actively for the benefit of society as a whole. His ideas were seconded by another radical man of the cloth, R. W. Dale of the Carr's Lane Congregational chapel. H. W. Crosskey, Chamberlain's minister at the Church of the Messiah, rounded out this clerical trio who spoke and wrote of the need for a socially-oriented Christian action. Their idealism was also put to practical use: Dale worked closely with Chamberlain in the National Education League; and both Dale and Dawson served along with Chamberlain on Birmingham's first school board.

Whether or not Chamberlain was persuaded by the notion that municipal reform was divinely inspired is unknown. More likely the civic gospel served as a justification for Chamberlain's own tendency to control and manage very firmly the affairs of the city.[3] As mayor of Birmingham from 1873 to 1876, he vigorously extended the authority of that office in pursuing municipal policies. In so doing, Chamberlain ran the town council and its associated committees as though its members were his employees.[4] A local newspaper observed that Chamberlain was in the habit of 'rattling through' the business of the council. Motions were made and questions put 'so rapidly that people ... found themselves giving their votes at the very moment they had intended to make a speech or move an amendment'.[5]

Chamberlain's success in Birmingham politics was directly related to his thorough understanding of the exercise and nature of power. The institutions of local government in Birmingham, as in other major cities in mid-nineteenth-century Britain, had become highly politicized, especially since the reforms of the 1830s. Conflicts between entrenched local elites and newly emerging reformers, expressed in party allegiances, were common. Even such ostensibly mundane municipal bodies as highway surveyors or improvement commissions became battlegrounds as conservatives, liberals, and radicals struggled for political dominance. To win, to gain the levers of power, was the prize.[6]

In such a volatile political climate, municipal policies had to be carefully formulated to attract as much support as possible. Equally important was energetic and resourceful leadership. Chamberlain's mayoralty was well marked by these crucial characteristics. In addition, Chamberlain's plans, as he articulated them, were coherent and practical. He wished, he said, to enhance the quality of life for Birmingham's inhabitants by making the city more efficient. He also hoped to modernize and beautify the city centre.

Chamberlain's first project, to provide an adequate supply of gas to the city, was emblematic. Municipal gas was not a new idea: Manchester had finished such a project as early as 1817, and other cities followed this example. But Chamberlain brought an unusual dispatch and financial expertise to the project. By obtaining low interest loans, Chamberlain smoothed the path for a municipal takeover from the two existing private gas companies. An expanding population and consequent demand for gas would help alleviate the financial burden, he claimed, and could earn a profit in the years to come. Thus rates need not be increased. Municipal gas, Chamberlain assured the city, would pay for itself. After its approval by both town council and ratepayers, the proposal went before parliament. Acting as the town's counsel, Chamberlain guided it skilfully through two parliamentary committees of inquiry. Once the measure became law, Chamberlain arranged to be elected chair of the town council's new gas committee: he thus followed through administratively on his own proposal.[7] The construction of gas street lamps became a visible symbol and reminder of Chamberlain's role in providing cheap public gas for the city. Profits accruing from the successful gas venture allowed Chamberlain to tackle a second important municipal issue – a more efficient and less expensive water supply. As in the case of gas, the object was to obtain for the city the right to supply water by buying out a private company. Because of the success of the gas scheme, there was little opposition to Chamberlain's plan for water and he enjoyed an easy victory.

A larger scheme which tested Chamberlain more acutely was an inner city redevelopment project. Overcrowding and unsanitary conditions plagued many of the urban centres of the country: Birmingham was no exception. To organize and shape opinion on this issue, Chamberlain convened a national conference on sanitation in early 1875. The conference, combined with a local sanitary committee's report on the disgraceful slum conditions in Birmingham, was influential in prompting Disraeli's government to pass the Artisans' Dwelling Act. Granting local authorities the power to condemn and raze slum dwellings and then to construct new housing, the Act provided Chamberlain with a unique opportunity to demonstrate his capacity for administration and governing. Indeed, the Birmingham plan became a pilot project for the Act. As in his earlier reforms, Chamberlain advocated economies of scale to reduce costs, instead of proceeding bit by bit. In his words, 'bold action will be, in the long run, the cheapest and the most profitable' approach.[8]

Chamberlain's vision of the project, however, was somewhat at odds with the spirit of the Act. Rather than renovating the city's slums for the benefit of the poor, he decided to build a new commercial centre – in effect, to use the Act for the marketing of Birmingham as an economic centre of the Midlands. To this end, Chamberlain 'reached new heights of audacity'.[9] Circumventing regulations set by the Act, he negotiated, manoeuvred, and pushed his plan through. Ultimately 40 acres of slums were demolished and 9,000 inhabitants were displaced.[10] Corporation Street, lined with shops and office buildings, emerged as the bustling hub of the city. Only a few dozen working-class houses were constructed.[11]

Chamberlain's unceasing activity consolidated his power and authority in Birmingham. Re-designing the mayoralty from its traditional role as an impartial ceremonial office into a dynamic policy-making institution, Chamberlain dominated Birmingham as no other municipal officer in the city's history. To maintain his power and authority as the executive head of the city, he created a formidable band of advisors, made up of relatives and political operatives. Meeting in Chamberlain's home or in the council offices, these loyalist supporters pledged themselves completely to advance the schemes of their chief. They advised on municipal policy, raised money, and organized a highly efficient electoral machine.

Chamberlain himself proved remarkably deft in bringing together a coalition of electors. Each succeeding election revealed his ability to appeal to diverse strands of the population. His most enduring alliance was formed between the large industrialists and the trade unionists. Coming up from the ranks in his father's firm, Chamberlain had developed an easy and accommodating style with working men. He learned their aspirations and drive for respectability. This association no doubt significantly influenced the emerging radical programme that he developed in the early 1870s. If he seemed to falter in providing working-class housing under the Artisans' Dwelling Act, he argued that only through commercial development could a vibrant economy benefit both capitalist and labourer.[12] These economic benefits, he claimed, fitted hand in glove with political progress. Thus, a radical platform would serve both masters and men.

Chamberlain's municipal programme can be viewed as a laboratory where he experimented with practical measures in devising his radical theories. Recent research has shown that this was a task even more difficult than has been realized. It was once thought that Chamberlain's alliance with the workingmen of Birmingham represented the apex of a relatively smooth functioning alliance between classes. Birmingham was regarded as a city whose structures of work – hundreds of small shops operating independently and relatively peacefully with factory owners – were rooted in economic and political consensus. But in fact these small units of production were as much riven with strife as larger factories. The primary tension occurred between workers and the small manufacturers, many of whom had been originally been artisans. These smaller producers were often forced to impose severe constraints upon their workers, such as increased workloads, in order to compete effectively with larger firms. Workplace tensions naturally followed.[13] Chamberlain was able to recognize such divisions of interest, surmount them, and when politically necessary, to appeal to the workers over the heads of their employers.

Chamberlain's success in Birmingham, both in governing and in establishing a popular electoral base, helped revive his ambition for higher political goals. He began to cultivate a wide circle of political and personal friends during the mid-1870s. His aim was to establish a distinctive political and critical voice in national politics. His primary target was – perhaps surprisingly – the Liberal Party. Denouncing what he saw as an ineffective Liberal leadership, he condemned especially their policy of drift and their apparent abandonment of a progressive platform. Writing to Morley in late 1874, he complained: 'we Radicals are allowing the moderates to have it all their own way'. Incensed by what he considered a general apathy, he requested space in the *Fortnightly Review* to 'knock on the head all this cant about the country being tired of progress'.[14]

But Chamberlain's article, when it appeared, must be regarded as disappointing.[15] Largely ignoring the 'Four Freedoms' enunciated a year earlier in the *Fortnightly*, this article revealed him still searching for a definitive radical programme. Condemning the Game Laws; castigating the Education Act of 1870; charging the late Liberal government with 'nagging' and inconsequential legislation; and mocking the timidity of Liberal principles: none of this advanced Chamberlain's own political principles.[16] Even his catalogue of need – urban pauperism, turbulent agricultural labourers, and strained relations between capital and labour – seemed commonplace. Chamberlain's conclusion, however, gave a clue to his real aim: 'the Radicals must at once combine and organize in support of their principles'.[17] By unifying, the radicals could force the Liberal Party – the timid party – to meet them halfway. It was clear that the route to radical political power in the nation, and through it to his own power, lay in creating a sufficiently large organization which could force an alliance upon the Liberal Party.

In the midst of his triumphant mayoralty and his plans for a wider political role, however, tragedy once again struck his family. Chamberlain's second wife, Florence, died in childbirth on 13 February 1875. Her newborn child died the following day and was buried in the same coffin. Chamberlain and Florence had been married for seven years. She was the cousin of Chamberlain's first wife, Harriet. As the daughter of the prominent Birmingham businessman, Timothy Kenrick (Harriet's uncle), Florence brought numerous advantages in her marriage with Chamberlain, just as Harriet had. By all accounts, she was an excellent match and the perfect Victorian helpmeet for her husband.[18] Nearly twelve years younger than her husband, the shy and retiring Florence nevertheless took an active interest in Joe's political career. She shared his radical views, kept indexed press reports of his speeches, edited his articles in the *Fortnightly Review*, and served as hostess to visiting politicians. She also bore four children – Neville, Ida, Hilda, and Ethel – and was an attentive stepmother to Austen and Beatrice.[19]

Florence's death had a devastating impact upon Chamberlain and reopened the wounds that he had borne at the death of Harriet. In a black-edged letter of mourning, he wrote to R. W. Dale that there was 'not a fibre in my whole being which has not been roughly torn asunder. You may judge how desolate & solitary I feel & how dark & difficult my future life seems to me.'[20] Shortly after Florence's funeral, he left Birmingham and travelled abroad, first to the continent and then to Scotland. Upon his return, he offered his resignation to the town council, but was refused. For support, he relied on the comfort of family and friends, especially from Collings and Morley. But most of all, he steeled himself against the loss by a hardening of sensibility and a determination – after an initial inclination to withdraw – to keep busy. Several months after Florence's death, he revealed his plan to Morley: 'to work double tides – to work constantly and not to think'.[21]

This strategy was not always successful. More than a year after Florence's death, after becoming a Member of Parliament for Birmingham, Chamberlain confessed to his friends that he could not enjoy this long-sought honour. 'I feel so terribly depressed', he wrote to Morley, 'that I catch myself continually wishing that this wretched business of life were over once for all.'[22] In an echo of this letter, Chamberlain wrote Collings the following day that 'everything reminds me of what might have been and recalls my present loneliness. I can neither look back nor forward with any satisfaction …'[23] Long after Florence's death, he experienced bouts of depression even as he consciously directed all his force and energy 'on the immediate work & duty of the present': his only reward was the 'grim satisfaction' that he was at least carrying on 'without unmanly weakness'.[24]

The long-term significance of Florence's death on Chamberlain is difficult to estimate. Garvin believes that 'a certain mocking grimness settled into him'.[25] Marsh thinks that her death hardened him and dulled a sympathy for the misfortunes of others.[26] Perhaps more important, Marsh believes that he lost his religious faith and thereafter staked his life and career on his own force of will. He may also have become more manipulative to gain his own ends. Yet it is also true that Chamberlain in the midst of his own misfortune could be solicitous, even tender, to his closest friends. When Jesse Collings left Birmingham for an extended continental and Egyptian tour for reasons of health in the winter of 1876, Chamberlain wrote that he missed his good friend, and offered detailed advice for rest and relaxation. If the Egyptian air were not bracing enough, Chamberlain recommended Switzerland, urging Collings to remain until he had explored every hill and mountain.[27]

Chamberlain's bursts of good will toward Collings and his mourning for Florence did not, however, interfere with his ambitions. He was elected to parliament in the summer of 1876, in a by-election that had been brought about through the intrigue of Chamberlain and his loyal supporters, who forced the resignation of George Dixon, then MP for Birmingham. Dixon, who had been Chamberlain's friend and ally in the educational struggles of the past several years, was less than pleased – even though he was compensated by assuming Chamberlain's former chairmanship of Birmingham's school board.[28]

Once in parliament, Chamberlain eventually was able to overcome his lingering sadness and bouts of morbid introspection, as well as the public cloud engendered by his political manipulations in Birmingham. He was from the first a conscientious and active member of the House. Although radical at heart, he accepted the Liberal whip. His maiden speech was well received, and soon afterward he established himself as a cool and competent speaker. He set about learning the rules of the House and meeting the great political men of the day, not all of whom he respected. W. E. Forster, his nemesis from the educational struggles, he described privately as 'an old baboon'.[29] Clearly, Chamberlain was unimpressed by the stature of established parliamentarians.

Chamberlain's primary goals during his early years as an MP were twofold. First was to establish a commanding reputation in the House of Commons. Almost as soon as he arrived at Westminster, he organized a 'party' of six MPs on the principle of the Officers' Committee of the National Education League; that is, 'perfect loyalty one to another & entire absence of all personal considerations'.[30] The party, so quickly launched, soon sank without a trace. But one of the six was Sir Charles Dilke, who became a close friend and social mentor. A sophisticated world traveller and man about town, Dilke provided a welcome London retreat for Chamberlain at his Sloane Street address during parliamentary sessions and it was there that Chamberlain began to meet leading political figures. Complementary radicals, Dilke and Chamberlain often saw eye to eye on political matters. Both men in addition shared personal tragedies. Dilke's first wife had also died in childbirth only a year before Florence. Most important to Chamberlain was his gradual realization that Dilke was not only loyal – a quality that Chamberlain valued above all others in his friends – but that Dilke was also curiously dependent in some intangible way upon Chamberlain's dominant personality. Dilke could be relied upon to do Chamberlain's bidding.

Chamberlain's second goal was to continue his attempts to organize radical opinion outside parliament. By creating a new organization for disseminating radical propaganda in the countryside, he could speak with a greater voice in the House of Commons as the representative of a national movement. By 1877 Chamberlain was ready. In that year, he organized the abolition of the National Education League and its resurrection as an organization with more explicitly political goals. The National Liberal Federation (NLF), as it was called, drew upon the old League's network of information and contacts and incorporated the electioneering practices of the Birmingham Liberal Association (BLA) which had had earlier successes in municipal elections. Originally devised in the 1860s by William Harris, an exceptionally able wire-puller and a member of the Edgbaston Debating Club, the BLA had become a formidable (and hierarchical) organization. Beginning at the ward level, party members elected delegates to a Central Committee, known as the Four Hundred (later, the Six Hundred). From the Central Committee, a smaller group was elected to the Central Executive of about one hundred. Only eleven of these were in turn elected to the Management Committee.

The National Liberal Federation was a natural outgrowth of the old Education League in a way consonant to Chamberlain's greater ambitions. Chamberlain could not have been unaware of the growing strength of nonconformity in the country-side, especially in the north and west.[31] Nonconformists had largely made up the membership of the League: Chamberlain hoped to carry nonconformist support into the more explicitly political Liberal Federation. He left nothing to chance. The NLF would be Birmingham-managed, as had been true of the National Education League. Birmingham delegates were paramount at national gatherings and in committee meetings. The officers of the NLF were drawn very largely from the lead-ership of the old League or from the BLA. The secretary of the NLF was Francis Schnadhorst, former secretary of the BLA, and perhaps the most assiduous of all Victorian politicos. The guiding hand behind the NLF – as everyone knew – was of course Chamberlain himself.[32]

Within a few years, the NLF had grown into a formidable organization. By 1884, nearly half of all local Liberal Associations (88 out of 198) had affiliated with the NLF. Especially prominent in the NLF were those Associations in the larger boroughs with populations over 30,000.[33] As the head of a potentially formidable political organization, Chamberlain could speak with some authority. Popularly known as 'the caucus', the NLF gave Chamberlain exceptional national visibility as a parliamentary novice. In the House of Commons for only a year, he had vaulted ahead of his colleagues in capturing the attention of his party. But he also raised alarms. The governing Conservatives took anxious note, and even some Liberal lead-ers were apprehensive, especially at the personal power that the caucus could give to Chamberlain and his radical views. To deflect criticism that the NLF was controlled exclusively by a Birmingham radical clique, Chamberlain publicly asserted that it was 'essentially democratic' and that it did not make opinion, but merely expressed it.[34]

To allay Liberal suspicions of the NLF, Chamberlain concocted a grand gesture to lend legitimacy to the new organization: he invited William Gladstone, the Liberal leader, to the first national meeting of the NLF. The meeting, held in Birmingham in May 1877, was a great success. So large were the numbers at Bingley Hall (estimated at 25–30,000) that reinforced barricades were brought in to control the crowd and glass had to be removed from the roof. Gladstone himself enjoyed the adulation, and used the occasion to lambast Disraeli's foreign policy.[35] A month after the meeting, Chamberlain pushed home the lesson of Gladstone's appearance by proclaiming that the former prime minister had expressed 'cordial sympathy' with the aims of the new organization. Chamberlain claimed further that Gladstone had also 'frankly admit-ted the claims of the Radicals ... to recognition and fair consideration in the party councils'.[36]

In private, however, Chamberlain was more candid about the purpose of the NLF. He confided to Morley that the caucus was a necessary weapon against 'all that club management & Pall Mall selection which has been going on so long and which has made of the Liberal Party the molluscous, boneless, nerveless thing it is'. In contrast to the moribund Liberal Party elite, the caucus represented 'force, enthusiasm, zeal, activity, movement, popular will and the rule of the majority'.[37] There is little doubt that Chamberlain was committed to using the caucus as an instrument to purge the Liberal Party of its more moderate members, especially the aristocratic Whiggish elements. As he put it to Morley, he was determined to 'd – n the Whigs high and low'.[38] Once purged, a new party could be built from the ruins of the old – a party more radical, more popular, and more vigorously led.[39]

Chamberlain's decision to make his mark on the Liberal Party came at a fortuitous time. After Gladstone's defeat in early 1874, the fallen prime minister had not only resigned as party leader but had largely retired from politics, spending much of his time on his Welsh estate at Hawarden writing religious tracts. With Gladstone removed, the leadership fell into a relative vacuum, shared as it was between the Whiggish Lord Hartington in the Commons and Lord Granville in the Lords. Chamberlain's aim was to discredit the existing Liberal leadership in the hope that Gladstone would eventually return to head the party with the help of the radicals. Grateful to his friends, Gladstone might suitably reward them.[40]

Complementary to his scheme of working within the Liberal Party in order to undermine it was Chamberlain's policy of working directly against the Conservatives. Disraeli's government, in power since 1874, had become increasingly popular primarily because of its imperial policies. Gaining control of the Suez Canal, engaging in warfare in Africa and Afghanistan, and bestowing upon Queen Victoria the title 'Empress of India' all stirred patriotic fervour. When Disraeli sent the British fleet to Constantinople and called up the reserves in 1878 as a warning to Russian designs on Turkey, bellicose sentiment was further inflamed. Jingoism was the order of the day.

Any Liberal opposition to Disraeli clearly ran against the political tide. But it provided an opportunity for Chamberlain to construct a distinctively anti-imperial electioneering cry. He chose for special condemnation the government's policy on the Eastern question, the most important of Disraeli's various imperial theatres of operation.[41] Dormant since the Crimean War, national struggles in the Balkans and the Middle East flared in 1875, where competing Russian and Turkish interests led to war. The Disraeli government sided with the Turks on the grounds that Russian success could threaten the British route to India through its enhanced influence in the eastern Mediterranean. The Liberals on the other hand – Gladstone most famously among them – supported Russia primarily on religious and moral grounds: the Turks had massacred thousands of rebellious Christian Bulgarians within their empire.

Chamberlain's opposition was politically calculated. Having decided to use the NLF and the radical programme as a transforming agent of the Liberal Party, Chamberlain naturally wished to see the Liberals in power. Whatever weakened the Conservative majority in parliament would serve that goal. And in opposing Disraeli, he would simultaneously support Gladstone, who had emerged from his Welsh retreat in 1876 to begin a crusade against Turkish atrocities in Bulgaria. Staking a claim to Gladstone's gratitude, Chamberlain began his own campaign against Disraelian imperialism in the late 1870s. His speeches, widely reported in the press, harshly criticized Disraeli's aggressive policies abroad. Before a crowd of 5,000 at Birmingham's Town Hall in January 1878, for example, Chamberlain charged Disraeli with reckless diplomatic and military policies, and lashed out at Disraeli's attempt to 'juggle into war'. Chamberlain claimed that Disraeli had put the powder 'a little nearer to the candle: ... an accident would do the rest'. He also doubted the wisdom of propping up the Turkish empire, 'a decaying barbarism'. 'Anything was better than the Turks', he told the crowd.[42] On other platforms, Chamberlain declared that the Conservative government was merely attempting 'to satisfy the vulgar enthusiasm of music-hall patriots', and warned that the inevitable outcome of Disraeli's policy would be 'the waste of blood and treasure'.[43] Summing up the Conservative policy as all 'brag and bounce',[44] he attacked it as a fruitless bullying tactic bound to fail. To lend muscle to Chamberlain's blows, the NLF sponsored nearly 130 meetings of protest throughout the country.[45]

Disraeli appeared at first unassailable. His diplomatic victory at the Congress of Berlin in 1878 seemed a vindication of his policy. But eventually the limitations of even a modern industrial nation attempting to control far-flung territories was revealed – and in dramatic form. In February 1879, a tactically sophisticated Zulu army of 20,000 men, using a combination of stealth and speed, annihilated a British force of 1,200 at Isandhlwana in South Africa. In September of that same year, the entire British mission at Kabul, the capital of Afghanistan, was slaughtered by mutinous Afghan soldiers – an action that led inevitably to the Third Afghan War. The dangers of an extended empire were becoming manifest. Equally important to the decline of Disraeli's fortunes were falling domestic agricultural prices and a depression in trade. By late 1879, there was growing optimism among the Liberals that in any future general election, they held a winning hand. It was the opportunity that Chamberlain had worked for.

4

MINISTER OF THE CROWN

A political error in judgement by Disraeli gave Gladstone and the Liberal opposition the opportunity to regain the government. Misreading by-election returns in February 1880, the prime minister dissolved parliament and called a general election in early March.[1] To the stunned surprise of the Conservatives, the election returned a substantial majority for the Liberal Party, 351 seats, over the Conservative minority of 239. Irish Home Rulers came in at a respectable 62 seats, reflecting an emergent nationalist movement in Ireland.

After half a dozen years in opposition, Gladstone had a relatively free hand in choosing his ministers. In doing so, he attempted to balance diverse factions.[2] Of the twenty who served in the cabinet, nearly half were Whigs, the most prominent of whom were the Duke of Argyll, Earl Spencer, and the Marquis of Hartington, heir to the Devonshire dukedom. Important mainstream Liberals were Sir William Harcourt and W. E. Forster. Gladstone was the sole Peelite/Liberal. To represent the radical element in the cabinet, the aging John Bright, MP for Birmingham, was chosen – though his selection was based more upon past services than for any hope of future ones. The most surprising cabinet choice of all was Gladstone's selection of a second member of parliament from Birmingham, Joseph Chamberlain.

Most observers expected that, if a second radical were added to the cabinet, it would be Chamberlain's friend and colleague, Sir Charles Dilke, who had established a solid reputation in the House since his election in 1868. Chamberlain had been in parliament only four years and had no previous cabinet experience. Nevertheless, Chamberlain vigorously pushed himself forward and intrigued for the cabinet position. Immediately after the election, he wrote directly to Dilke staking his claim. Acknowledging Dilke's strength in the House of Commons, he declared his own influence was greater in the country. Chamberlain also claimed that the recent Liberal victory owed as much to the National Liberal Federation as it did to Gladstone. He attempted to tie his fortunes to Dilke's by proposing 'a thorough offensive and defensive alliance' in which they both would refuse to accept all offices, whether of cabinet rank or not, unless both received offers.[3] Chamberlain reinforced this notion in a letter to Morley a few days later by suggesting that it would not be worthwhile for Dilke 'to go in alone' because outside the cabinet he and Dilke 'would be very strong' together.[4]

On another front, Chamberlain explicitly informed Sir William Harcourt – who was serving as emissary between Gladstone and various cabinet hopefuls – that if he were left out of office, he would organize a 'pure left' party in the country and would sponsor radical candidates in all borough elections. If Dilke were given cabinet office, he would however be willing to accept the Secretaryship of the Treasury, an office without cabinet rank. Chamberlain concluded his remarkable exchange with Harcourt by issuing a veiled threat to the new prime minister: 'if Gladstone would not yield he must take the consequences'.[5]

Gladstone would not have been moved by Chamberlain's bluster, but he would have been swayed by Chamberlain's public championing of radicalism and reform which provided a needed counterweight to an otherwise centre-right political tone in the new cabinet. In any case, Dilke's hope for high office was blunted by his firm belief in republicanism – a creed no longer held by Chamberlain – which raised difficulties with Queen Victoria. Thus Chamberlain entered the cabinet as the new President of the Board of Trade, the same department in which Gladstone himself had first taken office four decades earlier. Dilke was brought into the ministry as under-secretary at the Foreign Office without cabinet rank.

Chamberlain was neither shy nor intimidated as a cabinet neophyte. He seemed determined in his brashness. When the new cabinet travelled to Windsor Castle for their swearing-in ceremony, Chamberlain described the scene to his sister, Clara. Marching in, bowing before 'a quiet little Lady of 60', the cabinet then knelt on one knee and took the oath of allegiance. While still kneeling, Chamberlain reported, there was suddenly thrust 'a small, fat, red hand … under each of our noses and respectfully mumbled [over] by us'.[6] At his first cabinet meeting that same afternoon, Chamberlain spoke bluntly, urging a 'complete reversal' of Disraeli's imperial projects, including Britain's annexation of the Transvaal. He also recommended the dismissal of Sir Bartle Frere, High Commissioner in South Africa, who had been responsible for the Zulu Wars.[7] Only Harcourt supported Chamberlain.[8]

Chamberlain was equally provocative during his tenure at the Board of Trade. President of the Board was not a high-ranking cabinet office and fell well below secretaries of state (such as those for Foreign Affairs or for War) both in status and pay. Its concern was with the administration of tariffs and the promotion of trade – matters sufficiently familiar to Chamberlain. In this sense, the office suited him. Yet his tenure at the Board was often marked by conflict. Although he understood the intricacies of trade and tariffs and mastered the statistical problems easily, he had more difficulty in piloting significant legislation through parliament. Smaller measures passed readily enough: a grain cargoes bill to prevent shifting cargoes on ships at sea; and a seaman's wages bill to guarantee fairer payment and better treatment of sailors. A patents act, designed to encourage artisan innovation, and a bankruptcy act, protecting creditors in bankruptcy cases, were enacted only after some delay. Chamberlain's Electric Lighting Act of 1882, though successfully passed, enjoyed little success. It had an adverse affect upon the growth of the electric industry because it restricted to a limited number of years the time in which private developers could realize their profits before municipal authorities were given the right to purchase the new enterprises.[9]

Chamberlain's most difficult endeavour at the Board was his attempt to pass a merchant shipping bill.[10] Its origins lay in the indisputably high mortality rate among seamen in the mercantile marine. In the 1870s, hundreds of merchant sailors died at sea each year. Chamberlain forged an alliance with Samuel Plimsoll to undertake a campaign against what they considered a tendency among ship-owners to engage in risky practices, including overloading and undermanning.[11] In addition, Chamberlain claimed that ship-owners not only allowed leaky vessels to sail, but that they also over-insured them in order to gain substantial profits should these ships go down.

Chamberlain proposed a drastic alteration of the laws relating to marine insur-ance, and – in order to shift the responsibility for the death and injuries of seamen to the ship-owners – to bring the owners under the recently passed Employers' Liability Act of 1880. In so doing, Chamberlain alienated a powerful economic interest well represented in the House of Commons. Ship-owners protested that theirs was a dan-gerous and uncertain business and that the loss of life was merely a reflection of unfortunate circumstances of weather and natural hazards. They were also strong believers in 'free commercial enterprise' and objected to government interference with what they considered the sanctity of contract between ship-owners, underwrit-ers, and their seamen.

Once the battle was joined, each side hardened its position. Chamberlain repeat-edly refused to provide the Chamber of Shipping and the British Ship-Owners' Company with a review of proposed legislation. His speeches created the impression that ship-owners were themselves directly responsible for maritime casualties. Tarred with a broad brush, and fearful that the passage of the bill would imply an admission of guilt to Chamberlain's charges, even responsible and sympathetic Liberal ship-owners were driven to oppose the measure.

By March 1884, support for the bill in official quarters was waning. Eddy Hamilton, Gladstone's private secretary, reported that Chamberlain was 'getting into hot water'.[12] Chamberlain had in fact proceeded clumsily. Too little consultation, too much confrontation, and not enough compromise reflected badly upon the President of the Board of Trade.[13] Under pressure, Chamberlain wrote to Gladstone tendering his resignation. Gladstone refused. A month later, Chamberlain returned obliquely to the topic of resignation, couching it in curiously personal terms. Maintaining that he had done everything in his power to mollify the opposition, Chamberlain wrote that nothing would satisfy the ship-owners but the abandonment of the bill, and 'the humiliation of the Minister in charge'.[14]

Fortified by Gladstone's reassurance, Chamberlain returned to the attack. A heav-ily denunciatory speech in the House of Commons in May 1884 set out his strongest case yet against the owners. Then, in a questionable tactic, Chamberlain utilized the National Liberal Federation to bring pressure upon the ship-owners. A million copies of his May speech were circulated by the NLF, along with letters requesting that each local Liberal association pass resolutions in favour of Chamberlain's proposals and contact members of parliament to request their support.[15] But it was too late. Within a few weeks, the bill was withdrawn, bringing to a close the most galling experience he had yet known in political life.[16]

The withdrawal of the merchant shipping bill was not based wholly upon Chamberlain's stirring of a hornet's nest among ship-owners. Gladstone and the cabinet were also concerned that the shipping bill could lead to a defeat in the Commons, unacceptable at that moment because of the delicate manoeuvring around an impending franchise bill, far more important than Chamberlain's measure. The development of the franchise bill, which became the Reform Bill of 1884 – the third great electoral reform after 1832 and 1867 – and Chamberlain's role in it, is instructive.

As a part of his radical initiative, Chamberlain had pressed upon the cabinet an extension of the vote as early as 1880. But Gladstone urged delay on the grounds that such a 'big bill' had to be carefully planned for and introduced in its place on the legislative calendar.[17] Delay for the bill can also be accounted for by the government's preoccupation with imperial issues in South Africa, Ireland, and Egypt during the early years of the ministry. Chamberlain in the meantime was champing at the bit and had his own views of the delay. He believed that radical notions were unwelcome to the ministerial majority, who frequently 'ignored or outvoted' him and his fellow radical, Sir Charles Dilke.[18] There was some truth to this, but Chamberlain himself was partially to blame. Hampered by his self-inflicted wounds suffered at the Board of Trade, Chamberlain had been unable to mount an effective platform from within the government to implement his radical campaign for social and political reform.

By late 1882, however, Chamberlain was ready to begin a countrywide initiative 'out of doors' beyond the confines of parliament and cabinet to place radical reforms at the top of the political agenda. He was convinced that recent by-election losses for the Liberals indicated the need for a fresh approach by the government. As he put it in a letter to Dilke: 'the country – (*our* country that is – the great majority of Liberal opinion) is ripe for a new departure in constructive Radicalism & only wants leaders. So if we are driven to a fight, we shall easily recruit an army.'[19]

In a series of lengthy speeches throughout late 1882 and 1883, Chamberlain made his case for a radical programme while simultaneously denouncing the Conservative opposition. The first of his speeches, delivered at the annual meeting of the Council of the National Liberal Federation held at Ashton-under-Lyne (Lancashire) on 19 December 1882, called for an extension of the franchise to all householders in the country. In a speech redolent of classic utilitarian doctrines, Chamberlain promised that franchise reform would enable 'the whole force of the party of progress' to carry out 'the will of the people' and to secure 'the greatest happiness of the greatest number'.[20] In the following year, Chamberlain sharpened his rhetoric, attacking the Conservative opposition on a wide range of issues. In March 1883, at a meeting of the Birmingham Junior Liberal Association, Chamberlain charged the Conservatives with wilful obstruction in parliament. He especially criticized the record of the Conservatives on Ireland. Claiming that Lord Salisbury was merely the spokesman of an aristocratic order whose sympathy must always lie with landlords, Chamberlain condemned him as a representative of a class 'who toil not, neither do they spin'.[21]

Chamberlain's speechifying continued into the summer and autumn of 1883. In early July, he spoke as chairman of the Cobden Club annual dinner at the Ship Hotel in Greenwich. Eulogizing Richard Cobden, a founder of the Anti-Corn Law League and a popular agitator in the 1840s, Chamberlain drew a parallel to the 1880s. Like Cobden, Chamberlain, too, advocated radical measures because he was strongly convinced of the necessity of having 'full confidence in the people'.[22] In late November, Chamberlain spoke at the annual meeting of the Bristol Liberal Association. He reviewed the great social needs of the day – freedom of education, better housing for the poor, and improvement in the condition of agricultural labourers. These reforms, he maintained, could only be settled 'when the whole of the people take a part in the work of legislation'.[23]

Several days later, Chamberlain was in Wolverhampton, a guest at a banquet held by the local Liberal Club. Afterward, he spoke before nearly 3,000 in the Agricultural Hall. He urged his urban listeners to help open the electoral door for their country cousins: 'they are your own flesh and blood; they are your fellow-workmen; they are animated by the same principles.'[24] By mid-December he was back in Birmingham. Before a crowded audience in the Town Hall, he summarized the purpose of his campaign. 'We only want', he said, 'that the whole nation should be consulted.'[25]

To promote further what he called 'constructive radicalism', Chamberlain planned with T. H. S. Escott, who had replaced Morley as editor of the *Fortnightly Review*, a series of articles outlining in detail the radical programme. Each article was written by a specialist, with Chamberlain's evident hand shaping the argument.[26] From midsummer 1883 until January 1884, the appearance of these articles in serial form complemented Chamberlain's stumping the countryside for the reform cause. His clear and consistent message captured the attention of the country. Encouraged by his reception, Chamberlain was determined to press forward even more energetically. As he put it in a letter to Labouchere: 'it is now the policy of all Radicals to keep on driving at the franchise question & to refuse to be drawn aside into the discussion of foreign affairs or any other matter.'[27]

Chamberlain's speeches naturally raised the ire of Salisbury and the Conservatives; but Liberal feathers were also ruffled. There was particular unease in the cabinet that Chamberlain's tirades would force the government's hand on reform. Hartington, who from his Whiggish perch was always fearful of raising the popular pitch too high, appealed to Gladstone and hinted vaguely at resignation unless Chamberlain could be muzzled. That the tone and tenor of Chamberlain's speeches had become intemperate was the general sense, too, among moderate Liberals in the House. Peer-baiting was no doubt popular at some mass meetings; but Chamberlain's use of the biblical injunction at Birmingham in March 1883 (which became known as his 'toil and spin' speech) was widely seen as inflammatory. Gladstone, circumspectly, attempted to moderate Chamberlain's tongue, but with indifferent success. In any case, Gladstone was reluctant to suppress Chamberlain entirely: the radical leader was performing good work by preparing the ground in his own way for franchise reform.

By the autumn of 1883, even before Chamberlain's country campaign was finished, Gladstone set the Attorney General, Henry James, to work drafting a franchise bill.[28] It was a high priority for Gladstone – 'the question of questions' as he put it to Hartington in late October.[29] Cabinet discussions on the franchise began on

25 October 1883, before the opening of parliament's autumn session. In successive weeks, the franchise occupied considerable attention from cabinet members as they thrashed through the details of the proposed bill.

It was soon clear that extension of the franchise would be the simpler half of the proposed reform. Early on in the discussion, the government realized that an enlarged franchise must be accompanied by a redrawing of electoral districts, based upon the shifts in population that had taken place since 1867. Redistribution emerged, in fact, as the sticking point of the reform measure. Conservatives were not averse to the idea of franchise reform, but only if existing boundaries of electoral districts were redrawn would they actively support it. Salisbury feared that otherwise Conservative minorities in largely Liberal urban areas would consistently be denied parliamentary representation.[30] Gladstone and the cabinet decided, however, to separate franchise extension from redistribution in presenting the reform package to the House of Commons. The proposed bill essentially extended to the counties the borough householder franchise enacted in 1867. Franchise first, followed by redistribution, was their strategy. Initially, all went well. The Conservative opposition in the House of Commons seemed unable to mount a successful counterattack, perhaps because of Sir Stafford Northcote's inadequate leadership. By late June 1884 franchise extension passed the Commons in good order and was sent to the House of Lords. Here it met a different fate. Within ten days, the bill had been technically delayed, but was in fact defeated.

Now began several months of lengthy consultation and agonizing attempts at compromise between the two political parties. Given Chamberlain's activity in the countryside in 1883 and his prominence in raising high the reform standard, one would have expected from him a prominent role in the negotiations. But it was not to be. The delicate balancing of various interests and the careful manoeuvring among political claimants required a softer touch. Chamberlain was known as a 'bruiser', an argumentative and uncompromising man, and a man who would more often sneer than smile.[31] Therefore, the leadership of the reform legislation passed (perhaps to Chamberlain's chagrin) to his friend and fellow radical, Sir Charles Dilke.

Only recently elevated to the cabinet as President of the Local Government Board from his undersecretaryship at the foreign office, Dilke now came into his own. He had established a reputation as an efficient administrator and as a master of legal and parliamentary detail in his work at the foreign office. Additionally, his regular attendance and dutiful adherence to the rules of the House had earned him wide respect.[32] Working behind the scenes, often with the Conservative leadership, Dilke gave invaluable service in hammering out the final details of the reform bill.

Effectively excluded from the closed circle which undertook negotiations, Chamberlain once more sprang to action in the countryside, undoubtedly hoping to keep his name before the public. His theme was the obstruction of the House of Lords: those who neither toiled nor spun once again became Chamberlain's targets.[33] Within a month of the Lords' delay of the bill, the first of his political meetings took place in Birmingham on 4 August 1884. Taking advantage of an August bank holiday, crowds from the surrounding Black Country and large Midland towns within a 30-mile radius of Birmingham jammed the streets. A procession of trade societies and political clubs marched through the town with banners and bands during the afternoon, rendezvousing at a 70-acre tract in Soho where six platforms stood to accommodate speakers. Some groups had constructed parade floats: the St Paul's Liberal Association carried the model of a ship in full sail in support of Chamberlain's merchant shipping bill. The Cornwall Works Liberal Union bore aloft a large representation of a rusty fly-wheel in reference to a recent speech by Salisbury in which he had compared the House of Lords to the fly-wheel of the Constitution. A delegation of the National Agricultural Labourer's Union held small sticks headed by corn and grass as well as a flag with the motto: 'We demand the vote as our right.' The Amalgamated Carpenters hoisted saws, planes, and other tools elevated on rods, and carried a punning banner with the words: 'Deal with us on the square; you have chiselled us long enough.' Other signs were more direct: 'Away with the House of Lords' and 'Abolish the Lords' among them.[34] Significant among the banners were several venerable ones last unfurled in 1832. The symbolism was unmistakable: public agitation, which had once forced the pace in a great reforming year, was again challenging a stubborn House of Lords.

That evening, an estimated 20,000 at Bingley Hall heard the Birmingham radical establishment in full cry. On the platform were Chamberlain cronies J. Powell Williams, George Dixon, Francis Schnadhorst, and Jesse Collings. Also present were Henry Broadhurst, formerly a stonemason, a 'tramping artisan', and Liberal MP for Stoke since 1880; and Joseph Arch, former farmworker and founder of the Agricultural Labourer's Union. The star attractions were John Bright and, of course, Chamberlain himself. After Bright's lengthy and rambling remarks, Chamberlain spoke directly to a resolution condemning the House of Lords. Carrying out the theme of that afternoon's marching men, Chamberlain made explicit the necessary right of the expression of public opinion, and the effectiveness of its traditional role in British politics. The 'opinion of the streets', he reminded his audience, had been 'a mighty force in our political history'. Chamberlain's speech also carried a veiled threat. He warned that 'fierce outbreaks of popular passion' in the past caused 'a great destruction of property' and shook monarchs on their thrones. Indeed, in 1832, the obduracy of the House of Lords had brought the country 'almost to the verge of revolution'. As a tool of the Tories, the recalcitrant Lords had never contributed 'one iota' to popular liberties or popular freedom, and had always protected 'every abuse and sheltered every privilege'. Chamberlain concluded as he began, criticizing the House of Lords as 'irresponsible without independence, obstinate without courage, arbitrary without judgment, and arrogant without knowledge'.[35]

Chamberlain's other speeches in October were similar in tone. At Hanley (near Stoke), Chamberlain portrayed the Liberal meetings as 'a real uprising of the people' against the Lords' 'chucking out' of the reform bill. At Newtown in Montgomeryshire, he condemned a system of government whereby a tiny minority could 'block the way of the rights and privileges of millions of their fellow citizens'. The following day at Denbigh, Chamberlain spoke to a crowd estimated at 10,000 who heard him ridicule the Lords as 'ancient monuments'. Calling to mind the injustice perpetrated by the Lords upon dissenters, he also brought a message of reprisal into this fiercely nonconformist stronghold. 'As a Dissenter', he told the cheering thousands, 'I have an account to settle with them, and I promise you I will not forget the reckoning.'[36]

Chamberlain in full oratorical flight could no doubt rally the faithful. But he also exacerbated tensions during the crucial negotiations on the redistribution bill. A slanging match between Chamberlain and Salisbury led to mutual threats of broken heads. Harsh words on the stump prompted violence in at least one instance when the Conservative Lord Randolph Churchill, who had marked a Birmingham seat for his candidacy at the next general election, made an appearance at a Conservative rally at Aston Park on 13 October 1884. A rival Liberal meeting clashed with Churchill's supporters, and although there was no loss of life, the riot was serious enough to pro-voke considerable complaint – not least from Lord Randolph, who held Chamberlain personally accountable. When parliament reopened, Churchill's motion of censure on Chamberlain was defeated – though more narrowly than expected, reflecting some disapproval of Chamberlain on the part of moderate Liberals.[37]

In spite of heated words, an agreement on reform was in hand by late November 1884. After reaching an accord with the Liberal government on the main outline of redistribution, the House of Lords passed the franchise reform on 5 December. Adult males who owned or were tenants resident in houses in either boroughs or counties were the heart of the new electorate. Two million new voters were added to the regis-ter, many of whom were agricultural labourers. There remained only the details of the redistribution bill to be worked out between Liberal and Conservative negotiators. With Dilke's diplomacy and Gladstone's leadership, the redistribution bill wound its way through the House of Commons during the next few months.

When political attention shifted to parliament, the wind was taken from Chamberlain's sails in the countryside. The battle for reform was won: there was little reason for additional appeals to the country. But Chamberlain was determined not to be cast out of the public eye. In January 1885, he gave three major speeches setting out the radical implications of the franchise reform and the redistribution bill. These speeches were as controversial as his earlier public pronouncements. They were also the most coherent and comprehensive programme for radical reform ever advocated by a cabinet minister.

Chamberlain's first speech was given before the Birmingham Artisan's Association on 5 January. An audience of glassworkers, plumbers, telegraph clerks, pen-makers, and printers (among others) heard Chamberlain announce the beginning of a new era – a 'Radical millennium', a 'reign of democracy' – in the wake of the reform bills. The old order, Chamberlain predicted, was giving way. The centre of power had shifted as two million men 'in factory and in field' had been added to the voting lists under the new franchise bill. For the first time in England's history, the toilers and spinners formed the majority of the electorate. But to gain full political rights, Chamberlain warned, it was more necessary than ever to band together. The Liberal Party must itself be reorganized and new policies implemented to meet the require-ments of a democratic era. The aristocracy, he implied, were the outdated heirs of an outworn social class. A democracy should not be content with the dominance of a class of men who, 'having already annexed everything that is worth having', expected everyone else 'to be content with the crumbs that fall from their table'. It was time, Chamberlain emphasized, to talk more about the obligations, and less about the rights of property. Then, in a telling rhetorical question long remembered, Chamberlain asked: 'what ransom will property pay for the security it enjoys?'[38]

Ten days later, Chamberlain reaffirmed his radical themes at the Ipswich Reform Club. Advocating better urban housing and land reform for rural workers, he condemned the lot of the agricultural labourer as especially oppressive. For too long the squire, the farmer, and the parson had been insensitive to the labouring life 'of unremitting and hopeless toil'. A wise government, 'representative of a whole people', would not allow the country to become merely a paradise for the rich and a purgatory for the poor. To fund social projects in both urban and rural areas, Chamberlain not only proposed a graduated income tax so that the wealthy paid their fair share: he also hinted at the need for inheritance taxes on the wealthy and a tax upon unearned increment of land.[39]

Returning to Birmingham for his third speech, Chamberlain shared the platform with John Bright before an estimated crowd of four to five thousand in the Town Hall. Here, Chamberlain put forward additional matters needing reform: payment to members of parliament; abolition of plural voting; and restriction of parliamentary oaths of office for new members of parliament. Referring to land reform, he stressed again the need to assist small owners and tenants. Declaring that the sanctity of public property was greater than that of private property, Chamberlain maintained that some compensation should be demanded from those who plundered the property of others to take it for their own: 'With all this spoliation ... it is the poor who suffer, and not the rich.'[40]

In giving these speeches, Chamberlain once again operated without ministerial sanction. Even had the cabinet been informed, it would certainly not have approved the texts of his speeches. Although Lord Carlingford praised Chamberlain's Ipswich speech as 'clever and remarkable', he thought that Chamberlain too often took positions 'quite different' from the ministry in proclaiming 'his own policy' and in bidding 'for the favour of the coming democracy, as if he were an independent politician'.[41] Lord Hartington informed the Queen at Osborne early in 1885 that the cabinet as a whole was 'very much annoyed' with Chamberlain's language during the past two years, especially his proposals on taxation amounting 'almost ... to socialism'.[42] Hamilton also took a serious view of Chamberlain's bravura performances. He recorded in his diary that Chamberlain's wild talk was 'frightening people'; and that there was considerable resentment at his posing as the poor man's only friend.[43]

Most serious of all was Gladstone's response. Often uneasy with Chamberlain's lack of deference, Gladstone now saw the actions of his uncontrollable minister as mutinous. It was important for members of the government, as Gladstone plainly put it, not to forfeit party unity by advocating contentious issues in public that may offend cabinet members. Speeches out of doors and appeals to the public which seemed to create policy and to pledge legislation without cabinet consultation or consent could raise questions about the efficacy and strength of that government.[44]

In reply, Chamberlain admitted that no minister had the right to advocate opinions contrary to the principles of a government of which he is a member.[45] Beyond that Chamberlain was unwilling to go. He justified his appeal to the country by claiming that popular government (which the new reform legislation, he claimed, had in large measure created) was inconsistent with 'official etiquette formerly imposed on speakers'. A new public duty had come into existence. Ministries must now recognize and use the public platform as an 'indispensable' instrument of government.[46]

There seems little doubt that Chamberlain enhanced his political strength and gratified his personal need for power in cultivating a national constituency in the early 1880s. His country campaigns of 1883–5 were logical extensions of his earlier behaviour. In every political role he played or public movement he charted, Chamberlain drove hard to attain leadership. His success was partly bound up in his dynamic manner of speaking and his ability to cast striking phrases. Unlike Gladstone, who sought to instruct from a high moral plane with his labyrinthine pronouncements, Chamberlain exhorted and aroused directly and forcefully. Compared to Gladstone's resonant cello, Chamberlain on the platform was a thumping brass band. Chamberlain's speeches were often rough, irreverent, threatening affairs; but to his supporters, they were humorous, incisive, sympathetic, and on occasion, even sensuous. 'Pushful Joe' combined with 'Our Joe' could be a potent combination.

Chamberlain's ability to attract attention and to capture and influence friends and supporters in the public sphere was becoming widely recognized. In private conversation, too, his certitude, earnestness, and enthusiasm often drew out deep affective responses.[47] No better example of Chamberlain's ability to fascinate and beguile can be found than in the celebrated, if abortive, relationship between Chamberlain and Beatrice Potter, who would become the beautiful and austere saint of social engineering after her marriage to Sydney Webb. In the summer of 1883 Beatrice's father had taken a London house in Prince's Gardens, very near Chamberlain's recently purchased residence. Beatrice met Chamberlain and his daughters at a dinner party at a neighbour's house. She was 25 and he almost twice her age at 47. A young woman of serious intent who was searching for her own role in life, Beatrice was much struck by Chamberlain's passionate determination 'to benefit "the many"'.[48] His strong belief in social justice as evident in his public statements rang true to her own sympathy for the disadvantaged in society. In January 1884 she invited Chamberlain to her father's holiday retreat in the Wye Valley. Here she made an unsettling discovery. Behind Chamberlain's radical opinions lay very conventional views on women and domestic life. He required, as he put it, 'intelligent sympathy' from women; but, as Beatrice rightly interpreted him, 'intelligent servility' was what he meant. Whenever Beatrice attempted to establish a dialogue, or to qualify his statements, 'he smashed objection … by an absolute denial, and continued his assertion'.[49] He was, Beatrice concluded, both an enthusiast and a despot.

In spite of this unpromising confrontation, Beatrice was invited to Highbury, Chamberlain's Birmingham home, two weeks later. After dinner on the first evening, Beatrice and family members were escorted to the Town Hall to hear the great man. When he rose slowly and stood silently for a few moments before he began speaking, the crowd of several thousand 'became wild with enthusiasm', waving hats and hand-kerchiefs in salute to their chief. At the sound of his voice, Beatrice reported, the crowd 'became as one man'. During the speech, Beatrice noticed that with great intensity every thought, every emotion, 'was reflected on the face of the crowd'.[50]

Beatrice's experience at the meeting led her to understand Chamberlain's remark-able sway over an audience. His power as a leader and a controller of the political sphere was based upon an intuitive ability to extract the wishes of his audience or his constituents and to impose forcibly those wishes upon others who might be more indifferent to the issues at hand. It was to this power, power over others, Beatrice believed, that Chamberlain owed what happiness there was in his life. As she wan-dered with Chamberlain through his orchids at Highbury the morning after his speech, Beatrice was struck again by this realization – that he was less interested in pleasing her than in forcing her to think as he thought and to feel as he felt.

In later years, Beatrice continued to lament Chamberlain's lack of sensitivity to others as 'undermining the usefulness of his public life'.[51] She believed that his strong reactions to any perceived personal slight and his desire to punish those who disa-greed with him were caused by the deaths of his first two wives: from lost happiness, he turned 'to love of power'. Personal power became his single-minded aim. As he rose higher in political life, he kicked at those beneath him and flung those above to the ground if they interfered with his progress.[52]

Perhaps Beatrice Potter's negative impressions were the result of her unfulfilled love affair with Chamberlain; but her astute remarks proved remarkably accurate in the years to come. In his contentious world of politics, complemented by his need for control and power over others, Chamberlain consistently broke free from those who threatened his sense of certainty and right action. Beatrice also understood that family, personal friends, and – if he were to marry again – a wife could only be assured of his affection and warmth if they devoted themselves, 'body and soul to him'.[53] Liberal associates, parliamentary acquaintances, and political allies would all learn this in time.

5

THE MAKING OF AN
IMPERIALIST

Shortly after Chamberlain's January 1885 campaign, the attention of the cabinet and of the country was sharply diverted from domestic issues. The shocking news arrived from north Africa that General Charles Gordon, head of a British mission at Khartoum in the Egyptian-controlled Sudan, had been murdered and the city taken by a band of armed religious dervishes led by the Muslim Muhammed Ahmed, who claimed to be a Mahdi or guide, and successor to the Prophet. Because Gordon's mission had been expressly sanctioned by Gladstone's government, public obloquy fell as much upon the Liberal government as upon the Mahdi.

The capture of Khartoum and Gordon's death, in fact, were the climax of a series of imperial misadventures which were ultimately destructive of Gladstone's second administration. The theatres of operation were on the continent of Africa, both north and south, and in Britain's nearest imperial province, Ireland. The circumstances of these imperial events were involved in a crosscurrent of historical precedent, ministerial misinformation, and personality conflicts all set with the cauldron of party politics. Gladstone and his Liberal government had not intended to become involved in African affairs during their term of office. Indeed, they had pledged themselves during the election campaign of 1880 to roll back Disraeli's proactive foreign and colonial policy. This did not mean either a Liberal retreat from the empire or a quiescent foreign policy. Gladstone himself was never opposed in principle to intervention abroad. He was quite willing to protect imperial security and to maintain stability among nations. His main concern was to avoid 'needless and entangling engagements'.[1]

Chamberlain's own view of colonial policy was initially not so distant from Gladstone's. He, like Gladstone, wished to maintain the integrity of the empire, to protect its subject peoples, and to guarantee its benefits to Great Britain. Beyond that, he believed, it was hazardous to go. Thus, Chamberlain held reservations about an increased British presence in Egypt after Disraeli's purchase of the controlling shares in the Suez Canal in 1875. Protecting the Canal could mean an Egyptian protectorate. This in turn, he feared, might lead to the occupation of Syria; and 'what we should have to take to protect Syria I do not know'.[2] Avoiding (what might be called in modern terms) a domino effect was merely prudent.

Chamberlain denied, however, that Liberals supported a policy of 'peace at any price'. Liberals, Chamberlain insisted, had 'imperial instincts' as much as the Conservatives and were 'keenly alive to the responsibilities and duties of a great nation'. It was not, therefore, Disraeli's imperialism *per se* that Chamberlain opposed. If Disraeli used imperial projects for 'worthy objects' – perhaps toward a humanitarian end – Chamberlain did not object. But Disraeli too often directed imperialism to 'ignoble party purposes', or what Chamberlain called 'rowdy patriotism'. This was essentially the thrust of Chamberlain's speeches during the election campaign that brought the Liberals to power in 1880.[3]

It was a supreme irony that the Liberals, intending to repudiate Disraeli's aggressive imperial policy, found themselves increasingly involved in imperial affairs after 1880. Their reluctant but relentless imperial advance is best demonstrated in Egypt, where Chamberlain had already detected troubling signs. Growing numbers of British and other European nationals in the late nineteenth century had exacerbated tensions with the indigenous Egyptian population. In September 1881 a nationalist uprising led to the creation of a de facto independent Egyptian government headed by an army officer, Arabi Pasha. In June 1882 a xenophobic riot broke out in Alexandria with a loss of life to resident Europeans, and injury to a British consular official. To restore order, the Gladstone government ordered a naval bombardment of Alexandria and its occupation by British troops. Within the next few months a British military expedition of 35,000 men defeated Arabi's army at Tel-el-Kebir. The British were now paramount in Egypt, and had taken a firm first step on the eventual road to Khartoum.

The ministry had not been of one mind in its decision to invade Egypt. Anxious cabinet meetings and a worried correspondence between Gladstone and his foreign secretary revealed the division between hard-liners and soft-peddlers. Within the cabinet Bright was for peace; but Hartington, leader of the strong Whig contingent, readily opted for military action. Reluctantly, Gladstone, for a variety of reasons, went along with the notion of intervention.[4] The radical Dilke, whose interventionist views were widely known, was also active in supporting a military expedition.[5] Something of a surprise, however, was Chamberlain's acceptance of military force. Both Bright, who resigned from the cabinet in protesting the invasion, and John Morley (from outside the government) expected more from their radical colleague than his acquiescence to the cabinet's decision. To radicals like Morley and Bright, the cabinet's rationale for military intervention – that Arabi was merely an opportunistic adventurer and did not represent the wishes of the Egyptian people – was specious.[6]

Chamberlain attempted to justify his behaviour by arguing that Britain must always support both its interests and its duties abroad. Britain's interests in Egypt were twofold: to discourage French ambitions in that strategic region; and to protect the security of the Suez Canal and the route to India. Britain's duties were designed to promote progress in Egypt itself, especially 'the greatest possible development of representative institutions' among the Egyptians.[7] Chamberlain's defence of the government's Egyptian policy involved him in an extended argument with his radical allies. Bright charged Chamberlain with using 'the stock arguments of the Jingo school'. Chamberlain, half apologetically, attempted to exculpate himself. The cabinet as a whole, he maintained, had been convinced that British forces could depose Arabi quickly, and then retire from the field. Chamberlain also believed that British unilateral action may well have staved off a wider European intervention in Egypt, and possibly a European war as well.[8] Bright was not convinced. He concluded sorrowfully his correspondence with Chamberlain: 'The past is past but it leaves an ugly future – and for "Radical" members of the Cabinet an awkward one to discuss.'[9]

Writing to Morley, Chamberlain excused the cabinet's actions on similar grounds. Intervention was the only logical course of action to follow after Arabi's provocations. Having intervened, Chamberlain assured Morley, England would turn the invasion into a 'real benefit for the Egyptian people' by establishing institutions guaranteeing their liberties. Once that was accomplished, Britain would leave the country.[10] But, as with Bright, Chamberlain's expedient appeal to an altruistic civilizing mission through the instrumentality of British military forces failed to convince.

That the Egyptian crisis had precipitated a drift toward imperialism on Chamberlain's part is well borne out in a revealing letter written in late 1883. Chamberlain, who had been negotiating with T. H. S. Escott to complete the series of articles on the radical programme for the *Fortnightly Review*, advised against any references to foreign policy. His reason, as he admitted to Escott, was that he (along with Dilke) was 'a little jingo'; and he was fearful that he might be too jingoistic for the present 'popular sentiment on the subject' which he saw as increasingly non-interventionist.[11]

Chamberlain's growing imperial sentiment was only one of the many contending voices in the cabinet in the aftermath of the invasion of Egypt. Hartington and the Whigs wanted to remain in Egypt as long as necessary to shore up British interests. But Harcourt advocated full withdrawal from all of north Africa. Eventually, a compromise emerged: withdrawal from the country as a whole, but not from the Canal. A relatively small British presence would remain with sufficient authority to keep the Canal open to British shipping, at least until a stable and friendly Egyptian government could be established.[12] Chamberlain was broadly in support of this policy.

Events far from Westminster, however, soon overtook ministerial decisions. An armed religious movement to the south of Egypt in the Sudan (then an Egyptian dependency) had begun to move from the western mountains toward the Nile. The Mahdi-led Muslims swept all before them, overrunning isolated Egyptian garrisons, and capturing men and arms. By late 1883 the security of Egypt's southern border was threatened. To check their advance, Sir William Hicks led an Egyptian army of 10,000 into the Sudan. Caught by surprise not far from Omdurman, the entire expedition, including Hicks, was annihilated in September 1883. The path was now clear for the Mahdi to continue his advance toward the Upper Nile.

The impact of these events upon the cabinet was immediate. Early withdrawal from Egypt was no longer an option. Cabinet attention now shifted to minimizing the threat of the Mahdi to Egypt and to the Canal itself. Acting now as the protectors of Egypt, the cabinet decided to withdraw all remaining civilians and garrisons from the Sudan, leaving the Mahdi to his own devices. To facilitate the withdrawal, a cabinet committee engaged General Charles Gordon, an adventurous and charismatic military leader who had some knowledge of the Sudan. But Gordon, arriving at Khartoum, 1500 miles south of Cairo, was soon trapped by the Mahdi. After much delay, a British military expedition under General Wolseley was sent up the Nile to rescue Gordon: it reached Khartoum on 28 January 1885, 48 hours too late.

The advance of British forces up the Nile into the Sudan, and the widening arc of British power in north Africa, heightened the concerns of Chamberlain's closest radical colleagues. John Morley had become particularly uneasy at the continued British presence in Egypt even before the Gordon mission. As editor of the *Pall Mall Gazette*, Morley could exercise some influence, and in late 1882 he reminded Chamberlain of his obligation to support the radical principle of anti-imperialism.[13] In a public rebuke of Chamberlain, Morley spoke to his constituents at Newcastle in January 1884. His brief admonitory speech warned those from 'any quarter, in their own camp or elsewhere' that he 'would protest to the very last' any new ventures which would create a second Ireland in the Mediterranean, with all its expense and difficulties of governing.[14]

When Wolseley's rescue mission entered the Sudan in force, Morley's fears came to pass. To Chamberlain, he wrote: 'war in the Soudan is an affair of political conscience with me'.[15] Chamberlain immediately took issue with Morley. Charging him with 'Utopianism', Chamberlain argued strongly that the government should pursue the Mahdi as retribution for Gordon's death. If Britain ignored the Mahdi or were to 'turn tail', a signal of weakness would be sent to other European powers. 'We must', he insisted, 'show these fierce fanatics that we are strong, as they respect nothing but physical force.' Chamberlain was also convinced that Khartoum must be retaken.[16] The cabinet, however, decided against another Sudan expedition, and General Wolseley was withdrawn. Thus the Sudan was, in Matthew's words, 'put on ice' until the following decade.[17]

Morley's criticism of Chamberlain's dawning imperial sentiment was echoed by other radicals who opposed the government's policy in Egypt such as Sir Wilfrid Lawson, MP for Carlisle; Leonard Courtney, MP for Liskeard; and Peter Rylands, MP for Burnley. Perhaps the most vocal radical was Henry Labouchere, MP for Northampton. Labouchere had initially supported Egyptian intervention, but by August 1882 he had changed his mind, and began to use his journal, *Truth*, as a battering ram against the government. Chamberlain's attempts to soothe Labouchere, assuring him that he was opposed to a protectorate,[18] were unpersuasive, and Labouchere remained a critic both in and out of parliament. The most vociferous and directly personal attacks on Chamberlain, however, continued to come from John Bright. When invited to Highbury in April 1885, Bright was angry enough to respond in a stinging letter that 'the time is not pleasant for our meeting'. He came near to repudiating Chamberlain as a political colleague: 'It is fortunate for you that the Tories are so bad – or I think many people would begin to look at them with some favour.'[19]

Chamberlain dismissed the complaints of his radical colleagues. The lesson he had learned from the Egyptian imbroglio was that a firm determination to use force when necessary and an unquestioned pre-eminence of British interests over local aspirations should govern colonial and foreign policy. Advocating decisiveness, he deplored the 'policy of drifting' which too often characterized cabinet discussions during the Egyptian crisis.[20] In an attempt to retract his earlier declarations, he claimed that his position was centrist – one which steered 'between Jingoism and Peace at any price'.[21] If Chamberlain did not advocate the full-scale annexation of new territory for the empire – a policy of the Jingoes, he would claim – he was clearly willing to establish a British supremacy in those countries where British interests were at risk.

Chamberlain's experience as a member of the Liberal government in the 1880s was the political crucible in which he came to think imperially not only about Egypt but also about the world at large. Arguments with his radical critics convinced him that they were wishful thinkers, ignoring the realities of global power. He no longer agreed with many of his radical colleagues on imperial matters. In contrast to Bright and Morley, who retained a strong suspicion of state intervention abroad, Chamberlain believed that Britain should always act where interest and duty dictated.

Apart from the strategic lessons he learned from Egypt, Chamberlain was also probably influenced by his official position in the cabinet. As President of the Board of Trade he was determined to push forward the interests of 'the commercial classes' who had felt neglected in the past.[22] Since 80 per cent of the Suez Canal traffic lay in British hands, Chamberlain had a special responsibility in protecting that vital shipping lane. This important commercial consideration, combined with strategic concerns in north Africa led Chamberlain increasingly down the path of imperial necessity. Indeed, Robinson and Gallagher believe that Chamberlain's Egyptian experience during the 1880s made him by the end of that decade 'a fierce retentionist'.[23]

Complementary to Chamberlain's first-hand experiences in imperial affairs as a cabinet minister was his timely reading of a theoretical justification of Britain's imperial role in world affairs. J. R. Seely's *The Expansion of England*, published in 1883, was not only a bestseller but also 'a brilliant intellectual success'.[24] Seely's intent was not to defend the empire – an empire which had been created, in his famous phrase, 'in a fit of absence of mind'.[25] Rather, he hoped to explain what the empire had become. Too often, the individual colonies making up the empire had been thought of as mere possessions, instead of extensions of England. The colonists had not lost their English citizenship by moving abroad: they carried that citizenship with them. Thus colonists were 'of our own blood ... united with us by the strongest tie'.[26] In short, colonies were 'a great augmentation of the national state':[27] as they grew in number, a more expansive England was created. Seely's vision likely fired Chamberlain's imagination for a role he himself could play in an extensive empire. He had moved in a natural progression from municipal officer to Member of Parliament to cabinet minister. In each phase, he had honed his skills as leader and manipulator of public opinion. It would not be unusual for a man of such manipulative and controlling instincts to be attracted to the prospect of greater opportunities for power on a global scale.

Chamberlain's growing imperial designs and personal drive for the exercise of power beyond the borders of Britain during the 1880s finds its earliest expression in his involvement with the Irish question. For the first time, Chamberlain took a leading role in formulating imperial policy as it related directly to a British colony. Ireland's re-emergence as a pressing public issue was an unpleasant surprise to the Gladstone ministry. Gladstone himself believed that Irish matters had been settled when he initiated substantial reforms during his first ministry of 1868–74. Disestablishment of the Irish Church in 1869 and the Land Act of 1870 seemed to meet Irish grievances. But poor harvests, low agricultural productivity, and tenant farmers' inability to pay their rents provoked a round of tenant evictions in the late 1870s. In 1879, the Irish Land League under the leadership of Charles Stewart Parnell was formed to protect tenants' rights by direct action, primarily through rent strikes and other forms of intimidation. The League's systematic recruitment of the Irish tenantry became an important stimulus to the demands for Home Rule in the waning days of Disraeli's government.

The turmoil in Ireland caught the attention of the Gladstone administration within a few months of its formation. As the number of agrarian incidents rose, the government was driven to a decision between the two traditional legislative alternatives for dealing with Ireland – coercion or conciliation.[28] Chamberlain's initial instincts were for conciliation as the best means to protect Irish tenants from landlord exploitation. The cabinet was of like mind and sent to the Commons the Compensation for Disturbance Bill to prevent unfair evictions. After its defeat in the House of Lords, disorderly outbursts from Irish tenantry accelerated in late 1880. As the threat to public safety increased, the mood of the cabinet shifted. Led by Chamberlain's old nemesis, W. E. Forster, now Chief Secretary to Ireland, the Whiggish element in the cabinet was bent on coercive measures. Chamberlain strongly opposed any such legislation, arguing that 'the widespread disaffection of the Irish people grows out of causes of just complaint'.[29] After 'several stormy sessions',[30] a Crimes and Arms Bill permitting confinement of suspects without evidence was brought forward in early 1881 over the objections of Chamberlain, Bright, and Gladstone himself.

Once these coercive measures had passed, the swing of cabinet opinion moved again toward conciliation. Designed to balance the punitive Arms Bill with a more constructive social programme, a new land bill favouring the rights of tenants was introduced. Implementing in principle the famous 'three F's' – fair rents, free sales, and fixity of tenure – the bill facilitated rent reduction through the court system. Tenants thereafter need not rely upon the unauthorized tactics of the Land League to ensure a fair and equitable rental.

During many months of cabinet and parliamentary debate, Chamberlain's views underwent a palpable shift. Although he remained sympathetic to the Irish tenantry, he grew to distrust Parnell and the Land League.[31] He also disliked the politics of obstruction engaged in by Parnell and the Irish nationalists in the Commons. Their tactics of filibuster even against the government's conciliatory measures seemed counterproductive to Chamberlain and delayed remedial legislation. He was fearful, too, that the ultimate object of the Irish leaders was an independent Ireland. Therefore, he supported the arrest in October 1881 of Parnell and others who were sentenced indefinitely to Kilmainham Jail in Dublin.

Chamberlain's support of coercion in Ireland, coming as it did before the Egyptian crisis broke the following year, prompted a public rebuke from Morley in the pages of the *Pall Mall Gazette*. Stung by his friend's criticism, Chamberlain denounced the Land League's 'revolutionary programme'. He assured Morley that coercion was still 'hateful' to him; but it now seemed inevitable. 'For heaven's sake', he urged, 'do not let us "Wobble".'[32] Morley, he suggested, could perform a valuable service for the government by using the pages of the *Pall Mall Gazette* to 'pitch into the Tories' who were using the events in Ireland for their own purposes.[33] Morley objected, declaring that the *Gazette* had already condemned coercion; and in any case, he wasn't 'a spaniel who will run to pick up any dirty stick that Gladstone throws'.[34] Chamberlain's irritation became threatening: he promised that if the Irish continued their 'irreconcilable attitude', their leaders would 'rot in Kilmainham'.[35] Furthermore, he was prepared to 'use every means' to put down the existing Irish agitation.[36]

In public, Chamberlain was more moderate. In a speech at Liverpool before the NLF in October 1881, he defended suppression of the League on the grounds that it had become an organization dedicated to secession from the Union. An independent Ireland, hostile to British interests, could not be tolerated by any political group whether conservative, liberal, or radical. If the Union were broken, the two countries would become 'a standing menace one to the other'. Therefore, he must say to Ireland what the northern states said to the south on the eve of the American Civil War: 'The Union must be preserved.' Within that indissoluble link, Ireland would be guaranteed 'equal laws, equal justice, equal opportunities, equal prosperity'.[37] The ideas of this powerful speech, as we shall see, remained Chamberlain's consistent policy toward Ireland in the years to come.

Chamberlain and the Liberal government under Gladstone won the early rounds against the Land League. With Parnell in jail, Ireland appeared to be calm in the early months of 1882. But unexpectedly an opportunity arose for Chamberlain which once again revealed his eagerness to manoeuvre for advantage in manipulating the levers of power. On 15 April 1882, a Captain William O'Shea, Home Rule MP for Clare, sent an unsolicited letter to Chamberlain. Professing an intimate knowledge of Parnell's intentions, O'Shea wrote that in return for the release of Parnell from prison and the passage of a rent arrears bill giving greater protection from eviction to tenants, the Irish leader would discourage agrarian outrages in Ireland. Chamberlain saw the importance of this initiative and quickly opened negotiations with Parnell through O'Shea. Gladstone, too, was brought into the scheme. Within a fortnight, under the terms of the 'Kilmainham Treaty', Parnell was released, the Arrears Bill was promised, and a 'new departure' in Irish–British relations seemed possible.[38]

As so often was the case with Ireland, however, unexpected events caught the politicians off guard. They began with the resignation of the Chief Secretary for Ireland, Forster, on the grounds that Parnell's guarantees of cooperation with the Liberal government under the terms of the 'Treaty' were inadequate. Almost immediately, rumours began to circulate that the new Chief Secretary would be Chamberlain. His friends believed that his astute and determined negotiations with O'Shea and Parnell had brought closure to a complicated issue, and that he deserved appropriate recognition.[39] Chamberlain himself did little to scotch the rumours; instead, he actively promoted them.[40] Nonetheless, to the general surprise of many, not least of all Chamberlain, the post was first offered to Andrew Marshall Porter, a Presbyterian and Liberal MP for Londonderry, who turned it down. Gladstone then turned successfully to Lord Frederick Cavendish, brother to the Whig leader in the cabinet, the Marquis of Hartington. Within hours of his arrival in Dublin, Cavendish and his parliamentary undersecretary, Thomas Burke, were murdered in Phoenix Park by assassins wielding surgical knives. For a third time within a week, a Chief Secretary was sought. And, once again, Chamberlain was overlooked. Cavendish's successor was George Otto Trevelyan, Liberal MP for the Hawick Burghs (in the Scottish borders) and nephew of the great Whig historian, Lord Macaulay.

Chamberlain's aspirations to play a larger role in Ireland were only momentarily postponed, however. In the aftermath of the Phoenix Park murders, he reopened the line to Parnell.[41] Now supporting a conciliatory policy, Chamberlain fought against a Crimes Bill put forward by Harcourt as Home Secretary. But Chamberlain lost the argument in cabinet. The Bill, to be in force for three years, enhanced powers of arrest, established curfews, and created a special tribunal for the most serious crimes. Coercion was balanced, however, by conciliation as an Arrears Bill also passed into legislation. Although Chamberlain in effect had gained little for his efforts, he had signalled his continuing interest in Irish affairs.

Between 1882 and 1885, Ireland was relatively tranquil, and the government was able to turn its attention toward franchise reform and to imperial issues far from home. In the meantime, Parnell was becoming less visible as a leader of the Irish nationalist cause, partly because of his growing involvement with Katherine O'Shea (their daughters were born in 1883 and 1884). But Parnell was also secretly at work enhancing the effectiveness of the Irish parliamentary party and preparing it for the next phase of Irish nationalism – the agitation for Home Rule, destined to be the rock on which successive ministries, whether Liberal or Conservative, were to founder.

By late 1884 it was clear that in any forthcoming general election Irish MPs dedicated to Home Rule could present a formidable challenge to the Liberal government. Gladstone himself estimated that the Liberals would lose about 25 seats in Ireland, with the Home Rulers returning nearly 80 MPs.[42] That Irish affairs would become once again dominant in the House of Commons was guaranteed by the expiration in September 1885 of the 1882 Crimes Act. The scene was set for negotiation between the Liberal ministry and the Irish leader to forestall parliamentary obstruction during the coming months.

The main problem for Gladstone and his cabinet colleagues in the initial stages of the Home Rule campaign was to discern what Parnell meant by the term. Did he intend Home Rule as a euphemism for separatism and ultimately independence? Or would he be willing to settle for some lesser form of Irish self-government that maintained ties to Britain? Chamberlain was certain of his own position. As he explained it to a radical colleague, W. H. Duignan, he would resist Home Rule 'by force to the end of the chapter'[43] if it was the first step on the road to independence. But he had no objection 'in principle' to Home Rule so long as it was confined to an expansion of responsible local government to Ireland. In fact, Chamberlain believed that Ireland had a right to a local government 'more complete, more popular, more thoroughly representative, & more far reaching' than anything that had yet been proposed.

To implement Home Rule, he advocated a Central Board in Ireland which would deal specifically with Irish issues such as land, education, railways and other communications. The Board would also have the power of taxation for specifically Irish projects. Matters such as military and foreign affairs would be handled at Westminster. In lieu of a ministerial united front and Gladstone's apparent indecision about Home Rule, Chamberlain had stolen a march. His Central Board scheme was another example of his determination to formulate a policy independent of the cabinet and then to set about energetically in carrying it out.

He arranged for Duignan to disseminate his ideas to leaders of the Irish Nationalist Party. He entered into negotiations with Captain O'Shea, who served as intermediary to Parnell. And he shared with Gladstone the substance of the ongoing negotiations. But as the talks informally progressed between Chamberlain and Parnell (through O'Shea) in late 1884 and early 1885, a fatal misunderstanding emerged. Parnell made it clear to O'Shea that a Central Board could only be a temporary solution, and could never substitute for an Irish parliament, the flagship of the nationalist cause. A Central Board in Parnell's view would have only administrative, not legislative, functions. O'Shea, it seems, never transmitted this vital piece of information to Chamberlain. Thus Chamberlain continued to believe that Parnell would accept a Central Board as the foundation stone for Home Rule, whereas Parnell believed that Chamberlain was willing to regard the Board as secondary.[44]

When Chamberlain presented his Board scheme to the cabinet in early 1885, he faced immediate opposition. Weakened by internecine struggles and still reeling from the news of Gordon's death at Khartoum, ministers were not eager to undertake such a significant task as the reform of Irish local government. Chamberlain's argument to Earl Spencer, the Lord Lieutenant of Ireland, that the Board was 'our last card' and could, if established, reduce the drive for separatism among Home Rulers was not persuasive.[45] Even Gladstone, though he favoured the scheme, gave it only tepid support. On 9 May 1885, the Central Board was rejected by the cabinet.[46] Within a month, the demoralized government, already on its last legs, resigned on a defeat over the budget in the House of Commons. A Conservative interim government under Lord Salisbury immediately assumed office.

6

FLUCTUATING SCHEMES

When the Conservatives under Lord Salisbury formed a minority government in June 1885, the country fell into an electoral free-for-all. Liberals, radicals, conservatives, and the Irish Home Rulers struggled vigorously in preparation for the upcoming election. Central to the political discourse was Ireland, and more specifically the fate of Home Rule. There was little agreement among political leaders on Irish policy. Hartington – as the representative of the hard-line Whigs/Liberals – urged his party to pledge 'an uncompromising resistance' to Irish demands.[1] In contrast, the Conservatives, hoping to cling to office, entered into a bargain with Parnell and the Irish. In return for Irish support, the Conservatives would replace coercion with a policy of conciliation. Gladstone, more shrewdly, kept his options open. Maintaining his distance from both the Conservatives and Parnell, convincing Hartington that the solution to Ireland was still in play, and assuring Chamberlain that he 'shed tears over the grave of the Central Board',[2] Gladstone was well placed to operate politically from the centre.

As the electioneering evolved in the summer and autumn of 1885, however, one politician emerged as the commanding figure. A powerful speech-maker, a superb organizer of public opinion, and an exceptional strategist, Chamberlain was in his element during these critical months. His electoral platform contained three well-defined planks. The first concerned Ireland. Understanding the importance of settling the Irish question, he once again entered into private negotiations with Parnell. Chamberlain proposed that he and Dilke visit Ireland to see at first hand Irish conditions: this would signal Ireland's importance to the national political agenda. It would also, of course, undoubtedly give the radical leaders substantial favourable publicity and redound to their electoral benefit in England.

The second plank of his platform revived and extended the idea of a Central Board which had been so recently turned down by the cabinet. Chamberlain now proposed the creation of National Councils not only in Ireland but in Wales and Scotland as well. Such Councils would have both local administrative and legislative authority. If Parnell accepted the offer, Chamberlain could hope to rely upon the support of a numerous group of Irishmen in any new parliamentary constellation. The canny Irish leader, however, had decided not to nail his colours precipitously to any mast, and to wait for an opportune moment to accept the highest bid – even if it came from the Conservatives. Indeed, at the very moment that Chamberlain began his Irish initiative, Parnell was entering into secret conversations with leading Conservatives. Only when the Irish national press strongly attacked the proposed tour did Chamberlain realize that the Irish leader had apparently double-crossed him. Parnell's cavalier treatment of his offer obliged Chamberlain to cancel his visit. Outraged that his initiative was so publicly and contemptuously rejected, Chamberlain never forgot the snub.[3]

Chamberlain had better luck with the third plank of his platform – an expanded radical social programme. His inspired articles in the *Fortnightly Review*, published serially since 1883, were at the heart of his message. Now gathered into more accessible book form and published during the election campaign, *The Radical Programme* examined from the radical point of view social and political issues that concerned the country.[4] Chamberlain did not rely only on printed matter. Drawing upon his various country campaigns of the past several years, he refined and sharpened his appeal to the mass of the electorate in a series of major speeches around the country. The detail and scope of Chamberlain's electioneering had a controlled power and force that kept him continually in the public eye during the campaign.[5]

Even from the distance of more than a century, Chamberlain's 'unauthorized programme' (as it came to be called) remains a striking departure from the politics of that day in its direct appeal to agricultural labourers and working-class voters newly enfranchised under the Reform Act of 1884. The tone was set in his first speech in the port city of Hull in August 1885. Addressing an assembly of several thousand, Chamberlain proclaimed that his first object was 'to elevate the poor, to raise the general condition of the people'.[6] In recognition that working-class families too often lacked the resources to pay primary school fees for their children, he proposed the repeal of that part of the 1870 Education Act requiring parental financial contributions. Chamberlain also advocated 'some scheme of graduated taxation' for working families. To improve the lot of small farmers and agricultural workers, he urged 'decent cottages and fair allotments at reasonable rents, and with security of tenure'. This was widely known as the promise of 'three acres and a cow'. Using the model of municipal government familiar to a former mayor of Birmingham, Chamberlain also promoted the creation of popularly elected bodies of local government as instruments of empowerment in implementing these new programmes.

A month after the Hull meeting, Chamberlain delivered a speech at Warrington (Lancashire) reiterating the need to elevate the poor by 'a levelling up which shall do something to remove the excessive inequalities in the social condition of the people'.[7] For too long, social and economic inequities had been ignored: 'We have to ... grapple with the mass of misery and destitution in our midst, co-existent as it is with the evidences of abundant wealth and teeming prosperity.' To meet these greater social needs, it was necessary to put aside 'the convenient cant of selfish wealth' and to re-examine such stock phrases as 'the eternal laws' of supply and demand, the 'necessity' of freedom of contract, and the 'sanctity' of private property.

Within a week, Chamberlain had travelled to Scotland, a Liberal stronghold, bearing the radical message to Glasgow and Inverness. To Glaswegians he predicted that free education would 'put their feet upon the ladder which leads up to the storehouse of knowledge', promising that 'every poor man's cottage' could become 'as healthy as the palace of the rich'.[8] Chamberlain also took a stand upon an issue particularly lively in Scotland – the disestablishment of the Scottish Church. Led by Scottish nonconformists, the liberation movement had gained significant strength during the recent Gladstonian ministry. Chamberlain, reluctant to speak at length upon this complex religious matter lest it detract from his social programme, neverthe- less acknowledged local nonconformist fervour. He mentioned his own dissenting background and stated his opposition to state aid to religion. If left to him, said Chamberlain, he would 'free the Church from State control, whether in England, or in Scotland or in Wales'.[9] Although he cautioned the Scots on making this issue dominant in the campaign, his critical remarks against established churches were to haunt Chamberlain when the votes were counted.

At Inverness a few days later, Chamberlain's arrival at the railway station brought out a considerable crowd, including a large number of working-class Scots. In his speech that evening, Chamberlain dwelt upon the Highland Clearances, a 'black page' in the history of the private ownership of land.[10] He condemned the depopulation of thousands of industrious, hardworking toilers of the soil who had been forced from their homes and placed upon 'barren patches and seacoast shores' where they could no longer earn their living. It was time, Chamberlain said, to review a system of land- ownership which had permitted such exploitation and had placed 'such vast powers for evil in the hands of irresponsible individuals'. When presented with the freedom of the city the following day, Chamberlain returned to the theme of local government's responsibility for enhancing the welfare of the people. Declaring the present era 'the age of municipal enterprise', Chamberlain reminded his audience: 'We no longer build palaces for our princes, but we build schools for the children of our poor.'[11]

By mid-October, Chamberlain was again working the English constituencies and nearing the end of his country campaign. He continued his balanced presentation in appealing to both rural and urban audiences. In an important speech at Trowbridge (Wiltshire), where he was introduced as 'the man of the future', Chamberlain spoke to a mainly agricultural crowd. He emphasized again the importance of freely elected local authorities in every village and in every county which would guarantee 'and gratify that heaven-planted craving in every labourer's heart to have some closer and more direct connexion with the land'.[12]

Chamberlain concluded his campaign in an urban setting, delivering speech after speech throughout November in Birmingham. Calculated for a national audience, these speeches were also designed to foster a strong Liberal turnout in the newly cre- ated (under the reforms of 1884–5) electoral districts of the city. From three all-city seats, Birmingham now was made up of seven single-member seats. Chamberlain had chosen for himself the heavily working-class constituency of West Birmingham. He was also active in other Birmingham constituencies supporting radical candidates such as William Kenrick, the brother of his first wife, Harriet, and now alderman of the city; Powell Williams, his chief political operative and also an alderman; John Bright; and Henry Broadhurst, the labour leader.

Chamberlain was not only energetically campaigning against the Conservatives; he was also strenuously taking on the Liberal leadership. Writing to Gladstone, he insisted that in any future Liberal administration, he and Dilke must be able to speak and vote as they wished on education and local government reforms. If Gladstone could not accept these conditions, Chamberlain warned, the radicals would remain outside the government.[13] For Hartington, who had labelled the radical plans as 'Socialist' and illusory,[14] Chamberlain had harsher words. In his Warrington speech, he publicly condemned Hartington as an antiquated Rip van Winkle, asleep while the world moved forward. Privately, he was more severe. To Harcourt, Chamberlain declared that Hartington was 'up in a balloon', unaware of public opinion and the need for radical change. Hartington had 'for months past' gone 'out of his way to throw dirt on every single thing' that Chamberlain had proposed. In retaliation, Chamberlain threatened to 'run a Radical in every constituency' to diminish the Whigs. 'If Hartington wants war', Chamberlain warned, 'he can have it.'[15]

By presenting a 'definite and practical' programme for what he called the 'Radical Party', Chamberlain believed that he could attract a majority among Liberal voters in the countryside.[16] He was also convinced that the reforms of 1884–5, especially the expansion of the suffrage, gave him a unique opportunity. The new electors, he predicted to Harcourt, are 'Radical'.[17] He made a similar prediction to Lady Dorothy Neville: 'We are going to sweep the counties and with my programme.'[18] By winning a radical majority within the Liberal Party, Chamberlain would become the natural heir to Gladstone upon his retirement. The power and influence he had sought in the House of Commons would at last become his.

Indeed, it would seem that Chamberlain operated from a position of strength. The riddled Liberal leadership gave his natural drive and thrust for power a clear opening. His acquaintance with countryside campaigning, his contacts long established and well organized, and his excoriating style of speaking were advantages not held by any other politician.[19] Lengthy columns in *The Times* charted his sweep through the country and attested to his popularity at public meetings. *The Times* also editorialized that Chamberlain's campaign was undeniably the most prominent and his programme the most clearly delineated of any Liberal candidate.[20]

Yet the Liberal campaign proved a disappointment. Early returns from the counties suggested that the Liberals were slated for victory, but later borough results tended toward the Conservatives. Thus, the Liberals – traditionally strong in the cities and weak in the counties – encountered a surprising electoral reversal of electoral fortune. Final election tallies did not represent a clear-cut defeat; but neither was it the victory that the Liberals and Chamberlain had hoped for. Party totals in the new parliament were Liberals 334 and Conservatives 250. The Irish Nationalists, with 86 MPs, held the balance. Indeed, by cooperating with the Irish, Salisbury could open parliament and even remain in office for a time. Post-election consequences were more serious for Chamberlain. Within a year, he was cast out of the Liberal Party, lost the opportunity for leadership, and became the head of a splinter group of dissatisfied Liberals with limited prospects.

What had happened to Chamberlain's optimistic (some would say arrogant) predictions? And what role did he play in dashing Liberal hopes? It must be said that Chamberlain both helped and hindered his party's cause. There is little doubt that his energetic stumping the countryside in late summer and early autumn of 1885, especially in the rural areas, had brought his powerful and charismatic presence to thousands of new voters. Chamberlain had already identified the newly enfranchised agricultural labourers as a possible target for his radical platform during his speaking tour in January 1885.[21] This was a shrewd appeal. Recent historical work has shown that the rural working class, who had long been electorally silent, were ready to cast aside their traditional deference toward county elites. Vehemently anti-aristocratic, they were more radical than the Liberal rank and file.[22]

Whether or not the radical message itself was as important as the mere sight and sound of Chamberlain on the hustings is a matter of debate. Historians disagree, for example, about the impact of 'three acres and a cow' on the agricultural vote.[23] Chamberlain himself, not surprisingly, believed that the 'Cow' was effective in the agricultural districts, and would have achieved even more 'if the Whigs had not been such asses' in their attempt to discredit 'this admirable cry'.[24] But there was a possible unanticipated effect. Compulsory land purchases for agricultural labourers could take more land from farmers than from the gentry or great aristocratic landlords. Farmers thus likely viewed Chamberlain's plan with some apprehension. A divided rural electorate possibly prevented the Liberals from carrying the counties in greater numbers.[25]

Other points of Chamberlain's programme encountered opposition from the electorate. Free education, for example, seemed on the face of it to appeal directly to upwardly striving working-class parents who wished their children advantageously placed. But urban workers feared that the loss of fees in schools might simply encourage local authorities to increase the rates to make up the shortfall. Even more controversial was the potential impact of Chamberlain's proposal upon the future of denominational (voluntary and religious) schools and their rivals, the secular board schools.

At this time, denominational schools still far outnumbered board schools (14,600 to 4,295). To make education free for all children – whether enrolled in denominational or board schools – the state must provide aid to both kinds of schools. To denominationalists, state control inevitably following upon state aid could threaten their independence. To nonconformists, state aid without accompanying secular controls was completely unacceptable. Chamberlain never addressed this dilemma effectively. This unnerved his nonconformist radical supporters. The most dramatic expression of this came at a meeting of the National Liberal Federation (NLF) in October 1885, which decisively rejected free education unless it was explicitly tied to secular management. Before the election campaign was over, many of Chamberlain's firmest supporters, including Bunce of the *Birmingham Post*, Schnadhorst of the NLF, and John Morley could no longer support this important plank of the unauthorized programme.[26]

Another damaging blow to Chamberlain's campaign was the surprising and sudden emergence of the disestablishment of the Church as an election issue.[27] The fault was largely Chamberlain's. Within a fortnight of his Glasgow speech in mid-September, during which he had both encouraged dissenting opinion and dampened their expectations, Chamberlain reopened the debate. In a public statement he now encouraged the Scots to send as many 'disestablishers' as possible to parliament in order to assure that question 'a prominent place' in a forthcoming Liberal government. A few days later at a speech in Bradford, Chamberlain explicitly endorsed disestablishment not only in Scotland, but England as well.

The Conservatives accurately sensed that disestablishment would play to their advantage among moderate Liberals. They promptly launched a 'Church in Danger' campaign. In an important speech in early October, Lord Salisbury denounced Chamberlain as the leader of a party whose disestablishment policy was 'fraught with frightful disaster to the nation'. In an echo of Salisbury, Michael Hicks-Beach, the Conservative Chancellor of the Exchequer, condemned disestablishment as a 'public crime': he also proscribed Chamberlain's unauthorized programme as 'social revolution'.[28] Lord Randolph Churchill, a candidate for one of the Birmingham seats, took the charge straight to Chamberlain's back yard. Chamberlain, he claimed, having taken up 'Socialistic theories', could not be trusted to govern. Should Chamberlain come to power, he would lead the country astray with 'curious' and 'eccentric' legislation.[29]

Given his tendency to strike vigorously at his opponents when attacked, Chamberlain returned blow for blow. Speaking in Birmingham in early November, he reminded his audience of the enormous endowment of the Church of England, a matter of material interest 'especially to the working classes'. He hinted at restoring 'to the people … this vast property which is now diverted for the services of a sect'.[30] Chamberlain's fighting words not only inflamed the clerical hierarchy but the more militant parish clergy as well. Anglican pulpits rang with religious and Tory fervour: 'VOTE FOR THE CHURCH' was their resounding cry. Liberal candidates began to feel pressure from constituents. A few days before polling began, Dilke – fighting for his seat in Chelsea – wrote Chamberlain that London shopkeepers 'were very hot on the church question' and that many of his nonconformist friends were urging him to repudiate disestablishment.[31] The following day, Dilke pledged to his constituents that he would oppose disestablishment in parliament. Other Liberal candidates were forced to give similar pledges, including Morley, who had written the chapter on disestablishment in *The Radical Programme*. The matter was serious enough for Gladstone to chastise Chamberlain directly. He particularly thought that Morley's piece in *The Radical Programme* was 'outrageously unjust'.[32]

There is little doubt that Chamberlain's independent radical campaign invigorated the electorate and may have played an important role in attracting new voters into Liberal ranks. But a general sense among Liberal politicians was that Chamberlainite radicalism had gone too far and had paid a high electoral price.[33] The cry of 'Church in Danger' – in addition to flaws in the platform on free education and suspicions concerning the compulsory land scheme – alienated enough Liberal moderates to diminish their party's prospects in the new House of Commons.

It may be said that if Chamberlain were sensitive to the opportunities of the new electorate, he was not sensitive to the ramifications of what could be considered a self-serving campaign. Determined to enhance his power and authority in the country at large and in any post-election ministry that may be formed, he pulled out all the stops of every electoral issue and pushed every possible lever of persuasion to obtain a victory, thus ignoring his party's best interests.

An additional example of Chamberlain's inability to reign in his need for power and control, and the lengths to which he would go occurred during the closing days of the campaign when he attempted to manipulate the election to his own ends by dishing the prime minister himself. Gladstone had remained magisterially aloof throughout the campaign, in part because of a serious throat infection and his subsequent convalescence. But he had not been idle. Foremost upon his mind was the condition of Ireland and the need to settle the question of its governance. Hints to his colleagues and former ministers as to the direction of his thought were tentative and inconclusive. In truth, he was steadily moving toward the establishment of a Home Rule government in Ireland. It was a momentous decision. His plan was not merely to redress historic Irish wrongs, but to provide a badly needed rallying cry for the Liberal Party – one that would unite left, right, and moderate wings into a consensual partnership for their next term of office.[34] Home Rule would thus displace Chamberlain's radical social programme, which had divided Liberal Party members for so many months. The first manifest sign of Gladstone's intent occurred on 17 December 1885, just prior to the closing of the polls. On that day, several metropolitan newspapers published a story that Gladstone had settled on a plan of Home Rule: this was the famous 'Hawarden Kite' flown by Gladstone's son Herbert in an attempt to prevent any opponents of Home Rule from gaining the upper hand. From that time onward, Home Rule dominated political discussion in all political parties.

The Kite, as we now know, had in fact been induced at least partly by the Machiavellian behaviours of Chamberlain himself. In early December, electoral straws in the wind indicated that the Liberals would lack sufficient parliamentary seats to govern effectively on their own. That being the case, Chamberlain decided that it would be best if the Conservatives were to remain in power for the foreseeable future. Once installed in office at the sufferance of the Liberals, a Conservative ministry might very well put a wrong foot forward, thus discrediting them in the eyes of the country – especially if they appeared to truckle to Irish demands. Any future general election after a failed Conservative government would, Chamberlain surmised, benefit the radical-led Liberals, who could sweep all before them and return to parliament with a greatly enhanced majority. As Chamberlain put it to one correspondent: 'I am clear that we had better bide our time & rub the Tories' noses well in the mess they have made.'[35] Conspiring with his closest political friends, Chamberlain convened a radical summit at Highbury during the first weekend of December. In attendance were Dilke, Morley, and Shaw-Lefevre.[36] Within a week, Dilke made public Chamberlain's plan of encouraging a Conservative ministry when he spoke before a radical club in Chelsea.

With the news of Dilke's speech, the Gladstonian inner circle could only draw the conclusion that Chamberlain, Dilke, and the radicals were attempting to deny the fruits of a victory to the Liberals and to exclude Gladstone from office. At that point Herbert Gladstone took it upon himself to fly the Kite that would kick the radicals and kill the plot. Chamberlain, like his radical colleagues, was taken aback by the Kite. In grappling with the political dimensions of a possible Home Rule Bill underwritten by Gladstone, Chamberlain seems to have panicked. Hearing rumours of the Kite the evening before it was revealed in the press, Chamberlain dashed off a letter to Dilke in which he abruptly changed course. 'We must temporise', he counselled. 'It will be better to stick to Mr G.'[37] In other words, Chamberlain had suddenly decided to drop the plan to support the Conservatives in their attempt to form a government. Furthermore, he told Dilke, he planned to speak in that sense at Birmingham the following day. Admitting that his reversal could place Dilke in an awkward and exposed position, he attempted to smooth it over by claiming that his behaviour would puzzle the press to their advantage: 'they will perhaps think it is some astute Machiavellianism on our part to differ slightly at times.'[38]

But Dilke's prompt response clearly indicates that he was not mollified. Complaining that Chamberlain's behaviour was 'rough on me', Dilke rightly observed that if he followed Chamberlain in his volte-face, it would appear to everyone that he took political positions 'for personal reasons of a not very creditable nature'.[39] Chamberlain's reply came as close to an apology as he ever managed. 'Have I turned round?' he asked rhetorically. 'Perhaps I have, but it is unconsciously', he answered. He assured Dilke that he would publicly refrain from any word that would contradict Dilke's public utterances. He confided further that he had not retreated from his belief that Gladstone's Irish scheme was 'death & damnation' and that they must 'try & stop it'.[40]

Publicly, however, Chamberlain held out an olive branch to Gladstone. In a speech to the Birmingham Reform Club on the day of his letter to Dilke, he backed away from his original plan of favouring an extended life for Salisbury's government. Additionally – in what can only be described as a brazen lie – Chamberlain praised Gladstone and gave him a blank check with reference to Ireland. 'I have so much faith in the experience and the patriotism of Mr. Gladstone', he told the meeting, 'that I cannot doubt that if he should ever see his way to propose any scheme of arrangement, I should be able conscientiously to give it my humble support.'[41]

In the next several days, Chamberlain wrote other colleagues in an attempt to find his footing on shifting political sands. To Harcourt, who had an open line to Hartington, Chamberlain seemed to hint at an alliance with Hartington against any Gladstonian form of Home Rule. Yet he was clearly angered by Hartington's lack of support during the election campaign. Hartington had behaved 'so d – d unfriendly', he complained, that he had 'no hope and no desire for co-operation with him'.[42] Harcourt replied that Hartington was not 'half as unfriendly to you as you are to him'. Harcourt also assured Chamberlain, rather too optimistically, that Hartington would respond favourably to friendly overtures.[43]

Chamberlain also engaged in an extensive dialogue with Morley. Tension between the two old friends, which had arisen during the final years of Gladstone's ministry, continued after the fall of the Liberal government. Morley believed that Chamberlain's radical programme bore the taint of a doctrinaire authoritarianism.[44]

During the election campaign of 1885, Morley often urged Chamberlain to temper his demands. Morley himself was a passionate supporter of Irish nationalism: of all Liberal politicians, he was the most committed to Home Rule. During the election campaign, he was one of the few parliamentary candidates who paid attention to Irish affairs. To Morley, British dominance of Ireland was a case of imperial subjugation. For this reason alone, he believed that the Irish should have a say in their own governance. In September 1885 he had written Chamberlain that he could not 'refuse to consider the question of some sort of autonomy' for Ireland.[45] Morley's later remarks in the autumn confirmed his intention to advance Ireland to the forefront of public discussion. In an important speech to his constituents at Newcastle on 22 December, he urged Gladstone to prepare a detailed scheme of self-government for Ireland. Two days later, Chamberlain sent a strong letter 'entirely' disapproving of Morley's speech.[46] He claimed that there were only two possible options for Ireland, either his own scheme of National Councils or complete separation. No compromise was possible. Chamberlain flatly declared that he would not be 'dragged … into a policy' which 'would be fatal to the greatness & influence of the country'. Had he been on the platform at Newcastle with Morley, Chamberlain continued, he would have risen to his feet to protest against 'the dangerous tendency' of Morley's argument. Not content with political disagreement, Chamberlain added a personal note. For a long time, he and Morley had been 'drifting apart': it was 'a bitter disappointment … to think that we are not destined, as I once hoped, to tread the same path in political life'.

Morley rejected Chamberlain's attempt at intimidation. He reminded Chamberlain that their argument over the Sudan had prompted the same response. He chastised his friend for bringing 'the thunders of excommunication into play whenever we do not take precisely the same view of things'. 'Am I to be debarred from saying what I think – saying it, mind you, as I did at Newcastle, in particularly careful, sober, well-weighed words?' Morley claimed that he had no designs on a great position in government: 'I have no ambition to be an admiral of the fleet', he assured Chamberlain. 'But', he continued, 'I'll be hanged if I'll be powder monkey.'[47]

Chamberlain was not persuaded by the advocates of moderation. His belief that Home Rule was unpopular in England inclined him to take a strong stand against any overly generous Home Rule initiative on Gladstone's part.[48] Thus his reasons for opposition to Home Rule were partly political. Chamberlain was also motivated by a sense of frustration at the course of recent events. Cabinet rejection of his Central Board scheme and the Liberal leadership's apparent lack of appreciation of his contributions to the party all were grievances uppermost in his mind. In early December, he lashed out in anger, 'brimming over with differences, grievances, soreness', at a private dinner party. Criticizing Hartington as 'personally offensive', he was also 'furious' at Gladstone, declaring that he would not accept 'any arrangement' with Parnell and the Irish.[49]

It is clear from his comments that Chamberlain was additionally motivated by a growing animus against the Irish nationalist movement and against Parnell most particularly. This had begun when Parnell brusquely turned down the planned

Chamberlain and Dilke offer to visit Ireland in the summer of 1885. That the radical leader took it personally[50] was made manifest publicly when Chamberlain addressed a conference of Liberal associations in September 1885 at Warrington. There he condemned Parnell's advocacy of a single-chambered independent parliament sitting in Dublin as tantamount to establishing within thirty miles 'of our own shores a new foreign country, animated from the outset by unfriendly intentions toward ourselves'.[51] Chamberlain claimed further that Parnell's 'unhesitating, uncompromising demand' would lead to 'the dismemberment of the British Empire'. It was time, he continued, for Ireland with a population of only four millions to cease their threats against the remaining thirty-two millions in the kingdom. The Irish response was predictable. The *United Ireland*, for example, rejected outright Chamberlain's 'brute-majority argument' by reminding Chamberlain that Ireland once had nine millions: but England had bled them 'down to four'.[52] Should the 'rich and many' attempt 'to bully us who are poor and few', the editorial warned further, 'Ireland yet had its resources and would come off best in a game of tormentation'.[53]

To establish a foothold in this uncertain and overheated political climate, Chamberlain took the lead in attempting to elicit from Gladstone a more precise sense of what he proposed with regard to Ireland. A meeting in early January 1886, between himself, Harcourt, Dilke, and (most significantly) Hartington decided to force Gladstone's hand. Hartington was delegated to communicate their dismay at what they considered Gladstone's abrogation of leadership and to urge a meeting of party members to discuss Ireland. Gladstone, reticent and distant in his Welsh fastness, did not respond.

Meanwhile the Conservative government under Salisbury, following the general election, was preparing to resume office. Their minority status and doubtful relations with the Irish nationalists in parliament, however, guaranteed slim prospects. When the Conservatives' decision to introduce a coercion bill for Ireland was made known in the House of Commons on 26 January 1886, their fate was sealed by the combined opposition of Liberals and Irish. Salisbury resigned two days later. This tactical suicide was doubtless designed to place in Gladstone's hand a poisoned chalice. But Gladstone accepted the challenge and began to form his third administration in late January 1886. Offices filled in the new Liberal cabinet would at last give a clear indication of Gladstone's Irish intentions. Chamberlain's role was crucial. Would he be offered a position? And equally importantly, would he accept?

From its earliest moments, the formation of Gladstone's third ministry was characterized by unfortunate circumstances and misunderstandings. Rather ominously, both Hartington and Bright – from different ends of the political spectrum – declined office. When Gladstone invited Chamberlain into the cabinet – partly as recognition of his services to the Liberal election campaign and partly to muzzle him – the offer was made grudgingly. Gladstone first suggested the Admiralty; Chamberlain declined and asked instead for the Secretary of State for the Colonies. Gladstone refused him such a prestigious position, and counter-offered with the Board of Trade, Chamberlain's cabinet office. Chamberlain in turn demurred. After lengthy negotiations, Chamberlain was ultimately given the Presidency of the Local Government

Board – Dilke's former office and of less status than most other cabinet positions. Chamberlain at last accepted, but it had been an awkward and for Chamberlain a demeaning interchange.

Given Chamberlain's suspicions of Gladstone's intentions toward Ireland, it may seem surprising that he accepted office. Perhaps he believed that Gladstone would give up Home Rule; or that he could be persuaded to modify it in acceptable ways. More likely, Chamberlain believed that he had to remain near the centre of power in order to sustain his intrigues for gaining his political and personal ends. But Chamberlain's frustration at the aging Gladstone's tenacious hold on the Liberals and the events of his entrance into the cabinet fatally tainted his tenure as a member of Gladstone's government.

Chamberlain's sense of grievance in the early days of the ministry was heightened at every turn. When Gladstone chose Morley as Irish Secretary Chamberlain was momentarily shocked.[54] Morley – the visionary, the impractical, the literary man – had not only equalled Chamberlain in the race to power but had bested him by receiving an important office of state with a seat in the cabinet. Moreover, Gladstone soon made Morley one of his closest confidantes. In contrast, Chamberlain was deliberately excluded and remained outside the innermost circles of the cabinet where the crucial decisions on Ireland were being made during February and March 1886.[55] The breach between Chamberlain and his former Liberal colleagues was widening on both political and personal grounds.

Meanwhile, there were unsettling signs from Birmingham that the official mouthpiece of local liberalism, the Birmingham Liberal Association, was beginning to question Chamberlain's opposition to Home Rule. The Liberal agent Schnadhorst informed Chamberlain in mid-February that support for Gladstone in Birmingham and the country as a whole was strong and was generally disposed toward settling the Irish Question along Gladstonian lines.[56] Chamberlain thus found himself increasingly in a state of political insecurity, both in parliament and among his most loyal local supporters. In the weeks and months that followed, he attempted to use every opportunity to re-establish his dominance in Birmingham and to regain his reputation in the country at large. It is often difficult to follow his twists and turns, especially when his private comments were often at odds with his public actions.[57] His ideas evolved as events dictated.

Because his 'unauthorized programme' had failed to capture the Liberal Party for the radicals, Chamberlain had to reposition himself within the new national political discourse framed by Gladstone. He had little choice but to refine his ideas about Home Rule and thus to meet Gladstone on his own ground. At first, he fell back on earlier notions of devolving authority to local governing agencies in Ireland. Expanding the concept of National Councils, he advocated a federation of separate parliaments in England, Scotland, Wales, Ulster, as well as southern Ireland. These would deal with internal matters. An imperial parliament sitting at Westminster, made up of representatives from each of the several parliaments, would be concerned with such matters as the colonies and foreign affairs. Chamberlain also insisted that Irish representatives be in attendance at Westminster during the discussion of foreign and imperial matters in order to maintain an imperial connection between Ireland and England. Excluding them would suggest that the Dublin parliament would be all but independent from the imperial parliament and the constitutional and traditional subordination of Dublin to Westminster would be undermined, inevitably speeding the day of independence for Ireland.[58]

As Chamberlain crafted his Home Rule plan, the development of a second strategy – closely allied to the first – became apparent. If he were unable to capture the Liberal Party through his private intrigues and rousing country campaigns, perhaps he could reshape party politics to his advantage by establishing a new party. Creating a new political grouping – one freed alike from the trammels of staid Conservative domestic policies and of timid Liberal forays in foreign and colonial affairs – Chamberlain could take the attractive features of each into a centre-left coalition. Such a party could combine a dynamic domestic social reform programme with a vigorous colonial and foreign policy.

The natural constituency for Chamberlain's plan would be the radical Liberals whom he had courted for so long. But how could these progressive social reformers support an openly imperial policy toward Ireland? Would not their progressive instincts promote – as they had in Morley – an inclination toward a self-governing Ireland? Chamberlain was convinced that middle-class radicals were increasingly unsympathetic to Irish demands. Indeed, during Gladstone's second administration of 1880–5, Irish obstructionist tactics within parliament and disorderly agitation and violence in Ireland itself had inclined some radical MPs and constituency leaders toward coercive measures.[59] Upon those radicals, Chamberlain would stake his scheme: a majority, he hoped, would follow him in rejecting any overly generous Home Rule plan while at the same time maintaining their commitment to social reform. From this core of dissatisfied radicals, he could build a broader coalition.

The rewards to Chamberlain of following this twofold plan were clear enough: in either case, he could achieve sufficient authority and political control to attain the power he craved. But this path to power held dangers as well. The central obstacle, as it always had been, was the remarkable physical stamina and the high moral reputation of the prime minister. If Chamberlain were perceived as the intriguer that he was, tacking and shifting at each breath of the political breeze, the simple contrast between himself and Gladstone could wreck his scheme.

But Chamberlain, driven by his need for power, could not check his dysfunctional plotting. An instructive example occurred in the weeks just prior to the formation of Gladstone's third ministry. In a letter to Escott, editor of the *Fortnightly Review*, Chamberlain proposed an article setting out a radical view of the Irish crisis. The article would argue (in direct reference to his strategy outlined above) that radicals believed Ireland to be 'as much a part of the Empire as London or Yorkshire' and they were 'no more willing to consent to the dismemberment of the Empire' than other politicians.[60] Chamberlain's article duly appeared in early February 1886.[61] Signed 'A Radical', it reviewed various Home Rule plans, finding flaws in nearly all. One plan alone was favoured, that of Chamberlain's own National Council. Such a plan was, as 'A Radical' put it, 'essentially a proposal for the extension of local government on municipal lines'. The existing governing structure of Dublin Castle would be abolished as new administrative bodies came into being. The supremacy of the Crown and the British parliament would remain intact. There would be no interference with the chief institutions of the empire. If such a Council worked for Ireland, similar councils could be extended to Scotland and Wales.

This largely self-serving article concluded on a more constructive note. Chamberlain rightly noted that agrarian discontent had historically fuelled Irish independence. 'Outrage, disorder, contempt of the law, hatred of England, and the demand for legislative independence' – all these may be traced to the imposition by the English of an alien land system upon Ireland. Thus the real issue for Ireland should be the land question, not separation from Britain. A renewed consideration of Irish land must now be taken up 'and this time in frank concert with the Nationalist party'.

Here, then, was Chamberlain's main message to the radicals: it was their duty to recognize the primacy of economic and social issues (land) over constitutional and political ones (Home Rule). 'The demand for Home Rule must stand over till the more urgent and more vital question is decided', he declared.[62] By detaching the land question from Home Rule, Chamberlain could simultaneously appeal directly to the more progressive elements among the radicals, shift the parliamentary agenda away from Home Rule toward social and economic reform, and yet at the same time signal his own willingness to accept a limited Home Rule plan. He could thus emerge as a sensible political leader with a responsible alternative to any Home Rule plan espoused by Gladstone.

On the very first test of the sincerity of his proposals, however, Chamberlain failed. A few weeks after the publication of the *Fortnightly* article, Gladstone introduced to the cabinet (on 13 March 1886) his proposal for land reform in Ireland. Irish landlords would be bought out for £120,000,000 – the whole sum of which would be credited against the Exchequer. This was a first step toward a massive transfer of land to Irish tenants. Such a significant social and economic reform would, Gladstone hoped, give stability to a new Irish government to be established in Dublin.[63] Chamberlain, from his seat in the cabinet, interrupted Gladstone's presentation, immediately condemning the land scheme. He was, he said, appalled at the estimated costs. He also demanded that Gladstone reveal his Home Rule programme. Neither a land bill nor Home Rule, Chamberlain claimed, could be judged in isolation. Gladstone, surprised, protested that he had not fully worked out the details on either land reform or Home Rule, though he admitted that a separate Irish parliament sitting in Dublin seemed the most viable scheme. Gladstone urged Chamberlain to have patience with his Irish policy. Nothing was yet definitive. He had, he assured Chamberlain, worked as hard as his age would permit to fashion merely 'a *plan*' of Irish government, not a completed proposal: 'bricks and rafters which are prepared for a house are not themselves a house'.[64] Indeed, Gladstone was very willing to negotiate the terms of his land purchase bill: in fact within a week, he had reduced the guaranteed extension of British credit by half, to £60,000,000. But Chamberlain was unmoved: he resigned with effect from 26 March, never again to sit in a Liberal administration.

Chamberlain had effectively reversed his position as stated in the *Fortnightly Review* a few weeks earlier, and now claimed that both land reform and home rule must stand or fall together. More to the point, he summarily resigned his office in what appeared to be a fit of pique. Why had he reversed his position? Perhaps Gladstone's proposals in the cabinet suggested too comprehensive a Home Rule plan for Chamberlain's taste. Or perhaps Chamberlain finally had his fill of Gladstone's secret dealings with other members of the cabinet. There is no doubt, too, that Gladstone's hints of a separate Irish Parliament sitting in Dublin, coming as it did officially from the mouth of the prime minister, would trump any Home Rule plan that Chamberlain might devise. Only by discrediting Gladstone's land reform could Chamberlain clear the way for his own. In his letter of resignation to Gladstone, written for publication, Chamberlain declared he could not support the prime minister's land purchase bill because of its cost: it would add substantially to the national debt, and would also likely increase taxes. More to the point, such a financial burden born by Great Britain would not benefit the existing imperial union: on the contrary, the proposed scheme would be used 'to purchase the Repeal of the Union'.[65]

Chamberlain's motives for criticizing Gladstone's Irish land purchase plan may be questionable; but he voiced the opinion of many. There was a strong opposition to Gladstone's financial clauses. The general feeling was that enough had been done for Ireland. An additional burden on English taxpayers in order to give preferential treatment to Irish tenants while ignoring English farmers was unacceptable. Under pressure, Gladstone withdrew the bill as a political liability.[66] When Gladstone brought forward his Government of Ireland Bill on 8 April, therefore, it was Home Rule without the land purchase plan.[67] Chamberlain's contributions in defeating land reform had helped guarantee that the constitutional issue of Home Rule would be tackled first in parliament – in direct opposition to the recommendations of 'A Radical' in the *Fortnightly Review.*

The Home Rule Bill, briefly summarized, provided for a unicameral Irish parliament responsible for devising indigenous solutions to internal social and economic problems. Irish MPs were to be specifically excluded from Westminster. Foreign affairs, defence, and international trade were left to the imperial parliament at Westminster. Thus Ireland would rule itself from Dublin within an imperial framework. Through this Bill, Gladstone believed that he had created a full and fair device for satisfying Irish constitutional grievances. His aim, as Matthew points out, was to promote social tranquillity in Ireland: he never intended to provide an opportunity for Irish separation.[68]

Now officially broken with the Liberal leadership, Chamberlain could freely campaign against the Bill. His main thrust was that the Bill would inevitably lead to the creation of Ireland as a separate state. But he seemed unsure how firmly he should hold that position. To Labouchere, he initially signalled a willingness to compromise. 'We are all fortunately agreed', he wrote, that the principle of Home Rule had to be accepted in some shape.[69] He was also convinced that there was not 'the least difficulty' in allowing the Irish representatives to be at Westminster even when voting on non-Irish questions.[70] Yet scarcely a week later, Chamberlain stiffened his terms, writing to Labouchere that he was determined to 'retain Irish representation on the present footing'.[71]

Chamberlain's hostility to the proposed Home Rule Bill was more straightforwardly expressed in a series of letters to Harcourt, who was now Chancellor of the Exchequer in Gladstone's cabinet. Harcourt had urged on Chamberlain a conciliatory strategy toward Gladstone and Home Rule. He had also expressed his hope of remaining friends with Chamberlain no matter what their divergent views may be. Chamberlain rejected this overture, doubting that 'private intimacy and regard' could be maintained between them if they were driven apart on political issues: 'we shall have to take the gloves off very soon', he warned Harcourt. 'I do not expect any compromise or concession', he added. 'I imagine we shall fight the matter out to the bitter end and break up the Liberal Party in the process.' In a mood of self-pity, he blamed the prime minister for the impasse: 'Mr. Gladstone was so determined to deny to me the slightest influence or following that he never took the trouble to consider the possibility of removing my opposition.'[72]

Chamberlain's anger and frustration at his apparent failure to stem the growing support for Gladstone and Home Rule spurred him to take the offensive. One of his first steps was also one of the most remarkable. In late March 1886, only a few days before his resignation from the cabinet, he initiated contact with Hartington, offering with 'extreme cordiality' to serve under him should Gladstone resign.[73] Thus Chamberlain attempted to reverse at a stroke the strident rivalry which had characterized the relations between the two men since the late 1870s. Chamberlain's reversal may have been received by Hartington with understandable reserve, but within a few weeks, the two were exchanging correspondence with fair regularity. By early May, Chamberlain felt confident enough in Hartington to reveal the newest version of his Home Rule strategy. Should Gladstone abandon his insistence on excluding the Irish MPs from Westminster, Chamberlain would be willing to vote for the second reading of the Home Rule Bill – but only on the understanding that this concession was a step toward recasting the entire Bill. Chamberlain also insisted on additional changes, such as a separate assembly for Ulster; the complete subordination of any Irish assembly to Westminster; and the maintenance of the existing tax system whereby Westminster would collect all taxes and then disburse appropriate revenues to Ireland as needed for education, local government, and the like.[74] On 14 May 1886, Chamberlain, along with thirty-two followers, attended a Liberal Unionist meeting at Devonshire House. The Chamberlain–Hartington alliance was now publicly acknowledged.[75]

In the meantime, and in a no less transparent manoeuvre, Chamberlain had opened communications with the Conservatives. Within a day or so of courting Hartington in late March, he discussed with Salisbury's nephew, A. J. Balfour, a possible Radical–Conservative alliance against the Whigs. Such an alliance would be founded on Chamberlain's proposals of reform and local government for Ireland with the understanding that, should the Conservatives believe it necessary, coercion would not be ruled out. The Radicals, Chamberlain asserted, would 'allow the Irish to manage and mismanage their affairs as they please up to a certain point, [but] with a determination of coming down and crushing them if they go beyond that point'. Speaking off the record, Chamberlain also outlined his beliefs on government. He complained about the current constitutional state of affairs hindering the executive branch of government. His ideal was a democratic form of government in which the people might have power, but only power enough to determine 'general principles'; thereafter, elected officials should carry out those principles as they saw fit. 'My Radicalism', he emphasized, 'desires to see established a strong government and an Imperial government.'[76]

In addition to his manoeuvring among parliamentary colleagues, Chamberlain was active in attempting to manipulate opinion in the countryside. To Arthur, his brother, Chamberlain indicated that strong measures had to be taken to firm up a united front against Gladstone's version of Home Rule. He asked that Arthur see J. T. Bunce, editor of the *Birmingham Daily Post*, 'to keep him straight'.[77] Arthur, in reply, reported that Bunce was reluctant to take a stand against Gladstone, fearing that Chamberlain would then attempt to ally with Hartington to displace the prime minister. Arthur's efforts to place a favourable leader in the *Post* were apparently unsuccessful: in Arthur's words, Bunce was 'such a pig that if you tell him what you want said – he won't say it'.[78]

Chamberlain himself took direct action at an important meeting of the Birmingham Liberal Association in late April. In a lengthy speech, he reiterated the important points of his Irish policy. Relocating Irish representatives from Westminster to Dublin, he claimed, would guarantee an ultimate separation: Irish representatives must therefore remain at Westminster. In addition, Chamberlain emphasized the need to uphold the rights of Protestant Ulster in any arrangement which bound them to the predominantly Catholic southern counties of Ireland. Most particularly, he regretted that 'so vast a change' should have been brought forward 'without some consultation with the other leaders of the Liberal party'.[79] Although the Birmingham meeting had generally gone well for Chamberlain and his radical supporters, it closed on an inauspicious note. A knot of Gladstonians, led by Schnadhorst, attempted to delay a motion in support of Chamberlain.[80] The attempt failed, but it was a portentous sign.

Indeed, considerable opposition to Chamberlain's position on Home Rule was emerging during the spring of 1886. Provincial newspaper accounts frequently attributed unworthy motives as the rationale for Chamberlain's opposition to Home Rule. He was charged with acting on a 'vulgar ambition', lacking a 'moral force', and allowing his chagrin at Gladstone's slights to determine his policy toward Ireland.[81] A report from the Dundee region of Scotland was typically discouraging. Although merchants and manufacturers opposed Home Rule, the professional class was divided and workingmen and shopkeepers overwhelmingly favoured Home Rule – as did the agricultural labourers. All the open meetings in the district were enthusiastic for Gladstone. 'Chamberlain has sadly lost ground', the report concluded.[82]

Equally disheartening for Chamberlain was the strengthening Gladstonian opinion in the Liberal stronghold of West Yorkshire, and its political centre, Leeds. Characterized by a firmly rooted nonconformity and led by the Leeds Liberal

Association (modelled upon the Birmingham caucus), one might have expected sub-stantial support for Chamberlain's Irish policy. But the local influence of the *Leeds Mercury*, under the editorship of T. Weiss Reid, was critical. Reid was a friend of Herbert Gladstone, who sat for one of the Leeds constituencies and was the son of the prime minister. In addition, Reid's earlier experiences with Chamberlain's political behaviour had been inauspicious. In 1874, Reid had been repelled by Chamberlain's abortive Sheffield campaign during which the radical leader had exco-riated Gladstone and the Liberal leadership with 'sneers' and 'bitter and flippant' remarks.[83] From that time forward, Reid was convinced that Chamberlain's primary motive was his own political advancement.[84] Thus, Reid did his best to insure that Liberal meetings throughout the West Riding in 1886 pledged their support to Gladstone's Irish policy. So successful was he that – it was widely reported – former Chamberlain supporters began removing his portrait from their walls. Perhaps most damaging of all was the action of a special general meeting of the council of the National Liberal Federation in early May. Recognizing that the time had come 'for the permanent settlement of the Irish question', the NLF passed a resolution sup-porting both Gladstone and the Home Rule Bill.[85]

Chamberlain was not unmoved by the rapid decline in his political fortunes and by the aspersions cast on his motives. He confessed to Dilke that he was 'disgusted by some of the attacks' and that he could not abide 'the persistent malignity of inter-pretation of all my actions and motives'.[86] He complained especially of those 'who have left my side': he could never again treat them 'with the slightest real pleasure of confidence'.[87] Nevertheless, he promised to 'fight this matter out to the bitter end'.[88] And indeed, as the time neared for a vote on the second reading of the Home Rule Bill in parliament, Chamberlain – undeterred by the bad news from the countryside – increased his efforts to win enough votes in the Commons to defeat the Bill.

Perhaps his most notable action to win support from wavering radicals was his recruitment of John Bright against the Gladstonian Home Rule Bill. This was a shrewd move. Bright had long been a supporter of Gladstone, and had a reform-ing record on Ireland. In addition, his reputation among working men was solid. Chamberlain masked his intentions by feigning an interest in compromise. In a letter written in mid-May 1886, he urged upon Bright the role of a conciliator: 'you & you alone can effect it', he wrote. No one would dare call Bright a traitor 'or to impute to you, as they impute most unjustly to me, personal and interested motives'.[89] Two weeks later, Chamberlain invited Bright to attend a strategy session of opponents of Gladstone's Home Rule Bill a few days before the all-important vote on its second reading. Implying that he himself was inclined to abstain from voting on the Bill, Chamberlain hoped that Bright's presence at the meeting would 'help us to come to a right conclusion'.[90] Bright wrote in reply that he would personally vote against the second reading of the Bill, but he intended neither to speak nor to advise anyone else how to vote. Bright additionally suggested that if enough MPs should abstain during the division, it could have a beneficial twofold effect: first, by sending a signal to Gladstone, it might encourage him to compromise; and second, such abstentions would disincline Gladstone to dissolve parliament and thus spare the country 'from the heavy sacrifice of a General Election'.[91] Bright then gave Chamberlain permission to read his letter to the meeting.

At this critical meeting in Committee Room 15 of the House of Commons, some three dozen Liberals and a dozen Hartingtonians showed up. By then, it was well known that the vote on the second reading of the Home Rule Bill in the House of Commons would be very close. The Chamberlainites could make the difference. If they abstained, the Bill would go through; but if they opposed, it would be defeated, likely provoking a general election. Two events at the meeting decided its outcome: a promise from the opposition Conservatives that they would not oppose dissident Liberals at an ensuing general election; and the reading of John Bright's letter. The meeting decided almost unanimously to vote against the second reading of the Bill.

When he learned the news of the meeting the following day, Bright swiftly wrote to Chamberlain that he was 'surprised'.[92] His previous letter to Chamberlain had been intended, he said, only 'to make it more easy for you and your friends to abstain from voting in the coming division'. Had he guessed the outcome of the meeting, he would have said 'something *more* or *less*'. Even now it was not too late to abstain in the hope of preventing a dissolution of parliament 'which may for the Liberal Party turn out a catastrophe, the magnitude of which cannot be measured'. But Chamberlain turned down Bright's suggestion. Claiming that although he had at first been inclined to abstain, he became convinced 'on further reflection' that such a course 'would hardly have been consistent or honest'.[93]

The episode of Bright's letter has been cited by historians as a critical incident in the final days of the Home Rule deliberations. John Morley, in his biography of Gladstone, for example, writes that Bright's letter was 'the death-warrant' of the Bill.[94] Michael Hurst calls it a 'momentous letter'.[95] Roland Quinault thinks that Chamberlain was genuinely swayed by the letter to vote against Home Rule, and that this decision to follow Bright's example 'sealed the fate' of the Bill.[96] Other historians fault Chamberlain's use of Bright's letter. Richard Jay is convinced that Chamberlain, by reading only selected parts of the letter, misled the meeting.[97] Patrick Jackson supports this view.[98] Garvin, however, who gives this episode full attention, claims that Chamberlain not only read the entire letter, but he was at that point genuinely neutral and open-minded as to the fate of the Bill.[99] Yet Garvin himself provides convincing evidence, in reprinting Chamberlain's letters to Hartington and Harcourt, which clearly indicate his hardening position on Ireland, as we have seen.[100]

It seems obvious that Chamberlain, pretending neutrality, had manipulated Bright to announce publicly his opposition to Gladstone's Home Rule Bill. That Bright gave somewhat contradictory advice in his letter meant little to Chamberlain. And whether or not the whole letter was read seems irrelevant: the tone of the letter was plain. By hitching the old radical to his campaign against Home Rule, Chamberlain could justify his own position, and stiffen the backs of his supporters. The episode shows Chamberlain at his most cunning and devious.

The final vote on the second reading of the Home Rule Bill in the House of Commons on 8 June 1886 was a fitting climax to the country campaign and political manoeuvring that lay behind it. The Bill was beaten by 30 votes, 341 against and 311 in favour, with 93 Liberals in the majority. It would seem that Chamberlain had done well. He had been one of the most vociferous critics of the Bill, had worked hard in the constituencies against it, and had intrigued mightily against the Bill's proponents. An examination of the Liberal vote against Home Rule, however, provides a more mixed picture of Chamberlain's stature and influence. The fact is that virtually all of the cabinet, most mainstream Liberals, and a majority of the radicals followed Gladstone into the division lobby. Only a minority of Liberals deserted Gladstone, and of these only some three dozen may be termed Chamberlainites – the others followed Hartington, or voted for a variety of reasons of their own against Home Rule.[101] Still, Chamberlainite votes were enough to defeat the Bill in the House of Commons.

'Pushful Joe', by alienating friends and colleagues in his determination to attain power and challenging so forcefully the prime minister on the supreme question of the day, had miscalculated. He had, furthermore, spent without profit the coin of his own reputation. But Gladstone, too, must share the burden of responsibility in the failure of his Home Rule Bill. Politicians of his own day were well aware that Gladstone had often patronized and ignored his ambitious cabinet colleague.[102] Modern historians have concurred.[103] In fact, the prime minister was not far behind Chamberlain in his need to control his political and personal environment.[104] Gladstone's tendency to govern from on high by executive prerogative – a tendency that made him often appear overbearing and dictatorial – served him ill during the Home Rule crisis. Chamberlain, sensitive to slights, no doubt keenly felt this side of Gladstone when it was directed at him. In the final critical days, Gladstone was particularly dismissive of Chamberlain.[105]

Perhaps if Gladstone had been willing or able to conciliate Chamberlain, to take him into his confidence, to parley with him directly, history would have taken a different course. After all, both men sought Home Rule for Ireland. But from what we know of Chamberlain, it is difficult to imagine that Gladstone or anyone else could have captured him for the Home Rule cause. Even had he been brought within Gladstone's charmed circle, Chamberlain would not have relinquished his need for power and his determination to take advantage of the variegated play of politics in 1886.

Immediately after the defeat of the Home Rule Bill, Gladstone – as widely predicted – dissolved parliament and called for a general election, the second within a few months. The parliamentary campaign of June and early July 1886 had the feel of a civil war as embattled Liberals fought one another as much as they fought the Conservatives. Gladstone, in his 77th year, was energized by a kind of crusading spirit against the opponents of Home Rule. His strenuous electioneering was carried out in stump speeches, assiduous letter writing, and urgent telegrams. He assailed the apostate Liberals as much as the Conservatives. His theme, repeated often, was that opponents to his Home Rule scheme represented the traditional classes who had always been against the masses, the bulk of the nation. The classes had always been wrong: the masses always right.

Chamberlain's campaign, in turn, focused almost wholly on the Gladstonian Liberals and Parnell's nationalist Irish Parliamentary Party. He was clearly working in alliance with the Conservatives as part of an unofficial Unionist coalition. He damned Parnell as 'the puppet of forces greater than himself' and as a man whose 'springs are moved by the dynamite conspirators of America and by the National League'.[106] Gladstone, he charged, was not above 'juggling with figures'.[107] Chamberlain also accused Gladstone of attempting to destroy the empire; of misrepresentation and slander; and of dividing the Liberals into warring factions.

The consequences of contesting Liberals fighting for the upper hand gave the Conservatives an easy ride. In contrast to the previous election, Gladstonian Liberals lost heavily – down from 334 seats in 1885 to 196. The Conservatives gained proportionately: from 250 to 316. Irish seats remained virtually the same at 83. The new Liberal Unionist political grouping, headed by Hartington and Chamberlain, polled 74. Chamberlain's political base of operation had been sharply diminished. How would he now play his hand?

7

IN THE WILDERNESS

For nearly a decade after the defeat of Gladstone's Home Rule Bill, Chamberlain existed on the margins of political life. Without the prospect of high office, he operated in parliamentary life as a gadfly to the Conservatives and a scourge to the Liberals. His party allegiance was confined to a wing of the Liberal Unionists whose recognized chief was Lord Hartington and his band of Whigs. With them Chamberlain now made common cause. Together they numbered approximately eighty in the House of Commons, but only a handful, no more than a dozen, could be counted as firm Chamberlain supporters. The Liberal Unionists had no distinctive set of policies: their stated intention was to support the Liberals when possible and the Conservatives when necessary. Their anomalous position in the House of Commons was nicely symbolized by Chamberlain's insistence that he and Hartington sit in the House of Commons not with Conservative MPs, but on the front opposition bench with Gladstone. For several years this proximity was as provocative as it was curious.

From his Liberal Unionist base, Chamberlain continued to manoeuvre for place and position – sometimes edging toward the Liberals with the hope of unification; and sometimes moving closer to the Conservatives to keep his political prospects alive. At first glance, this was perhaps the most fruitful strategy he could have devised. By occupying a centrist position he could maintain maximum flexibility. But his initial impulse after the defeat of Home Rule was to restore his affiliation with the Liberals. The way, however, was blocked by Gladstone. The old man kept the Liberals together by the force of his moral leadership and by his insistence that Home Rule must take precedence above all other legislative initiatives. That Gladstone had 'wrecked' the Liberal Party and that the country was now 'in for a prolonged period of reaction' remained Chamberlain's firm conviction. At the same time, he believed that Gladstone was 'the only man' who could 'undo the mischief that he has wrought'.[1] Should the aging Liberal leader retire, Chamberlain believed that 'all would come right pretty quickly'. If, however, Gladstone remained active in politics, then the preferred strategy of Liberal Unionists must be to delay, to 'lie low' until 'the inevitable disappearance of the G.O.M. from the scene'.[2] Counselling patience to fellow Liberal Unionists, Chamberlain hoped that after a time of Conservative power during which Gladstone's influence might fade, Liberals could regroup, gather strength, and turn out the Conservatives.[3]

But Chamberlain himself was not a patient man at the best of times. As the weeks passed into months, he began to doubt the likelihood of either a Gladstonian retirement from parliament or a retreat from Home Rule. By September he seemed to be flailing and his strategy sounded increasingly desperate. He even suggested to Hartington that all Liberal Unionists should temporarily retire from parliament and let the Conservatives 'fight it out' with the Gladstonians and Parnellites.[4] As he confessed to R. W. Dale, the state of Liberal politics was 'almost enough to make one despair'.[5]

Denied the corridors of power and made uneasy by Gladstone's continued intransigence, Chamberlain was led to a bold proposal in late December 1886. Speaking to the Liberal Divisional Council of West Birmingham, he offered a substantial olive branch to Gladstone and his supporters. He believed that it was possible to make 'an honest attempt' to carry out 'all those important reforms' on which both Gladstonian and Liberal Unionists could agree.[6] Of any remaining points of disagreement, he advised 'time and ... experience and frank discussion' for their resolution. To begin, Chamberlain urged a small group of Liberal leaders 'sitting around a table and coming together in a spirit of compromise and conciliation'. Thus was born the idea of the Round Table Conference.

Chamberlain's proposal was direct, imaginative, and unexpected. It was also politically astute: if the Gladstonians refused his offer, the onus of a continued Liberal division would be theirs. If, on the other hand, the Gladstonians accepted and reunification was achieved, Chamberlain's reputation (and his power) could only be enhanced. The responses to Chamberlain were immediate and varied. Gladstone himself was circumspect. Noting coolly that the trial balloon was undoubtedly 'a new fact of great weight' in showing that Chamberlain had altered his former position of 'extreme hostility', Gladstone nevertheless made it clear that there was little that Chamberlain could bring to the main body of the Liberal Party. His followers were small in number and they lacked the quality that would 'make up for [their] defect in quantity'.[7] In sum, Gladstone believed that the Liberal leadership 'must be on ... guard' and act with 'very great caution' with regard to Chamberlain.

Morley, equally cautious but willing to listen, raised an important question: was Chamberlain 'simply foxing' as he did all through the previous parliamentary session?[8] Earl Spencer shared Morley's doubts. 'Chamberlain seems to be playing a new part', he wrote to Gladstone. But he thought it a false role: 'I fear that his attitude of conciliation is not very genuine ...'.[9] Harcourt was more encouraging. Although he recognized that Chamberlain may be open to any plan 'so long as Mr. G. eat dirt',[10] Harcourt also believed that Chamberlain's offer was made in 'a real spirit of conciliation'.[11] He hoped Morley would 'go in hot and strong for a compromise with our old friends and not mince matters too much if the thing can be done'.[12] With some hesitation, Morley acquiesced. Accordingly, on 30 December 1886, Chamberlain met with Harcourt at the latter's London residence in Grafton Street. They met again the following day, this time with Morley in attendance.

With preliminaries out of the way, there quickly followed two official meetings in mid-January 1887, and a final meeting in February. Spokesmen for the Liberal

Unionists were Chamberlain and G. O. Trevelyan.[13] The Gladstonians were represented by Harcourt, Morley, and Lord Herschell.[14] The meetings began auspiciously. Although Hartington refused to participate and Gladstone and Morley remained sceptical, both Harcourt and Chamberlain initially made optimistic pronouncements. Chamberlain assured Harcourt that 'the outlook is brighter for Liberalism than I could possibly have hoped some weeks ago'.[15] After the first two meetings, Chamberlain remained positive: he reported to Hartington that the Conference had been conducted 'in a very friendly & conciliatory spirit'.[16]

Harcourt echoed Chamberlain. In a letter to Gladstone, he praised a general agreement among the conferees that there should be an Irish legislative body for purely Irish affairs. In addition, Chamberlain's land scheme in aid of Irish tenants and his federal Home Rule plan modelled on Canada's constitution was favourably received. Although the divisive issue of representing Irish interests at Westminster was glossed over and Ulster remained a stumbling block, Harcourt thought that 'very substantial progress' had been made.[17] The weekend following the January conferences found Chamberlain at Malwood, Harcourt's country estate. Here the talk revolved around Irish issues. In a lengthy letter to Morley (then at Sandringham), Harcourt relayed his impression of Chamberlain's sincere desire for reconciliation 'on the most reasonable terms'.[18]

In spite of these happy auguries, within a month of Chamberlain's Malwood visit, the Conference had collapsed, the Liberals were more fiercely divided than ever, and Chamberlain once again isolated. What had happened?[19] It is difficult and perhaps beside the point to apportion blame. Of ill will and suspicion on both sides there were aplenty. But it seems that Chamberlain's impatience, intransigence, and prickliness were the proximate cause of the breakup. It is apparent from the very first that Chamberlain, in spite of his initial favourable comments, had not entered the Conference in a compromising mood. More likely, his agenda all along had been merely to place blame upon the Gladstonians for the Liberal division over Home Rule.[20]

Indeed, within a fortnight of the Malwood colloquy, even before the Round Table broke up, Chamberlain initiated a brisk and aggressive campaign against Home Rule and its supporters.[21] In a speech to his constituents at Birmingham on 29 January 1887, he – in Garvin's words – 'poured volleys into the Gladstonian and Irish ranks'.[22] Characterizing the political situation as 'unsatisfactory and changeable', Chamberlain declared that the Irish question had subsumed all others. Badly needed social reforms were delayed because the Irish leaders, 'like spoiled children', were demanding 'an impracticable form of government'. Gladstone and his supporting cast of Liberals were equally at fault. They had adopted a new doctrine, 'a complete subservience to a minority', abjectly surrendering to 'a foreign and anti-English conspiracy'. There were, Chamberlain concluded, limits to the concessions which Liberal Unionists could make.[23]

Morley was outraged at Chamberlain's wide-ranging attack on the Gladstonian Liberals and their allies, the Irish. Chamberlain's remarks displayed 'a peculiar want of loyalty to the idea of the Conference' – a conference that Chamberlain had himself proposed.[24] 'Whoever heard', he asked Harcourt, 'of one of the parties to a friendly discussion of this kind … going out at intervals to fire broadsides into those whom he has just left?' Morley's anger brought from Harcourt an admonition. But the waspish Morley could not resist retaliating. During a speech before his constituency in Newcastle on 9 February, he obliquely lashed out at Chamberlain's behaviour by insinuating that he was motivated by 'pettiness', 'personality', ' sourness', and 'bitterness'.[25] Riled by these remarks, Chamberlain complained to Harcourt that Morley's speech was 'personally most offensive to me'.[26] Furthermore, he reserved the right to make a full public reply at a time of his own choosing.

In spite of this disruption to the spirit of the Conference, Harcourt argued against its dissolution. Gladstone, who was spending much of his time at Hawarden deep in Irish matters, agreed. Thus the third meeting of the Round Table went forward on 14 February 1887 at Trevelyan's Grosvenor Crescent house. All five conferees had, it seems, a convivial dinner. Within a few days, however, came a warning of further storms. At a luncheon hosted by Lady Dorothy Neville, Chamberlain met by chance Harcourt's son, Lewis. Chamberlain confided that he had just written a letter about disestablishment in Wales 'which will make your hair curl'.[27] The letter, published in *The Baptist*, a nonconformist journal, duly appeared on 25 February and was widely reprinted by the major newspapers. Garvin admits that it was 'a hot, raging blast' and a 'militant outbreak … incompatible with diplomacy'.[28] Gardiner believed that the letter 'blew the Conference out of the water'.[29] Marsh concurs that Chamberlain's remarks brought the Round Table Conference 'to a halt'.[30]

Re-reading the letter from the distance of more than a century may temper this judgement, but there is little doubt that it – combined with Chamberlain's Birmingham speech of a few weeks earlier – undermined Gladstonian confidence in Chamberlain's good will. In *The Baptist*, Chamberlain asserted that any delay in Welsh disestablishment must be laid at Gladstone's door. Gladstone's distraction with Home Rule had not only affronted Welsh dissent, but Scottish crofters and English agricultural labourers as well. They all had to wait their turn and a 'delay of their hopes' until the Irish question had been settled. In a harsher version of his Warrington speech many months earlier, he declared: 'Thirty-two millions of people must go without much-needed legislation because three millions are disloyal …'.[31]

Even the optimistic Harcourt was quick to criticize the letter 'as a studied and irritating attack' on Gladstone.[32] He condemned outright Chamberlain's 'outburst of temper', claiming that it had dashed the hopes of the Conference. 'You complain of the bitterness displayed against you', he wrote heatedly to Chamberlain, 'but I wish sometimes you would consider how much you do to provoke it.'[33] Harcourt also accused Chamberlain 'of carrying on war *à l'outrance* in public whilst arranging affairs *à l'aimable* in private'.[34] Chamberlain was defiantly unrepentant. Declaring that the Gladstonians would never accept him into the Liberal Party until he had suffered 'complete acts of submission and penitence', Chamberlain refused to engage in what he called 'abject surrender'.[35] Furthermore, he wrote, 'every thing your friends say or do offends me … In these circumstances, we are always on the edge of the volcano …'.[36]

Continuing recriminations led to a mutual decision to terminate the Round Table. Hard words among the conferees did not subside for months and inflamed feelings lingered far longer. Morley and Harcourt on one side, and Chamberlain on the other, remained warily alert for any signs of hostile remarks or deliberate intentions to wound. Each side threatened to publish the private correspondence of the other in order to show bad faith. Old grievances were raked up and renewed. Imagined slights and thoughts of revenge characterized these exchanges.[37] Morley's private assessment of the proceedings of the Conference and the consequent failure of Liberal reunion was closest to the mark. In a disheartened post mortem to the Round Table, he wrote Chamberlain that it was discreditable 'to us all that things should have come to their present desperate pass. There must be some more or less rational way out of it, if we could only find it. It seems to me as if the difficulties were mainly at bottom personal.'[38]

We have followed the episode of the Round Table Conference in some detail because it clearly demonstrates once again that Chamberlain could not separate the personal from the political, even when the damage to his own aspirations and policies was severe. The failure of the Round Table also held portents for the future. It was the last opportunity for a Liberal reunion, and a turning point in party politics. Although some Liberal Unionists drifted back to Gladstone, many remained under the dual leadership of Hartington and Chamberlain until their gradual absorption into the Conservative Party. The divided Liberals spent most of the next two decades in political opposition. Most importantly for Chamberlain, the failure of the Conference forced him to rethink his own political destiny, leading to a gradual acceptance of his fate as a political outsider for the remainder of his active life – a lost Liberal, but never a Tory. His drive for power remained undiminished; but his path to power, now broken, was no longer clear to him.

Perhaps to recover his political direction, Chamberlain took to the public platform in the aftermath of the Round Table. Throughout April and May 1887, Chamberlain was on the road in Scotland. His ostensible aim was to immerse himself in the social and economic conditions of some of the poorest of the British population – the fishermen and crofters of the Highlands and Western Isles.[39] But his on-site investigations and speeches soon revealed a broader intent – a continuing Liberal Unionist campaign against Gladstone, the Liberal majority, and their Irish allies. This message he took to other parts of Scotland. At a meeting of the Ayr National Radical Union, Chamberlain condemned Irish leaders for consorting with 'the apostles of dynamite, of outrage and assassinations'.[40] A noon meeting the next day at the Ayr Town Hall found Chamberlain attributing treasonous motives to the Irish. He claimed that the 'present disastrous situation' in the Liberal Party had been created by an alliance between the Gladstonian Liberals and 'the irreconcilable foes … the enemies of this country'.[41] The following evening at the Edinburgh Music-hall (a meeting also sponsored by the National Radical Union), Chamberlain condemned the 'project of veiled separation' put forward by the Gladstonians as tantamount to handing over the administration of law and justice in Ireland 'to a set of ruffians'.[42] At Glasgow, Chamberlain brought the cheering meeting to its feet in a rousing attack upon the Irish leadership. He would, he declared, do everything just and reasonable for Ireland; but he would not break up the United Kingdom, even though the eighty-six Irish members of parliament 'should be backed up by all the assassins and all the dynamite-mongers of the United States of America'.[43]

Having roused the Scots, Chamberlain took his increasingly inflammatory rhetoric to another Celtic stronghold later that year. Largely overlooked by historians, Chamberlain's Ulster tour in October 1887 revealed the dangerous degree to which Chamberlain was willing to pursue personal power – even at the cost of inciting the entrenched hatreds and rivalries that had long existed between Protestant Ulster and the Catholic southern counties. The tour began on the evening of 10 October when, accompanied by Collings, Chamberlain departed from Birmingham's New Street Station. Travelling overnight, the train arrived at the port of Stranraer in southwest Scotland the following morning. Later in the day the two companions took a steamer to Larne. A special train brought them to Belfast. Upon arrival, they were met by carriage and driven along an avenue decked with flags and thronged by an enthusiastic and cheering crowd. That evening, Chamberlain delivered his first important address in Ireland at the Ulster Hall. To his audience, he posed an important rhetorical question: 'How is it that Belfast continues to increase and multiply while Cork and Waterford decline?'[44] The answer Chamberlain gave at length. Belfast, representing Ulster, included people of protestant Scots-English descent who made up 'almost all the cultivated intelligence' of Ireland. That population, though a minority in Ireland as a whole, also included 'the greatest part of its enterprise and a large proportion of its wealth'. It was loyal and law-abiding. In short, Belfast and Ulster were connected 'by ties of race, and religion, and sympathy, with the greater nation of which it is proud to be a part'.

Chamberlain developed this theme the following evening in a second speech at the Ulster Hall. *The Times* reported that 'thousands' filled the building, with as many more outside unable to gain admittance.[45] To this receptive audience, Chamberlain set out his doctrine of the 'two Irelands'. To the north was 'an Ireland which is prosperous and loyal and contented'. To the south was 'an Ireland which is miserable and dissatisfied and continually under the control and leadership of agitators who profit by the disturbance they create'. There were also two races in Ireland – one which had historically shown 'all the qualities of a dominant people', and the other which had 'always failed in the qualities which compel success'. It would thus go against nature, he concluded, to place a naturally dominant race under the weaker. It followed, too, that he was not in favour 'of submitting Ulster to a Dublin Parliament'.

The following day, Chamberlain travelled north to Antrim, Ballymena, and Coleraine. Cheering demonstrators along the way shouted slogans of 'Chamberlain for ever', 'The Union for ever', and 'No Home Rule'.[46] At Ballymena, Chamberlain demanded a 'separate treatment for Ulster' as 'a cardinal condition' for any Irish settlement. At Coleraine, Chamberlain first spoke to a large gathering in the Corporation Hall, and later in the day under a marquee at Fairgreen where some 5,000 were in attendance. He encouraged his listeners 'to prevent any weakening or loosening of the bonds which bind you to Great Britain'. He warned that any change in the constitution along the lines advocated by Gladstone and Parnell could lead, if not to anarchy and civil war, then certainly to commercial disaster and national bankruptcy. On his final day of speeches, 14 October, Chamberlain visited Portrush and Bushmills to see the Giant's Causeway. Afterwards, he had lunch at the Causeway Hotel, and then delivered a short speech in which he once again stressed differences in national character between Ulstermen and 'the southern race'.[47]

Chamberlain's triumphant northern Ireland tour seems to have lifted his spirits; but the reaction among his former Liberal colleagues who supported Home Rule was, as might be imagined, highly critical. Morley condemned the Ulster tour as a desperate political gamble. 'The ground has crumbled away from under his feet in England', Morley explained to Harcourt, 'and he hopes to find some solid foothold in Ulster ...'.[48] Morley's 'last lingering fragment of faith' in Chamberlain's honesty had been destroyed by the violent language of the Ulster tour. Harcourt concurred: 'Nothing could be more malignant or dishonest than his line and his language', especially when one remembered that six months earlier Chamberlain had agreed to the Round Table Conference on the basis of support for a Dublin parliament.[49] Furthermore, it was 'impossible to conceive anything more deliberately dishonest than his present denunciation of an Irish parliament'. Harcourt condemned particularly Chamberlain's divisive remarks on Ireland: 'His appeal to race prejudice and religious bigotry is very disgraceful.'

Morley and Harcourt did not suggest that Chamberlain's behaviour was motivated simply by a prejudicial anti-Catholic view of southern Ireland. Rather, Chamberlain seemed to be appealing to a volatile Ulster electorate for political gain. Indeed, Chamberlain's visit to Ulster was at least in part designed to exacerbate Gladstone's problems with Home Rule.[50] In a letter to Hartington at the conclusion of his Ulster campaign, Chamberlain said as much. 'Do not forget Ulster', he urged, 'it is a terrible nut for the G.O.M. to crack.'[51] By trawling in troubled waters, Chamberlain hoped to find some morsel that would provide political nourishment. Chamberlain also hoped to firm up his Liberal Unionist supporters to prevent them from returning to the Gladstonian fold.[52] That this was a realistic concern, as Chamberlain revealed in a letter to Hartington written before his departure to Ulster. He reported despairingly that Liberal Unionists in all parts of the country were asking 'what the issue is wherein we still differ from our old colleagues'.[53] Chamberlain feared that the Gladstonians were 'winning hand over hand' and that the present political situation for Liberal Unionists was becoming 'untenable'. He was, as he confessed to Hartington, at his 'wits end to know how to treat the situation in public & what to say to prevent the disappearance of our following in the country'. By playing the Orange card, Chamberlain could signal unequivocally to his Liberal Unionist supporters as well as his new Conservative allies that he was determined to resist the demands of Home Rule, and that this firmly held policy largely defined Liberal Unionism.[54]

In his attempt to create a viable Liberal Unionism, Chamberlain wished not only to retain a close political bond with Ireland: he also hoped to preserve those elements of his radical past that undergirded his plans for domestic social and economic reforms as they related to Ireland. These were not always complementary policies and revealed a weakness in his centrist strategy. This was clearly borne out in his somewhat contradictory positions in the Irish debates during the parliamentary session of 1887. The Salisbury ministry, led by its less than progressive right wing, was determined to bring law and order to Ireland. Initiating a broadly coercionist policy, they proposed as their first important legislative measure a Criminal Law Amendment Act. Designed to become a permanent part of the Irish legal code ('perpetual coercion'), it increased the powers of courts to try stipulated criminal conspiracies, including actions against rent payment and unlawful assembly. The Crimes Act also allowed changes of venue for jury trials and created so-called 'proclaimed districts' (to 'proclaim' was to put down by proclamation) in which certain parts of the Act could be enforced in specified parts of Ireland. These extensive powers strengthened the hand of the government in maintaining order in Ireland, and enhanced its flexibility of response.[55] The Act, passed in July 1887, provided the new Irish Secretary, Arthur Balfour, with a coercionist tool that he employed with vigour and in doing so earned his reputation as 'Bloody Balfour'.

Chamberlain supported the measure as necessary to public order, but only on the condition that it be combined with remedial measures. In pressing letters to Balfour, Chamberlain made the case for a necessary conciliatory carrot to follow the coercionist stick.[56] The Crimes Act, he observed, would undoubtedly 'strengthen the position of the landlords'. But something must also be done for 'the efficient protection of the tenants'. He recommended an Irish land reform scheme along the lines he had proposed in the recently disbanded Round Table Conference. In late March 1887, the ministry introduced its Land Bill in the House of Lords. But there the Bill soon encountered stiff opposition from some of the government's own supporters. With Chamberlain leading the way, the Liberal Unionists successfully brought pressure to bear on the obstinate peers.[57] The new Act contained two important provisions: it enabled county courts in Ireland to grant stays of eviction; and it guaranteed Irish tenants 'judicial rents' – that is, rents based upon existing market conditions, especially important during the existing economic depression in Ireland.

Chamberlain might well have been pleased. By supporting both coercive and conciliatory measures, he could claim that Liberal Unionism had played a useful and distinctive part in furthering parliamentary legislation. But it had been at a cost. Gladstonian Liberals did not thank him for his active role in the passage of the Crimes Act; nor did the more conservative MPs in Salisbury's ministry welcome his participation in upholding tenant grievances.

Chamberlain's anomalous political position was underscored in the controversy over the third important Irish measure of the 1887 session – the suppression of the Irish National League under the jurisdiction of the Crimes Act. The League, which had been established in 1882 as a successor to the Land League, had two aims: national self-government (Home Rule); and the economic development of Ireland (land reform). In late 1886, the Secretary of the National League devised a scheme whereby tenants, if denied rent abatements by their landlords, would pay the rents into an escrow account managed by a board of trustees. The Plan of Campaign, as it was called, would then use the accumulated funds to subsidize evicted tenants.

Should these funds prove insufficient, the resources of the National League would be employed to bail out the tenantry.[58]

Chamberlain opposed the government's suppression of the League. In essence, he opposed putting into operation the very Crimes Act that he had voted for. He declared publicly that it was an inappropriately severe measure, and that in any case the League was declining in popularity and effectiveness.[59] By outlawing the organization, Chamberlain believed, the Conservatives would only encourage Irish agitation. Privately to Hartington, Chamberlain enlarged on his reasons. The proclamation would be 'suicidal', he claimed, because it would revive the parliamentary controversy over coercion that was proving unpopular in England.[60] If the government proceeded, he warned, he felt himself free 'to take a perfectly independent course'. And, indeed, in late August 1887, Chamberlain and a handful of the Liberal Unionists voted in support of Gladstone's motion against the Conservative government's suppression of the League. Thus, within the course of a few months, Chamberlain had voted for a strong coercion bill, and then in effect voted against its implementation in a specific case.

Chamberlain's attempts to find a suitable political platform for attaining his goals of personal power and political office had, by late 1887, proven fruitless. His undoubted talents as organizer and debater had been overshadowed by his reputation as an intriguer and political opportunist. With neither political prospects nor support from a sufficiently large band of influential patrons or followers, he had fallen far from the ranks of respected statesmen. No longer trusted by mainstream Liberals, he had yet to win the confidence of his new Conservative allies. His apparent reversals on the government's Irish legislation had also damaged his credibility. Isolated and weakened by unfavourable by-elections and defections from Liberal Unionist ranks, Chamberlain's fortunes, in the words of historian Peter Fraser, 'sank to their nadir'.[61] The tarnishing of Chamberlain, as Garvin notes, placed him 'in the most execrable plight' and posed an urgent question for the Conservative government: 'what on earth to do with him'?[62]

Salisbury's answer to this question was to send Chamberlain to America to chair a Fisheries Commission in late 1887. For five months Chamberlain negotiated outstanding differences between America and Canada on fishing rights in the Gulf of St Lawrence. It was a far cry from his higher political hopes. Nevertheless, Chamberlain was able to turn this third-rate diplomatic endeavour into a notable success. He travelled widely in the United States and Canada, earning a respectful hearing for British interests. His intelligence, self-possession, and blunt speech won him attention and admiration in both countries. In addition, his emerging sense of an imperial mission was strengthened. Equally important to his private life, he met the woman who was to become his third wife and new mistress of Highbury.[63]

Upon his return to Britain in March 1888, Chamberlain had the opportunity to begin afresh. Indeed, Marsh argues that he discovered in America new resources, both politically and personally.[64] A new love, certainly, but had he changed his own quest for power and authority? The answer is clear. Neither the prospect of marriage nor a sense of renewal at home had diminished Chamberlain's 'inner anger'; nor had his driving energy been curbed.[65] Two absorbing and familiar issues captured his attention as he re-entered political life after his American adventure: Unionism and its future; and Ireland and the case of Parnell.

The future of Liberal Unionism in Birmingham was particularly at risk in early 1888. Defectors such as William Harris, an early Chamberlain supporter, and the neutral stance of R. W. Dale weakened Chamberlain's local influence. Gladstonians had also captured most of the divisional organizations in the city. Upon his return to Highbury, Chamberlain immediately set out to revitalize Liberal Unionist grass roots support in Birmingham. He also cultivated the leading Birmingham Conservatives, hosting them at dinner parties at Highbury, and encouraging Conservative candidates to stand for municipal offices. It was a tribute to his energy and determination that this electoral alliance was successful enough to win 14 of the 16 town council seats in November 1888.[66]

Chamberlain's attempts to sustain an independent Liberal Unionist Party which would remain collegial with the Conservatives rarely ran smoothly, however. Conflicts were not uncommon, especially over policy and legislative matters. In parliament, Conservative backbenchers, mistrustful of his political loyalty, were reluctant to support Chamberlain's brand of Unionism. Equally problematic were disputes between local Conservative and Liberal Unionist agents in the constituencies. It must be said that Chamberlain did little to ease these tensions. This can best be illustrated by the famous case concerning Lord Randolph Churchill's desire for a Birmingham seat in 1889.[67] Churchill had frequently paid court to Birmingham electors since the reform legislation of 1884, and had made a fair running at the election of 1885, losing by fewer than 800 votes out of a total of 9,200 cast. Indeed, Churchill's sound electoral showing in the Central Division of Birmingham had tapped an emerging Conservative political sentiment. In May 1888, during the early stages of what proved to be John Bright's final illness, Chamberlain – now an ally of Churchill in the Unionist alliance – offered Bright's seat to Churchill when it became vacant. When the old radical died in March 1889, therefore, Churchill expected selection by the Birmingham Conservatives: he also hoped for approval, given Chamberlain's previous assurances, from the local Liberal Unionists.

But Chamberlain in the meantime had reconsidered Churchill's candidacy. Writing to his son, Austen (then a budding politico), Chamberlain remarked in December 1888 that it was 'rather too bad to have to give up one of our few Lib. Unionist seats'. He expressed an additional reservation: 'Randolph must not be too exigent. We *can't* go on our knees to him …'.[68] And in a later letter: 'I wish he would himself say openly that he would not stand.'[69] Not only had Chamberlain's support for Churchill ebbed: behind the scenes he had begun the search for a Liberal Unionist candidate in place of Churchill. Powell Williams, MP for Birmingham South, Chair of the Executive Committee of the new Birmingham Liberal Unionist Association and, more importantly, Chamberlain's political agent, had entered into negotiations with John Bright's son, Albert, to stand for his father's vacant seat. When Bright died on 26 March, matters came to a head. Word of Chamberlain's stratagem – carried out by Williams – reached Churchill, who, as Williams reported to Chamberlain, 'spoke somewhat bitterly about you, and expressed his opinion that you were "play-ing a game".[70] Game it was; but an important game for high stakes – for power and control over the political life of Birmingham. On 2 April, Chamberlain, acting with Hartington and the Conservative Michael Hicks Beach, made it official: they advised Churchill not to stand. In a by-election two weeks later, Albert Bright was returned with a substantial Unionist majority for his father's seat.

Clearly, Churchill was caught in a power play of Chamberlain's making. Chamberlain had broken an earlier promise, had secretly lobbied for a substitute candidate, and then simply thrust Churchill aside. The reason for Chamberlain's behaviour is apparent. Churchill, popular among the Conservative rank and file, could become a rival to Chamberlain within his own domain. Indeed, Churchill, among all Conservative politicians, could pose the greatest threat to Chamberlain's attempt to straddle both Liberal and Conservative positions. In addition, Churchill was a pow-erful and vivid public speaker, much in the Chamberlain mode. Chamberlain simply could not tolerate a rival within his own sphere of influence.

Once the news of Chamberlain's actions toward Churchill began to circulate, there was an outcry among Birmingham Conservatives.[71] Chamberlain was forced publicly to defend himself. Writing to the editor of the conservative *Birmingham Gazette*, Chamberlain went on the attack, denouncing the 'monstrous charges of treach-ery and breach of faith which have been so freely made by certain members of the Conservative Party'.[72] Churchill responded to Chamberlain's allegations by writing directly to Chamberlain, with a copy to the *Birmingham Post*.[73] He set out in detail the extended negotiations between Chamberlain and Birmingham Conservatives over the past several months. Churchill declared that Chamberlain had violated an election pact whereby Conservatives would support Liberal Unionists for the Birmingham city council elections of November 1888 in return for which Chamberlain and his Liberal Unionists would support more Birmingham Conservative candidates for parliament. Birmingham Conservatives had kept up their end of the bargain, co-operating 'very loyally and energetically' during the municipal elections. It was time, Churchill suggested, that Chamberlain cease to provoke, and begin to conciliate: 'you seem to consider', Churchill continued, 'that you can catch Conservative votes with vinegar …'. Birmingham Conservatives, active members of the Unionist alli-ance, no longer wished to be 'hewers of wood & drawers of water to yourself & your friends'.

The disagreement, now made public, brought delight to the Gladstonians. Harcourt asked of Morley: 'Was there ever such an impudent turn as that taken by J. C. in his letter to the Tories? … Can the folly of temper further go?'[74] Morley agreed: 'J. C.'s absurd exhibition of temper will deepen men's distrust of him.' He added that Churchill's public letter 'will be as oil on the flames of Tory wrath in Birmingham'.[75] Harcourt in response thought it would be difficult ever to know the full truth of the matter, but for the present it could not be denied 'the Joe–Randolph cock-fight' was 'delicious'.[76]

The controversy continued to simmer over the next few years with the Conservative local association repeatedly attempting to renew what they considered a broken bargain, and Chamberlain stubbornly refusing to bend. Late 1889 is a case in point. In October of that year, Chamberlain complained to Hartington that the Conservatives were 'behaving disgracefully' to the Liberal Unionists.[77] Indeed, a few weeks later, Chamberlain's complaint – at least from his point of view – was born out. In early November, he recorded a meeting with J. Satchell Hopkins, President of the Birmingham Conservative Association, during which Hopkins requested a Conservative parliamentary candidate for Birmingham Central at its next vacancy. If Chamberlain did not cooperate, Hopkins threatened a withdrawal of support for the Liberal Unionists in any forthcoming municipal election.[78] But Chamberlain continued to dodge the issue, and to forestall a resolution of the matter.

Two years later, the dispute still simmered and had become serious enough for Chamberlain to approach Lord Salisbury directly. He urged the prime minister to speak out on the importance of the Liberal Unionists to the Unionist alliance. If the Conservatives were too grasping in Birmingham, he warned, three or four seats could be lost at the next general election.[79] Not long after, bad feeling between Chamberlain and local Conservatives widened to include a neighbouring constituency, rural East Worcestershire, where a parliamentary seat had become vacant. The ensuing by-election particularly interested Chamberlain. The seat lay within the sphere of his direct influence, for Highbury itself was just inside its northern boundary. It had previously been held by a Liberal Unionist. And, most important from Chamberlain's point of view, his eldest son, Austen, had been selected as its Liberal Unionist nominee for parliament.

As the price for their support, local Conservatives insisted that Austen pledge himself against any legislative attempt to disestablish the Church of England – a not unreasonable request for Conservatives to make. Chamberlain, however, was reluctant to agree. If Austen denied any prospect of disestablishment, radical non-conformists would be antagonized and their votes lost. Denouncing the Conservative 'intrigue', Chamberlain held fast. Should Austen be forced out, he warned Wolmer, Salisbury's son-in-law, he would demand another Liberal Unionist in his son's place 'as we will on *no* account allow a Conservative to have the seat'.[80]

Within a few days of his letter to Wolmer, Chamberlain sought mediation from Arthur Balfour, then Irish Secretary. Claiming that the Liberal Unionists of East Worcestershire were 'furious' at the demands of the Conservatives, Chamberlain threatened retaliation. Given Conservative obduracy, why should the Liberal Unionists 'move a finger or give a vote' to any Conservative?[81] Balfour duly interceded, pointing out to constituent Conservatives that the Liberal Unionists had supported the Conservative Party 'through six stormy sessions' and that it was best not to emphasize the differences between the two Unionist parties, but rather to concentrate on their similarities.[82] Balfour also counselled against 'superfluous pledges' at election times. Perhaps Balfour's entreaties worked: in any case, Austen was returned for East Worcestershire at the by-election and was also successful a few months later in the general election of 1892.

As Balfour had well noted in his letter, Chamberlain and the Liberal Unionists had given good service during the Salisbury government, in office since 1886.

Indeed, Chamberlain and Salisbury had discovered surprising similarities and an understanding of each other's political position which brought them together in an unacknowledged personal and political alliance. Both believed, for example, in the efficacy of a strong state – Salisbury to strengthen Britain's diplomatic hand against rival European powers; and Chamberlain to promote social justice at home. Chamberlain also realized that he could appeal directly to Salisbury's self-consciously Burkean instinct for gradual and unavoidable reforms. David Steele has in fact made a strong case that Salisbury had within him a genuine, if limited, reformism which complemented Chamberlain's own.[83] Salisbury's acceptance of much of the substance of Chamberlain's reformist programme, as Steele amply demonstrates, allowed the Conservative prime minister to engineer a new Conservatism as Unionist ideas displaced antiquated Tory views. Complementary to Steele's explanation for Salisbury's ability to bend to reform is Michael Bentley's belief that Salisbury in fact distrusted the capacity of his own aristocratic class to preserve their social and political privileges. Chamberlain's strength of purpose and forceful presence, if brought into fruitful collaboration, could stiffen the spine of the traditional ruling elite.[84]

Above all, Salisbury understood Chamberlain's drive for power. He believed that Chamberlain's showy radicalism could be brought to heel if the prospect of office and influence could be his. Treated with respect and a modicum of deference, Chamberlain might be useful to the Conservative leader. In this, Chamberlain was quite different from the unpredictable Churchill, for whom even the attainment of power could not bring responsibility in office. In short, after a disagreeable beginning in the early months of the Salisbury ministry, Chamberlain was able to find an accommodation, if not with all his Unionist allies, at least with their chief.[85] Thus, at specific points during the legislative programme of 1886–92, Chamberlain nudged a willing Salisbury forward in a progressive direction.

A good example of how the Chamberlain–Salisbury partnership worked was the passage of the Local Government Act of 1888.[86] For more than a decade, successive governments had attempted to replace the Court of Quarter Sessions as the governing body of the counties. A wholly unrepresentative institution made up of Justices of the Peace appointed by the Lord Lieutenant, Quarter Sessions had the reputation by the late nineteenth century as an antiquated and self-interested group of country gentry. Given his interest in local government, Chamberlain was an early spokesman for replacing the JPs at Quarter Sessions with an elective body which had the power of compulsory purchase for allotments. This demand had been fundamental to Chamberlain's 'unauthorized programme'.

Liberal governments in the past had not been opposed to such a scheme; but the press of cabinet business continually delayed its introduction and enactment. In addition, Chamberlain, whose influence in Gladstone's ministry of 1880–85 had been limited at best, could never exert an effective pressure for such a bill. Freed from the constraints of Gladstone's governing agenda, Chamberlain vigorously pushed his social programme upon the Salisbury government. Chamberlain's persistence was clearly evident in the ultimate passage of the Local Government Act of 1888, accomplished through hard-earned compromises.[87] Directly elected County Councils, who in turn selected one-third of their members as aldermen, were created. They managed most county business. This satisfied Chamberlain. Supervision of county police, however, was placed in the hands of a committee whose membership was equally shared between the Court of Quarter Sessions and the County Council. The police clause thus allowed Salisbury to put at ease Conservative backbench opinion, which feared disorder in the countryside if a democratic County Council were wholly in charge of the police.

Chamberlain's greatest contribution to the Salisbury government, however, lay in his continued support for its Irish policy. Although unalterably opposed to what he called 'separatist' Home Rule, Chamberlain was willing to grant unionist Home Rule – a form of local self-government that was moderate enough to please most Conservatives. But if Chamberlain's Home Rule policy and support of coercion for Ireland endeared him to the Conservative government, the Liberal and Irish opposition viewed him with loathing. To the Gladstonians, he was a pariah: to the Irish, a Judas.

Chamberlain's frequent and rancorous disputes with Liberals and especially Irish MPs in the Commons contributed to one of the most contentious chapters in modern British political history. Exacerbating the conflict was the mutual personal hostility between Chamberlain and Charles Stuart Parnell. Relations between the two men had fallen far from the early 1880s when they had been willing to engage in negotiations over the future of Ireland. Since then, Chamberlain's own political future had darkened. Conversely, Parnell's stature as a leader of the Irish had made him the 'uncrowned king' of Ireland. Among the Gladstonians, Parnell was widely regarded as the legitimate voice of an oppressed people.

Liberal Unionists and Conservatives, however, were always prepared to believe the worst about the Irish leader. Parnell's commanding speeches in the House of Commons, his grip on the southern Irish electorate, and his mysterious ability to elude imprisonment on charges of treason continued to enrage and perplex the Unionist alliance – Chamberlain not least among them. When, therefore, *The Times* published on 18 April 1888 a letter purportedly in Parnell's own hand that tied him to the Phoenix Park murders of Lord Frederick Cavendish and his private secretary several years earlier, Unionists were elated. They at last had proof implicating Parnell with the most extreme terrorist atrocities in Ireland. It cannot have gone unnoticed, however, that the putative Parnell letter appeared on the very day of the crucial vote of the government's Crimes Act. We now know that the timing was more than a coincidence. A conspiracy had been hatched between the Unionist *Times* and Richard Pigott, a failed journalist and inept forger, to smear Parnell and thus to ease the passage of the coercion bill. [88]

During the time that Parnell sought to unmask what he knew as the plot of some unknown forger, the Conservative government searched for a legal means to investigate the Irish leader. They hoped, by damaging Parnell's reputation, to derail the Home Rule project and to remove the Irish question from public discourse. It was Chamberlain who persuaded the government to appoint a special judicial commission with wide powers of inquiry. As the commission was being formed, Chamberlain began on his own, in late July 1888, a campaign against Parnell designed to discredit him.[89] In a series of debates in the House of Commons, Chamberlain claimed that, in secret negotiations between the Irish leader and himself, Parnell had agreed to accept a Central Board for Ireland as a substitute for an Irish parliament. Chamberlain strongly implied that the Irish leader betrayed his parliamentary comrades and his followers in Ireland by repudiating the very scheme that he himself had helped to formulate.

Parnell, denying that he had ever accepted a Central Board as a substitute for an Irish parliament, relayed to the House his own memory of Chamberlain's intrigues when a member of Gladstone's ministry. Playing upon Chamberlain's tendency to leak ministerial secrets, Parnell informed the House that Chamberlain was 'always most anxious to betray to us the secrets and counsels of his colleagues in the cabinet'.[90] Parnell followed up his charges in an open letter to *The Times*, challenging Chamberlain to publish such evidence as he had on the Central Board scheme.[91] The following day, Chamberlain publicly accepted and promised to provide 'a full statement' of all relevant communications between himself and Parnell in 1884 and 1885.[92]

Unfortunately for Chamberlain, his own private papers bore out Parnell's contention that he had never claimed a legislative function for a Central Board scheme. This Chamberlain learned in his conversations with O'Shea while preparing for his response to Parnell. Chamberlain also discovered that O'Shea had systematically misled him about Parnell's intentions during the negotiations of 1884–5, and in turn had misled Parnell about his, Chamberlain's views.[93] Chamberlain, having publicly promised to do so, had no option but to reply to Parnell. His letter, which appeared in *The Times* on 13 August 1888, was a complete vindication of Parnell's position. Chamberlain admitted that a review of his correspondence corroborated Parnell's claim that he had not intended a Central Board to serve in place of an Irish parliament. 'I do not think therefore', Chamberlain wrote, 'that upon this point there is now any conflict of testimony between Mr. Parnell and myself.'[94] It was, as Lyons notes (in an understatement) 'more than a little surprising' that Chamberlain had pitched himself headlong into such a public error.[95] Chamberlain's dawning realization of his mistake is amply revealed in the letters he wrote to his American fiancée, Mary Endicott. Confiding to her that the Parnell affair was 'a most unfortunate business', he confessed that 'it will take all my wits and all the courage I can muster to fight my way out of it'.[96]

With Chamberlain's public humiliation, Parnell's ascendant star continued to rise. The Commission, which began its inquiry on Parnell in September 1888, conducted 129 sittings. Even before the final report in February 1890, it was clear that Parnell would be vindicated. When Pigott was exposed during the hearings, a cheering crowd accompanied Parnell as he walked down the Strand to give evidence at Bow Street. Pigott himself had fled in disgrace to Madrid, and there died by his own hand. The general impression grew that Parnell had been made the victim of a political witch-hunt. When Parnell appeared in the House of Commons in March 1889 during the debate on the Address, he was greeted by a standing ovation of Liberals and Irish, led by Gladstone. A week later, at the Liberal Eighty Club, Parnell shook hands with Earl Spencer, who had been Lord Lieutenant of Ireland at the time of the Phoenix Park murders. Parnell's apotheosis (as Lyons has it) occurred in late December 1889, when he was invited to the Liberal sanctuary, Gladstone's home at Hawarden Castle in northern Wales. Mutual admiration and a constructive dialogue between the two men represented the highest hopes for Home Rule in Ireland.

Within a week of this meeting, however, all bets were off and the unravelling of the Liberal-Irish alliance began. O'Shea, on Christmas Eve 1889, petitioned for a divorce, citing Parnell as co-respondent. During the next several months, as the shabby details of his domestic deceit with Katherine O'Shea were gradually made public, Parnell's reputation sank. At the divorce trial in November 1890, Parnell made no appearance. Long before then, the political stature of the Irish leader had been destroyed by a tide of moral censure. Gladstone and the nonconformists of the Liberal Party, no less than the Conservatives, freely condemned him. Nor did an adulterous relationship bring joy to Ireland. The once firmly united Irish Nationalist MPs split on the issue. Within a year of the trial, Parnell was dead, most likely of pneumonia complicated by kidney disease.[97]

The only remaining mystery in Parnell's public downfall was O'Shea's timing in his petition for divorce. He undoubtedly had known of his wife's affair with Parnell for some years, perhaps as early as 1881.[98] Why did O'Shea delay his suit for divorce? Money may have been the primary reason.[99] The O'Sheas had long been dependent upon Katherine's wealthy aunt for financial assistance. Known for her strict moral code, Aunt Ben would have been shocked by revelations of marital infidelity. Upon her death in May 1889, however, when O'Shea discovered that he had received nothing from her legacy, such a constraint no longer existed.

Additional personal and political motives undoubtedly set in train the divorce proceedings at just the moment of Parnell's greatest triumph. O'Shea, no doting husband, had hoped to gain political benefit from Katherine's attachment to the Irish leader and for a time, he was not disappointed. Throughout the 1880s – as a dubious kind of protégé – O'Shea traded on Parnell's influence in consorting with the councils of the great. Additionally, with Parnell's assistance, O'Shea was elected to parliament as MP for Galway in early 1886. Four months later, however, O'Shea unexpectedly resigned and his parliamentary ambitions came to an abrupt halt.[100] O'Shea's resignation was likely prompted by his uncomfortable recognition that many members in the inner circle of the Nationalist Party were well aware of Parnell's relationship with O'Shea's wife, and that they objected strenuously to such an obvious payoff to a compliant cuckold.

Realizing that he could no longer rely upon Parnell for political favours, O'Shea probably felt increasingly aggrieved. To see Parnell go from strength to strength during the events of 1889 may have provoked him beyond endurance. Yet he needed some encouragement to take what was, as he well knew, a momentous decision both to divorce his wife and to bring down Parnell. Imagining O'Shea making such a decision on his own is difficult: he was always a small-stakes player. The possibility that Chamberlain himself may have played a role must be considered. As we know,

O'Shea had been in contact with Chamberlain on and off for a number of years, most recently in their collaboration against Parnell in the late summer of 1888. The two men had good reason to wish Parnell harm. Certainly in their own day, rumours linked the two in a plot against the Irish leader: Chamberlain, it was said, not only instigated O'Shea's divorce, but helped to finance it.[101]

Historians have taken various views of the matter. Garvin denies the charge outright.[102] Lyons takes the story more seriously. He notes that in late 1889 O'Shea had informed Chamberlain of Parnell's involvement with his wife, and thus Chamberlain was aware of an opportunity to damage Parnell. But, as Lyons also notes, there is no solid evidence of Chamberlain's complicity.[103] Curtis takes essentially the same tack, arguing that although 'a Chamberlain–O'Shea axis may sound highly plausible' it must remain a hypothesis until convincing evidence is brought to light.[104] Thus Curtis falls back upon the ambiguous Scottish legal judgment of 'not proven'. The most recent analysis by Marsh, however, is more damning. Marsh states outright that Chamberlain encouraged O'Shea to ignite the bomb under Parnell. Once Chamberlain learned from O'Shea that he contemplated divorce from his wife on the grounds of adultery with Parnell, it was an opportunity 'sweet enough' for Chamberlain to meddle in.[105] Further extenuating circumstances include O'Shea's continuing letters to Chamberlain over the next many months, informing him of the sad details of the divorce proceedings and offering advice on legislative matters. In one intriguing instance, O'Shea presumed to ask from Chamberlain a loan of £800. More surprisingly still was the fact that Chamberlain gave him half the sum, begging off the remainder because of his own financial troubles.[106]

Whatever the truth may be about Chamberlain's involvement, the immediate consequences of Parnell's downfall were clear enough. With Parnell out of the way, the drive for Home Rule was weakened, the Liberal-Irish alliance was damaged, and Unionism was strengthened. More important for Chamberlain was the removal from parliament of one of his bitterest foes; and the removal, too, of a rival for power in parliament. Parnell's fall thus seemed a harbinger of good fortune for Chamberlain. Within a few months of Parnell's death, another fortuitous funeral took place. The old Duke of Devonshire, Hartington's father, died. Hartington, by his elevation to the House of Lords, left Chamberlain as the sole leader of the Liberal Unionists in the House of Commons.

But problems remained for the ambitious Chamberlain. He had to extend his authority beyond the limited group of Liberal Unionists to include his Conservative allies if he wished to create a vehicle for his own political power. Here a fundamental obstacle persisted. Having secured a measure of cooperation with Salisbury and displaying a staunch opposition to Gladstonian Home Rule, Chamberlain had yet to win the trust of the main body of Conservatives. His radical background and interest in social reforms continued to give pause to the average Conservative. There were also unsettling signs in the country at large that support for the Liberals was reviving. The public was tiring of the heavy-handed Conservative coercionist policy toward Ireland. By-elections were turning against the Salisbury ministry. Chamberlain was not yet out of the wilderness.

8

THE PURITAN MAID

By the late 1880s, Chamberlain's political career presented a mixed record. He had been a reasonable success in his first cabinet office at the Board of Trade, where he proved diligent and energetic. If he had achieved less legislative success than he had hoped, his administrative skills and organizing talents were nevertheless notable. His ability to articulate a reformist programme, both in parliament and in the countryside, was widely recognized, even by his opponents. He had become a leading spokesman for the progressive wing of the Liberal Party and the most dynamic politician of his era.

Yet in all his official actions were elements of discord and strife that earned him as many criticisms as accolades. This was not merely a political division of opinion: Chamberlain's critics spanned the spectrum. Liberals and Conservatives alike, while acknowledging his abilities, condemned his single-minded efforts to advance himself at the expense of others. They suspected that his ambition and arrogance reflected a determination to establish himself at whatever cost as the supreme political power in the nation.

Perhaps more surprisingly, given Chamberlain's progressive tendencies, were the suspicions of his character among radical colleagues. A. J. Mundella, for example, the radical MP for Sheffield, had experienced Chamberlain's arrogance at first hand in the general election of 1874, when the Birmingham intruder thrust himself forward as an ostensible Liberal ally to Mundella at Sheffield. The years following did not increase Mundella's respect. During Chamberlain's organization of the National Liberal Federation, Mundella condemned him as 'designing' and a born intriguer who only wanted 'as many puppets as he can get in the House in order that he may manipulate them'.[1]

The radical MP for Liskeard, Leonard Courtney, whose advocacy of proportional representation had raised Chamberlain's ire, had so little affection for the radical leader that he refused to serve under Chamberlain at the Board of Trade in 1880. Courtney's wife, Kate – sister of Beatrice Potter – had an even more negative view of Chamberlain. Following a lengthy political conversation with Chamberlain in the summer of 1885, she deplored his 'detestable' authoritarian tone. Should Chamberlain become the dominant power in the Liberal Party, he would be only too likely, Kate feared, to transform the party into 'an organised petty tyranny' and there would be no such thing as 'real freedom in political life'.[2]

Chamberlain's dominant and aggressive personality and his belligerent behaviours were a trial to his friends as well as to his political colleagues. He often carried differences of opinion to extremes. The best example may be found in his relations with John Morley. We have already encountered tension and controversy between the two men. But the early years of their friendship were far different. Morley, as a middle-class radical, was drawn strongly to Chamberlain's energetic leadership in fostering radical causes. From his vantage point as editor of the *Fortnightly Review*, Morley provided an important readership for Chamberlain's radical platform. Chamberlain, in turn, supplied practical political experience to leaven Morley's literary and philosophical treatises. This arrangement was apparently formalized during a week's working holiday in Paris in 1875, when they devised a partnership designed to utilize their complementary talents.

Before long, their political affiliation ripened into an equally close personal relationship. Chamberlain's unburdening himself when his second wife died brought a deep sympathetic response from Morley. Soon, Chamberlain was confiding to Morley about his depression and his ill health. Headaches and gout – 'like a bad toothache in your big toe'[3] – were particularly plaguing. Morley assured him that his 'bad spirits' were not surprising given the cause, and that he felt keenly for his friend. He wrote after one visit: 'The picture of you sitting alone in your garden has haunted me.'[4] Chamberlain regularly invited his new friend to Birmingham. They went on a dozen holidays together. Morley recalled those days in his memoirs with great fondness: 'for thirteen strenuous years', he wrote, 'we lived the life of brothers'.[5]

Most striking about Morley's characterization of Chamberlain, however, were the terms of their friendship. Apart from their agreement on political issues, Morley was taken with Chamberlain's 'resolute energy, tenacity of will, vehement confidence'.[6] He was also attracted to Chamberlain's stamina, zeal, swiftness in debate, and firmness of character. Morley once twitted Chamberlain for being 'a masterful cuss';[7] but in fact Morley in general applauded an imperious quality in public men. Advice, publicity, and praise – Morley gave all to Chamberlain, who in turn found attractive qualities in the reflective and literary Morley. Most particularly, Chamberlain sensed that Morley was capable of subordinating his own ambition and placing himself in the service of another. As Chamberlain approvingly put it to Collings, Morley was 'entirely free from "personality" and thinks only of the cause & how he may help it'.[8]

When Chamberlain entered the cabinet in 1880, it seemed that the time had come for their political and personal partnership to yield practical dividends. But there were signs of strain. Morley opposed both the imperial adventure in Egypt and coercion in Ireland. Using the forums of the *Pall Mall Gazette* (he became editor in 1880) and the *Fortnightly Review* (the editorship of which he retained until 1882), Morley began to criticize the government's policy, culminating in a vigorous campaign against any increased British presence in the Sudan.[9] Morley's election to parliament for Newcastle in 1883 gave him added visibility as an opponent to government policies, and more specifically to Chamberlain's advocacy and justification of those policies. The man of words was beginning to challenge the man of action in his own theatre of operations.

Yet, for a time, the two remained friends. Thanking Chamberlain for a barrel of Birmingham oysters at Christmas in 1883, Morley wrote that he would 'drink to the health of the giver, who will always be the closest to me of all my friends'.[10] Chamberlain's response was equally amiable: 'I do not know what I should do without the one or two warm friends I have been happy enough to find in a journey which has not been quite so fortunate as casual observers might suppose.'[11] Acknowledging a similar gift at Christmas 1884, Morley assured Chamberlain that 'time strengthens our friendship – instead of blunting it'.[12] Within a year, this could no longer be said. The controversy over Home Rule ended their political alliance and their personal friendship.

Chamberlain's friendship with Sir Charles Dilke followed a similar course to that of Morley. Dilke and Chamberlain were initially drawn together in their pursuit of common radical goals. From the first, they unabashedly schemed against the Liberal leadership to further the radical cause. With complementary skills, they were ideally suited for their task. Dilke was dull in speech, but administratively adept and with an encyclopaedic knowledge of parliamentary and political affairs. Chamberlain was in contrast infused with a power to command, and a mesmerizing and demagogic speaker in parliament and the countryside. Their compact was fully demonstrated in the first two years of the Gladstone ministry as they stood together on important issues.[13] After Dilke gained entrance to the cabinet in 1882, he and Chamberlain sat together opposite Gladstone at the cabinet table. Their hurried notes and written comments to one another during cabinet meetings suggest an almost schoolboyish camaraderie and flouting of authority under the stern eyes of the prime minister.

Perhaps most important to Chamberlain in their friendship was a curious strain of deference in Dilke.[14] Like Morley, Dilke was willing to serve in a subordinate position to Chamberlain – illustrated by Dilke's surrender of a claim to a cabinet position in the face of Chamberlain's energetic persistence in 1880. Other instances of Dilke's submissiveness were equally striking. In a plaintive letter in late 1882, for example, Dilke wrote that he had not heard recently from Chamberlain and was fearful that he had vexed him in some way. Two days later, Dilke confessed he had been worried about Chamberlain's mood until he saw him: 'You dispelled the clouds in a moment … by your smile.'[15] Earlier that year, Dilke offered, should Chamberlain become Chief Secretary to Ireland, to join him in Ireland 'and spend the whole autumn and winter with you as your chief private secretary'.[16]

Dilke's fidelity and Chamberlain's strength fulfilled a need in each as they pursued power within the Liberal Party. Thus their alliance held firm during their unceasing intrigues in the final months of the Gladstone government. So confident had they become by January 1885 that Chamberlain urged caution to avoid suspicion they were prematurely involved in 'dividing the lion's skin' of a dead or dying Liberal leadership.[17] Certainly, prospects seemed favourable. Irreconcilable cabinet factions,

Gladstone's loss of vigour, and declining public support for mainstream liberalism gave them an unusual opportunity. Furthermore, Dilke's reputation had been substantially enhanced during these months because of his contributions to the Franchise and Redistribution Bills and his strong line in parliament defending the British presence in Egypt and the Sudan. Chamberlain, for his part, had been canvassing the country on behalf of the radical cause, and his name shone brighter than ever among the electorate. When Gladstone's ministry collapsed in early June 1885, bringing the Conservatives briefly to power, the way seemed paved for a revivified radical-led Liberal Party. As Chamberlain put it to Dilke: 'A little patience & we shall secure all we have fought for.'[18]

Within a month, however, every prospect of radical success had been destroyed. On 20 July Dilke learned that an outraged Donald Crawford, a Scottish lawyer and politician, intended to file for divorce citing him as co-respondent. The Dilke scandal has been a source of historical curiosity from that time to this.[19] There seems little doubt that Dilke was incautious in his sexual adventures, but whether or not he had taken Mrs Crawford to bed was never proven. Two trials only revealed for a certainty that Dilke had been indiscreet with Virginia Crawford's mother, Mrs Eustace Smith, some years earlier. But even this information, made public in a court of law, raised substantial questions about Dilke's moral character. Inevitably, his political standing was damaged, and although he continued to serve ably in the House of Commons for many years afterwards, Dilke could no longer hope for high office.

Chamberlain's role in the scandal has been questioned, especially as it related to a mysterious visit to his house in London by Virginia Crawford only a few days before the scandal broke. But Dilke's most recent biographer is surely right in absolving Chamberlain of any complicity in attempting to bring down his friend and political ally.[20] Any sexual scandal made public would have damaged the political schemes of the two partners. In fact, Chamberlain offered staunch support to Dilke during the most active days of the scandal. He invited Dilke to Highbury where he spent much of that troubled summer. At Dilke's marriage to Emilia Pattison in October 1885, Chamberlain served as best man. Chamberlain frequently advised his friend, and was in court to lend him moral support. Even after the scandal, Chamberlain kept up with Dilke, dining at his London house and refusing to drop him even though he was 'down in the world'.[21] But it was clear to Chamberlain that he alone must now bear the burden of regenerating the Liberal Party. Dilke was of no further use.[22]

Of all Chamberlain's close political allies, Jesse Collings remained the most steadfast.[23] After the death of Chamberlain's second wife, he and Collings left precipitously on an extended tour for the continent and Algiers before returning to Birmingham. This may have been the crucial experience which created the foundation of their friendship. Thereafter, they confided frequently with one another. Each looked after the other's health, with Collings playing almost a maternal role in his concern for Chamberlain's welfare. It seems, too, that among all of Chamberlain's friends, Collings had the capacity for teasing and jesting with Chamberlain, who accepted it surprisingly well. Chamberlain, in a mock complaint, once claimed that Collings was 'always chaffing me'.[24] When, for example, Chamberlain encountered a delay in the marriage plans with his third wife, Collings pretended to be delighted that for once Chamberlain was 'not getting things' all his own way.[25]

Collings also provided a useful political sounding board for Chamberlain. He remained close to his humble origins (his father was a bricklayer) and could provide Chamberlain with a direct opening to the world of work that Chamberlain had experienced only at second hand. Collings was especially interested in allotments and small holdings for agricultural labourers, and took an active role in the National Agricultural Labourer's Union in the 1870s. He later founded the Rural Labourers' League in 1888. After his election as MP for Ipswich in 1880, Collings brought his interest in land reform to the House of Commons.[26] Throughout all of his political life, however, Collings never deviated in his loyalty to Chamberlain and never questioned any policy of his chief. His subservience and unconditional positive regard for Chamberlain maintained their friendship.

Apart from his friends and close political colleagues, an abiding source of comfort and solace was Chamberlain's Birmingham home in King's Heath, just beyond the fashionable suburb of Edgbaston. At Highbury, Chamberlain not only hosted dinner parties and large garden gatherings: he also held strategy sessions for his political intimates. Highbury was the central focus of Chamberlain's growing political empire: his London residence at Prince's Gardens was a poor second as a nerve centre for his ambitions. Nearly every weekend during parliamentary sittings, Chamberlain took the train north toward home and Highbury.

The house itself, built to Chamberlain's specifications in 1880, was a notable example of a new kind of domestic structure popular among the business and political elite of the late nineteenth century. Set within 18 acres of grounds, Highbury was a miniature replication of the grand estates that had traditionally served the aristocracy as a physical manifestation of its power and ruling authority.[27] Yet Highbury was placed squarely in the suburbs and was close enough to Birmingham's city centre to secure firmly its urban affiliations.[28] Highbury's architecture has been labelled 'modern Venetian Gothic'. Externally finished with red-tinted brick and white stone trim, the front facade is dominated by a large tiered series of bay windows from ground to roof, which are mirrored by two smaller bays of two storeys. The surrounding park initially included winding paths leading to secluded hollows and pools. In later years, the park provided sufficient pasturage for a herd of cattle, the hobby of Chamberlain's eldest son, Austen. The main conservatory, reached directly from inside the house through the drawing room, was the dominant feature of the landscaped garden. Attendant greenhouses – two dozen in all – provided botanical laboratories primarily for Chamberlain's orchid culture, as well as for his azaleas, begonias, and cyclamens. Chamberlain spent many hours experimentally and systematically cross-fertilizing strains of orchids. His orchid catalogue listed the numbers and names of plants, dates when bought, value, native soil, and all other pertinent information. Naturalized bulbs, hollies, and rhododendrons also flourished. In the formal Dutch garden alone were planted nearly 8,000 bulbs of irises, tulips, and daffodils. To manage the cultivation took a full-time staff of two dozen gardeners.[29]

The interior of the house was characterized by a lavish use of coloured tiles and a variety of building materials. Parquetry in the floors, painted rafters, marbled pillars, and the huge hall one encounters almost immediately upon entering – large enough to be used occasionally as a ballroom – created a sense of exuberance.[30] On the ground floor at one corner of the house was Chamberlain's study, a large square room with an oak desk solidly placed and dominating the floor space. Lining the oaken shelves around the room were reference works, parliamentary blue books, *Hansard's Parliamentary Debates*, a reasonable number of French novels, and books on orchid lore. A smaller room adjacent to the library once served Chamberlain's secretary; it is now a gentleman's toilet.

Apart from its role as a centre of political activity, Highbury was also the domestic centre of Chamberlain's life. Both Chamberlain's wives had died before Highbury was built, but his sons and daughters provided a respectful and obedient family circle. Although lively and affectionate letters characterize the extensive correspondence between father and children, there was also a palpable emotional distance between them. Chamberlain's natural reserve and his tendency to manage their affairs, even to the smallest details, maintained a barrier rarely lowered.

This is not to say that the Chamberlain children were repressed or disadvantaged by their father's exacting standards. They were, after all, children of wealth and privilege who admired their father, took pride in his accomplishments, and were thoroughly solicitous of his welfare. The three younger Chamberlain children were less in the limelight than their elder siblings. Hilda and Ida wrote a book together on the natural history of the Riviera, and in their later years lived together in Hampshire and were active in local affairs. Ethel, the youngest child and the only one of Chamberlains' four daughters to marry (to Whitmore Lionel Richards), bore, it is said, the closest resemblance to her mother Florence. She died prematurely. The eldest child, Beatrice, considered the most widely read, was willing to tackle such difficult works as Benjamin Kidd's *Social Evolution* and to relax with the correspondence of Goethe and Schiller. She won Beatrice Potter's admiration for her 'large', 'beautiful', and 'simple warm nature'. But to Miss Potter's inquiring eye, Beatrice had only 'one great devotion' absorbing every day of her life – 'a passionate feeling for her father, a desire to protect him from all pain and to share with him every pleasure'.[31] Beatrice often served as a social secretary for her father and lived at Highbury until her father's death. She never married.[32]

Of Austen, his eldest son, Chamberlain entertained the greatest hopes. Consequently, his early letters to Austen when he was a schoolboy suggests that his father was determined to shape his son into an obedient and dutiful child. Once correcting his spelling, Chamberlain observed that in learning Latin, Austen seemed to have forgotten English.[33] Discovering a letter from one of Austen's friends, Chamberlain found that his 12-year-old son was smoking brown-paper cigars. 'I don't admire your taste', he wrote curtly. Additionally, he cautioned Austen not to leave his letters carelessly open if he intended to have secrets.[34] In other correspondence, Chamberlain chastised Austen for not replying about riding lessons, for an apparent lapse of manners in writing to a cousin, for doing poorly in English, for forgetting his (Chamberlain's) birthday, and for not writing lengthy enough letters.[35]

In later life, Austen remembered that all the children were somewhat in awe of their father, and 'certainly there was instant obedience'. Not that they feared their father, he wrote, 'except in the sense of over-anxiety lest we should not please him'.[36] Austen's desire to please his father went to the extent of dressing like him (including wearing a frock coat, silk hat, orchid, and monocle), adopting his politics, and hoping to succeed as his father had in public life.[37] Indeed, Austen had fair success in political life as a Unionist MP, cabinet member, and a leader of the Unionist Party. But he was throughout his political career clearly his father's son.

Neville, too, fell under the sway of his father's personality. Like Austen, he was schooled at Rugby, but was selected by his father for a career in business rather than politics. After Rugby, Neville took courses in applied science at Mason College in Birmingham. Later, he was apprenticed to a firm of accountants. The final stage in his preparation for business came about accidentally and ended badly. A chance meeting between Chamberlain and the Governor of the Bahamas, Sir Ambrose Shea, led Chamberlain to believe that there was a potentially profitable market in cultivating a local Bahamian plant, sisal, which reportedly produced a high-quality fibre for hemp. Just as he himself had been placed by his own father for entrepreneurial training, so Chamberlain sent Neville in 1891 to purchase several thousand acres of land and begin cultivating sisal plants on the small and barren island of Andros. Chamberlain also believed that such a commercial adventure would be an ideal way, as he put it to Neville, 'to show your manhood'.[38]

For five years, from the age of 22, Neville was solely responsible for the operation. Living alone and with little direct access to expert guidance, he worked unceasingly, eventually clearing 5,000 acres and employing up to 500 labourers in cultivating, picking, bailing, and shipping the plants to the United States. The geographical distance between father and son prohibited a close daily oversight of the project by Chamberlain, but he nevertheless took an active supervisory role over Neville's management of the sisal plantation. Ever the entrepreneur, Chamberlain explored each avenue of commercial advantage, prodding Neville to be aware of opportunities for profit. He was especially concerned about Neville's accounts, and offered frequent advice. In one instance, he requested 'some further explanations'.[39] He once asked Neville to send him sisal leaves pressed into a brick, so that he could take it to a paper manufacturer to ascertain its value for paper making. 'Do not', he cautioned his son, 'tell *anyone* what the object is.'[40]

Concerns about Neville's health also frequently punctuated Chamberlain's correspondence. He urged his son to get sufficient sleep and proper food, encouraging him to hire a cook. Extra help should be found if he became shorthanded. He was insistent, too, that Neville, whenever possible, take holidays. He especially recommended visits to nearby Cuba and Florida. 'Remember your health is the first consideration', he cautioned.[41] When Neville seemed reluctant to leave Andros, Chamberlain would command. In the spring of 1894, he wrote that Neville should return to Birmingham for the sake of his health. So that Neville would not mistake his intentions, Chamberlain underscored his request: 'this is not a matter for argument but a final decision ... which, I am sure, you will carry out'.[42]

Under his father's vigilant eye, Neville struggled to make a profit over the next few years. But the quality of the sisal was uneven; market prices declined; and labour problems were endemic. After several years of futile effort, Neville was called home. The venture had taken its toll on Neville. Even early on, he confessed in a letter home that he was 'low spirited and depressed ... heartily sick' and longing 'for civilization and comfort'.[43] The failure of the Andros project was additionally a blow to family finances: the loss of £50,000 meant that Chamberlain was forced thereafter to live off capital. Chamberlain's response to the disaster, however, was admirable. He refused to blame Neville. Using family connections, Chamberlain was soon able to place Neville in a large metal company in nearby Selly Oak. This became a springboard to greater business opportunities in Birmingham as Neville prospered. In time, of course, Neville fared well not only economically. Serving as city councillor and Lord Mayor of Birmingham, Member of Parliament, cabinet minister, and eventually prime minister, Neville attained the high office that his father never achieved.

Clearly, life for Chamberlain's children at Highbury was neither cheerless nor unpleasant. It was a place where they enjoyed their extended family (other Chamberlains and Kenricks lived nearby); entertained a wide network of friends; and met and discoursed with leading politicians of the day. But the children understood that the first rule of the house was obedience and that the patriarchal word was supreme. If not a tyranny, the household was governed under the strict laws of a benevolent despot. Their father assigned and decorated their rooms, was vigilant over their schooling, and demanded that his own priorities be paramount. It was understood that Highbury was for Chamberlain not only a place of relaxation; it was also a place of work. When preparing for his speeches, for example, Chamberlain would brood over them for days, becoming moody and withdrawn, smoking and working into the early hours of the morning. He rummaged through his notebooks for appropriate quotations, and consulted his record of what he said in earlier speeches to avoid repetition and discursiveness. Well before the date of a speech, he began writing it out entirely, and then reducing it to short notes as the final day approached.[44]

Throughout the early years at Highbury, there is little evidence that Chamberlain either thought about, or actively sought, a wife. His work was all absorbing. In the mid-1880s, however, his life took a more social turn as he savoured the perquisites of a cabinet minister in London's salons. Perhaps surprisingly, Chamberlain was a success, even with Tory hostesses such as Lady Dorothy Nevill, who admired his candour and his wit.[45] A more flirtatious relationship seems to have developed with Lady Dorothy Stanley. Extracts from her diary reveal a strong attraction between the young Lady Dorothy, then in her mid-20s, and the serious and decisive (and much older) politician. There were frequent visits. They discussed French novels. He sent her a signed photograph. She, in turn, gave him a gift of oranges. The more she saw of him, the more she trusted him. 'I like his simple directness', she confided to her diary. 'I do not think, as many do, that he is a subversive man ...'.[46] Although she found him 'dreadfully indiscrete [sic]', he was also 'flatteringly sincere & earnest'. His disclosures were, she wrote, 'safe with me'.[47] Lady Dorothy provided a willing ear to Chamberlain's vehement denunciations of the state of British politics, and of his ambitions in public life. To her, Chamberlain asserted his belief that he was certain to be prime minister one day. 'I have never doubted the power of will and determination', he told her: 'given health, given time I shall conquer.'[48]

In spite of his assurances to Lady Dorothy, however, Chamberlain was far from his goal in early 1887. With the Conservatives solidly in office and Chamberlain relegated to a minority splinter group, opportunities for seizing power were limited. He felt increasingly at a loose end. This had predisposed him to accept Lord Salisbury's invitation in August 1887 to lead a delegation to the United States, where negotiations concerning a long-standing fisheries controversy with Canada were to begin that autumn. Chamberlain was at first hesitant, expressing to John Bright his fear that domestic politics were such that 'many persons ... will blame me if I fail & ... will give me no credit if I succeed'.[49] But the prospect of travel abroad inclined him to accept an offer of escape.[50] Sailing from Liverpool in late October 1887, Chamberlain reached New York on 7 November.[51] It was the beginning of a journey more notable for its social consequences than for its diplomatic achievements.

Meetings in late November at the State Department in Washington, D.C., were not initially encouraging. Chamberlain reported to Salisbury that American protectionist sentiment, especially among members of the Republican Party, could delay or even sabotage the negotiations.[52] But Chamberlain was persistent and created a favourable impression among his American hosts. In the end, an acceptable treaty was concluded. It offered American fishermen entry into Canadian waters as soon as Canadian fish were admitted tariff-free into the United States. The boundary of Canadian territorial waters was also delineated. An important additional protocol essentially permitted these terms to be in force for two years until such time as the treaty proper was ratified by the American Senate.[53] By mid-February, 1888, Chamberlain's official duties were completed.

Apart from negotiating, Chamberlain found the time to travel in both Canada and the eastern United States. His views were not always favourable. He disliked the principal commercial streets of Washington – 'not equal to a second class street in Birmingham' was his brusque comment.[54] New York he dismissed as 'the ugliest big city I have ever seen'.[55] Visiting President Cleveland in the White House, Chamberlain thought that it was, like all American houses, 'kept much too hot by steam and hot water pipes'.[56] If Chamberlain found the American physical environment displeasing, he discovered more attractions in North American women and in the social whirl of American and Canadian society. Within a few weeks of his arrival, he wrote to his daughter, Beatrice, that 'the average of American female beauty is higher than ours. You see a very large number of nice looking girls in the streets and the proportion of good figures and of well dressed women is very large.'[57] In Canada, he discovered similar pleasures. At a dinner in his honour in Toronto, he claimed that a number of the prettiest women of that city were in attendance. 'This I am informed in the Papers', he wrote to Birmingham, 'because I am well known as a connoisseur in female beauty.'[58] Within a fortnight, he was again in Washington at a dinner party hosted by members of congress where he spied 'two very pretty young ladies. In fact I never saw so many bright and pretty women of all ages as I have here.'[59]

It is not surprising that, in spite of his varied impressions of America, he was having "'a high old time'".[60] In January 1888, he recorded a delightful round 'of continuous gaiety and hospitality'.[61] In one week alone, he had been at six dinner parties, three evening receptions, three balls, one supper, one theatre party, one luncheon, and various afternoon receptions.[62] Once the treaty had been signed, Chamberlain reported himself to be 'in rollicking spirits': he boasted to Beatrice that his popularity 'has continued to the end'.[63] This was no idle boast. Cecil Spring Rice, then a secretary in the British Embassy in Washington, reported in December 1887 that Chamberlain 'continues his course of popularity and is become a great element in this society'.[64] Chamberlain had also won respect by his cleverness and his blunt speech, especially against Ireland, 'arguing with ferocity and directness, sometimes pitted against a whole tableful of men'.[65]

Chamberlain's unusual burst of good feeling was doubtless due in part to the successful conclusion of the treaty and to the social delights of his hosts. But even more important was his meeting with Mary Endicott, whom he described to Beatrice as 'one of the brightest and most intelligent girls I have yet met'.[66] The daughter of William Endicott, President Cleveland's Secretary of the Army, and Ellen Peabody, Mary was well connected in American society. When not in Washington, her family lived in Salem, Massachusetts. Mary, like other women, found Chamberlain's earnestness and absence of superficial small talk attractive. After a whirlwind courtship of only a few weeks characterized by an overwhelmingly persistent campaign, Chamberlain won Mary's hand, if not yet her heart. His search, it seemed, for a wife and a mistress of Highbury was at an end.

But to bring about the marriage was less easy than Chamberlain had imagined. Mary's family, unnerved by the suddenness of it all, was taken aback. There was a considerable age difference: Mary was 23 to Chamberlain's 51. Mary's father was also fearful of political consequences. As a member of President Cleveland's cabinet, Endicott could foresee that his daughter's marriage to a well-known English politician who had opposed Home Rule could jeopardize Cleveland's re-election by antagonizing the Irish-American vote. Endicott therefore imposed conditions. The marriage was not to take place until after the impending election. Furthermore, announcement of the engagement was to be delayed as long as possible. In effect, the marriage would be postponed until November of that year.[67]

Chamberlain, in his initial state of euphoria, accepted these conditions. But he was willing to accept only on the grounds that he could write to Mary, and that she would be allowed to respond. Within hours of his departure from Washington, Chamberlain began a series of extraordinary letters. Often dozens of pages long written every day for the next nine months, the letters are a diary of his daily life and a summary of his political activities. But far more important are the paradoxical themes of love and devotion to his bride-to-be on the one hand, and, on the other, his anger and frustrations with his future father-in-law.[68] In short, these letters reveal much about Chamberlain's newly found capacity for falling in love; but they reveal more about his demanding tendency to manage, to exert control, and to establish dominance and power – characteristics we have already seen in his public life, now here fully revealed in his private behaviour.

Chamberlain's infatuation for Mary was obvious from the very first letter written before he left American shores. Mary was 'the sweetest of girls and the most entrancing of the witches of Salem'. As he wrote before her portrait, her kisses were still warm on his lips: 'you are my joy & my life & my love'. It was a 'wonder of wonders' that had brought 'this great & undeserved happiness to me'.[69] On board the *Umbria*, beginning his Atlantic voyage home, Chamberlain continued: 'I cannot live without you.' Awakening in the night, he finds her always in his thoughts.[70] In his later letters, he was equally romantic, and mawkish in the way that love in its early stages often is. He slept with her letters under his pillow. He pledged undying devotion and eternal love. He regarded her as 'something apart & sacred in the Holy of Holies where no one enters but myself'.[71] She was his 'second self'.[72] He sent her copies of his speeches, photographs, and (in one odd instance) a coil of copper wire left over from the installation of electric lights in his London home at Prince's Gardens.

Upon returning to Birmingham in early March 1888 Chamberlain immediately told his children, all of whom welcomed the news. Once in place at Highbury, however, Chamberlain was an anxious suitor. The distance was daunting, and often delayed communication. Late letters might bring a mild transatlantic reproof. He constantly suffered from what he called 'letter fever', and once confessed to being as 'cross as a bear with a sore head' at not receiving a prompt reply to one of his letters.[73] When Mary's letters were too short, he complained bitterly at being put on 'half rations'. It was, he moaned, 'the cruellest thing you have ever done ... I will not accept half lives or half letters or half anything. It is all or nothing ...'.[74]

He was especially concerned at the tardiness of a public announcement of their engagement. Hoping to return to the USA as early as May, he wrote in early April 1888: 'I cannot bring myself to contemplate a longer delay.'[75] When it was clear that he would not be welcome that spring, Chamberlain took a firmer position: 'It is right that your father and mother should know that they are making difficulties for us by insisting on this secrecy. We will fight them together ...'. He concluded the letter in anger: 'I am just as wild about it all as a tiger cat ...'.[76] In fact, Chamberlain's mood turned distinctly threatening as he attempted to force Mary's father to relent. He proposed sailing to America at once 'to settle the matter' unless he heard favourable news;[77] he urged Mary to 'speak plainly' to her father;[78] and he continually berated Endicott for his obduracy.[79] He also denounced 'this unnatural separation' as 'cruel and wicked'.[80] Well into the summer months, Chamberlain felt an intense bitterness against those who had 'unnecessarily, unwisely & with culpable weakness ... imposed this martyrdom upon me'.[81]

Threats having failed, Chamberlain played to Mary's sympathies. He complained of frequent depression and physical illness brought on by the separation and uncertainty. In late April, he had a 'nervous headache with acute pains that almost demoralised me ... I was almost wild with physical suffering.'[82] A few days later, he was both 'sick & angry beyond measure' at the continued delay, and declared that 'this odious & shameful concealment should cease'.[83] In later letters, he wrote of feeling 'awfully depressed', 'moody & depressed', 'depressed & anxious', 'almost in despair', 'horribly dull & depressed', 'very miserable', deep into 'the blues', 'depressed to an unusual extent', 'dull & played out', 'very low & out of spirits', 'low spirited', and 'settling down into a condition of chronic gloom & melancholy'.[84] In late June, he blamed the separation and delay for a lengthy bout of a 'frightful temper with everybody'. Warning his family at Highbury of his mood, 'they flee from me'.[85] He was convinced that the stress of separation caused an attack of gout, forcing him to hobble about Highbury in a cloth boot.[86] The separation had also begun to affect his work. 'You cannot think how hard it is to work with another absorbing anxiety always present.'[87] One may wonder how Miss Endicott bore up under this barrage. A letter from Mary to Jesse Collings gave a clue. Distressed at the delay and feeling awkwardly placed 'between two duties' (as daughter and fian-cée), she found the circumstances 'a sore trial'. She hoped that the marriage date could be hastened, but, as she resignedly concluded, 'for the present the matter has passed out of my hands'.[88]

Only when the marriage date was finally set for early November did Chamberlain's tone change toward Mary's father. He assured Mary that he had put aside all ill feel-ings about the delay, though he still believed it could have been avoided. He even seemed to forgive Mr. Endicott: 'I am sure that your father has meant everything for the best …'.[89] Chamberlain's relatively generous valediction to this wrenching episode was a rare incident in his personal and political life.

Chamberlain in the midst of his complaints to Mary was always careful to reassure her that his love and affection was unvarying. But he also made it clear that he had specific expectations of her role in marriage. In the marriage pledge, for example, he emphasized that she would 'have to promise to love, honour, and *obey me*'. These, he thought, were necessary conditions for a happy marriage. 'If you love and honour', he wrote, 'you will not have much difficulty or hesitation about obeying in any case in which I thought it necessary to command.'[90] Softening his requirements slightly, he predicted that they would never have a difference 'on any question of the slightest importance'.[91] As he put it, not entirely in jest: 'you no longer belong to yourself, you belong wholly to your tyrant & you have abdicated for ever your independence & freedom'.[92] 'You are to be', as he put it, 'my helpmate …'.[93]

It is not too much to suggest that Chamberlain, once he had encountered dif-ficulties in pursuing his 'Puritan maid',[94] was thrown into circumstances in which he could not exert his accustomed authority and power. Yet he seemed at times to understand himself and his motives. He once warned Mary that he was quite particu-lar and critical.[95] He characterized his true self as 'obstinate & self willed – very proud & arbitrary – very impatient of contradiction & masterful in temper'.[96] Obstructed by events which blocked his way or by stubborn individuals who refused to capitulate to his demands, Chamberlain's anxiety level often rose dramatically. He sometimes felt 'like a dynamite machine ready to explode at the slightest touch'.[97] At other times, he felt 'powerless to help either you or myself'.[98]

These revealing comments about his own psychological state in his letters to Mary provide the clearest evidence of Chamberlain's psychological state when his authority was questioned. Whether in friendship or courtship, as mayor or parliamentarian, Chamberlain could not countenance opposition to his ideas or policies. Friends must be subservient, wives must obey, colleagues must follow, opponents must be brought down. Allegiance to a particular political party was less important than its adherence to him. Consistency in political, social, and economic ideas might be sacrificed to his need for control. If Chamberlain should attain the highest political office in the land, these characteristics might well be heightened. Chamberlain's contemporaries fully understood this and thus many viewed with alarm his steady progress up the political ladder during the late 1880s and early 1890s.

Plate 1   Chamberlain: determined even as a young man

Plate 2 Chamberlain about the
time he courted Mary
Endicott

Plate 3 Mary Endicott,
Chamberlain's third wife

Plate 4   Exterior of Highbury, the powerhouse of Chamberlain's Birmingham years

Plate 5   Interior of Highbury

Price One Penny.   THE DART.   Saturday, May 1, 1880.

HE STOOPS TO CONQUER.

The Right Hon. J— C— (a Red Republican—kissing hands) : Let us dissemble. No matter. The time will come !

Plate 6   Queen Victoria, unhappy at the inclusion of the radical Chamberlain in
             Gladstone's second ministry

JUDY, OR THE LONDON SERIO-COMIC JOURNAL.—July 7, 1880.

CARRIED IN TRIUMPH BETWEEN WHIG AND RADICAL.

BUT IT IS SUCH A PITY THEY MUST PART COMPANY.

Plate 7 Chamberlain's radicalism appears to the conservative journal *Judy* as a threat to the ministry

Plate 8 But others had a more favourable view

DECEMBER 31st.]   THE OWL   [1880

"THE STRONGEST MAN IN THE CABINET"

(Vide Mr. Plunket's recent Speech.)

Supplement Gratis with "UNITED IRELAND." Saturday, Sept. 19th, 1885.

AN ERROR IN CALCULATION.

MR. CH———N.—We are thirty-four millions against your four, and by G——, if you give us any of your infernal tongue——
IRISH-AMERICAN.—Thirty-four millions against four!'. Husho, stranger, draw it mild! YOU are forgetting ME!. There are fifteen millions more where I came from

Plate 9 This famous cartoon captures the tensions between Chamberlain and the Irish nationalists

JUDY, OR THE LONDON SERIO-COMIC JOURNAL.—Dec 1, 1885.

RECENT PLATFORM DISPLAYS.
SHOWING WHAT DIFFERENCES ARE POSSIBLE IN AN UNITED CABINET.

Plate 10 Divisions continued within the cabinet as Chamberlain followed his own path

Plate 11 Chamberlain consorting with Conservatives Lords Salisbury and Randolph
Churchill during the heated debates over Irish Home Rule

TENTH Year, No. 503.   THE DART   Friday, June 11th, 1886.

LIBERAL TEMPLE

THE MODERN SAMSON.

Plate 12 Once again the strong man, Chamberlain pulls down the Liberal Party over the Irish question as Gladstone looks on in dismay

XXXV.—THE GREATEST SHOW ON EARTH.
UNDER THE PERSONAL MANAGEMENT OF MR. JOSEPH PUSHFUL.

THE GREATEST SHOW ON EARTH!! THE ENVY OF THE WORLD!!

THE BRITISH EMPIRE. UNLIMITED

IMPERIUM IN EMPORIO

UNDER THE PERSONAL MANAGEMENT OF MR JOSEPH PUSHFUL

ALL THE BEST BITS SECURED

SEE OUR SPECIAL LINE IN CROWN COLONIES

Plate 13 As Colonial Secretary in Salisbury's Conservative/ Unionist ministry, Chamberlain finds a wider scope in his pursuit of power

PUNCH, OR THE LONDON CHARIVARI.—October 31, 1896.

PREPARING HIS SPEECH.

Mr. Joe Ch-mb-rl-n (*to himself*). "'IN SHORT, GENTLEMEN—IF YOU ARE ONLY TRUE TO YOUR PRINCIPLES, ANY ONE OF YOU MAY BECOME—AS I HAVE DONE—A MINISTER IN A LIBER—I SHOULD SAY IN A CONSERV—I BEG PARDON—I SHOULD SAY IN AN UNIONIST GOVERNMENT.' H'M—RATHER CONFUSING—I DON'T THINK *THAT'LL* QUITE DO!"

[Mr. Chamberlain is announced to speak to-night, Wednesday, October 28, at the Jubilee Union of the Birmingham Debating Society.]

Plate 14 Chamberlain, facing a mirror, is somewhat confused about his party allegiance in this *Punch* cartoon

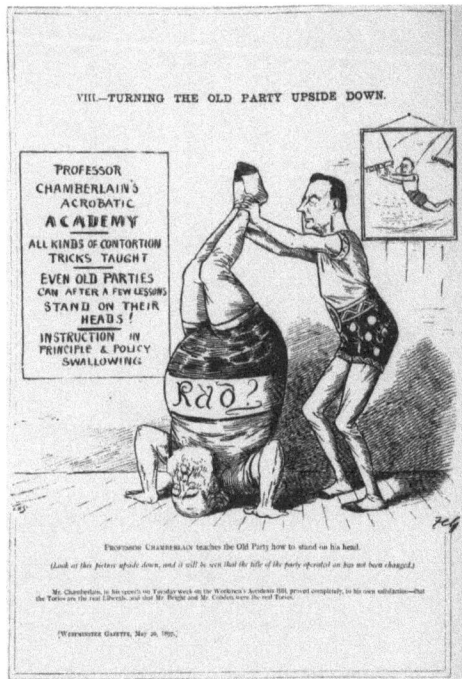

VIII.—TURNING THE OLD PARTY UPSIDE DOWN.

PROFESSOR CHAMBERLAIN'S ACROBATIC ACADEMY

ALL KINDS OF CONTORTION TRICKS TAUGHT

EVEN OLD PARTIES CAN AFTER A FEW LESSONS STAND ON THEIR HEADS!

INSTRUCTION IN PRINCIPLE & POLICY SWALLOWING

Rad?

PROFESSOR CHAMBERLAIN teaches the Old Party how to stand on his head.

(Look at this picture upside down, and it will be seen that the title of the party operated on has not been changed.)

Mr. Chamberlain, in his speech on Tuesday week on the Workmen's Accidents Bill, proved conclusively, to his own satisfaction—that the Tories are the real Liberals, and that Mr. Bright and Mr. Cobden were the real Tories.

[Westminster Gazette, May 26, 1897.]

Plate 15 Radical inclinations have not entirely vanished from the energetic Colonial Secretary

Plate 16 Once again before a mirror, Chamberlain considers assuming the appearance and mantle of a revered Conservative leader

Plate 17 A mad dog looking on the loose, Chamberlain threatens even Lord Salisbury, Foreign Secretary as well as Prime Minister in the Unionist ministry

Mr. C. (apostrophising portrait of William Pitt): It's wonderful, William, how much alike all we great Ministers are. You were hated in Europe in your time as I am hated to-day.

["Read your history, and you find the younger Pitt, one of the greatest of English Ministers; you find Lord Melbourne, you find the Duke of Wellington, you find Lord Palmerston—you find all those great Ministers who in their time upheld the honour and interests of the British Empire—you find them all complaining that they had not a friend in Europe . . . sometimes that is a consolation to me."—Mr. Chamberlain at Birmingham, January 6, 1902.]   [Westminster Gazette, January 8, 1902.]

Plate 18 Comparing favourably his own policies to former British leaders, Chamberlain is reassured

THE COLONIAL CONFERENCE AT THE COLONIAL OFFICE

From a Photograph by J. Russell and Sons, Baker Street

Mr. W. Holdernes   Sir J. Anderson   Sir J. Forrest   Sir W. Mulock   Lord Onslow   Admiral Custance   Mr. G. W. Balfour
Sir R. Bond   Mr. R. J. Seddon   Sir W. Laurier   Mr. Chamberlain   Lord Selborne   Mr. W. Patterson   Mr. Fuller
                                                                          Sir A. Hime   Sir E. H. Barton

Plate 19 Front and centre at the Colonial Conference of 1902, Chamberlain emphasized the need for strengthening imperial unity

A PERMANENT MEMORIAL.

"A scheme is on foot to erect in Mr. Chamberlain's constituency (West Birmingham) some permanent memorial of his mission to South Africa. The idea most favoured at present is a public clock with four faces, to be erected on a lofty pedestal in a prominent part of the division."—*Daily Papers.*

[Our artist respectfully offers the above elegant and appropriate design for the consideration of the projectors of the memorial.]

["*Daily Dispatch*," *March* 18th, 1903.]

Plate 20 The four faces of 'Big Joe' at the University of Birmingham reflect the different phases of Chamberlain's political career

PUNCH, OR THE LONDON CHARIVARI.—September 16, 1903.

THE UNREADY RECKONER.

PRINCE ARTHUR. "O, DEAR OPHELIA, I AM ILL AT THESE NUMBERS; I HAVE NOT ART TO RECKON. . . ."—*Hamlet*, Act II., Sc. 2.

Plate 21 Balfour, delivering the lines that Hamlet wrote to Ophelia (pictured here as Joe), is troubled by tariff reform

THE CHAMBERLAIN ORCHIDSTRA.

[The first meeting of the new Tariff "Commission" is fixed for January 15.]

Plate 22 A friendly and subservient Tariff Commission, led and staffed by Chamberlain

Plate 23 Chamberlain cooks the Liberal Unionist Council, leaving out an important ingredient, the Duke of Devonshire

CHANGE OF TASTE.

JOSEPH (the Chef). "DON'T LIKE THE OLD RECIPE. TOO RICH. FAR BETTER WITHOUT ALL THAT DEVONSHIRE CREAM."

[Mr. CHAMBERLAIN, finding the present constitution of the Liberal Unionist Council too "aristocratic" for his taste, is bringing forward a series of resolutions with the view of reconstituting the Council on the basis of a fuller representation of the Party.]

FOLLOW ME, LEADER.

The Hind Legs (log). "MY DEAR ARTHUR, OF COURSE YOU'RE THE ONLY CONCEIVABLE *HEAD*; BUT WE'RE GOING *MY* WAY!"

Plate 24 The Valentine Compact formally secured Chamberlain's power within the bedraggled Unionist Party, which had been soundly defeated in the election of 1906

Plate 25 Chamberlain and Mary on polling day, 17 January 1906

Plate 26 Tipping his hat to the crowds on polling day, Chamberlain concludes the final election of his life

Plate 27 A celebration of Chamberlain's 70th birthday at Bingley Hall, Birmingham

9

POWER DEFERRED

The Liberal Interlude

When Hartington became the 8th Duke of Devonshire and left the Commons, Chamberlain was the only viable replacement as the Liberal Unionist leader. Although an object of mistrust and suspicion because of his well-known tendency to political intrigue, Chamberlain had no rivals among Liberal Unionists and few among the Conservatives. His energetic skill at parliamentary debate, his understanding of the political process, his programmatic view of policy and legislation, and his indefatigable campaigning style assured him the leadership. As leader of the Liberal Unionists, Chamberlain could bring a coherence and organizational potency, thus far lacking, to his small band of supporters in the Commons. Additionally, as leader, he could legitimize his own search for power.

The Duke's languid approach to party organization and his tendency to delegate authority rapidly gave way to Chamberlain's military model. A muscular and commanding tone was evident from the outset. He insisted on a unanimous and unconditional election by the Liberal Unionists at an official party meeting. This was done at Devonshire House in February 1892, where 'the Duke' (as Hartington was thereafter familiarly known) formally relinquished the leadership to Chamberlain.[1] From top to bottom Chamberlain sought to centralize and put in order the Liberal Unionists. He reorganized the Liberal Unionist Party by installing a new Chief Whip. To firm up the Liberal Unionist Association in the countryside, he appointed J. Powell Williams, his Birmingham political agent. Never shy in parliament whether in government or out, Chamberlain could now speak with an official voice.

The most immediate political task facing Chamberlain as leader was the forthcoming general election in the summer of 1892. By-election results during the six years of Salisbury's ministry had not been encouraging. Of more than a hundred contests, the Conservatives had gained only two seats in contrast to the Liberal total of twenty-two. Characteristically energetic, Chamberlain quickly got off the mark in his campaigning. It was a strikingly modern platform. He advocated old-age pensions; workmen's compensation; courts of arbitration for industrial disputes; and eight-hour days for miners. Disavowing radicalism as his motive, Chamberlain claimed that social and economic issues could legitimately be undertaken by a Conservative Unionist government – or indeed by any government. In spite of his disavowal, he had clearly not forgotten his radical origins: he was determined to make substantial reform a centrepiece of the coming electoral contest.

Even before the campaign had begun, he had carefully laid the groundwork. As early as 1891, Chamberlain had established and chaired a parliamentary committee to examine the feasibility of old-age pensions. The following year, prior to the general election, he had set out his ideas fully in the *National Review*.[2] During the election campaign itself, Chamberlain asserted that 'the time has come when the State should recognize it as one of its first duties to aid and stimulate some provision for old age'. He further declared it was nothing less than 'a scandal' that old men and women 'who had led honest and respectable and laborious lives' should end their days in the workhouse under the stigma of pauper relief.[3]

Chamberlain also had much to say on the dominant constitutional issue of the day, Home Rule. Here he defended the status quo. He pointed out the opposition of Ulster to Home Rule; tarred Gladstone with the brush of Parnell; and denounced the 'unpatriotic conduct' of the Irish leaders. Above all, he criticized the Liberal obsession with Ireland. With Ireland blocking the way, it was impossible to move forward on important social issues. At Walsall, speaking in support of Frank James, a Conservative Unionist candidate, Chamberlain indulged in a breathtaking flight of sophistry to prove his point – and to prove additionally that the great Liberal principles of the past were now upheld by the Unionist Party. Which party, he asked rhetorically, now sought the greatest happiness of the greatest number? Not the Gladstonians, he answered: misguided Liberals had denied the happiness and welfare of thirty-seven millions of loyal subjects in order to attend to the 'exacting demands' of only three million Irishmen of doubtful loyalty.[4]

Campaigning especially hard in his 'Duchy' – Staffordshire, Worcestershire, and Warwickshire – Chamberlain stirred the voters to such a pitch that Conservative and Liberal Unionist candidates won 30 of 39 constituencies. Chamberlain himself substantially increased his majority in Birmingham West, drawing support from almost all sections of the electorate.[5] The Liberal Unionist Sir Henry James readily understood the importance of Chamberlain's achievement. He congratulated his new chief for his 'splendid successes in the Midlands'. Chamberlain now had, James believed, 'an enormous power – and it will be mainly the exercise of that power [by which] Home Rule can be defeated'.[6]

But Chamberlain's striking electoral success was not representative of the Unionist effort at large. The Unionist alliance lost 80 seats, including 18 formerly held by Liberal Unionists. The final tallies gave the Conservative Unionists 268 and the Liberal Unionists 46, for a total of 314. Gladstonian Liberals emerged as the largest party at 272, followed by Irish Home Rulers with 81, for a total of 353. In effect, the Liberals could form a government, but – as had been true after the 1885 general election – only with the aid of Irish MPs. Thus was Gladstone able to form the fourth and final ministry of his political career.

The Unionist defeat has been explained variously.[7] It may be that an enervated Unionist leadership, fatigued by six years of legislative labours, no longer interested the electorate. Or perhaps traditional Tories, offended by Salisbury's excessive social legislation and alienated by Chamberlain's influence, refused to support the Unionist alliance at the polls. Equally probable is the effective campaign carried out by the Liberals. In opposition to the Unionist alliance, the Liberals strongly advocated Home Rule for Ireland. This played upon a growing sentiment in the country that the Irish question ought to be 'settled'. Likely important, too, was a social agenda that the Liberals had devised well before the election. At a famous meeting of the National Liberal Federation (NLF) at Newcastle in late 1891, the chairman, Robert Spence Watson, reminded the Liberal Party of its heritage: 'For the people against class, against privilege.' Success for the Liberals at the polls, he claimed, 'would be another victory gained in equalizing and making more possible the conditions of life for the whole of the people ... higher, nobler, purer, and better than it had hitherto been'.[8] To that end the NLF pledged itself to address disestablishment, temperance, electoral reform, amendments to the laws on employer liability, and reform of the House of Lords. The 'Newcastle Programme', as it was called, became the official platform of the Liberal Party. Thus the Liberals broadened their appeal well beyond narrow Irish issues, which for several years had dominated their political thinking.

Although Chamberlain condemned the Newcastle Programme as 'nothing more nor less than a gigantic political waste-paper basket' containing bits and pieces of a political platform,[9] the Liberals at Newcastle had taken a leaf from Chamberlain's book. As Hamer has pointed out, Chamberlain pioneered 'programme' politics.[10] Avoiding single-issue formulations, Chamberlain believed that large and diverse programmes could more readily capture a wide band of supporters. His campaign for free land, free labour, a free church, and free schools in the early 1870s, the radical programme of 1885, and the social platform of 1892 stand as examples. Chamberlain also believed that merely enunciating programmes was not enough: some mechanism was necessary to prevent confusion and disorder among various reform issues. For Chamberlain, the mechanism was, quite simply, strong and decisive leadership which could bring coherence to the programme as a whole. Otherwise, election campaigns and governments alike could bumble along from one issue to another without establishing a clear legislative intent. Effective organization and leadership would additionally prevent an overloaded programme falling of its own weight or becoming dismantled piecemeal by the political opposition.

By the time of the election in 1892, it is also clear that Chamberlain's programmatic approach to politics had become an important part of his conception of a perpetual campaign. Never waiting until elections were called, Chamberlain was thoroughly involved in cultivating public opinion at all times. His skill in managing the electorate was based upon his understanding of the need for a reiterative public campaign which would both inform and instruct. To inform, Chamberlain stated his programme clearly and frequently. To instruct, he persuaded the voters in the rightness of his message. His national organizations, speeches in and out of parliament, and newspaper and journal articles were all attempts at monopolizing public information through a kind of political blitzkrieg. Chamberlain had, of course, genuine policy preferences in addressing social and economic issues. But he had also to think increasingly about employing a careful political strategy to preserve his own position within the party framework. As the leader of an opposition party in the House of Commons (as he was from 1892 to 1895), Chamberlain's primary task was to strengthen the alliance between his own small band of Liberal Unionists and the Salisburian Conservatives, while simultaneously preventing his Liberal Unionists from falling into the Conservative embrace. This tactic already had been employed to some extent during the previous Salisbury government. In addition, Chamberlain had to distinguish his brand of Liberalism from the mainstream Liberals while allaying the suspicions of the diehard Tories that he would in time betray their interests. Such political balancing acts, if successful, could keep Chamberlain an independent master of his own political party.

When the new Liberal government introduced its social programme to the House of Commons, Chamberlain played his cards carefully. Keeping the lines to Salisbury open, he neither rejected the Liberal proposals outright nor engaged in openly destructive tactics. He suggested, where possible, specific changes in the legislation that could be considered improvements; or he questioned on practical grounds the utility of the legislation. For example, during the extended debate on the Employers' Liability Bill, Chamberlain upheld the integrity of the Bill as a whole; but he also proposed amendments that would make it more attractive to the Conservatives. The Bill itself was an attempt to rewrite the Employers' Liability Act of 1880, which had favoured employers rather than employees in providing compensation for injured workers only when negligence of employers or their agents could be proven.[11] To avoid expensive litigation on the discovery of fault, some employers had devised a policy of 'contracting out' by which their workers received insurance with broader coverage than the law allowed. In return, workers in the event of an accident would waive any extensive claims for damages against their employers.

Liberals wished to prohibit contracting out: in this, they were firmly opposed by the Conservatives. Chamberlain, from his position as chief of the Liberal Unionists, acted as a political broker between the two political parties. He supported the Conservative position on contracting out, preserving voluntary arrangements; but he also advocated an extension of coverage on the principle of universal compensation. Quoting statistics from Germany, Chamberlain showed that nearly half of all workplace accidents were attributable neither to workmen nor their masters, but were inherent in the work itself. By removing the employers' liability clause, workers would gain a greater insurance coverage. In this case, Chamberlain's attempts at compromise failed: the Bill became bogged down in the Lords and was abandoned, not to be resurrected until the succeeding Conservative government.

Chamberlain also returned to his interest in state-sponsored pension plans. As a member of a royal commission established in 1893 to investigate pensions, he proposed a state-assisted voluntary scheme which would entitle workers at age 65 to a pension of 5 shillings weekly. It was a modest proposal, but one that carried an important principle. Not unlike his ideas for workmen's compensation, however,

Chamberlain's pension plan did not find immediate legislative support.[12] Indeed, even though Chamberlain did more than any other politician during the 1890s to promote old-age pensions, it appears that his attempt to follow through legislatively on this, as on other social and economic issues, was of limited success. This can be attributed in part to the continued reservations of his Conservative allies and in part to the disadvantages inherent in any attempt to follow a political *via media*. Chamberlain particularly was not always comfortable in the position of attempting to compromise between two opposing camps.

This was most dramatically demonstrated in the 1892–95 parliament during his strenuous resistance to the Liberal Government of Ireland Bill. Although somewhat more limited than the 1886 Home Rule Bill, the proposed legislation of 1893 nevertheless established an Irish legislature in Dublin with eventual power to legislate on land, the judiciary, and the police. The bill also provided for 80 Irish MPs to sit at Westminster who would participate in Irish and imperial issues, but not in British domestic matters.[13] From the time of its introduction by Gladstone on 13 February 1893, Chamberlain led the attack against the Bill. In fact, he seemed quite willing, even determined, to sow dissension. His contentious debating style provoked his political opponents. He was often at the centre of stormy debates. On one famous occasion, a fistfight broke out on the floor of the House over remarks made by Chamberlain.[14] On 2 September, after 82 nights of debate, the Bill passed the Commons by only 34 votes. A week later, the Lords threw it out by a 10 to 1 majority.

Having been severely tested once again in parliamentary battle against his former political friends, Chamberlain emerged as a hero among the Unionists. At an anti-Home Rule demonstration at Hatfield House in April, he was carried shoulder-high by a delegation of more than a thousand Ulstermen around the south court.[15] But Chamberlain's sense of triumph over the defeat of the Liberal Home Rule Bill was short-lived. From late 1893 through early 1895 a sense of uncertainty dogged Chamberlain: the winds of fortune blew both favourably and ill.

At first, events ran smoothly for Chamberlain. Within a few months of the defeat of Home Rule at the hands of the Lords, Gladstone resigned as prime minister. Age and infirmity, combined with a raging cabinet disagreement on imperial and naval policy, brought a sad end to a remarkable political career. It was an event Chamberlain had long hoped for. But his chance for the leadership of the Liberals was all but gone. The battle for the Liberal leadership was fought out between Lord Rosebery, the imperial aristocrat who succeeded Gladstone as premier, and Sir William Harcourt, Chamberlain's one-time confidant and now chief spokesman for the Liberals in the House of Commons. With Rosebery's succession as Liberal leader, Chamberlain's ambitions and opportunities for power within the Liberal Party were brought conclusively at an end.

Equally significant for Chamberlain's political career was a significant downturn in his personal fortune. As noted earlier,[16] Chamberlain in the early 1890s lost a substantial sum in a failed sisal-growing venture in the Bahamas. At about the same time, Chamberlain's investments in the Canadian Pacific Railway fell rapidly in value.

With the future security of his family at risk, Chamberlain had to decide whether or not to continue his political career. For him, there was no option: he would remain an active politician, even if the financial prospects of his wife and children were somewhat dimmed.[17]

In a frame of mind already darkened by financial worries, Chamberlain encountered increasing resentment and restlessness among Conservatives at his participation in the Unionist alliance. Essential differences on religion and education had never been resolved between the nonconformist Liberal Unionist leader and Church of England Conservatives. Equally important were conflicts over local politics. Conservatives had for years chafed at Chamberlain's exclusionary policies within his Midlands sphere of influence. Matters came to a head in the spring of 1895 upon the retirement of A. W. Peel, the Liberal Unionist MP for Warwick and Leamington, and Speaker of the House.[18] The Conservatives and Liberal Unionists were immediately at odds over his successor. Chamberlain began coaching Peel's son, George (also a Liberal Unionist), for the position. The Conservatives – grooming their own candidate – were equally adamant. A political brawl broke out in the constituency and rapidly spread to the Unionist leadership. When the national press took up the controversy, Balfour once again was forced to act: he rejected the Conservative candidate, and agreed to sanction Chamberlain's nominee, George Peel. But the Conservatives refused to accept Peel.

Chamberlain reacted quickly and forcefully against the threat.[19] Writing to his wife, Mary – then visiting her parents in Cannes – he characterized the Tories as 'bitter' and complained that they 'seemed bent' on making his position 'intolerable'.[20] To the Duke of Devonshire, he intimated a resignation from the leadership of the Liberal Unionists unless his wishes were followed. 'I remain a Liberal at heart', he wrote to the Duke, 'although I am loyally working with the Tories.' But he could not 'sacrifice everything without losing all the influence' he possessed.[21] On the same day, he informed Henry Chaplin, an influential Conservative backbencher and Chamberlain supporter, that if he were to play any effective future role in the Unionist alliance, it must be 'with the hearty – and not the grudging – assent of the Conservative Party'.[22] Eventually, the affair was smoothed over when a compromise candidate, Alfred Lyttelton, a Liberal Unionist, was accepted by all. But a lingering mistrust continued between backbench Conservatives and the rogue Liberal/Radical they considered Chamberlain to be.

The controversy over Speaker Peel's parliamentary seat prompted from Lord Salisbury an astute appraisal of Chamberlain's personality and behaviour. In a confidential letter to his son-in-law, Salisbury observed that Chamberlain had gotten himself 'into a peck of troubles' primarily because he suffered from 'a common defect' of earnest men: 'he cannot believe in earnestness on the other side'.[23] Chamberlain did 'not really believe in a convinced churchman, or a squire who retains his opinions honestly': thus, he did not realize that they are 'impervious to his powers of persuasion'. If Chamberlain continued to shape his political life 'on the Birmingham view' of squire and parson, they would never accept him as their leader. But if he could set aside his own strongly held views, 'this little breeze will very speedily be forgotten'.

Salisbury also admitted that the Conservative leadership had underestimated the feeling of local Conservative Party members when they agreed to an alliance with the Liberal Unionists: 'We looked at the matter purely from a Parliamentary point of view ... It never occurred to us to ask how the Conservatives in the constituencies might like it.' Salisbury expressed sympathy with those keen Conservatives whose job it was, especially in Liberal Unionist constituencies, 'to speak & spend, to labour & to intrigue in the less lovely details of a party struggle, with knowledge that the result' of that exertion might never lead to a Conservative victory. Chamberlain's refusal to countenance a shared approach to parliamentary representation could only exacerbate their frustration. Matters were not helped by Chamberlain's prickly nature, well understood by Salisbury. As he confided to Wolmer: 'I never came across so sensitive a public man before.'[24] Ironically, Chamberlain's contretemps with members of the Unionist alliance occurred only a few weeks before the general election of 1895 when Chamberlain once again vigorously took to the hustings to bolster the Conservative and Unionist cause.

The 1895 election is of particular interest because of its overwhelming rejection of Lord Rosebery's Liberal government. Most historians have blamed the Liberals for their own debacle. The divisive effect of Gladstone's resignation and the defeat of Home Rule, Lord Rosebery's ineffective leadership, and severe rivalries within the cabinet have all been advanced as explanations. Overall, the ministry's lack of direction suggested a loss of will in devising constructive legislation. By 1894 the Rosebery government was reduced to 'filling the cup' – that is, sending to the House of Lords a large number of reform measures with the anticipation that they would be rejected. The Lords, by their obstructionism, would (the Liberals hoped) alienate the countryside and provide a badly needed rallying cry. But the tactic was transparent: lacking a sincere reform programme, the ministry was, it seemed, merely engaged in a cynical electioneering trick.[25] Nominal Liberal supporters, discouraged by their party, abstained from voting, thus insuring a Conservative victory at the polls.[26]

Attributing Conservative success merely to Liberal failure, however, may do less than justice to the Conservative achievement. Popular Conservatism, especially in urban areas, had been on the rise some years before the election of 1895. Indeed, the three general elections of 1886, 1895, and 1900 had the highest Conservative votes of any of the 19 general elections from 1880 to 1951.[27] Apart from the brief Liberal interlude of 1892–95, which temporarily broke the string of victories, the Unionist alliance held office continually from 1886 to 1905. The reasons were various, as historians have noted. Pride in imperial achievements, the rising affluence of the population as a whole, and better organization among Unionist Party professionals have all been advanced.

Conservative political strategists also made headway in their appeal to middle-class voters by espousing the sanctity of property. The establishment of the Primrose League, with its faint trappings of a romantic, medieval past enrolled thousands of volunteer workers. Even children were socialized into the respectable conservative community as 'Primrose Buds'.[28] Conservative associations, often staffed with middle-class members, were established in nearly all constituencies. Active canvassing and better candidates completed the smooth operation of the Conservative election machinery.

Conservatives also courted the working class. During the 1895 election campaign, they denounced the Liberals as censorious killjoys for proposing a local veto bill which could close all parish public houses. They posed as defenders of the liberties of the people – including their right to down pints at the end of a long workday. By accepting the working-class culture of pub, football, and racing, and by convincingly labelling traditional Liberal municipal governments as both coercive and aloof from the interests of labouring men, Conservatives reversed traditional Liberal allegiances.[29] Unionists now claimed the mantle of true liberalism in opposition to (as they put it) the false democratic tyranny of the so-called Liberal Party. Over all, the Conservatives presented an attractive and plausible alternative to the Liberal platform, stressing bread-and-butter issues such as expanded foreign trade, assistance to working men who wished to purchase the homes they rented, and the creation of labour conciliation boards.[30]

Chamberlain was not unaware of the shifting political allegiances in the country. In Birmingham, as in other urban centres, Conservatives were making sharp inroads: the Conservative share of the Birmingham municipal elections rose from 23.2 per cent in 1868 to 41.5 per cent in 1885.[31] The reasons were not far to seek. Tightly governed by the caucus system and firmly directed from above by a Liberal elite, Birmingham workingmen were often treated unsympathetically, even by those reformers pledged to improve their material conditions. For example, construction costs of working-class housing sometimes operated inequitably by increasing local rates to the detriment of small shopkeepers. Workingmen who rented their lodgings were also at a disadvantage as landlords sought to offset rising rates with higher rents. In addition, the new construction and improvement of working-class dwellings was slow to come. Workers had a visual reminder of broken promises each time they walked down Corporation Street.

For many working-class Liberals who were becoming disillusioned with their party, Liberal Unionism offered an acceptable alternative. Chamberlain, well practised in courting working-class votes for a radical cause, now shifted his appeal to draw them into a Liberal Unionist alliance. Emphasizing the extension of social legislation, a limited Home Rule, and an expansion of imperial sentiment, he reached out to those working-class voters who were disaffected with the Liberal establishment, but who were reluctant to join Conservative ranks. It can be argued that Chamberlain's evolving Liberal Unionist platform was at least in part a direct consequence of his intention to retain power by offering a brand of liberalism that allowed him to keep his city's electorate under his own care and management.[32]

But there was a palpable danger to Chamberlain's plan. Liberal Unionism could also become a comfortable halfway house to conservatism. To capture and keep transient Liberals within his Liberal Unionist political orbit, Chamberlain relied upon his formidable organizing talents. Establishing a broadly based Midlands Liberal Unionist Association in the early 1890s, Chamberlain created a branch in every constituency in the three counties of his 'Duchy'.[33] By the time of the election of 1895, Liberal Unionism, under Chamberlain's leadership, was ready for battle.

Although Chamberlain's obvious attempts to create Liberal Unionism as a personal vehicle for his own political advancement continued to unnerve many Conservatives, they were not so foolish as to repudiate an effective electioneering cry.[34] Chamberlain's 'positive Unionism',[35] especially his pledge to benefit the material welfare of the people, won the approval of the Conservative rank and file. His election speeches in 1895 rang every change for the Unionist cause. In supporting Henry Morton Stanley (the newspaper magnate and African explorer) as a Unionist candidate for North Lambeth, Chamberlain exhorted 'the working classes' to pay more attention to the history and growth of the empire.[36] They would find, he predicted, that Stanley and others who discovered new markets and opened fresh outlets for trade did more for working people than all the items put together in the Liberal Newcastle Programme. Chamberlain also spoke for the unemployed, for the poor who lived in unsanitary conditions, and for those members of the working class who wished to own homes. Nor was he above raising xenophobic fears of immigrants who had begun to settle in large numbers in nearby Whitechapel. Such 'destitute aliens', he warned, could take jobs away from 'our own people'. Chamberlain did not neglect rural voters during the election campaign. At Stratford-on-Avon, lying solidly within an agricultural constituency, Chamberlain appealed to the farming vote by claiming that the Liberal Local Veto Bill would adversely affect public house owners, 'one of the very best customers of the farmers'. In addition, closing public houses would deny agricultural workers the pleasure and comfort of 'a moderate indulgence in drink'.[37]

Soon afterward he was at Selly Oak – then on the fringes of Birmingham – where he attacked the Liberals more vigorously than ever. By then, two-thirds of the House of Commons and been elected, and Chamberlain could predict with fair accuracy that the Unionists had won the most decisive victory of any incoming government since 1832. The overwhelming Unionist majority, he claimed, was a mandate against the 'crazy legislation' of the former Liberal government.[38] 'This country', he declared, 'has been governed during the last three years by a faction of disloyal Irishmen, of intolerant Welshmen, and of extreme teetotallers ...'. He condemned the preferential treatment of Ireland. He extolled the Empire. In criticizing the 'Little England' views of Harcourt and Morley in the late cabinet, he assured his audience: 'We are not degenerate sons of the men who have gone before us. They made the empire; we will keep it and extend it.' The Liberals were guilty of 'destructive legislation' that ignored social questions affecting the masses of the people.

In his speeches, Chamberlain also sought to repudiate the perennial charge against him that he was a traitor and a turncoat. He insisted that he had not joined the Conservatives; rather the Conservative Party was merely one wing of a national party, of which the other wing was Liberal. Unionism consisted of 'two branches of the same party.' The Unionist alliance had originally been brought into being for the purpose of preventing a separatist Home Rule for Ireland and thus preserving the empire. Since that object had been achieved, the alliance could now turn its attention to 'the national policy of progressive legislation.'[39]

The 1895 election campaign in retrospect witnessed the climax of Chamberlain's national campaigns for social reform. His interest in reform was unabated in the coming years; but his role as a member of the Unionist cabinet signalled a shift of emphasis. He was no longer to be primarily a domestic politician. A new ministerial office, as Secretary of State for the Colonies, gave him a global platform. The stage was set for his exercise of power on a worldwide scale.

10

POWER GAINED

The Colonial Office

It was surprising to many that Salisbury would offer any cabinet position to Chamberlain and equally surprising that Chamberlain would accept. The historian Michael Bentley muses openly on the puzzle: 'Why an established Conservative Anglican aristocrat should want to bring into this government an (at best) Unitarian screw-salesman from Birmingham with a record of radical destructiveness does not seem obvious.'[1] Sir William Harcourt, from a position of first-hand knowledge, thought if offered a position Chamberlain would not accept. 'Much as Chamberlain loved power', he observed to Hamilton, 'he did not care for office.'[2] Salisbury's offer of the cabinet to Chamberlain, however, made perfect sense. First, Chamberlain had given good service to the Unionist alliance for almost ten years. And, second, Chamberlain outside the ministry was a wounded tiger – far more dangerous to the government outside than inside, where he might be caged.

An additional surprise to political observers in 1895 was Chamberlain's choice of office. The Colonial Office had not been particularly important in the past. Indeed, until 1854 it had been a part of the Foreign Office. Britain's most important colony, India, had its own cabinet position. The same was true for Britain's nearest colony, Ireland. Chamberlain's interest in social reform would have seemed to incline him to one of the cabinet positions with responsibility for domestic matters. Salisbury himself thought as much and offered Chamberlain the Home Office, or failing that, the Chancellor of the Exchequer. But Chamberlain insisted upon the Colonial Office, the same position that he had first proposed to Gladstone in 1886. It was a choice, as we have suggested, that offered Chamberlain the greatest possible scope for his undoubted energies to pursue his goal of supreme power.[3]

With Chamberlain at the Colonial Office, Salisbury as prime minister and foreign secretary, and Salisbury's nephew, A. J. Balfour, leading the House of Commons, a powerful triumvirate led the Unionist Party and the country for the next seven years. A strong Liberal Unionist presence also characterized the new ministry. Of nineteen cabinet members, four were Liberal Unionists. In addition to Chamberlain there was the Duke of Devonshire as President of the Council; Sir Henry James in the House of Lords as Chancellor of the Duchy of Lancaster; and Lord Lansdowne as Secretary of War. The former Liberal Unionist, George Goschen, now a Conservative, was at the Admiralty. Other Liberal Unionists served in important subordinate posts: Jesse Collings at the Home Office; Powell Williams under Lansdowne; and Austen Chamberlain at to the Admiralty under Goschen. Salisbury's selection of his son-in-law, Lord Selborne (formerly Wolmer), as Chamberlain's undersecretary at the Colonial Office proved unexpectedly important. Ostensibly there to keep an eye on Chamberlain for his father-in-law, Selborne, a Liberal Unionist, instead fell under the sway of his chief and became his advocate and strong spokesmen for the government's imperial policy.[4]

During Chamberlain's early days as Colonial Secretary, his daughter, Beatrice, wrote of her father's intentions: 'Papa says he has written a series of essays on various points to be sent round the Department in order that they may understand his policy & act as one man …'.[5] Beatrice added that she thought it 'nice' that the Colonial Office should have a chieftain who would take the trouble to inform his colleagues of his plans. 'Nice' was not, however, the reputation that Chamberlain earned. His methodical work habits, imperious voice, peremptory manner, and needful orderliness were intimidating. Yet he also inspired a high level of performance, productivity, and loyalty among his subordinates. So long, that is, as they remained subordinate.

As we would expect, Chamberlain wasted little time in making his mark. Formerly a 'leisurely and sleepy place', the Colonial Office soon began to hum with a new energy.[6] Even the smallest details caught his eye. Deciding that the furniture and carpets were too shabby in the Secretary of State's room, he 'smartened-up' the place, including the installation of electrical lights in place of the candles that had provided illumination for generations.[7] Chamberlain's imperative need to manage his immediate environment was noted by a journalist who visited the Colonial Office. A glance at Chamberlain's room revealed that there 'was nothing superfluous, nothing out of place'. Every morning when the Colonial Secretary came to work, his desk was 'absolutely clear'. Not 'a paper in the room' could be seen.[8]

After clearing away office cobwebs, Chamberlain set out to reform antiquated practices at 12 Downing Street. To consolidate the sprawling worldwide colonial administrative system, he instituted an exchange programme between officials in London and service staff in the field. In response to the expanded duties of the Office, he increased the size of its staff. Lower-level staff more than doubled, from 24 to 51; and upper-level appointments also increased substantially, from 25 to 41. The Office itself was reorganized with the creation of two West African sub-departments, and an augmented South African department – these reflecting the growing importance of Britain's colonial ventures on the African continent during the Chamberlain years. Through these reforms and his own vigorous management, he substantially enhanced the reputation of the Colonial Office as an active and influential department within the cabinet.[9]

Broadly speaking, Chamberlain had three policies as Colonial Secretary: to develop the economic viability of the colonies; to consolidate and (where possible) to extend the power of the British Empire; and to create an imperial federation, a British version of the German *Zollverein*. These were obviously complementary policies. Economic power generated in the colonies would redound to the benefit of Britain and the empire as a whole; and within that empire an imperial customs union would guarantee trading advantages to every imperial participant.

Chamberlain's decision to bring the state more fully to bear upon governing the colonies came at a time of transition among British imperial thinkers. As the scale and complexity of imperial holdings grew during the nineteenth century, Britain was increasingly forced into a pragmatic acceptance of diverse governing practices. Self-governing white settlement colonies, Crown Colonies, amorphously managed protectorates, and quasi-governmental chartered companies had created a tangle of interwoven governing responsibilities. Furthermore, the distance between London and the imperial peripheries often fostered merely reactive responses in times of crisis, rather than considerate and prudent judgements. Financing administrative costs, especially military and policing, was no less daunting. The need for a more central-ized structure to the empire began to emerge in the 1880s. The idea of a 'constructive imperialism' – organized, coherent, and progressive –was attractive to Chamberlain.[10]

The origins of Chamberlain's imperial policies had gradually emerged as we know during his experience in Gladstone's cabinet in the 1880s. The Home Rule contro-versy doubtless had also influenced Chamberlain. He had spoken often enough of the strategic and economic necessity of Ireland's remaining an integral part of the empire. He had so argued with Morley in the 1880s. Nevertheless, a stronger case can be made that Chamberlain's experiences relating to Egypt were more crucial than Ireland in the evolution of his imperial thinking.[11] After the British naval assault on Alexandria in 1882 and its occupation by British troops, he had at first favoured retiring from Egypt as soon as possible. Subsequent cabinet debates, however, and the recognition of Egypt's strategic importance to the Empire had educated Chamberlain to a differ-ent way of thinking. In a letter of 1884 to his staunch Birmingham supporter, R. W. Dale, Chamberlain justified holding Egypt and the Red Sea littoral on the grounds of suppressing the slave trade in that area – a reason sure to please the nonconformist Dale. But Chamberlain also supported the occupation on military and diplomatic grounds – to prevent a scramble between Italy and France for Egypt.[12]

Chamberlain's views on Egypt and its centrality to his imperial designs strength-ened in the years to come. In late 1889 and early 1890, he went on an extended tour of Egypt. Accompanied by his wife, Mary, and (curiously) Jesse Collings, he sailed the Nile, viewed the ancient monuments, and marvelled at the great poinset-tias in Cairo. More importantly, he had an interview with the Khedive; conferred with high Egyptian officials, including the Prime Minister; reviewed the troops at Wady Halfa; and spoke to numerous local officials. British colonial officers such as Sir Evelyn Baring, Consul-General in Cairo, and Sir Francis Grenfell, chief of the Egyptian army, made the most distinct impressions upon him. The British presence in Egypt was, he concluded, essential for the orderly development of that country.[13] To Austen, he reported that he had no doubt of a positive future for Egypt if the English occupation were maintained; but if Britain retired prematurely, Egypt would return 'to the old conditions of corrupt and arbitrary administration'.[14]

Chamberlain was particularly impressed with the British development of public works in Egypt, especially the irrigation system that had substantially raised agricultural productivity in the Nile basin. His understanding of the utility of public works, fostered by his own experience as a radical mayor of Birmingham, now widened from its earlier municipal applications into a global dimension. This was the germ of his idea to foster an integrated colonial investment strategy between Britain and its overseas possessions.[15] These impressions he shared with his constituents shortly after his return from Egypt. In a speech to the West Birmingham Liberal Unionist Association in March 1890, Chamberlain issued a kind of manifesto, embodying his hopes for the British presence in Egypt.[16] He spoke of the 'old Egypt' which for centuries had been in 'a state of barbarism', its government 'inept, inefficient, and ignorant' as well as arbitrary, cruel, and oppressive – 'common characteristics of Oriental Governments'. But the new Egypt had experienced 'a total change'. Taxes had been reduced; public works and national education plans were in place; courts of justice had been established; and corruption had been extinguished. Admitting that he once had opposed the occupation of Egypt, Chamberlain publicly recanted. 'We have no right to abandon the duty which has been cast upon us', he said. The nation must continue 'this great work'. Unable to stand alone, the Egyptians themselves expected no less from Britain: they 'ask for your support and assistance'.[17]

Chamberlain was certain of the beneficence of the British mission in Egypt. He also recognized the benefit to his own political career that an imperial presence might bring. In 1892, he had advised Dilke not to go against the popular grain by advocating the evacuation of Egypt: 'be as Radical as you like', he wrote, 'be Home Ruler if you must – but be a little jingo if you can'.[18] In short, supporting imperialism abroad could mean votes at home. If he could harness imperialism, both in its domestic sentiment and its international implications, he could consolidate his hold on the Unionist alliance. Unionism – initially a slogan for unity at home – could become an election cry for unity within the Empire as well.

How Chamberlain used and promoted the imperial image to electoral advantage is additional evidence of his ability to employ national issues to advance his political and personal agendas. Imperialism, initially grounded in economic and diplomatic self-interest pursued by policy-makers in high places, had become by the 1890s an essential part of popular culture. Inundated by music hall patriotism, best-selling adventure yarns, museum exhibitions of distant lands, and photographic reproductions, Britons revelled in the stories and images of plucky lads and manly chaps on the edge of empire.[19] This new public imperial engagement combined traditional patriotism, commercial entrepreneurship, missionary zeal, and a sense of national superiority with a genuine interest in strange and exotic places. By recognizing and tapping into widespread imperial sentiment, Chamberlain positioned himself as the most prominent and articulate spokesman of Britain's imperial mission. Imperialism abroad he portrayed as a high-minded crusade for civilization and a beacon of light for millions in the undeveloped lands of Africa and the East. Imperialism at home could also have a direct economic benefit for British citizens, especially the working class. Imperialism was a patriotic duty uniting the nation as a whole, uplifting all

Britons regardless of party affiliation. These were the themes that Chamberlain developed in speech after speech during the final decade of his active life.

Building upon his observations in Egypt and his understanding of an evolving imperial culture, Chamberlain proclaimed his theory of 'undeveloped estates'. Governments must bear a greater responsibility than ever before in actively supporting the economic development of their colonies. To the House of Commons in 1893, Chamberlain extolled the virtues of 'our ancestors', who had created 'this policy of expansion' that led to the foreign trade by which 'a great part of our population lives'.[20] He believed 'that the people of this country have ... determined that they will take their full share' in carrying out the work of colonization. Britain, 'of all nations' was 'peculiarly fitted' for this work. Moreover, active colonization could be borne 'at a comparatively small expenditure'. In addition to encouraging private investment, the government should establish a railway network where possible in every colony. The industrial working classes of Britain would immediately benefit as builders of locomotives, manufacturers of rails and rolling stock, and exporters of coal.

On the eve of the election of 1895, Chamberlain reiterated his theme. At the annual dinner of the Jewellers' and Silversmiths' Association in Birmingham, he advocated taking 'every opportunity' of extending and developing foreign trade and 'especially of securing new markets'.[21] Governments, whether Liberal or Conservative had been negligent, he claimed, in improving the welfare both of colonial inhabitants and British citizens. 'It is not enough', he said, 'to occupy certain great spaces of the world's surface unless you can make the best of them. We are landlords of a great estate; it is the duty of the landlord to develop his estate.' The roads of ancient Rome had knit together that immense empire: 'What roads were then, railways are now.'

In one of his most famous speeches during the election campaign of 1895, Chamberlain enlarged further on government's responsibility to its colonies.[22] He warned that old markets were exhausted. Unless new markets were found, the loss of trade and unemployment were inevitable consequences. 'Great Britain, the little centre of a vaster Empire than the world has ever seen, owns great possessions in every part of the globe, and many of those possessions are still almost unexplored, entirely undeveloped.' What would a great landlord do, Chamberlain rhetorically asked, in a similar case with a large estate? The answer was obvious: a landlord would improve his property by promoting growth and creating markets for the products of his land. So should Britain manage the territories it controlled and governed. That was the task he would set himself as Colonial Secretary.

Chamberlain was as good as his word. Within a few months of assuming office, he set in motion his plans for state-assisted colonial economic development. He brooked no opposition in attaining the necessary power over international policy to achieve his aims.[23] His ideas and actions were most strikingly manifested in the three important crown colonies of British West Africa – the Gold Coast, Lagos, and Sierra Leone.

British trade had encountered substantial difficulties for more than a decade in West Africa. British merchants – both in coastal Africa and in Britain – had witnessed a general fall in prices as a consequence of a lengthy long-term depression in the last quarter of the century. In addition, within the African hinterland, trading routes had been interrupted and production limited as indigenous merchants and producers sought to adapt to the demands of new market conditions. These economic problems gave rise to well-organized pressure groups. Chambers of commerce in London, Liverpool and Manchester, the shipping interest in parliament, and various manufacturing and trading firms demanded government intervention to protect their interests.[24] An imperially minded Chamberlain was naturally sympathetic to their requests. He believed that his grand railway scheme was precisely the solution called for. It would not only extend markets, but also solve problems of production and distribution. Should political influence and military authority ride the rails into the African hinterland, so much the better for Britain.

Chamberlain's initial problem was to overcome the traditional caution of the Treasury, whose job was to protect rather than expend public monies. Arguing that railway construction would best facilitate the economic development of West Africa, Chamberlain pointed out that heavy steam-driven crushing machinery required for extracting gold at the inland mining sites in the Gold Coast could only be brought in by railway. In other colonies – such as Lagos and Sierra Leone – palm oil, rubber, and timber could most easily be transported in bulk to the coast by rail. Railways could also stimulate the growth of cotton, tobacco, and groundnuts.

The magnitude of Chamberlain's colonial scheme was disconcerting to the cabinet: his requests for funds were on an unprecedented scale. Opposition from Hicks-Beach, the Chancellor of the Exchequer, was particularly vigorous. Hicks-Beach was also concerned about Chamberlain's tendency to evade Treasury authorization for expending public funds on risky capital ventures in Africa. He complained to Chamberlain in late 1898 that 'we have [n]ever been informed by C.O. of what was going on; or been asked in any way to sanction the increase until the money has been spent'.[25] In response, Chamberlain proposed a colonial development fund based upon revenues from the Suez Canal shares owned by the government. Such a fund would be set aside from the general accounts of the Exchequer and earmarked specifically for the colonies. But the scheme was sabotaged by Sir Edward Hamilton, the Gladstonian Liberal and diarist, who was then serving as joint permanent under-secretary of the Treasury. Hamilton convinced Hicks Beach (and the cabinet) that removing the fund from the control of parliament would exempt it from official scrutiny, and would likely encourage irresponsible fiscal behaviour on the part of the colonies.

Undeterred by this failure, Chamberlain initiated on his own authority as Colonial Secretary the beginning of railway construction in both Lagos and Sierra Leone, and the completion of route surveys in the Gold Coast. This was an extraordinary action. In lieu of either parliamentary sanction or Treasury approval, he simply empowered the colonial governors to pass two separate sets of ordinances; the first to start construction, and the second to issue colonial stock for railway loans on the London market.[26] Chamberlain entrusted the implementation of this complicated scheme to crown agents for the colonies. Although agents were not members of the civil service, they were appointed by the Colonial Secretary and worked under his general supervision.[27] Among other duties, agents were responsible for negotiating with public works contractors and consulting engineers, and issuing and servicing colonial loans. Agents made their living by charging brokerage fees for all colonial loans and levying commissions on the purchase and shipment of stores. Senior crown agents often had additional special privileges, including a close relationship with the Bank of England. Thus, when the Lagos railway stock proved unmarketable, crown agents obtained short-term loans of £288,524 enabling railway construction to go forward.[28]

While Chamberlain was thrusting his way forward in West Africa, the Salisbury government had to play catch-up in endorsing their Colonial Secretary's independent actions. After an initial abortive try, the government induced parliament to pass the Colonial Loans Bill in 1899. It authorized loan payments for thirteen different colonies, including those development projects already underway. But capitalization for railways and improvements in West Africa went forward only slowly: investors tended to prefer the steadier dividends of American and Canadian railroad securities. The completion of the West African railway lines was thus delayed beyond Chamberlain's term of office.

Chamberlain's policy of 'developing the estate' occasionally went beyond the calculation of economic advantage to the mother country. He was also interested in colonial public health schemes. With the appointment of Dr Patrick Manson as Colonial Office Medical Adviser in 1897, Chamberlain began a series of steps that led to the establishment of the London School of Tropical Medicine. In later years, other British medical schools followed this lead by introducing tropical medicine into their curricula. Chamberlain also encouraged the Royal Botanical Gardens at Kew to extend its research into tropical botany with an eye to improving the diet in the colonies and to vary their crops for a more profitable export market. Chamberlain's initial concern was likely the creation of a healthier environment for colonial officers stationed in West Africa. The indigenous African population also ultimately benefited from the improved medical care and sanitary conditions brought about by the attempts to control malaria and related diseases.[29]

A similar story of Chamberlain's determination to develop the empire may also be found in the British West Indies. Because of the smaller scale of these colonies and their limited mineral deposits, railways were less important as flagships of development than in West Africa. Supporting and modernizing the sugar industry, the staple crop of the region, was the primary task. For some time, the Indies had been at a disadvantage in competing with heavily subsidized European beet sugar production: both Austria and Germany, for example, employed a generous system of export bounties. The economic decline of the Indies was exacerbated during the late nineteenth-century depression which drove down world sugar prices.

In tackling the problem, Chamberlain used a combination of tariff manipulations and financial assistance. By imposing selective countervailing duties on imports of bounty sugar from Europe into designated markets of the empire (in both India and Canada, for example), he sought to establish preferential treatment for West Indian sugar.[30] Chamberlain also proposed in 1898 floating a guaranteed loan of £750,000 to build central sugar factories in Barbados, St Kitts, and Antigua. The money was never raised, but Chamberlain was able to instigate a series of Colonial

Office grants-in-aid over the next few years, including funds for steamship subsidies, agricultural research, and most significantly £250,000 for the West Indian sugar industry.[31]

Chamberlain's robust pursuit of British interests abroad was not confined to colonial matters. Early in the Salisbury ministry, he was drawn toward an active role in foreign affairs. This was potentially awkward. Chamberlain was not known as a skilful negotiator. His blunt tactics were more suited for managing a business or bludgeoning recalcitrant political opponents than for the subtle world of diplomacy. In addition, any overt attempt to influence foreign policy could place him in opposition to Lord Salisbury, who was both prime minister and Foreign Secretary. Yet at first Chamberlain and Salisbury worked well together – as they had on domestic legislation during Salisbury's second ministry. There were, however, marked differences in diplomatic style between the bumptious Chamberlain and his Olympian chief. This was clearly evident in the early days of the ministry during a serious crisis in British Guiana, newly targeted by Chamberlain as one of his developing estates.

The western boundary of British Guiana had long been in dispute with neighbouring Venezuela, whose struggles for independence and nationhood in the early nineteenth century had made it wary of European intrusion. When gold was discovered along the frontier during the 1870s and 1880s, British prospectors flocked to the mines.[32] Some remained as settlers. With them came British authority and a strengthening of British claims to the contested boundary. Tensions heightened as border clashes ensued.

In 1887 the Venezuelan government severed relations with Britain, seized a British ship, and imprisoned its captain. By 1892 British colonial police and military posts faced their Venezuelan counterparts at various flashpoints. In 1894, Venezuela appealed to the United States to help settle the question. In the summer of 1895, the American Secretary of State, Richard Olney, sent a peremptory dispatch directly to the British Foreign Office. Evoking the Monroe Doctrine and demanding an immediate reply, Olney insisted on arbitration of the boundary question.

Salisbury's reaction to these events was to slow the pace and to respond in measured tones. Chamberlain, however, was from the first (as one historian has observed) 'all for belligerence'.[33] When a British police station was captured (but then quickly retaken), Chamberlain demanded the fullest possible compensation from Venezuela under the threat of force. In a letter to Salisbury in September 1895, he declared that settling of the Venezuelan crisis was urgent, for he had plans for the disputed territory: 'I am trying to get it developed and am in communication with firms in the city about it.'[34] The ante was raised by President Cleveland's sabre-rattling message to Congress. Reaffirming the Monroe Doctrine, Cleveland also asked Congress to establish a commission which would determine the boundary. Accompanied by bellicose newspaper comments, his words were received in Britain as an ultimatum.

Chamberlain became abusive. In an explosive letter to Selborne, he condemned 'the extreme sensitiveness and vanity of the Americans as a nation': they falsely believed 'that they are bigger & stronger & better than we are'.[35] He also severely criticized the government of the United States. The American Senate, he thought, was composed of parochial lawyers and self-interested politicians. Cleveland was a 'coarse-grained bully': his speech to Congress the 'greatest crime of the century'. Additionally, Cleveland's demands were an 'unnatural & altogether unprecedented extension' of the Monroe Doctrine – a doctrine that Americans tended to believe as they believed in their Bibles, 'as of divine inspiration'. Nor did Chamberlain accept an open and unconditional arbitration offered by the Americans. Britain, he maintained, had been 'in practical undisputed possession of the territory' for a century: 'We can no more arbitrate about this than we can about the Isle of Wight.'[36]

In rejecting arbitration, Chamberlain found Salisbury on his side. Both wished to honour 'settled areas' where British occupation was well established, and to have these areas excluded from arbitration. Salisbury also remained firm in denying the applicability of the Monroe Doctrine to Venezuela. But Salisbury was not convinced that the Americans were serious in their claims. Unlike Chamberlain, who was strongly combative and seemed almost proprietary in his comments on British Guiana, Salisbury downplayed American truculence. The whole contretemps, he thought, was merely a 'squall', engineered by the Democratic Party as 'a jingo flare-up' to aid President Cleveland in the forthcoming election.[37]

Alarmed by the prospect of war, and perhaps taken aback by Chamberlain's hard-line stand and Salisbury's reluctance to arbitrate, the cabinet advocated a softer tone toward the United States. This modified Salisbury's views, and Chamberlain's as well. Chamberlain played a more responsible role in early 1896 when he engaged in constructive diplomatic talks through an intermediary, Lord Playfair, with Thomas F. Bayard, the American Ambassador to the Court of St James. Later that summer – during a visit to the United States with his wife – Chamberlain unofficially discussed the matter *tête-à-tête* with Secretary Olney in Boston. With earlier hostile confrontations now giving way to reasoned debate, a peaceful solution became possible.

Ultimately a Boundary Commission was created, and its findings provided the basis for a settlement in 1899, a settlement essentially imposed upon Venezuela to its dismay. Most of the disputed territory was awarded to British Guiana. The United States, too, had gained. Its insistence on playing a role in arbitrating a dispute between a European power and a South American country tended to legitimate the Monroe Doctrine. The benefit to Britain was also substantial. The prospects of a war with the United States in the late 1890s was likely more than even imperial Britain could easily have managed.

Chamberlain's tendency to make intransigent responses when confronted with diplomatic crises was often in evidence throughout his career as Colonial Secretary. It was this characteristic that gave him the reputation of being 'impulsive'. So he may have been; but a more accurate reading would be that he acted quickly and decisively (and undoubtedly impatiently) in order to satisfy his own need for control, for command, for power. His tenure as Colonial Secretary provided ample opportunities for him to assume the mantle of power over the colonies. In the cases of West Africa and the Indies, he used that power to promote his imperial economic programme. The Venezuela crisis had shown how readily Chamberlain was willing to seize on a colonial conflict and amplify its difficulties to Britain's (and his own) advantage. Each success of this kind tended to encourage Chamberlain in his belief of the rightness of his actions, and to embolden him in his drive for power.

Chamberlain's economic development plans, well under way by the late 1890s, did not diminish his diplomatic truculence. Indeed, Chamberlain's policies in West Africa began to have an unsettling impact with wider ramifications in Europe. As British traders in their search for commercial advantage continued to push inland up the Niger River from the delta, French military units, operating principally out of Senegal, slowly began occupying the Upper Niger. This systematic advance was in part a reaction to British successes in East Africa along the Nile, and was intended by the French as compensation for their displacement in Egypt. British governments were pleased enough to see French imperial energy deflected to the West African tropics and away from the more strategically important Egypt and the Suez Canal. By 1897, however, French military outposts in West Africa had become thick enough on the ground to endanger free-ranging British traders, and possibly to threaten Chamberlain's schemes of economic development.[38]

Even before he had become Colonial Secretary, Chamberlain had developed an animus against the French, as his correspondence with Dilke reveals. Reviewing French imperial thrusts around the globe, Dilke complained in late 1894 that Britain must 'stand up for our rights'. The French would always yield, Dilke believed, because war would mean the destruction of the Republican government in France 'and the powers that be know this'.[39] In reply, Chamberlain agreed: 'I wish we had a chance of trying our policy. I believe the result would surprise some of the weak-kneed ones.'[40] Once in charge at the Colonial Office, he quickly abandoned the quiescent policy of previous British governments, taking swift and aggressive steps to halt French military advances.[41]

Moving decisively, Chamberlain operated from a two-pronged strategy. First, he sought to meet the French on their own ground in the field. Second, he aimed at establishing a beachhead at the negotiating table in Paris with the aim of capturing the diplomatic initiative. In accomplishing his first objective, Chamberlain created the West Africa Frontier Force, manned by Hausa and Yoruba troops with British officers. To impress upon the French his serious intent, Chamberlain appointed Frederick Lugard as commander of the Frontier Force.[42] Lugard, an experienced soldier, was as argumentative and obstinate as Chamberlain himself. In their first interview (described as 'stormy' by Lugard), the two men disagreed heatedly. Chamberlain held to a risky 'chessboard' strategy, by which British forces in small detachments would infiltrate French-held territory with the idea of positioning themselves face-to-face with similar French units. Lugard proposed a more circumspect navigation in force up the Niger, occupying both banks of the river, and offering some compensation to the French. Chamberlain denounced 'vehemently and angrily' Lugard's idea. Acting as Colonial Secretary, he simply imposed his views on Lugard.[43]

By the spring of 1898, the West Africa Frontier Force was in place – often in close proximity to French troops. Rival flags occasionally flew only a few hundred yards apart. In one incident, the British were opposed by French bayonets; in another, they had to thrust themselves bodily through a cordon of French soldiers. A single rifle shot could have had incalculable results. Such a consequence held no terrors for Chamberlain: 'even at the cost of war', he told Selborne, the French in West Africa had to be confronted.[44]

Recognizing the need for experienced logistical personnel in transporting the Force, Chamberlain had commandeered the Royal Niger Company and requisitioned their resources, particularly staff and river steamers. The Deputy Governor of the Niger Company was additionally ordered by Chamberlain to reinforce imperial troops with its own constabulary. But George Goldie, as the chief administrative officer of the Company, resisted Chamberlain. After all, the Company, though chartered, was private. It seemed as though Chamberlain were attempting to solidify his own power in West Africa by undermining and gaining control of the Company. Goldie also disagreed with Chamberlain's policy of economic development. Goldie's task, as he saw it, was to encourage trade, especially up and down the Niger, on behalf of the Company's shareholders – not to build extensive and possibly risky railways. He refused to be the tail of Chamberlain's imperial kite.[45]

Chamberlain thus was forced to fight on several fronts, initially against Lugard, and then later against both the French and Goldie. It was a task he relished. His hardened response to opposition was brought quickly into play. Lugard he had mastered quickly in conference. Goldie, at greater distance, must also be broken if he would not bend. Chartered companies, after all, were supported only because governments had been reluctant to assume the financial burdens of colonial costs. But Chamberlain represented an entirely different approach to colonial administration. Favouring state-sponsored development, he viewed the Royal Niger Company as an anachronism and welcomed an opportunity to assume its duties. To Salisbury he wrote that 'a very high line' had to be taken with Goldie: if necessary, the government would 'expropriate' the Company 'at once' – 'lock, stock, and barrel'.[46]

Complementing his military strategy, Chamberlain simultaneously stiffened British demands at the ongoing diplomatic negotiations with France. He refused, as he put it to Selborne, to 'allow this country to be bullied'.[47] Chamberlain was especially perturbed at the conciliatory stance of the British ambassador to Paris, Sir Edmund Monson, a Francophile who seemed disposed to accept French demands for both access to the Niger River and the retention of Bussa, an important river city. Chamberlain believed that the French were determined to break the commercial monopoly established by the Royal Niger Company. He peppered the Foreign Office with admonitions to resist the French: Salisbury then relayed Chamberlain's demands to Paris. Through his persistent diplomatic intransigence, Chamberlain was able to take control of the negotiations.[48]

Chamberlain's tactics succeeded. As the British military preparations in West Africa began to encounter French units in the field, French diplomats moderated their demands. They agreed not only to withdraw from Bussa, but from Ilo as well, a hundred miles further up the Niger. Thus the river for several hundred miles inland fell under British control. The French were also denied a corridor of access from the hinterland to the Niger. They were, however, granted recognition by Britain of some inland territories already in French hands. These terms were the basis of the final agreement – the Anglo-French Convention – signed in June 1898.

To Chamberlain has gone most of the credit for settling the controversy on terms favourable to Britain. Dragging the reluctant Salisbury in his wake (as Kanya-Forstner put it), Chamberlain 'charged at the French on every point in the dispute' yielding not an inch.[49] Michael Crowder praised Chamberlain's 'brilliant brinkman-ship'.[50] Obichere excuses Chamberlain's admittedly 'aggressive' brinkmanship as born of necessity.[51] Marsh thought his achievements 'stunning'.[52] Garvin, of course, pointed out Chamberlain's 'unfaltering nerve, steady shrewdness ... and energy' in the organization of colonial Nigeria.[53] Flint, too, gave Chamberlain high marks: the triumph 'was peculiarly and personally that of Joseph Chamberlain', who had carried out his policy 'with consummate skill, manipulating individual actors in the drama to suit his own purposes almost without their knowing what he was doing'.[54]

Historical judgement, nearly unanimous in its praise of Chamberlain's stand in West Africa, is also reflective of opinion at that time. In thanking the Colonial Secretary for memoranda on West Africa, Sir John Arthur Bigge, then Assistant Queen's Secretary, praised him handsomely from a royal quarter: 'The good firm attitude you have taken is the only way to make the French understand that we won't be bullied.'[55] 'Everyone looks to you', wrote Spencer Wilkinson in March 1898, 'as the man who is standing up for England.'[56]

Chamberlain's forward policy in West Africa, his staunch defence of British inter-ests around the globe, and his continued prominence in parliament guaranteed him a favourable public profile in the first years of his tenure at the Colonial Office. Indeed, he took every opportunity to consolidate his position as the leading spokesman for empire. When he was installed as Lord Rector of Glasgow University and awarded an honorary Doctor of Laws degree in November 1897, Chamberlain delivered a paean to British patriotism. Exalting patriotism as 'that greatest of civic virtues', he declared that without it there would be no 'splendid deeds of heroic bravery', and no advances in liberty and civilization so characteristic of Britain and the empire.[57] Quoting Shakespeare, Chamberlain recited the speech of the dying John of Gaunt extolling 'This blessed plot, this earth, this realm, this England'. It was the clear duty of patriotism, Chamberlain said, to help in the expansion of the Empire 'in which we seem to be fulfilling the manifest duty of our race'. In an often-quoted passage, he rhetorically asked: 'Is it contended that the weary Titan staggers under "the too vast orb of his fate" and that we have not the strength to sustain the burden of empire?' The answer was a resounding 'no'. Wherever the British flag flew, he assured his audi-ence, Britons were 'living as brave men and dying as heroes' in the performance of their duty and in the passionate love of their country. They only asked 'from us that their sacrifices shall not be in vain'.

During the next few days in Glasgow, he emphasized his theme again and again. Britain's imperial policy was one of 'beneficent intervention', he assured the Glasgow University Conservative Club: it was 'a policy of humanity, civilization, and pacifi-cation'.[58] Deriding his Liberal opponents, he called them a party of surrender. The Unionists, on the other hand, 'believe in the greatness of the Empire': 'We think that a nation, like an individual, is the better for having great responsibilities, great obligations.' In addition, Unionists had a realistic view of the world: 'We know that for us control over the markets is an absolute necessity, and that without it we could not possibly keep in comfort all the vast population which we have in these small islands.' Presented with the freedom of the city a few days later, Chamberlain made two major speeches – at St Andrew's Hall upon the presentation; and at a luncheon in the City Chambers where he dined with the Corporation. He spoke of the growing evidence that colonial fellow-subjects were drawing closer to Britain. The idea of a united Empire, once thought impractical, was becoming a reality: 'the future has for us in store a greatness of which our ancestors and we ourselves had never dreamt'.[59]

As his Glasgow speeches indicated, Chamberlain was untroubled by any doubt concerning Britain's imperial mission and in his role in sustaining it. Strengthened by his enhanced domestic political position and encouraged by his successes in West Africa, the West Indies, and South America, Chamberlain grasped for greater power. In a series of interrelated manoeuvres, he attempted to counter Salisbury's policy in China, sought alliances with Germany, and tried to suborn Portuguese colonial control in South Africa. Each of these we examine below.

China came dramatically to the government's attention as a result of Germany's sudden seizure of the port of Kiaochow (eventually absorbed by the modern port of Tsingtao) and Russia's acquisition of Port Arthur in the late 1890s. Both countries were taking advantage of the defeat of China in the Sino-Japanese War of 1895 and the concluding Treaty of Shimonoseki, which signalled the weakness of the Ch'ing Empire. And both countries were, in fact, following the example of Britain, which had held Hong Kong since 1842 and Kowloon since 1860, taken after two Anglo-Chinese wars earlier in the century. Since then, Britain had become the leading trading partner with China: British cotton goods were sent in exchange for Chinese tea and silk. Britain had also extended its influence over China by opening various treaty ports to international trade and installing a British Inspector-General who administered Chinese tariffs. Internal trade up and down the Yangtze River was largely in British hands, complemented by an extensive British consular network in China. In addition, Britain had a significant presence in both the commercial and governmental structure of China's largest city, Shanghai.[60]

It was not surprising that other countries sought to emulate Britain's success in the Far East.[61] China, with an immense population, defenceless after 1895, and vulnerable to foreign intervention, seemed to promise enough markets for all to share. In addition to commercial considerations, Germany's seizure of Kiaochow was primarily driven by its new policy of *Weltpolitik* – a determination to play a more active role in world affairs.[62] Specifically, its desire was for a naval coaling station, rather than the establishment of a colony on Chinese soil.

Russia, too, had been on the march to gain a greater influence in the Far East. After the port of Vladivostok had been established in 1860, Russian interest in uniting its vast territory with an east–west railroad rapidly increased. By the 1890s this project had been energetically taken up by Count Sergei Witte, Russian Finance Minister from 1892 to 1903. Such a trans-Siberian railway could also siphon off at least a portion of the China trade by transporting it westward overland. Extending an additional railway spur southward from the main trans-Siberian line toward a warm water port would enable Russia to overcome the difficulties of commercial transportation during those months when Vladivostok was ice-bound. Hence Russia's designs on Port Arthur.

The rapid establishment of two European powers on China's northern coast placed the Salisbury government in an awkward position.[63] Salisbury himself regarded the events in China with a benign eye: the Nile remained the centrepiece of both his foreign policy and his imperial strategy. To the public at large, however, the Russian incursion was a particular affront, coming as it did so soon after the German seizure of Kiaochow. Russian actions demanded some sort of British retaliation. But in a series of lengthy meetings in the spring of 1898, the cabinet under Balfour (Salisbury was frequently absent recuperating from bronchitis) decided not to protest Russian action. Instead, the ministry rapidly pushed forward a plan to establish a British naval base in north China as a counterpoise to Russia and Germany. The selection of Weihaiwei seemed a logical choice.[64] Placed almost midway on the coast between the recent German and Russian acquisitions, Weihaiwei – with its large and protected harbour – could sustain a vigilant British squadron. Weihaiwei's position on a peninsula at the entrance to the Gulf of Chihli at the upper end of the Yellow Sea also gave it a command of passage that could, if necessary, block Russian shipping. Most importantly, its seizure, the cabinet hoped, would satisfy public opinion for strong action.

The taking of Weihaiwei met with an unenthusiastic public response, however. Opponents gleefully pronounced the new acquisition 'woe-woe-woe' or 'wee-hee-wee'. Articles in public journals appeared with such titles as 'The Failure of our Foreign Policy' and 'Where Lord Salisbury has Failed'.[65] There were rumblings on the backbenches. The impression that Britain was merely responding impulsively to events over which it had no control suggested a lack of policy.[66]

Into this morass of international rivalry and diplomatic confrontation, Chamberlain plunged. He was determined to make his voice heard. For example, he was the sole opponent in the cabinet to acquiring Weihaiwei on the grounds that it implied Britain's acceptance of the actions of Germany and Russia.[67] Chamberlain argued instead for an aggressive policy that would neutralize the incursion of their rivals into China. Chamberlain was particularly incensed at Russia. At one point during a cabinet meeting in April 1898, Chamberlain apparently delivered a 'blood curdling' speech in favour of war against Russia.[68] Indeed, from the very first news of the Russian naval demonstration at Port Arthur, he sought some means of striking back. He approached Salisbury about an alliance with Japan – a rising military power with expansive aims of its own in the Far East.[69] Chamberlain also spoke with Kato Takaaki, the Japanese minister to London. Little came of this at the time, however.[70]

Chamberlain also made his impatience known to Balfour. In a secret letter in early February 1898, he warned Balfour that the government would be in 'grave trouble' unless it adopted 'a more decided attitude in regard to China'.[71] Russia, unlike Germany, has 'done us at every point'. Forcing out British ships in Port Arthur

– all the while pretending their occupation was only temporary and not in restraint of British trade – was a thumb in the eye to Chamberlain. If matters remained as they were, Chamberlain predicted that 'our prestige will be gone and our trade will follow'. But the cabinet refused to alter its accommodating policy toward Russia. When Salisbury returned to active politics after recuperating on the continent, he helped fashion the Anglo-Russian Agreement of 1899 which recognized legitimate 'spheres of interest' of each party: the Yangtze for Britain, and Manchuria for Russia.[72]

Even before the completion of the Agreement, however, Chamberlain began a series of steps that effectively initiated an independent foreign policy within the cabinet, reaching far beyond his duties as Colonial Secretary.[73] Motivated by his determination to punish Russian belligerence and to contain her advances, and by his own need for exploiting every avenue of power, Chamberlain devised a plan to secure Anglo-German friendship. His opportunity came in late March 1898, when the German ambassador to Britain, Count Paul von Hatzfeldt, entered into private and unofficial conversations with leading members of the British government in an attempt to smooth the way for better relations between the two countries.[74]

During the Hatzfeldt–Chamberlain conversations, Chamberlain quickly proposed an alliance between Britain and Germany. In doing so, Chamberlain was undiplomatically candid: he expressed concern about the crises in China and West Africa and confessed the failure of Britain's policy of diplomatic isolation. It was time for Britain to seek allies: of all possible allies, Chamberlain declared, he would prefer Germany. Chamberlain's astonishing and unexpected proposal, about which he had not informed a single member of the government, was turned down by the German State Secretary, Bernhard von Bulow, who saw it clearly as an alliance directed at Russia with no particular advantage to Germany.[75]

When Hatzfeldt informed Chamberlain a few days later of Bulow's response, Chamberlain was only moderately discouraged. Indeed, there was a strong second act to this diplomatic play, with the chargé d'affaires at the German embassy in London, Baron von Eckhardstein, starring in a supporting role. Eckhardstein had for several years been a favourite in the diplomatic and social circles in London, frequenting the salon of the Duchess of Devonshire and cutting a dashing figure in his hussar's uniform. He had also married the daughter (and heiress) of Sir Blundell Maple, MP, the Tottenham Court Road furniture magnate.[76] His English connections and his wish to make a name for himself as a power broker led him to seek a rapprochement with Britain by appealing directly to the German Kaiser.

Returning to London after his visit to the Kaiser in mid-April 1898, Eckhardstein reported to the key players, Balfour, Chamberlain, and Hatzfeldt, that the Kaiser was enthusiastic about the alliance project. But this was not the case, as the relevant German documents reveal. Eckhardstein had exaggerated. Only if the proposed alliance extended to Europe and addressed German concerns as well as imperial ones would the Kaiser agree. So matters stood until Salisbury returned on 1 May 1898. Awaiting him were Chamberlain's minutes of his conversations with both Hatzfeldt and Eckhardstein. In his covering letter, Chamberlain argued the need for an alliance with Germany. Overlooking Chamberlain's unofficial intrigues with a representative of the German government during his absence, Salisbury responded by suggesting that Germany must speak with one voice if it seriously wished an alliance.

A few days later, in an important speech before the Primrose League in the Albert Hall, Salisbury made public his views on foreign policy. The speech was designed to serve notice that he was once again in charge and that Britain would pursue a steady, strong, and independent course in international affairs. Recalling the 'despondency' felt by Britain in 1884–5 with the capture of Khartoum and the death of Gordon, Salisbury noted that much had changed since then. The 'Imperial spirit' had triumphed; vast territories had been reclaimed for civilization; and the 'sword of England' had done its work. Britain was fully competent to chart its own course. Pursuing this theme, Salisbury postulated that those countries with 'enormous power', where power grew every year, would naturally dominate those lesser nations where 'disorganization and decay' were characteristic. As weaker nations continued their decline, so the stronger, in proper Darwinian fashion, would play an increasing role 'in any re-arrangement' of states that might take place.[77]

Chamberlain, who could not have missed the implied criticism, responded several days later in a speech in Birmingham. Speaking at the tenth annual meeting of the Liberal Unionist Association, Chamberlain devoted his opening remarks in praise of the Unionist alliance and its achievements.[78] Then, referring directly to Salisbury's 'powerful and eloquent speech' of a few days earlier, he made the case for abandoning Britain's traditional foreign policy of 'strict isolation'. With the stronger states of Europe making alliances among themselves, new conditions had arisen, Chamberlain declared. Britain now 'stood alone' against the most pressing foreign threat – Russia's growing influence in China. That 'ancient empire' was in 'a position of practical impotence'. Unless Britain allied with 'some great military power', Russia could not be stopped. Unless the policy of isolation was abandoned, 'the fate of the Chinese Empire may be, probably will be, hereafter decided without reference to our wishes, and in defiance of our interests'.

Chamberlain once again had created a sensation. Imperial interests of the time, such as the China trade, could not but be pleased. British Russophobes also applauded. Liberal opponents, however, were taken aback. The young Asquith asked in the House of Commons: 'What have we done or suffered to be touting for allies in the highways and byways of Europe?'[79] Morley, as we might suspect, also denounced the speech. It was, in his opinion, one of 'the most flagitious ever made' by an English minister of state.[80] In the House of Lords, the Earl of Kimberley attempted to draw out Salisbury on Chamberlain's 'remarkable utterance' (as Kimberley put it). But Salisbury refused to rise to the bait, and downplayed the differences between himself and his Colonial Secretary. Nevertheless, Kimberley believed that it was 'plain enough' that Salisbury 'did not share C's opinions. It is quite certain that C. spoke entirely off his own bat.'[81] Even some Unionists seemed to have been embarrassed by Chamberlain's public break with Salisbury's policy. Apart from the political consequences, it was ungentlemanly.[82]

Historians since then have given a mixed response to the Birmingham speech, one of Chamberlain's most important public utterances. Garvin finds the speech among

Chamberlain's best, revealing 'intuitive prescience ... daring initiative, [and] telling idiom', showing him once again as a master of democratic leadership.[83] Grenville is less impressed. Admitting it a 'sensational' speech, he condemns it as a 'blunder' and a 'serious mistake', causing 'much mischief' at home and abroad.[84] It was no doubt a controversial speech: most importantly for our analysis was its evidence of Chamberlain's tendency – now long established – to pursue independent policies. Shortly after the speech, Chamberlain entered into a cabal (or 'ministerial council') of those in the ministry who favoured an alliance with Germany against Russia. Meeting at Chamberlain's London residence in Prince's Gardens in June 1898, this unofficial body commissioned the British ambassador to Germany, Sir Frank Lascelles, to discover the Kaiser's intentions concerning an alliance.[85]

By then, the merry-go-round of Anglo-German negotiations had become complicated by a diplomatic squabble in South Africa. Briefly put, differences between Britain and Germany had arisen over the Portuguese colony of Mozambique, especially the disposition of Delagoa Bay within that colony. Delagoa Bay and its port city, Lourenco Marques (now Maputo) was the key to South Africa: it was only 50 miles from the eastern border of the Transvaal and the shortest route to the sea from the inland cities of Johannesburg and Pretoria. Its harbour and strategic placement made it attractive to competing colonial contenders, including Cecil Rhodes, South African Boers, and the German navy, as well as British imperialists. Delagoa Bay had a special attraction for Britain in the 1890s: it gave an easy access to the South African interior and thus a ready means of maintaining control over the discontented white settlers of Dutch ancestry who accepted British sovereignty (or 'suzerainty' as it was called) only with great reluctance.

As parties to one of the oldest of European alliances, Britain and Portugal were likely to settle matters advantageously to both. Portugal's political instability and the parlous state of her finances offered an opportunity for an arrangement: Britain could provide a substantial loan in return for control of Delagoa Bay. But Portugal was a reluctant negotiator, in part because of its uncertainty about the intentions of Germany, which had developed capital interests in South Africa, and had become a heavy supplier of munitions of war and Krupp guns to the Boer regime.[86]

Chamberlain became involved in negotiations as early as 1896. In an attempt to expedite matters, Chamberlain reminded the Portuguese minister to London, the Marquis Luis de Soveral, that in previous treaties Portugal had ceded to Britain the right of pre-emption in the event of any anticipated transfer of control or sale of Delagoa Bay.[87] He also warned the Portuguese government that it was in its own interest 'to be friendly with England': if it refused the hand of friendship, the British government – which had 'much at stake' in the matter – 'must come to our own decision at once, and the opportunity of a mutually favourable arrangement may be lost'.[88]

This may have had the desired effect, for negotiations revived briefly in 1897, though with little success. Subsequently, negotiations languished for several months and were not resumed until early in 1898, when Portugal, alarmed by the German seizure of Kiaochow and by its possible implications for an active German acquisitions policy in Africa, sought reassurances in London. Renewed conversations between Soveral, Balfour, Chamberlain, and Francis Bertie (an assistant undersecretary at the Foreign Office), ran into rough water once again when the Germans discovered that negotiations were proceeding without them. The German ambassador to Lisbon, in an audience with the King of Portugal, made clear the Kaiser's displeasure. In addition to threatening the Portuguese, the German government simultaneously pressed Britain for compensation should the talks reach a successful conclusion.

Chamberlain was undismayed by the German initiative, and took an equally strong line with the Portuguese in an attempt to force them deeper into negotiations. In an interview with Soveral in early July 1898, he charged Lisbon with 'shilly-shallying', and declared that if the deadlock were not soon broken, 'all hope of a settlement' between Portugal and Britain would be at an end.[89] Portugal would have only themselves to thank if Germany (or France) 'took a Kiao Chow in Portuguese Africa'. After this verbal drubbing, Chamberlain tried a softer touch by promising Soveral that Britain would attempt 'an amicable agreement' with Germany.

Chamberlain in fact genuinely welcomed the German initiative as a way of pursuing his broader goal of a grand alliance with that country. Although this did not find favour with Salisbury, the cabinet overruled him in supporting the Colonial Secretary.[90] Shortly afterward, Salisbury, ill again, went on a recuperative holiday in France, leaving Balfour to negotiate with the Germans. Chamberlain, having earlier negotiated with the Portuguese, now attempted to influence Balfour in his talks with Hatzfeldt. Chamberlain made it plain to Balfour that, in spite of his larger aim of a German alliance, he was suspicious of Hatzfeldt. The German ambassador's tone entering the negotiations was not encouraging: Hatzfeldt spoke 'as an injured man who is being fleeced by usurers'.[91] Chamberlain took a strong line, urging an end to negotiations if Germany refused to uphold Britain's pre-emptive right over Delagoa Bay. Balfour, eager to settle with Germany, disagreed with Chamberlain's threatening tactics. To Balfour's way of thinking, the advantage offered by the proposed arrangement would be a 'public advertisement' to the Transvaal that Germany had promised non-interference in British South African interests.[92] Treading a careful path between Salisbury's broad reluctance to treat with Germany at all and Chamberlain's sticking at details, Balfour concluded negotiations in August 1898.

The Anglo-German Conventions of 1898 set out conditions for a joint Anglo-German loan to Portugal: they also shared joint security for the loan in the form of divided customs revenues in Mozambique. In an additional secret convention, the signatories decided upon a partition of Portuguese colonies based upon mutual spheres of interests in the event of loan default. The signatories also bound themselves to exclude any other country from establishing a presence in Portuguese colonies. And, finally, they settled on mutual compensation should either signatory gain an advantage in concessions or right of occupation in its respective sphere of influence.[93] This agreement signalled that some progress had been made toward formalizing Anglo-German relations. It did not necessarily guarantee a feeling of warmth or trust among the high officers of state, however. Indeed, Britain would soon experience a diplomatic failure and a passage of arms in South Africa that would alienate not only Germany, but would isolate it far more completely from the continent than had Salisbury's policy.

All in all, 1898 had been full of indecisive diplomatic encounters and potential imperial dangers. The year ended, however, with a distinct diplomatic victory, due in large measure to Lord Salisbury, with Chamberlain this time in support. Britain's determination to retain a strong unilateral presence at the Suez Canal had continued to fuel Anglo-French rivalry in West Africa. But France had never surrendered its Nile ambitions. In the summer of 1896 Captain Jean-Baptiste Marchand and a small expeditionary force were sent from the Congo to take possession of an abandoned mud-brick fort on the west bank of the White Nile, 400 miles south of Khartoum, still in Mahdist hands since the death of Gordon in 1885. By capturing Fashoda and claiming the adjacent region of Bahr-al-Ghazal, the French hoped to force the convening of a conference of European powers which might reopen the question of Egypt and the Sudan to their advantage. Fashoda could also provide an avenue for controlling some of the headwaters of the Upper Nile, and thus ultimately the lower reaches of that great river.[94]

To counter the French, and to engage in an important subsidiary mission of cleaning up the Dervish bands still in control of parts of the Nile, Salisbury dispatched General Sir Herbert Kitchener of the Royal Engineers, who was with Wolseley in the expedition to rescue Gordon and was, since 1886, the governor of the eastern Sudan. Kitchener's rapid success, first at Dongola and then Omdurman, just opposite of Khartoum at the juncture of the Blue and White Niles, secured the entire Nile to that point. From there, Kitchener and his forces steamed up the Nile toward Fashoda, where Marchand had already raised the French flag some months earlier. With a much superior force, including 100 Highlanders, 2,500 Sudanese troops, and machine guns, Kitchener took command on 18 September.

There followed several weeks of tension. Britain insisted on, first, Marchand's unconditional evacuation of Fashoda, and, second, the rights of conquest both of the Nile Valley and the adjacent Bahr-al-Ghazal. France stalled, hoping for some compensation to avoid a public humiliation. The delay stoked the British press, which quickly became belligerent. Shortly afterward, the Admiralty called up the Reserve Naval Squadron. The cabinet then placed the fleet on an emergency status. There was talk of war in high places.[95] Marchand's decision in late October to leave Fashoda for Cairo to file his official report, however, weakened the French case. A few days later, the French cabinet acquiesced to British demands. Within 48 hours, Salisbury announced the news in London. Additional negotiations eventually produced the Anglo-French Convention of March 1899, entirely in Britain's favour. No navigable outlet to the Nile Valley was granted to France; and the boundary between French Africa and the Sudan was drawn as Britain wished.

The French stand-down at Fashoda and their diplomatic defeat as well as the British re-conquest of the Sudan owed much to Salisbury. Chamberlain played only a minor role. Indeed, at the time of the battle of Omdurman, Chamberlain was en route to America with Mary to visit her parents. When he returned in mid-October, matters were well under way. Chamberlain, nevertheless, utilized the flood of patriotic and imperial feeling to his own and his party's advantage. Within a fortnight of Salisbury's public announcement of the French capitulation, Chamberlain began a round of speeches in Manchester reviewing the government's foreign and imperial policies, as well as its domestic legislation and social programmes. It had been six months since his last appearance on a public platform.

His first speech before the Manchester Conservative and Liberal Unionist Associations in the Free Trade Hall was a rousing event with 5,000 cheering supporters singing patriotic songs. Chamberlain first gave thanks to the 'ungrudging support' extended to the Unionist Party by their political opponents: Britain had been 'an absolutely united people' during the recent crisis with France.[96] But that did not prevent Chamberlain from criticizing the Gladstonian Liberals, who, he predicted, would soon be at work attacking the government 'with parrot-like iteration'.

In a speech the following day at a banquet given by the Manchester Conservative Club, Chamberlain emphasized the imperial achievements of the Unionist government, especially with regard to Africa and China. He began his speech by discussing what he called 'the progress of geography': where once the map of Africa had been a 'very large blank space', every inch of it had been almost completely filled in during the past three years,[97] driven by the competition among nations for a share in potential markets. It was, Chamberlain claimed, supremely important not to underestimate the value of those future markets: they were capable of 'enormous development'. All Britain wished for, he said, was 'our fair share'. This was why Britain insisted that the markets of China should be accessible to all 'through the open door'. How could Britain be certain that the door would remain open and that no nation 'will try to slam it in our face'? The answer was to seek agreements with other nations with common interests in maintaining 'a liberal trade policy'.

That Chamberlain had not forgotten social issues during his Manchester tour was revealed in a third speech in as many days. This time, speaking before the Manchester Liberal Unionists, Chamberlain reminded his audience that their Conservative allies had been apt pupils. Well-schooled by Disraeli and Lord Randolph Churchill, Conservatives heartily accepted the Liberal Unionist goal of 'improving the condition of the masses of the people and of securing the greatest happiness of the greatest number'.[98]

The Manchester speeches summed up Chamberlain's joint policies of imperial domination and (to a lesser extent) domestic social reform that he brought to a climax in 1898. After three years in office as Colonial Secretary, he had grafted onto his career-long radical interest in social legislation the imperatives of imperialism with its triple aims of economic development, market expansion, and extension of British power and prestige. He had enjoyed almost unqualified success in his endeavours. By a combination of defiant determination, unrelenting vigour, and purposive behaviour, Chamberlain had challenged the cabinet leadership, thrust aside opposition to his plans, and driven toward an independent national policy. There seemed no limit either to his ambition or to his grasping for greater power. But he was soon to encounter a severe check to his policies and actions. The contested field of play was, however, neither in West Africa nor the Nile region nor in Europe or China. Chamberlain's supreme test emerged in South Africa.

11

JOE'S WAR?

Although Chamberlain's role in the South African War of 1899–1902 (also known frequently as the Boer War) was central, its origins were too complex to be attributed to the actions of a single individual. South Africa's complex social and racial divisions, competition for its immense natural wealth, and political disputes over hegemony between the imperial government and local authorities made it the most demanding of all British colonial possessions. Originally settled by the Dutch East India Company in the seventeenth century as a fortress and supply station, South Africa also had an obvious strategic importance. By the time that Britain captured Cape Town in 1795 to prevent it falling into French hands during the Revolutionary Wars, South Africa contained a mixed population of subservient slaves and indigenous Khoikhoi dominated by a Dutch-Afrikaans-speaking white minority. As British influence in the Cape Colony increased and the number of British settlers grew in the early nineteenth century, conflicts with the Cape Dutch-Afrikaners intensified.

To escape from the British and to search for new land, thousands of Cape Dutch retreated into the interior during the 1830s and 1840s. Their hopes of independence, however, went unrealized. As the Boers (former Cape Dutch-Afrikaans farmers) trekked northward, they encountered indigenous African peoples who resisted their incursion. Warfare between Boers and the Xhosa flared ominously, forcing British Cape administrators to pacify the unstable frontier. British soldiers marching into troubled areas carried the flag and the authority of an annexationist colonial administration.[1] Thus, the boundary of British South Africa continually advanced along the path initially made by the Boer trekkers. Nonetheless, by the 1850s the Boers had retreated far enough to the north to establish – with relatively little interference from Britain – two Boer republics, the Orange Free State and the South African Republic (Transvaal).

During the time of the treks, the Cape British had been equally active in creating a second colony, Natal, which served as an outpost against the formidable Zulu. By mid-century, there were two inland Afrikaner republics and two coastal British colonies. From the 1860s, in a continuing expansionist dynamism, the British added Basutoland, the port of St Johns, Griqualand West (in 1871 after diamonds were discovered there), and most significantly for the opening drama of Chamberlain's active role in South Africa, the protectorate of Bechuanaland (Botswana) in 1885.

This extension of British colonial territory was matched by complementary political developments during the 1870s. First, the Cape Colony was granted self-government in 1872: this was a natural corollary of the Cape's geographical size, large population, and wealth. Second, a movement began for a South African Confederation centred on the Cape Colony which would unite British colonies and Boer republics into a constitutional state based upon the Canadian model. An attempted annexation of the Transvaal and its inclusion into such a federation, however, was effectively blunted during a short Anglo-Boer war when a British force was defeated at Majuba Hill in February 1881.

In succeeding treaties, British governments acknowledged the essential independence of the Transvaal, with the exception of British control over its foreign relations. This loose constitutional arrangement was an easy choice for the British to make at a time when the Transvaal was a poor, landlocked, ramshackle republic.[2] Dramatic economic changes, however, soon altered the political and ultimately the imperial relations in South Africa. In 1886, gold was discovered on the Witwatersrand in such quantity that before the end of the century, the Transvaal was the largest single producer of gold in the world. Additional discoveries of large deposits of coal completed the so-called mineral revolution in the Transvaal. Capital investment and accelerated economic development quickly transformed the Transvaal. Lured by tales of wealth, immigrants (Uitlanders, or Outlanders) – many of them British – flocked to the mines. In the fast growing city of Johannesburg, founded on the site of the mines, Uitlanders began to demand the rights of citizens and to pressure the South African government for redress of grievances.

South Africa's turbulent political and social conditions continued into the 1890s. Provocative incursions of expansionist-minded Boers, the frequent shifting of indefinable boundaries among warring chiefdoms, and the unauthorized expeditions of adventurers, hunters, and traders into the protectorate of Bechuanaland and beyond threatened stability in that region. As Colonial Secretary, Chamberlain was determined to bring order out of chaos: Cape colonies, Boer republics, black protectorates – all would be joined together under a benevolent but firm and orderly imperial power.

Chamberlain's attempt to set his imperial plan in motion, however, was nearly a disaster. Shortly after attaining office in 1895 Chamberlain was presented with an important official request from Cecil Rhodes, who was then both Prime Minister of the Cape Colony and Managing Director of the British South Africa Company (BSAC). Rhodes asked the Colonial Office to transfer 'at once' the protectorate of Bechuanaland to his own Chartered Company (as it was widely known).[3] Rhodes' request was not as peremptory as it may seem. Under the terms of its charter of 1889, the British South African Company was authorized to make treaties, to engage in mining, and to maintain a police force in an area vaguely designated as north of the crown colony of Bechuanaland, (known as British Bechuanaland, ultimately annexed into the Cape Colony).[4] The protectorate of Bechuanaland, as distinct from the crown colony of the same name, would eventually under the terms of the charter be transferred directly to the BSAC at some later date. In addition, the government approved the construction of a railway through the protectorate. And finally, the government agreed to encourage the Bechuana chiefs to grant concessions over land and minerals to the BSAC.

Until the time that the BSAC would replace the protectorate of Bechuanaland, Rhodes, never still in his imperial schemes, turned his attention elsewhere.[5] In 1890, the so-called Pioneer Column under the auspices of the BSAC traversed through the western part of the protectorate of Bechuanaland and then into Zambesia (later Southern Rhodesia) beyond the Limpopo River to exploit what resources they could find.[6] Soon, the paramilitary forces of the BSAC began expropriating land and cattle. Then, employing a series of pretexts, the BSAC forces provoked a revolt which flared into the Ndebele War of 1893–4. By this time, matters had gone well beyond the control of the Colonial Office, then in the hands of the Liberals. Eventually, the High Commissioner of the Cape, Sir Henry Loch, dispatched imperial troops to reinforce the BSAC, effectively subduing the rebels.

With Zambesia now in hand, the time had come for the protectorate of Bechuanaland to be used as a pawn in Rhodes' expansionist dreams. Rhodes' aim was to connect the Cape with the interior by railway through Bechuanaland and into Zambesia, thus both circumventing and surrounding the hostile Boer republic.[7] So encircled, the Transvaal would eventually be absorbed within an expanded Cape Colony. In addition, by building upon his base in Rhodesia north of the Transvaal, Rhodes could begin in earnest his grandest scheme of all – a railway extending from Cape Town to Cairo.

The Salisbury government was not averse to Rhodes' imperial aims. His work in South Africa accomplished much with little cost to the Treasury. There would be no apparent loss in handing over the protectorate of Bechuanaland to Rhodes and the BSAC. Still, Chamberlain, as a novice Colonial Secretary, wished to examine with care Rhodes' request. Perhaps he wanted more time to think about the practical consequences of Rhodes's imperial vision. Chamberlain was certainly suspicious of Rhodes, the BSAC, and their possible implications for his own plans for a centralized re-structuring of the Empire.[8] It also seems likely that Chamberlain was influenced by a campaign undertaken in England by three important client chiefs of Bechuanaland who opposed any transfer of their land to the BSAC.[9] Using collaborative chiefs in governing through a form of indirect rule had proven its worth in some cases.[10] Chamberlain had no wish to alienate summarily willing partners in his own schemes of imperial collaboration.

It should be noted, too, that Chamberlain would unlikely have responded quickly or eagerly to the demands of a man like Rhodes. They were too much alike, too driven by their own needs for power and control to come readily into an understanding of shared imperial designs. But Rhodes was more than a mirror image of Chamberlain. He represented the logical extension of Chamberlain's entrepreneurial ideals, radical approach to political and economic problems, and capacity for intrigue and manipulation. Operating beyond the bounds of parliamentary precedent and without the restraints of opposition political parties, Rhodes was in the purest sense an untrammelled freebooter.

In any case, when Rhodes approached the Colonial Office concerning the protectorate of Bechuanaland in July 1895, Chamberlain hesitated. Rhodes responded by asking for assistance from Lord Rosebery, the former Liberal prime minister and sympathetic imperialist. When Rosebery in turn consulted Ripon, the latter counselled against it: 'there is no saying wh[at] use an unscrupulous fellow like Joe might make of your intervention'.[11] Rhodes had better luck with two of his most trusted agents – Dr Rutherfoord Harris and Albert, Lord Grey.[12] During conversations which occurred intermittently from August to November 1895, Chamberlain learned from Grey that the real purpose of the proposed Bechuanaland railway concession was to provide enough land to serve as a base of operations to invade the Transvaal in support of an incited uprising of Uitlanders in Johannesburg.[13]

This was a remarkable revelation. Rhodes was in effect requesting through his agents ministerial support for the invasion of what was arguably a sovereign country. No better example can be found of Rhodes' propensity to act unilaterally outside accepted traditions governing international relations. Equally remarkable was Chamberlain's behaviour. By merely listening to these proposals, Chamberlain, as a Secretary of State, was indirectly condoning the plans and implicitly lending them sanction by the British government. Perhaps impelled by this daring scheme, in which he saw a way of finally settling the nettlesome Boer question, Chamberlain acted – but not entirely in favour of Rhodes. He effected a kind of compromise. Denying Rhodes's request of major concessions of land and minerals from the African chiefs in the protectorate, he granted only a strip of land along its eastern edge bordering the Transvaal. Thus Rhodes secured the so-called Pitsani strip (named for a small town located near the border), wide enough for the northward route of the railway line and wide enough, too, for a military staging point.

By December 1895 plans were fully in place for an attack using personnel and leadership from the BSAC. More than 7,000 armed men in Johannesburg were to rise in revolt. A signal would be sent to the Transvaal's western border where a detachment of 1,500 men would be waiting in the recently acquired Pitsani strip. They would then gallop across 175 miles of Boer-held territory to assist the revolt.[14] Precise timing, strong leadership, and working weaponry were all crucial to the success of the raid. In every instance the plan failed. Instead of thousands in revolt, fewer than 400 were recruited in Johannesburg and the uprising was broken off. Undeterred, Dr Leander Starr Jameson, leader of the border detachment and veteran of the Ndebele campaigns, rode out from the camp at Pitsani before dawn on 30 December 1895, with fewer than 500 troopers. Their vaunted Maxim guns, prone to overheating, were never brought into effective use as Boer commandoes picked off the invaders from the heights along their line of march. After several days' hard riding, the demoralized survivors surrendered before they reached Johannesburg. Historians have widely denounced the enterprise as a fiasco. As Rotberg sums it up, the plan was based upon 'a host of exuberant miscalculations'.[15]

Chamberlain understood the significance of Jameson's unheralded raid and the consequences of its failure. To the world, it was quite obviously an invasion, launched across a recognized frontier with the express purpose of overthrowing a legitimate government. As the highest officer of state who had a direct and unofficial involvement with the preparation for the raid, Chamberlain bore on his shoulders the primary responsibility. If his role should become widely known, his reputation and his political career would be in jeopardy. To be cast down from his pinnacle of power would be intolerable.

When the news of Jameson's crossing the border reached Highbury, therefore, Chamberlain sprang into action. Hurriedly leaving a dinner party, he boarded a midnight train to London. Upon arrival, he telegraphed Paul Kruger, President of the Transvaal, repudiating the raid. He also wired Sir Hercules Robinson, the High Commissioner, ordering him to restrain Jameson. He then contacted both the British and South African press informing them of his actions.[16] In the next 72 hours, he worked at a fever pitch. On 31 December he reported to Mary that he had 'a long & somewhat anxious day – seeing people – sending & receiving telegrams but the situation is still obscure'.[17] The following day, with still no word of Jameson's fate, Chamberlain wrote that he was not yet 'out of the wood'.[18] On 2 January, the hours 'of work and worry' provoked 'a very bad headache' forcing him from the Colonial Office to rest at his London home in Prince's Gardens.[19] It was there that he heard of Jameson's capture.

Chamberlain's apologists have taken his rapid response and firm repudiation of the raid as a sign of his shock at such an ill-founded and illegal action: thus his behaviour indicated his innocence of any knowledge of the plan. But it could as easily be argued that his actions signified a desperate attempt on the part of a co-conspirator to control and limit the damage of a failed plot. Indeed, Chamberlain's role in the Raid and the planned uprising in Johannesburg have long been a topic of historical debate. There is little dispute that he was aware of an intended uprising by the Uitlanders. This was widely known: even Kruger, it has been said, was aware of the plot. The debate, then, has centred on how much Chamberlain knew about the raid and how far he encouraged it in his official position as Colonial Secretary. Garvin, of course, exculpates Chamberlain entirely, if somewhat inconsistently. Peter Fraser echoes Garvin: Chamberlain 'was not a party to the intrigues of Rhodes and the Chartered Company'. A more recent view by Michael Bentley does not take sides, opining that Chamberlain's involvement 'may forever remain unclear'. But the general thrust of historical judgement has tilted against Chamberlain since the opening of important papers in South Africa in the 1940s. Emblematic of this shift in historical interpretation was Elizabeth Pakenham's change of mind. In her first account of the raid, she equivocated; but in the second edition of her work, she strengthens the case against Chamberlain's complicity in the raid. Perhaps she had been influenced by Denis Judd's earlier indictment of Chamberlain. Peter Marsh's verdict is straightforward: Chamberlain had been 'sucked into' Rhodes' conspiracies. Most recently, Judd and Surridge write that Chamberlain 'connived' at Rhodes' plan for the raid.[20]

In short, it would seem that Chamberlain was aware of both the planned rebellion in Johannesburg and equally aware of the Jameson-led raid. But he was not actively involved in the initial planning stages of either. He was, however, involved in and orchestrated to a fair degree the ensuing cover-up, using his official position to obstruct the parliamentary inquiry and thus to deny even a rudimentary knowledge of the raid. This will become apparent in the discussion that follows.

Apart from the likely damage to Chamberlain's personal reputation and to his standing in the Unionist government, the raid had potentially more serious consequences for the prestige of Great Britain. When implicating documents were taken from the captured raiders, a justifiably suspicious President Kruger publicly accused Chamberlain of conspiring with Rhodes in an attempt to bring down the Boer republic. If it could be proven that Chamberlain in his role as Colonial Secretary had aided or abetted the raid, it would be a direct violation of the London Convention of 1884.

That foreign governments were eager to fish in these troubled waters was soon evident. Within a few days of the raid, the German Kaiser sent a public telegram to President Kruger congratulating him in defending the independence of his country and repelling 'armed bands' which had attacked without provocation. German intervention in the crisis and the veiled threat in using the term 'independence' in referring to the Transvaal was not a bolt from the blue. For more than a decade, German and British rivalry was on the rise in southern Africa. Germany's occupation of South West Africa, its interest in Delagoa Bay, and increased German immigration and investments in railways and mining in the Transvaal alerted Britain to the exercise of the new *Weltpolitik* in that part of the world.[21] Occurring only days after the Raid, the Kruger Telegram was a clear expression of Germany's determination to use the opportunity provided by the failed raid to strengthen its hand in South Africa.

Luckily for Chamberlain, the Kaiser had miscalculated. The telegram redounded to Chamberlain's advantage by creating a backlash in Britain. Playing upon the public outrage that followed the publication of the telegram in *The Times*, Chamberlain seized his chance to create a diversion. He urged upon Salisbury an 'Act of Vigour' on the part of the government 'to soothe the wounded vanity of the nation'.[22] Among his recommendations were a strongly worded dispatch to Germany; the immediate preparation of troops for Cape Town; and an appeal to British colonies at large to complete their naval and military defences. Salisbury, however, preferred a more muted response: a flying squadron of British ships was dispatched immediately to Delagoa Bay. This warning was substantial enough to discourage further German encroachment and it satisfied British opinion that 'something' be done.

On the same day as his letter to Salisbury calling for action against Germany, Chamberlain launched a second diversionary tactic. Addressing Kruger, he demanded justice for the Uitlanders in the Transvaal, many of whom were British. By doing so, he hoped to place the Boers on the defensive, and shift the blame for the uprising and the raid from Rhodes and the BSAC onto the intractable Kruger government. By appearing to defend the rights of Britons, even if they lived abroad, Chamberlain sounded a Palmerstonian note which carried a warning. Unless citizens of the Empire were protected, wherever they were, armed intervention was a distinct possibility.[23]

Sending gunboats to South Africa and defending British immigrants in the Transvaal did not ease public doubts about the raid, however. Initial newspaper comment was wary, if not openly suspicious, about Colonial Office involvement. *The Times* believed that a 'serious responsibility' lay upon 'the shoulders of the

Colonial Office'. The *Daily Chronicle* had words of praise for Chamberlain as well as a warning. There was room for Chamberlain's 'active, clear, strenuous spirit in the development of this Empire of ours. Our race has still a mighty mission to perform on sea and land.' But it was also important 'to master the art of living with our neighbours'. The *Evening News* took an entirely different tack. Believing that the English in Johannesburg were in 'serious danger', the *News* criticized the 'red-taped weakness of the Colonial Office' which had blundered in recalling Jameson.

By the end of the first week, however, the press in general was lining up for Chamberlain. The *Daily Chronicle* had second thoughts. Chamberlain's actions following the raid, it wrote, have 'completely dissociated the governing forces of the Empire from the shadow of a shade of complicity with Dr. Jameson's action'. Even *The Times* found a firmer voice, praising Chamberlain extravagantly: the Colonial Secretary had shown 'steadiness of nerve, firmness of resolution, promptitude in deciding and acting upon obscure and complicated facts, and a large-minded grasp of the whole situation'.[24]

The general exculpatory tone of the press doubtless gave Chamberlain a sense of relief. Within a fortnight of the raid, he wrote to Lady Dorothy Nevill that his cabinet colleagues were unanimous in their support: 'Lord Salisbury & my colleagues have been most generous … & have allowed me a free hand …'. Although some troubles were 'still in store', he hoped 'that all danger is past'.[25] Chamberlain's optimism was, however, premature. Questions soon began to surface about the relationship between the Colonial Secretary and Rhodes once it was apparent that the Chartered Company had both instigated and then carried out the raid using Company troops led by a Company agent. It appeared that the Company was in breach of international law and very probably guilty of criminal actions.[26] Why had the Colonial Secretary not acted against the Company?

Indeed, it would have been difficult for Chamberlain to take such action: the Chartered Company was indispensable for the consolidation of British influence both in South Africa and Rhodesia. Other alternatives were simply unacceptable to Chamberlain, and one may presume, to the cabinet as a whole. Neither withdrawal, nor a reversion of the Company's charter to the British government, with its inevitable costs to the public treasury, could be countenanced. Equally important in Chamberlain's reluctance to act was his uncertainty about the position that Rhodes would take in any likely inquiry into the raid. Rhodes knew everything. Only he could reveal the depth of Chamberlain's complicity in the plot to overthrow the Transvaal government.

To parry the thrusts of continuing suspicion and criticism, Chamberlain adopted two strategies. The first was to go on the offensive in a public campaign to justify his colonial policy and to uphold the integrity of the government. Here he was in his element. For example, in late January 1896, serving as chairman of a banquet honouring Lord Lamington, the new Governor of Queensland, Chamberlain referred directly to the 'incidents' in South Africa. He cautioned his audience to remember the tendency 'to attach too much importance to sensational occurrences which pass away and leave no traces behind'. No doubt a few mistakes had been made and would continue to be made in colonial matters, Chamberlain admitted, but there was consolation in the far greater record of imperial successes. Britain, 'alone among the nations of the earth', had been able not only to establish colonies all over the globe, but had also been able to secure 'the loyal attachment' and 'the general good will' of those under the British flag.[27]

Chamberlain's second strategy was potentially more risky: he agreed to a public inquiry. The outcome of the inquiry, more than either the attempted insurrection or the raid itself, posed the greatest threat to Chamberlain's reputation. Such an inquiry would be difficult to control and might discover hitherto hidden evidence as to the origins and execution of the raid. Nevertheless, he had no choice but to bow to public pressure for an official accounting of the raid. From early 1896 until mid-1897, therefore, Chamberlain, acting in his capacity as Colonial Secretary, energetically helped to devise and then to direct the parliamentary inquiry on the raid. His aim, however, was not to facilitate the inquiry but to subvert it. He understood that the wider the net cast by the inquiry and the longer the investigation, the better for all the plotters. By delay, obfuscation, and transparent witness tampering, he attempted to defuse the various components of the entire Transvaal fiasco: the uprising; the Raid; the role of Rhodes and the Chartered Company – and his own complicity.[28]

Chamberlain was wholly successful in his efforts. He was greatly aided by procedural difficulties inherent in the complexities of the case. The example of Jameson is instructive. After his capture and extradition to England, questions arose about his trial venue. Should Jameson be tried in a criminal court; and, if so, what would be the charge? What would be the relationship between that trial and a parliamentary inquiry? What role should be played by the concomitant investigation of the Chartered Company underway in the South African Cape House of Assembly? Always in the background was the relationship between Jameson's action as leader of the raid and the wider conspiracy. Once it had been decided that the parliamentary inquiry should be postponed until Jameson's criminal trial was concluded, the desirable element of delay (from Chamberlain's point of view) was achieved. In late July Jameson was tried before Lord Chief Justice Sir Charles Russell and found guilty of charges under the Foreign Enlistment Act and sentenced to 15 months imprisonment.[29] With Jameson out of the way, the next question was the composition of the parliamentary committee to hear the evidence concerning the raid. Ten members were chosen including, curiously enough, Chamberlain himself, who was bound to become a prime object of the committee's investigation.[30] Once formed, the committee met briefly in August 1897, and then adjourned until the next parliamentary session.

Well before the inquiry got underway, Chamberlain was busily shoring up his defences. Undoubtedly Rhodes was central to the inquiry. Chamberlain was soon at work recommending to him a tactical approach. He counselled Rhodes through an intermediary, Reginald Brett, to admit that 'like everyone else', he was aware of a possible revolution in Johannesburg and that it was his duty as Cape Prime Minister to prepare for such an event.[31] But Rhodes should also claim, Chamberlain urged, that he had no intention of using military force 'except upon an emergency', such as a threat to British lives and property. Even then, he would not have initiated action without the consent of the High Commissioner, Sir Hercules Robinson. If, in addition, Rhodes could prove that there was 'a Dutch-German conspiracy', it would be accepted as a 'good excuse' for his actions and it would 'undoubtedly tend to divert the issue and share the blame'.

Within a few days, Brett had arranged a meeting between Rhodes and Chamberlain.[32] At that meeting, on 6 February 1896, Chamberlain apparently promised Rhodes that the Company's charter was safe.[33] The way was now cleared for a public exoneration of Rhodes. A week later, speaking in the House of Commons, Chamberlain commended Rhodes 'for the great services he has rendered' in Africa, and suggested that if he had committed a great wrong, he could repair it with a greater right.[34] Although Rhodes was forced to resign as Managing Director of the Company, the Company's charter was not revoked. Chamberlain's support was undoubtedly crucial to Rhodes' rehabilitation. Rhodes might now serve as the image of the selfless imperial servant that Chamberlain wished to convey.

In spite of this evidence of collaboration between Chamberlain and Rhodes, there remained a potentially divisive issue jeopardizing their fragile alliance.[35] The parliamentary inquiry might discover unpleasant facts about the uprising and the Raid. Rhodes had from the first objected to an inquiry, knowing full well that a public disclosure of his deeper conspiracy might jeopardize his reputation and authority in South Africa. The uncertain prospects of the official investigation prompted desperate measures. In effect, Bourchier Hawksley, Rhodes' solicitor, threatened blackmail. Hawksley warned that if an inquiry were held, Rhodes and other ringleaders of the plot would claim that they acted with Chamberlain's encouragement. Furthermore, they could produce a series of telegrams to prove it. In June 1896, copies of several dozen telegrams had been sent to Chamberlain at Highbury. Although none of the telegrams were from Chamberlain, they nevertheless seemed to implicate him on two grounds: that he gave the Pitsani strip to the Chartered Company for the specific purpose of facilitating the Raid; and that he had actively been involved in the timing of the Johannesburg uprising.

At first, the telegrams seemed damning. But after their examination by Chamberlain, Meade, Selborne, and other Colonial Office officials, they were used to Chamberlain's advantage.[36] He sought, and received, support from Salisbury.[37] He could now call Hawksley's bluff, threatening to make the telegrams public, presumably on the grounds that others would be seen as more culpable than he. This effectively neutralized the attempt at blackmail.[38] Conclusive evidence that Chamberlain was well aware of the plot came not from the telegrams, however, but from an exchange of letters between Lord Grey and Chamberlain a few months before the inquiry began.[39] Doubtless prepping for the inquiry, Chamberlain had written Grey reminding him of a private conversation they had had a year earlier in which Grey (as Chamberlain acknowledged) explained the need for a military base in Bechuanaland to support an expected revolution in Johannesburg. Indirectly admitting that he may have made 'casual expressions' or 'incidental remarks' that could have been misconstrued, Chamberlain nevertheless insisted that the conversation contained privileged information: he was sure that Grey would never violate such a confidence. In his letter, Chamberlain held out both a carrot and a stick. If Rhodes voluntarily appeared as a witness at the inquiry, he would be free to decide whether or not to answer certain questions. But if the incriminating telegrams were published, Chamberlain warned that the slender thread 'on which hangs at present the future of the Company and of Mr. Rhodes's connection with its territories' could be broken.[40]

Chamberlain was particularly concerned about Grey's role in the inquiry. A strong supporter and confidant of Rhodes and a member of the board of the British South Africa Company, Grey was deeply involved in the Jameson Raid.[41] At the time of the inquiry, Grey was serving as chief administrator of Rhodesia and was understandably reluctant to return in order to testify. Indeed, he thought that the Commons inquiry 'should be allowed to fizzle out'.[42] He was thus not reassuring in his response to Chamberlain's query. If asked by the committee of inquiry whether or not he had informed Chamberlain of the impending Johannesburg revolution, Grey wrote that he would answer in one of two ways. He would either refuse to answer; or he would state that he had in fact told Chamberlain privately that the long expected uprising of the Uitlanders would shortly take place.[43]

Efforts to orchestrate the cover-up extended to Colonial Office subordinates. A few had to be sacrificed to protect their chief. Foremost among these were Edward Fairfield, head of the South African Department in the Colonial Office; Sir Graham Bower, Imperial Secretary to the High Commissioner for South Africa; and F. J. Newton, resident commissioner of the Bechuanaland Protectorate, who was stationed at Mafeking.[44] Fairfield was spared by a stroke he suffered in November 1896, from which he died several months later. Bower and Newton, on the other hand, who had known of Rhodes' plans, were pressed into denying that Sir Hercules Robinson, the High Commissioner of South Africa, had a prior knowledge of the plans. If Robinson had been implicated, it would close the circle of official complicity at the highest levels in both South Africa and Britain in the plan to bring down the Transvaal government. Bower and Newton were persuaded to testify that although they knew of the plans, they failed to tell Robinson.[45]

When the parliamentary inquiry began in February 1897, Chamberlain and his co-conspirators were well prepared: witnesses had been coached; incriminating telegrams had been neutralized; and threats had been issued. Perhaps the crowning achievement was Chamberlain's management of the inquiry itself. Watchful of his own interest and certain of the loyalty of the Colonial Office, he played a confident and vigilant role as a member of the committee. During the testimonies of witnesses, he often intervened directly to stress his own innocence. In at least one instance, he lied in his testimony before the committee of inquiry.[46] Hoping for at least an inconclusive report, Chamberlain was more amply rewarded with a vindication of his claims of innocence. His refusal to take responsibility for any foreknowledge of the uprising and denial of complicity in the Raid were never firmly challenged. The final report completely exonerated both Chamberlain and Sir Hercules Robinson.

In his attempts at eviscerating the committee of inquiry, Chamberlain had an unsuspecting ally in Harcourt, who became leader of the Liberals after Rosebery's resignation in 1896. Harcourt had a clear political incentive to discover embarrassing and even fatally damaging evidence against his erstwhile colleague and friend. And yet he seemed particularly credulous of Chamberlain and his colonial comrades. Harcourt was tentative and superficial in his questioning of witnesses, rarely probing at weak testimonies. Opportunities were certainly numerous enough. Rhodes, Hawksley, Bower, and Chamberlain himself all took the stand at one time or another. But committee members, often led by Harcourt, could not break down their evasions and denials.

Chamberlain, working from inside the committee of inquiry, had a particular advantage in outmanoeuvring Harcourt. A startling example occurred late in the inquiry's deliberations when Flora Shaw, a noted journalist for *The Times*, was called before the committee.[47] The committee's specific interest in Shaw was a series of telegrams between her and Rhodes, one of which purported to claim that Chamberlain himself was attempting to expedite the uprising in Johannesburg in late December. This famous 'hurry-up' telegram seemed to give direct proof of Chamberlain's integral connection with both the uprising and the Raid. There is little doubt that Chamberlain instigated the telegram: he was concerned that any delay might give the Transvaal an advantage by allowing them more time to form a firmer bond with an interested Germany. In addition, Anglo-American relations had suffered a setback with President Cleveland's ultimatum on 17 December 1895 over Venezuela. By resolving the Transvaal stalemate immediately, the decks could be cleared for any additional unpleasantness with the United States. Events thus seemed to Chamberlain to require an accelerated pace for the planned uprising and raid. These thoughts Chamberlain shared with Shaw, who in turn sent the incriminating telegram.[48]

When Shaw was summoned to appear before the Committee, she wrote Chamberlain hoping to meet him for 'a talk'.[49] Chamberlain declined, but designated his private secretary, H. F. Wilson, to serve as intermediary. On the reverse side of Shaw's note, Chamberlain wrote a brief set of instructions before forwarding it to Wilson: 'If there is anything she desires to know she might see you and tell you what she wants.' Chamberlain additionally asked Wilson to solicit from Shaw important information. He would like to know the answer 'beforehand' to the following question: had she mentioned 'in the course of any conversations with me' Jameson's plan (that is, the placing of troops on the border to facilitate an insurrection)? In an obvious prompt, Chamberlain wrote that he did not remember Shaw ever saying a word on the subject, but he would nevertheless like to know her recollection.[50]

The following day, after speaking with Shaw, Wilson sent a lengthy reply to Chamberlain.[51] The answer to his question was 'no'. Wilson reported that Shaw was determined to adhere to this denial 'as far as possible'. In addition, she would refuse to give the committee details of other conversations on the grounds that communications with a Secretary of State were confidential. She assured Chamberlain that the three telegrams that she had sent to Rhodes were on her own responsibility. Rhodes' telegrammed replies were of little importance: in any case, she had not preserved them. Chamberlain must have been well pleased with this rehearsal. At the inquiry, Shaw was fluent, articulate, and convincing in her denial of any incriminating knowledge that would be relevant to the proceedings. With this final hurdle surmounted, Chamberlain was at last in the clear.

Given Chamberlain's talent for managing and manipulating behind the scenes, it is not surprising that the Liberals, including Harcourt, were unable to fasten blame upon the Colonial Secretary during the course of the inquiry. Yet Harcourt was not entirely gullible.[52] Later, in fact, he changed his mind. Although he remained convinced of Chamberlain's innocence in promoting the raid, he came to believe that Chamberlain was deeply implicated in the planned Johannesburg uprising. But this to Harcourt was a venial sin. Far more serious was the imperial irresponsibility of Rhodes. To Harcourt, Rhodes was the most culpable of all the plotters, and the most dangerous. Harcourt was determined to bring down the 'colossus'. His hope was the resignation of Rhodes and a stern censure of his imperial adventurism. In short, Harcourt had his own agenda before the inquiry. Following the tracks of Chamberlain through a conspiratorial jungle would have been diversionary in the pursuit of his primary objective.

Although there has been substantial criticism of the committee among contemporaries then and historians since,[53] Chamberlain survived the inquiry in a stronger position than he had entered it. Indeed, Rhodes had been far more damaged than Chamberlain. Forced to resign from high office and an object of suspicion from former political friends in the Cape Colony, Rhodes also lost his plans for the Bechuanaland Protectorate which thereafter remained under the Crown. The Colonial Office under Chamberlain also emerged from the shadow of the Raid, strengthened by new recruits – staunch imperialists and firmly loyal to their chief.[54] In London, Fred Graham replaced the deceased Fairfield at the South Africa desk and Edward Wingfield became permanent undersecretary succeeding Meade. Conyngham Green became British Agent at Pretoria in the Transvaal. George Fiddes was appointed secretary to the new British High Commissioner in Cape Town. These joined Selborne, already at the Colonial Office as permanent undersecretary. Most important of all was the appointment of a new High Commissioner for South Africa, Alfred Milner, in April 1897.

Milner was cut in the Chamberlain mould. Intelligent, forceful, a committed imperialist, he was a dynamic counterpart to his London chief. Unusually well qualified for his post, Milner had won a scholarship to Balliol, become president of the Union, and been awarded a fellowship to New College. He had worked as a journalist for ten years under Morley and then W. T. Stead at the *Pall Mall Gazette*. Later he became private secretary to Goschen, Chancellor of the Exchequer under Salisbury. Later still, he served as undersecretary of finance in Egypt under another leading proconsul, Lord Cromer. From 1892 to 1897 Milner was Chairman of the Board of Inland Revenue at Somerset House, work for which he was honoured by a knighthood. As a first-rate administrator and with proven relevant experience, he caught Chamberlain's eye and was a natural selection to the highest governmental position in South Africa.

Like Chamberlain, Milner believed in the benevolent force of the state to foster social policies, and thus was not shy in exerting its power, even military power, to bring about needed changes.[55] Indeed, Milner was willing to push Chamberlain forward when the Colonial Secretary seemed reluctant to act. Yet at first both men were cautious in the era following the Jameson Raid, explainable in part by the fact that there were some positive signs from the Boer government. Uitlander grievances were being addressed – including extension of the franchise, an education reform, and the creation of a municipal council in Johannesburg with some places reserved for Uitlander representation.[56] But there was a point beyond which the Boers were unwilling to go – the acceptance of British 'suzerainty' or paramountcy over the Transvaal.

Once Kruger, the champion of Boer independence, had been re-elected president of the South African Republic in early 1898, British policy as enunciated by Milner changed from conciliation to confrontation. The Colonial Office did not follow at first, and held to a more moderate course. This was through no love for Kruger[57] but rather the belief that time was on the side of British patience, and that a persistent anti-Boer attitude might be unpopular in Britain as well as provocative to European opinion. Nevertheless, Milner knew his man. Chamberlain, he believed, would eventually come around if handled properly. In a letter to Rhodes, he warned against pushing Chamberlain too hard. 'He is', wrote Milner referring to Chamberlain, 'very bold and loves the forward game. But it would be a mistake ... to get Chamberlain to take up anything he could not carry with his colleagues, ... for it will be a long time before we get another Colonial Minister, who is so likely to back up big schemes of expansion and to damn Treasury objections to them.'[58]

Complementing Milner's work in the field as a leading proponent of a forward policy against the Transvaal was Lord Selborne at the Colonial Office. Encouraged by Selborne, Milner decided to increase the pressure against the Transvaal. During a visit to England in late 1898 and early 1899, Milner began an anti-Boer campaign by cultivating a variety of opinion makers. At meetings, dinners, and weekend house parties, he sought out politicians, journalists, men of money with South African interests, and even the royal family, whom he visited at Sandringham.[59] Upon his return to South Africa in late January 1899, Milner created machinery – primarily through a controlled newspaper press – which could manufacture public opinion in both South Africa and Britain and create the issues that ultimately justified war.[60]

To stiffen what he called 'the wobblers' in Britain, Milner raised the level of criticism of the Boer regime in his official dispatches to the Colonial Office. In May 1899, he sent to Chamberlain perhaps the most famous of these – the so-called 'Helot's Dispatch'. In it he condemned in scathing terms Kruger's refusal to liberalize the Uitlander franchise. Upholding what he termed the legitimate and 'vehement demand' among the Uitlanders for enfranchisement, Milner believed that the turmoil in the Transvaal would never end until they had attained their 'fair share of political power'. Because the majority of Uitlanders were British citizens 'accustomed to a free system and equal rights', they felt deeply their subjection to an inequitable political system. Milner deplored the 'spectacle of thousands of British subjects kept permanently in the position of helots, constantly chafing under undoubted grievances, and calling vainly to Her Majesty's Government for redress'.[61]

With Milner pushing for war, there was little that the Transvaal could do to halt the slide. Even when a moderate wing among the Boer leaders gained some influence in the spring of 1899 and sponsored a conference on outstanding issues at Bloemfontein in the Transvaal's sister republic, the Orange Free State, no agreement was reached on the Uitlander franchise question. When the conference broke up in disarray war was only four months distant. Actions on both sides hastened that day forward. In the Transvaal, Kruger's position on the franchise question was upheld in a series of patriotic meetings throughout the country. The insistent theme was the preservation of Transvaal independence and the denial of any British right to intervene in its affairs. Simultaneously in Britain events moved toward a climax, with Chamberlain at last taking the reins from Milner's hands. In mid-June, a Blue Book of dispatches (including the 'Helot's Dispatch') was presented to the House of Commons for public scrutiny.

During the early weeks in the summer of 1899, the cabinet, meeting frequently on South Africa, sanctioned in general terms Chamberlain's continuing attempts to pressure the Transvaal into additional reform measures for the Uitlanders. Chamberlain's ostensible aim was to push to the point of war – always insisting upon the dual themes of Uitlander reforms and British sovereignty – but not beyond it. The Transvaal in turn implemented a few (not insubstantial) reforms for the Uitlanders, including a guaranteed number of Uitlander seats in the Transvaal Volksraad and a lowered residential requirement for the franchise. But the British government would not accept these terms unless coupled with an agreement to establish a joint Boer-British inquiry to monitor the reforms. The Boers refused on the grounds that such an inquiry was an unwarranted interference in the Transvaal's domestic affairs. The cycle of apparent concessions followed by fresh demands characterized these final weeks of confrontational diplomacy.

Meanwhile Chamberlain had begun a public campaign in Britain against the Boers. In a policy statement of some length given at the Town Hall in Birmingham in late June, he spoke 'plainly', as he told his audience, about 'the Transvaal question'.[62] He reviewed in detail the history of British relations with the Transvaal for the past 20 years – a history fraught with war, broken promises, and hostile intent on the part of the Boer republic. Above all, Chamberlain criticized the policy of the Transvaal government as 'oppressive and unjust', 'a menace to British interests', and 'a serious danger to our position as the paramount Power in South Africa'. More specifically, he deplored the Transvaal's policy with regard to the Uitlander population – a policy that had gone 'from bad to worse'. The Uitlanders were the citizens of 'the paramount power'; yet they had been treated as if 'they belonged to an inferior race'. If Britain did not support its citizens in the Transvaal, British subjects to the south in the Cape Colony could be put at risk; at the very least, their loyalty would be severely strained. There could even be wider implications. Britons around the globe serving in the empire might feel abandoned or alienated. Thus Britain, Chamberlain asserted, had reached 'a critical and a turning point in the history of the Empire'. The empire must continue to grow 'great and glorious' unimpeded by the 'aggression of the Boers'.

Chamberlain's militant tone had been encouraged by Selborne. In a confidential letter to his chief a few days before the speech, Selborne urged Chamberlain to tell the country 'the whole truth' – that Kruger could not be trusted and that a supreme crisis now faced Britain in South Africa. The public must be informed that Britain had embarked upon a policy from which it could not retreat without 'disastrous consequences' and 'humiliation'. Indeed, retreat would be 'a permanent sign that the rising star in South Africa was Dutch & the setting [sun] British'.[63] The following day, during a nine-hour debate on South Africa in the House of Commons, Chamberlain returned to his theme. Britain, he said, had the right to protect its own subjects, whether at home or abroad; and it had special rights 'as suzerain Power' in the Transvaal to guarantee franchise reform for the Uitlanders. It was no petty reform, Chamberlain assured the House, but an issue touching upon 'the power and authority of the British Empire'.[64]

Chamberlain's public campaign against the Transvaal government continued into the late summer. Speaking from the grounds at Highbury in August to a ward meeting of the Birmingham Liberal Association, Chamberlain once again reviewed the iniquities of a rigid and archaic Transvaal government. Charging Kruger with unacceptable procrastination, he declared that the Boer president 'dribbles out reforms like water from a squeezed sponge'.[65] All Britain asked was common justice and reasonable reforms. The sands, he warned, were 'running down in the glass'. The government would not cease its demands until it had 'secured conditions which once and for all shall establish' Britain as 'the paramount Power in South Africa'.

Most discouraging to the Boers was the realization that Britain was determined to demand concessions without surrendering something in return.[66] To the Transvaal government, the negotiations were wholly one-sided and to their disadvantage. For the British, an acknowledged sovereignty over the Transvaal was its primary imperial aim – nothing less would satisfy. Chamberlain believed, in his persistent way, that by wearing down his opponents, he would succeed. Therefore, until very late in the negotiations, little planning for war had been undertaken: only a modest increase in British troops had been implemented by July 1899. Not until September were 10,000 additional troops sent to the Transvaal as a sign of British firmness.[67] Such a show of strength, Chamberlain thought, would surely force Kruger's government to capitulate to British demands. Instead, the Transvaal government – now united by what seemed the threat of an invasion far beyond the scope of the Jameson Raid – issued its own ultimatum on 10 October 1899. The following day, the Orange Free State joined with the Transvaal in its struggle for independence.

Chamberlain's responsibility for the origins of the Boer War has been much debated. Critics such as Drus, Marais, van der Poel, and Wilde believe that Chamberlain, having failed to accomplish his aims during the Jameson Raid, was determined to achieve them through war. In contrast, Andrew Porter takes exception to what he calls this 'Afrikaner' interpretation of Chamberlain as the 'the arch-villain' who, 'in a wholly disreputable plot', pursued 'a vigorous anti-Boer policy from the time he reached office'.[68] Porter argues further that Chamberlain, with the exception of some details of timing and emphasis, had the support of the cabinet in pursuing his South

African policies.[69] He never acted alone or secretively. Grenville very largely supports Porter in exculpating Chamberlain from 'starting' the war; nor, he maintains, did Chamberlain 'consistently plot for war'.[70]

Other historians have shifted the grounds of the debate by criticizing the notion of human agency as a major cause of the war. Marks and Trapido, for example, condemn an overemphasis upon the personalities and motivations of such actors as Chamberlain and Milner.[71] Perhaps influenced by J. A. Hobson's powerful denunciation of imperialism, they argue that imperial economic interests were at the heart of the war fever. Simply put, gold was the prize, not British political dominance over the Transvaal. Astute and conspiratorial mining magnates sought to create a modern state in the Transvaal with an efficient bureaucracy, an effective policy force, and a reputable judicial system. These essential conditions, combined with mechanisms to control and direct labour, would promote stability and guarantee an economic and political climate profitable to mine owners.

Marks and Trapido base their conclusions in part upon the work of Geoffrey Blainey who postulated that the 'deep mining' gold mining companies (as opposed to the shallower 'outcrop' mines nearer the surface) were the main instigators of political change in the Transvaal.[72] Deep mines had to be more heavily capitalized and their profits were endangered by Kruger's policies. For example, the dynamite monopoly held by the Transvaal government rendered explosives, so necessary to the deep mines, artificially expensive. Tariffs on imported foodstuffs and obstructive labour policies also depressed mining profits. Blainey clinched his argument by noting that two of the chief plotters of the Jameson Raid were members of deep mining companies – Rhodes was joint managing director of Consolidated Gold Fields of South Africa; and Alfred Beit, one of the richest of all South African millionaires, was a partner in Wernher, Beit and Co. In short, a strong case could be made that capitalist greed and drive for profit was significant in causing the South African War.[73]

There is little doubt that some economic context to the war must be considered. But human agency and the imperial factor also played roles. Important decision-makers such as Chamberlain, Milner, and Selborne, voicing the aspirations of an imperial culture, were strategically placed to have a significant impact upon events. Did they act to seize the gold and to protect imperial economic interests? To some extent, surely. But the evidence is overwhelming that their primary consideration was to enhance and consolidate the empire.[74] Selborne, in an important memo to his father-in-law, Salisbury, took note of the mineral wealth of the Transvaal, but not in crude material ways. He believed that the Transvaal was 'the key to the future of South Africa' as the richest and most populous part of that region: it might become 'the natural capital State and centre of South African commercial, social and political life'.[75] Such a union could even lead to the creation of a United States of Africa with the power to exclude Britain and the Empire.

Milner, too, in his copious correspondence rarely refers to the need for an expropriation of riches either for the benefit of British mine owners, or for the imperial government. Acting in proconsular fashion, he was determined to deny the aspirations of the Transvaal for an independent state.[76] To this task, he brought an autocratic temperament, a capacity for work, and an imperial vision matching Chamberlain's. Milner and Chamberlain acting together, one dominant in southern Africa, the other the master of metropolitan imperialism, cannot be ignored as the fundamental force that shaped British policy which ultimately led to war.[77]

Yet it must be said that Chamberlain neither initiated nor provoked war.[78] He thought of an armed force 'more as a means of keeping matters astir, as an intimidating factor in negotiating', rather an instrument for bringing on war.[79] This was consistent with his language and behaviour in other times of imperial crisis during his tenure as Colonial Secretary. He had no reason to think that his confrontational style, his pursuit of power and authority, and his insistence on having his own (and Britain's) way would not prove as successful in South Africa as it had on numerous earlier occasions. Against the French in West Africa, Portugal in southeast Africa, the Germans and Russians in the Far East, or the Americans in their own hemisphere, he had been largely victorious. Chamberlain made a fundamental miscalculation, however. If the British had forgotten about the Jameson Raid, Boers and their sympathizers had not. Shortly after the Raid, the alliance between Rhodes and the Afrikaner Bond – the political party of the Dutch in the Cape Colony – was broken, forcing Rhodes' resignation as premier.[80] Rising young Boers, such as Jan Smuts, found their sympathies increasingly with Kruger. Smuts, after a successful student career at Stellenbosch and Cambridge, settled in Cape Town in 1895. Two years later, after the Raid, he moved to the Transvaal where he was appointed State Attorney by Kruger. Smuts was dismayed by the limited investigations of the British parliamentary committee of inquiry following the Raid. He began seriously to question the general trend of Chamberlain's policy toward the Transvaal.[81] The views of another prominent South African is equally instructive. W. P. Schreiner was also educated at Cambridge and later the Inns of Court. He returned to the Cape Colony a confirmed moderate and believer in imperial federation. He was against the franchise restrictions imposed upon the Uitlanders in the Transvaal. He was additionally a friend and supporter of Rhodes. The Jameson Raid changed everything: he resigned his position as attorney general (Rhodes was then Cape premier) and began to view British aims and policies with an increasingly sceptical eye. During Chamberlain's series of speeches critical of Kruger in the summer of 1899, Schreiner wrote to his friend John Edward Ellis, a Liberal MP who became a notable British 'pro-Boer'. 'Can it be', he asked, 'that no ... settlement is desired?' Chamberlain's speeches rendered any peaceful accommodation difficult between Britain and Boer. Chamberlain's main error lay in assuming that Kruger, if pressed hard enough, 'will yield *everything*'. To Schreiner, Chamberlain gave the impression of simply picking quarrels, and thus causing a reaction against any concession on the part of Kruger.[82]

Distrust and doubt bred suspicion and fear. It was widely believed that the Jameson Raid was merely a foretaste of what was to come: Britain would strike again. Britain's continued demands for internal reform were thus viewed as mere pretexts for turning the screws upon the Transvaal government, and upon its supporters in the Cape Colony. For the Boers, war with Britain would primarily be defensive, designed to hurl back British imperial ambitions. To prepare itself against overt aggression, the

Transvaal from 1896 onward devoted more than a third of its annual budgets to defence expenditures. Purchases included thousands of the latest model rifles and howitzers from the German firm of Krupps; Creusot heavy guns from France; and from Britain, the newest Maxim-Nordenfeld quick-firing field guns. Substantial stores of shell and rifle ammunition filled Transvaal arsenals. To operate their new equipment effectively, Boer artillery officers were either sent abroad for training in Germany and the Netherlands or in some cases schooled by German gunners in the Transvaal itself.

By the autumn of 1899, the Boers were well prepared for any eventuality. When diplomatic efforts failed, they chose to initiate a pre-emptive strike which would create a buffer between them and the Cape Colony. On 12 October 1899, a Boer patrol sabotaged a railway line near Mafeking, Bechuanaland, and then shelled a stalled British armoured train from a distance of some 700 yards. Within 48 hours, a Boer force of eight to nine thousand had surrounded Mafeking and its British garrison of about a thousand men. A few days later, 300 miles to the east, the Boers invaded the British colony of Natal and threatened Ladysmith, headquarters of the main British force in South Africa. Again, effective Boer artillery, operating in conjunction with accurate rifle fire, boxed in the British. The third tactical investment by the Boer offensive occurred at Kimberley, which lay between Mafeking and Ladysmith, but much further south in the Orange Free State. It, too, was soon besieged by well-coordinated and fast-moving Boer troops. Within the next few weeks, commandos had invaded the northern fringes of the Cape Colony, annexing the occupied districts into the Boer republics. Well-equipped, operating along protected interior lines in defence of their homeland, and possessing unrivalled familiarity with a difficult terrain, confident and resolute Transvaal commandos swept all before them.

British troops were unable to gain a footing in the months that followed. Poor planning, sloppy intelligence, and half-hearted reconnaissance in the field merely exacerbated problems of an indifferent military leadership. Bewildered officers and men were lost by the hundreds at the three pitched battles of Stormberg, Magersfontein, and Colenso, all fought within a few days of each other in December 1899. Known collectively in Britain as 'Black Week', these military engagements, added to the ongoing sieges of British forces, were a shock to the British public. No less dismayed were the government's ministers, Chamberlain chief among them. Stunned by the initial losses in October, he confessed to be 'broken in spirit' after Black Week.[83]

But Chamberlain's depressed mood was brief: he quickly recovered to become the government's chief spokesman in rousing a martial spirit in the country. Even before Black Week, he had taken the lead in unequivocally setting out Britain's war aims. The object of the war, as he told the House of Commons, was 'to maintain our existence as a great power in South Africa' and more specifically, 'to remain the paramount power'.[84] For nearly two decades, he charged, the Boer republics had 'persistently, by imperceptible steps' attempted 'to oust the Queen from her suzerainty, to throw off the last trace of subordination': now they had taken off the mask and shown what their object had been all along – 'to be a sovereign independent state'.[85] Denying that it was a war of greed and rapacity to secure gold and territory from a weaker state, he reiterated the necessity of fighting for justice for the Uitlanders and for good government against a tyrannical oligarchy. In addition, it was the duty of imperial powers and the burden of civilized societies to pursue the work of 'the general progress and advancement of mankind', even though this might result in war. Britain need not shrink from war for such good causes: indeed, it was to war that the nation owed 'its position in the world, its security, and its liberty'.[86]

In spite of Chamberlain's fighting words, the government continued to lose ground in South Africa. This provided an opportunity for the Liberal opposition to begin a critical campaign against the government's record. On 5 February 1900, the Liberals moved an amendment to the Address condemning the government for its mishandling of the war. Chamberlain's response ushered in a new phase of political conflict. Admitting that the government had made mistakes and that the war was at 'a critical stage', he deprecated 'those who gloat over the misfortunes of the country'.[87]

Chamberlain's attacks upon the Liberal opposition grew more heated in the following months. At a meeting of the grand committee of the Birmingham Liberal Unionist Association in May, Chamberlain criticized the leader of the Liberal opposition, Sir Henry Campbell-Bannerman, by name. Questioning Campbell-Bannerman's patriotism, Chamberlain suggested that he had encouraged Kruger to resist the demands 'of her Majesty's Government'.[88] Developing the theme of a disloyal opposition, Chamberlain sought to associate the Liberal policy of Irish Home Rule with their criticisms of the war. Speaking to a Conservative meeting in London in June 1900, Chamberlain condemned the Liberals as the anti-imperial party. Those who would have granted Home Rule to Ireland, he said, were the very men 'who did their utmost to prevent the expansion of the Empire'. Those who would have betrayed their fellow loyal subjects of the Crown in Ulster were now ready to desert the Uitlanders in the Transvaal. In contrast to the Liberals, Chamberlain declared, the Unionists had fought 'shoulder to shoulder against the forces of dissension and disorder'.[89]

The Unionist political strategy against the Liberals, spearheaded by Chamberlain, was a calculated risk. To skewer the Liberals as wrong-headed, meek-minded, even disloyal might very well produce results, but only if the war could be won. Should the war go badly, Liberal faultfinding would be vindicated. As it happened, Britain slowly gained the upper hand against the Boers. The sluggish and unlucky General Sir Redvers Buller was replaced by the more energetic Field Marshal Lord Roberts as Commander-in-Chief in South Africa, along with the innovative Lord Kitchener as his Chief of Staff. Improved military leadership was matched by the increasing experience of troops in the field. Perhaps most importantly, the massive influx of men and matériel began to tell. By the end of February, both Kimberley and Ladysmith had been relieved. Mafeking was rescued in mid-May, after 217 days of siege. Three weeks later Johannesburg was taken and the British entered Pretoria, the capital of the Transvaal. The conflict in South Africa seemed nearly over. To his wife, Mary, Chamberlain wrote in late summer that the war was 'dribbling out'.[90] On 1 September both the Transvaal and the Orange Free State were annexed to the British

Empire. Within a fortnight Kruger had left the Transvaal, travelling to Delagoa Bay where he boarded a cruiser supplied by the sympathetic Dutch. He died an exile in Switzerland in 1904.

Victories in the field for the Unionists had the gratifying effect of disarming their domestic foes as well. The war had fractured the Liberals. By the summer, they had devolved into three recognizable factions: the 'Little Englanders' who opposed the war; Liberal imperialists who supported the war; and a middle group who found some merit in each of the two other factions. 'A pretty kettle of fish!' was Kimberley's appalled judgement.[91] The truth was that many Liberals of every stripe had some sympathy with the imperial ideal long before the war. Liberals also recognized the force of a popular imperialism among the electorate at large. Thus it was difficult for them to find a position from which to criticize Chamberlain's imperial policies. Campbell-Bannerman's pre-war speech before the National Liberal Federation at Hull in March 1899 is illustrative. Liberals were not afraid of the responsibilities of empire, he assured his audience. But Liberals had always opposed 'the vulgar and bastard imperialism of irritation and provocation and aggression'.[92] Power in the service of empire, Campbell-Bannerman concluded, could only be justified in the service of moral ends.

Of course, Chamberlain could easily respond that upholding the rights of British citizens abroad was indeed not only an imperial responsibility, it was also a moral imperative. The Uitlanders, under Kruger's tyrannical regime, must be protected. Once the war was under way, the moral issue could be subsumed under patriotic fervour. Patriotism plus morality was a forceful component of popular imperialism. But patriotism languished in the face of initial British losses. Only after the despair of Black Week had passed and been replaced by British success at arms could an effective appeal be made to the electorate. An opportunity came after the lifting of the siege at Mafeking in May 1900. Chamberlain – seconded by Balfour – urged an election as soon as possible in order to capitalize on the victory. Salisbury, more cautious, delayed until autumn in the hope of even better news from South Africa.[93] Parliament was therefore not dissolved until 25 September with elections following soon after.

The election battle presented a scenario tailor-made for Chamberlain. With relish, he went on the attack. No other government minister was as active as he. The 'sledge-hammer work'[94] of his speeches began in his own constituency of West Birmingham. Speaking from a makeshift platform erected in the playground of the Camden Street Board Schools to a crowd of two to three thousand, Chamberlain made much of Liberal divisions. Liberals were, he said, 'a party of shreds and patches'.[95] Indeed, he thought the Liberals were scarcely a party at all, but rather 'a conglomerate mixture', a 'congeries of disconnected and antagonistic atoms'. More seriously, he condemned the Liberal 'Little Englanders' for communicating with the enemy. They had encouraged the intransigence of Kruger. It was proof, Chamberlain claimed, that the Liberals lacked a constructive policy in an imperial age: they only knew the 'policy of scuttle'.

Two days later Chamberlain spoke outside his Duchy at Oldham in support of Winston Churchill, the son of his old ally, Lord Randolph. Newly returned from

South Africa, young Churchill had pled with Chamberlain to speak on his behalf.[96] When Chamberlain arrived at the Empire Theatre, he found a crowd of 4,000 listening to a band playing patriotic airs. In his speech he again charged the opposition with encouraging the enemy. During negotiations, some members of the Liberal opposition had told Kruger to 'stand firm' and he "'would give Master Joe another fall"'.[97] Nothing, said Chamberlain, could have been more unpatriotic: those who acted thus were as culpable as Kruger in initiating the war. Campaigning two days later in the pottery town of Tunstall, Chamberlain elaborated on his charge that the Liberals had acted in collusion with the Boers. He urged his audience to heed the advice of the mayor of Mafeking, who reputedly declared 'every seat lost to the Government was a seat gained by the Boers'.[98] The following day, campaigning at Bilston for the Unionist candidate for South Wolverhampton, Chamberlain strongly implied that some Liberals had written 'disgraceful and discreditable', even possibly treasonous, letters to Boer leaders.[99] In other speeches at Stourbridge (for Mid-Worcestershire), Coventry, Warwick and Leamington, Burton-on-Trent (Staffordshire); and the Cannock Chase Colliery Company in the Litchfield division of Staffordshire, Chamberlain's message was the same.

Once the campaign had concluded, however, Chamberlain's message and mood shifted to a more uplifting, almost spiritual exhortation as he extolled the benefits of the empire and the need for its preservation. In a post-election address to the Fishmonger's Company in London, he claimed that the empire had been 'born anew'.[100] It was now an empire of 400 millions, comprising 'almost every race under the sun'. These varied peoples had become, Chamberlain claimed, 'one family'. It was bound together by mutual sentiment, common ideals, and noble aspirations. It was an altruistic empire, having brought 'freedom and justice and civilisation and peace' to all its 'dependent races'. In the future, he believed, even 'more progress will be made'. To Canada and Australia could now be added all of southern Africa. It was, he said, 'a foreshadowing of that greater federation … of kindred nations' which would strengthen the empire and 'in the good providence of God, the empire will fulfil its mission'.

However elevating Chamberlain's imperial message may have occasionally sounded, his Liberal opponents remembered most his relentless and distinctly negative campaign. If the Liberals were often divided by the war, they were united in their detestation of Chamberlain. In a letter to Morley, Harcourt recalled Chamberlain's temper and bullying nature: 'He showed it before in his violence in 1880 and 1885 and again in 1892.'[101] The Liberal imperialist Herbert Asquith denounced Chamberlain's role in the election as a 'fit of vulgar debauch' and thought he had 'the manners of a cad and the tongue of a bargee'.[102] Kimberley doubtless spoke for many centrist Liberals in his belief that Chamberlain 'outdid himself in violence & unfair statements'.[103]

Chamberlain's patriotic and imperial themes vigorously pursued in the countryside and his characteristic dynamic platform performances had much to do with the success of the so-called 'khaki' election.[104] Conservatives won 334 seats; Liberal Unionists, 68; Liberals, only 184; and Irish Nationalists, 82. The overall majority for the combined Unionists was 136 – not as large as in 1895, but a substantial win nevertheless. It was also notable in that it was the third Conservative and Unionist victory in the previous four general elections.

It is, however, important to remember that the general election of 1900 was the climax of a much longer campaign against the Boer republics. A latent popular imperialism, Chamberlain knew, could be goaded into a patriotic war only if roused by effective propaganda. The diplomatic pressures against Kruger, widely publicized during 1898 and throughout 1899 by Chamberlain, Milner, and others was an important first step. Once the war was under way, pro-war pressure groups complemented the work by the Unionist leadership. Among these groups, the Imperial South African Association, founded in 1896, was the most active. It published pamphlets, supplied speakers to working men's clubs, raised a special fund for the election of 1900, and campaigned against pro-Boer candidates[105]. Some of the most influential newspapers of the day also supported the war, such as the *Daily Mail* and *The Times*.[106] So fervently did *The Times* support the war, especially in its attacks upon pro-Boers as unpatriotic, it gave rise to suspicions that the newspaper was in league with the Colonial Office. The pulpit, too, was used to promote the war. Church and Chapel invoked both the sanctity and the wrath of God on the side of Englishmen.[107] With such allies supporting Chamberlain and the war, and with public opinion in general taking on 'a moderately khaki colour',[108] it was not surprising that Campbell-Bannerman was in despair at the election result. 'I confess', he wrote to Ripon in October 1900, 'that the thing which concerns me most is to find that Chamberlainism *pays* with our countrymen. They worship a forcible man, and a clever man, and if his methods are vulgar, dishonourable, unfair, they only smile and approve.'[109]

Not long after the election however, it was evident that the Unionist government's optimistic pronouncements about an imminent victory were premature. Peace negotiations in South Africa had faltered and eventually failed. It was soon clear that if one war were over – the conventional war of opposing massed troops – another war, equally deadly, of guerrilla tactics was about to begin. Several thousand Boer commandos – now divided into small raiding and reconnaissance parties – continued to attack trains, cut telegraph lines, and bombard British posts. On occasion, they briefly occupied outlying towns, and when possible, struck at British encampments.[110] More seriously, regrouped Boer commandos, several hundred strong, from time to time staged concerted attacks upon unsuspecting British forces in a return to the conventional tactics of the first stage of the war. Resourceful as ever, the Boers were once again confounding British military thinkers.

As the war dragged on into 1901, British tactics gradually altered to meet changed circumstances. Chamberlain himself played an active policy role in the guerrilla phase of the war. His suggestions included the creation of a mobile armed elite corps of troops and using Boer prisoners as hostages in trains travelling through dangerous districts.[111] The main military objective, however, was to limit Boer mobility and to deny them protective cover. Under the leadership of General Kitchener, the size and scope of the intelligence service was greatly expanded so that efficient espionage could warn of impending Boer plans. In addition, thousands of small blockhouses laid out on a fixed grid pattern were built to increase surveillance. Connected by barbed wire and linked by an effective communications system, the blockhouses also served as barriers toward which Boer detachments could be driven by brigade-sized British flying columns in hot pursuit.[112] These purely military operations complemented a scorched earth policy which had been implemented as early as March 1900. Stripping Boer homesteads of food, burning their crops, and firing their buildings became common practices of British troops. A logical extension of this policy was to provide some accommodation and shelter for the wives and children of Boer commandos. Thus were initiated the 'concentration' camps, notorious in the latter phases of the war. Designed to resettle the population and to remove the territory of civilians, crops, and livestock, this was the final piece to the interlocking plan (the Kitchener 'chain of attrition', as Nasson puts it)[113] to force the surrender of Boer insurgents.

The concentration camps in time contained more than 100,000 inmates, both black and white. Crowded conditions and poorly maintained sanitary facilities led to successive epidemics of measles, dysentery, pneumonia, and whooping cough. Death rates were extraordinarily high, especially among children, reaching 344 per 1,000 in the latter months of 1901. The scandal created by the camps redounded against the government. The Liberals realized their opportunity. On 14 June 1901, Campbell-Bannerman gave a major address before the National Reform Union. In it, he castigated those who were responsible for 'this terrible war' and accused the government of pursuing an 'insane policy of subjugation and obliteration' against the innocent. Prudence and justice had been abandoned: the war was being carried on 'by methods of barbarism in South Africa'.[114]

During a lengthy debate in the House of Commons on 2 August 1901,[115] Campbell-Bannerman repeated his attack upon the government's policy of 'devastation' in South Africa. He was joined by a host of other anti-war speakers, including the young firebrand from Wales, David Lloyd George; the radical Henry Labouchere, MP for Northampton; and several Irish Nationalists. The length of the war with no end in sight and its escalating cost were the common refrain. Chamberlain was forced into a defensive response. Condemning Boer guerrilla warfare as 'a stage of brigandage and outrage', he justified firm measures. He claimed that farm burning had been 'entirely abandoned as a general policy'; but he also admitted continuing isolated cases came to the government's attention. He admitted, too, 'a lamentable mortality' in the concentration camps. But he maintained that the camps were intended as a 'humane' policy – to protect innocent civilians in a war zone.[116]

Liberals now had a focus for their attacks on the government's war policy. In the latter months of 1901, their public speeches in and out of parliament, letters to the editor of important newspapers, town meetings, and reinvigoration of 'pro-Boer' pressure groups all testified to a quickening of Liberal political fortunes.[117] The country as a whole also seemed wearied by the conflict. But at last overwhelming British resources eventually wore down Boer resistance. At Vereeniging, on the Transvaal–Orange Free State border, a treaty was signed on 31 May 1902. The two republics lost their independence but the Boers themselves gained a general amnesty. The treaty also granted significant financial benefits, including economic aid and renewal and reconstruction relief for war victims.

Although there appears to have been widespread relief in Britain at the conclusion of this long and costly war, there is little doubt that Chamberlain's reputation remained high, especially among his imperial supporters. Typical was Henry Birchenough's tribute in *The Nineteenth Century*.[118] During the past several years, Birchenough claimed, there had emerged 'one great idea and one striking personality, the idea of a united Empire and the personality of Mr. Chamberlain'. Of all Englishmen, Chamberlain alone 'had both the will and the power' as well as the office to further British imperial aims. Such a man, Birchenough hinted, whose 'quickening spirit pulsates through every branch of national life with vitalizing power', would guarantee an 'infusion of fresh vigour into every state department' should he ever become prime minister. The admiring Amery sums it up: Chamberlain had displayed during the war a 'tactical genius and relentless determination' as well as 'firm yet conciliatory leadership'.[119]

Secured by a flood of support and good will, Chamberlain decided to consolidate public opinion behind his imperial mission. In November 1902, he set out on a lengthy tour of South Africa. It was almost a royal procession: the colonial monarch viewing his possessions.[120] Indeed, he was given a majestic send-off – a grand banquet at the Birmingham Town Hall, followed by a parade through the city to the cheers of many thousands, escorted by the Warwickshire Imperial Yeomanry, and the whole route illuminated by 4,000 torch bearers. Within a week, Chamberlain and his wife (accompanied by three aides) were at London's Victoria station where they were greeted by a host of dignitaries, including Balfour, who was now prime minister, Field Marshal Roberts, and half the cabinet. Boarding the royal train to Portsmouth, Chamberlain and his party embarked on HMS *Good Hope*, one of the newest cruisers making her maiden voyage.[121]

The initial leg of the trip was notable for its encounter with a violent storm as the ship approached the Bay of Biscay. Even the naval officers became ill with the tossing of the ship: only six of twenty appeared at dinner. But, we are told, Chamberlain never turned a hair, staying up late into the evening, sitting aft in the Admiral's cabin, smoking his long black cigars.[122] The remainder of the journey at sea was uneventful. Following a direct course to South Africa, the ship made several important side-trips. First touching at Port Said, the party proceeded by train on to Cairo, where Chamberlain had last been in 1890. Three days later, they were on their way through the Red Sea and into the Indian Ocean. Within a week, the *Good Hope* docked at Mombasa, the main port of the East African Protectorates. From there, a train took Chamberlain and his party inland to Nairobi. Returning to Mombasa and detouring briefly at Zanzibar, the ship reached Durban on Christmas Day 1902. By sailing from Egypt, down the eastern coast of Africa, and disembarking in Natal, Chamberlain had symbolically underscored British power from Cairo to the Cape. The intended message was clear: war had not weakened Britain; it had added to its imperial strength.

In the next two months, Chamberlain travelled from Durban to Ladysmith in Natal to Johannesburg and Pretoria in the Transvaal, passing through Mafeking in Bechuanaland on his way to Kimberley in the Orange Free State – cities and towns which only months before had been flashpoints of the war. Nor did he neglect back-veldt country towns, often travelling by wagon on untracked paths, sometimes lingering over the relic-strewn and still littered battlefields. His days were filled with the daily dispatches, telegrams, and office memos that made up the usual work of a Colonial Secretary. But he was also adding substantially to his professional duties by the burdens imposed on his official tour – granting interviews, greeting deputations, attending dinner parties, and making speeches before legislative bodies throughout South Africa. His aims were to implement the peace under an aura of reconciliation and to bring together defeated provinces within a federated South Africa. Chamberlain was firm and direct in all his pronouncements. He demanded complete acceptance of the peace treaty, an effective representative political system, a working partnership with the imperial government, and loyalty above all. His words were not always welcome. Jan Smuts reported that Chamberlain rarely met with Boer leaders: when he did so, he was insulting and unresponsive.[123]

Chamberlain had little time for introspection on his journey; but his wife, Mary, serving as a kind of reflective amanuensis, wrote letters home to her mother recording her impressions.[124] Everywhere, she wrote, there was a friendly welcome from Boer and British alike: 'it is an expression', she wrote, 'of the deep sense of Imperialism which has become so well rooted during these last years'. This was, she thought (in a loyal echo of her husband), 'a most encouraging sign for the future unity of the British Empire'. Only occasionally did she notice that some farmers 'seemed a little glum'. She was more taken with the bag of uncut diamonds given her at the Kimberley mines. At Mafeking, she comments, with a striking lack of recognition of the implications of the imperial gaze, that she saw a group of Mashona boys, 'quaint little black figures in white shirts and blue cloths, holding Union Jacks'.[125]

The final leg of the overland journey was an extensive trek through the Cape Colony concluding at Cape Town, from which Chamberlain departed on 25 February 1903, sailing for home on the Union-Castle liner *Norman*. Within three weeks, Chamberlain arrived in Southampton to be met by an official reception held in recognition not only of his imperial influence but also of his popularity as a politician in the country at large. Flags and banners (one of which bore the legend 'Southampton welcomes home Britain's Imperial Statesman') greeted him at Ocean Quay. He was also met by a large crowd and an address from the mayor of Southampton, who praised Chamberlain for his 'untiring devotion to the welfare of the Empire' and for his 'welding together in one indissoluble whole' Great Britain and her colonies.[126] Further ceremonies accompanied his arrival at Waterloo Station in London. Prime minister Balfour, numerous MPs, colonial representatives such as Lord Strathcona, High Commissioner for Canada, and various other business and political figures were on hand. The Chamberlains' arrival at Prince's Gardens a short time later concluded their odyssey. They had been gone nearly four months.

Chamberlain's South African tour was unique. There was no precedent for a minister of the crown making such a journey on the soil of a defeated enemy. Chamberlain had brought to South Africa his career-long experiences of appealing to a mass electorate. Nothing could better prove his undiminished appetite for political influence, his dominating energy, his drive for power, and his capacity for forming public opinion than this arduous journey of over 16,000 miles taken in his 66th year. It was, as well, a portentous voyage. His success in South Africa would influence his decision within a few months to take a fateful step in British political history that would reshape party politics for years to come.

12

TARIFF REFORM

The Final Struggle for Power

Chamberlain's triumphant return from South Africa could not mask the costs of the South African War. The size and scale of its operations and the extent of British losses paralleled those of the Crimean War half a century earlier.[1] Nearly 450,000 troops had been put into the field; of these 22,000 had perished including those who died of disease and illness. Of the approximately 70,000 Boer troops, over 7,000 died. Twenty-eight thousand South African civilians (mostly women and children) had perished in concentration camps. Lives lost were matched by treasure spent: some £217,000,000 were needed to fight the war.

Equally significant were the intangible costs of war. Military priorities caused inevitable delays in such projects as educational and social reforms. The most notable wartime casualty on the home front during the war was in fact Chamberlain's enthusiasm for reform. The fate of his long-delayed plan for old-age pensions may serve as an instructive example. Well before the war, when he was out of office during Salisbury's second administration, Chamberlain had publicly advocated a startling and novel proposal – that the state should assume some responsibility for its aged poor.[2] In speeches during the early 1890s he had deplored the conditions by which 'the masses of the people' had not received 'their fair and full share' of the nation's wealth, reminding the country that the only relief available to elderly paupers was under the degrading system of the poor laws.[3] He recommended that the government permit post offices to open accounts 'for the purpose of superannuation'. These accounts would be voluntary individual contributions, the safety and security of which would be guaranteed by the government. By 1895, he was proposing a partnership between the state and private Friendly Societies to bring the scheme to fruition. Each would share in creating a fund that would grant a pension of 5 shillings for those over 65. For Chamberlain, it was more than a matter of social justice. He warned that unless the elderly poor were helped, there could arise from the working classes an agitation that would prove 'a danger to social order'.[4]

Popular interest in old-age pensions began to appear among the electorate during the Boer War. In the Khaki Election of 1900, pensions became a dominant issue in Chamberlain's own duchy. East Birmingham, a constituency dominated by employees in heavy industry (such as the city gasworks and the Metropolitan Carriage Company, makers of railway rolling-stock) actively supported such a plan.[5] J. V. Stevens – a Gladstonian Liberal, city councillor, and secretary of the Amalgamated Tin Workers – made a strong showing on a platform supporting non-contributory pensions.[6] Chamberlain's influence eventually carried the day in East Birmingham when the Unionist candidate won the election. But the emergence of Stevens as a working-class candidate advocating working-class legislation could be a portent, as Chamberlain well understood.

To co-opt a possible self-initiated working-class social programme, Chamberlain invited interested parties (among them friendly societies and trade unions) to put forward a viable old-age pension scheme. In response, a meeting of the Trade Union and Co-operative Congress in January 1902 enthusiastically adopted a resolution favouring non-contributory pensions of 5 shillings a week for every citizen over the age of 60. Chamberlain was taken aback. A non-contributory pension scheme could throw the expense of the plan completely onto the shoulders of employers or burden the state with fiscal demands. He condemned the proposal outright.

Chamberlain's retreat from pensions was no doubt prompted in part by the realization that his conservative Unionist allies would never favour such a plan. But it is also apparent that Chamberlain, while encouraging working-class organizations to come forward with a pension plan in the waning days of the Boer War, was simultaneously attempting to convince the Chancellor of the Exchequer, Hicks Beach, to maintain high levels of military expenditure. He argued that British failures during the early stages of the war had left 'an uneasy feeling' that the country had been unprepared. He believed that military expenditures, in order to meet future defence needs, should not be reduced unduly.[7] It would seem, then, that Chamberlain was willing to entertain a contributory pension scheme but less willing to consider a non-contributory plan, largely because of retrenchments necessary in the social sector to provide funds for pressing military costs.[8] Imperial issues, not domestic reforms, were now his first priority.

There are other signs that Chamberlain's support for social legislation weakened in the final years of his political career. This was particularly noticeable during the lengthy struggle over educational reform. The last comprehensive reform of primary schools had been Gladstone's Education Act of 1870. In that act, a compromise had been struck to allow a dual system of denominational, or voluntary, schools to exist alongside the newly created secular schools created by the new School Boards. Since then, conflict between voluntary schools and Board schools continued unabated.[9] Voluntary schools, however, gradually lost ground to the better financed Board schools. Alarmed at this trend, the Unionist-leaning Church of England requested financial aid from the government. In response, supplementary funds were provided by parliament in 1897 to rescue the declining voluntary system. Thereafter, the Conservative government found itself contributing piecemeal to educational needs, whether voluntary or Board. Grants to necessitous schools, pensions for teachers, and the creation of a new Board of Education were all examples of increasing governmental involvement.[10] Such an ostensibly even-handed approach did not, however, ease traditional fears among nonconformists concerning secular funding of religious education. From their point of view, the use of public monies to support Anglican and Catholic schools was an abomination.

One would have expected Chamberlain to play an active part in the controversy, given his nonconformist position during the education debates of the late 1860s and early 1870s. But it is clear that political exigencies had shifted his views. In a letter to R. W. Dale in 1891, he admitted that he could no longer address 'specifically nonconformist questions' because nonconformists had continued to support Home Rule in opposition to Unionist policy. He denounced nonconformists as 'more fanatical, more bitter, more selfish & more unscrupulous than I have ever known the champions of the Church to be'. As he put it to George Titterton, a local Birmingham supporter, education issues had too often become lost 'in purely partisan disputes'.[11] Besides, he had been persuaded that something had to be done to 'save the Voluntary Schools from extinction'; otherwise, more than half the primary student population would be without schools. Unmentioned to either Dale or Titterton was the equally obvious reason that, as a prominent member of the Unionist Alliance, he had no wish to offend Anglican sensibilities.

The looming contest between Church and nonconformity over education came to a head in 1901–2, just as the Boer War was winding down. Temporary and ad hoc supplementary funding for denominational schools was nearing its end, and once again the question of declining standards in the voluntary schools became salient. The government, now led by Balfour since Salisbury's resignation in July 1902, was determined to deal comprehensively with the problem.[12] Only by granting rate aid to voluntary schools could a sound bill be devised. Chamberlain, as the leading Liberal Unionist in the coalition government, was placed in an awkward position. Unwilling to jeopardize his standing with the Conservative wing of the Unionist Alliance, he could hardly oppose such an important governmental social programme. Yet his support for the education bill could bring upon him, above all other government ministers, considerable obloquy from the powerful nonconformist pressure groups. Adverse electoral consequences were sure to follow.[13]

Chamberlain's tactic was to adopt a low profile in public, and in private to assume the role of a cabinet Cassandra. He repeatedly warned that any attempt to favour denominational schools would not only inflame the Liberal opposition but would also alienate the government's Liberal Unionist allies. This had some effect, as Balfour initially trod cautiously. A compromise measure was drafted and given a second reading by the House of Commons. It would abolish Board schools and create new local education authorities. It would also allow the new authorities to make grants to voluntary schools if an agreement could be struck with the managers of local voluntary/denominational schools. This 'local option' clause satisfied nonconformist demands for some measure of control over voluntary schools.

During the committee stage of the Bill in the summer of 1902, however, strong Anglican supporters within the Conservative Party rallied. The 'local option' was dropped from the Bill, making rate aid for voluntary schools mandatory. Another amendment decreased the statutory control that local authorities might exert over voluntary schools. An outcry from nonconformist Liberals had an immediate electoral impact at the North Leeds by-election on 30 July when a substantial Conservative majority was overturned by a radical Baptist who had fought the election entirely on the education issue.[14] In chapel-going Wales, where the Act was regarded as 'the legislative incarnation of the Antichrist',[15] public opinion was especially roused. Balfour was savaged, as his private secretary noted, by 'the Hot Gospellers of every Chapel of bellicose Nonconformity'.[16] Austen Chamberlain had a firsthand indication of nonconformist sentiment that summer while touring the Scottish islands on the royal yacht. After a landfall to see the Ramsay sheep dog trials, he was travelling behind King Edward's carriage when he heard someone cry out: 'God save the King & down with the Education Bill!'[17] Nonconformists were stirring far and wide.

As the nonconformist tide of opposition rose, Chamberlain sounded a new series of warnings to his ministerial colleagues. To Balfour, he predicted 'certain political destruction' for the Unionist Party.[18] 'Our best friends', he informed Devonshire, 'are leaving us by scores and hundreds and they will not come back.'[19] 'Why could we not "let it alone"', Chamberlain wrote despairingly to Brodrick, 'and leave the reform of primary education to our successors?'[20] Chamberlain's premonitions were borne out when the Liberals took up the nonconformist cause with gusto. Harcourt reminded the House of Commons that Chamberlain had been in the forefront of the nonconformist educational programme when he had first entered parliament, but had now turned against it. Harcourt also charged the government with crafting a bill designed to further the interests of the Church of England.[21] Harcourt's criticisms in the Commons were seconded by Earl Spencer, who, as leader of the opposition in the Lords, actively campaigned against 'the miserable Education Bill'.[22]

The strength of nonconformist feeling soon threatened Chamberlain himself. A conference of the Birmingham Liberal Unionist Association held in late September 1902 strongly condemned the proposed Bill. Chamberlain's worst fears were about to be realized. If he could not hold his own constituents, the Unionist Alliance itself might be endangered. At Highbury, he immediately called an emergency session of the Association. His address and the subsequent discussion seems to have quelled the revolt, especially after his admonition that should the government be defeated on its education bill, a new government of Home Rulers, pro-Boers, and Little Englanders would have ruinous consequences for Britain's foreign and colonial policy.[23]

Out of the swirl of controversy, a Bill eventually emerged. Overall, the Bill attempted to rationalize the educational system by abolishing the popularly elected School Boards and replacing them with a local educational authority, essentially a committee of the county or county borough council. This had the advantage of removing the contentious electioneering during School Board elections, which had continually inflamed sectarian disputes over education. This structural change also had the effect of removing school policy from the direct control of the electors in each community. In short, efficiency and an orderly administrative approach were bought at the expense of a democratic management of schools.[24]

In spite of his ambivalent feelings about the Education Act, Chamberlain's interest in educational reform remained firm. Even during his busiest days as Colonial Secretary, he was fully engaged with an educational project of his own – the establishment of a university in Birmingham. It was, as Marsh notes, not only a logical outcome of his past municipal and regional endeavours in promoting the social progress and enhancing the prestige of the city and the surrounding Midlands: it was also perhaps the finest of all his achievements.[25] The new institution would become the first civic university in England. Building upon Mason College, an existing local technical college, Chamberlain (who was a member of its Council) extended the range and scope of the college's narrow curriculum to include the humanities and a faculty of commerce. In addition, the new institution focused on applied science to benefit local industry and engage in important original research. Chamberlain particularly wanted to train what he called the 'captains of industry' – those who served in middle managerial and technical positions.

Chamberlain involved himself in all aspects of the University's early years. Securing the University charter, setting the curriculum, hiring its principal officers, and stating its mission were among his most important contributions. In typical fashion, Chamberlain staffed important positions with his acquaintances and kinsmen. The vice-chancellor, university treasurer, and chair of the University Building Committee, as well as some Council positions (the Council was the main governing body of the University) all went to relatives and political allies. Chamberlain was not motivated, however, purely by nepotistic considerations. His political prominence and national influence had a direct benefit to the University. As Chancellor, for example, Chamberlain was instrumental in appointing Sir Edward Elgar as professor of music in 1905. Perhaps Chamberlain's most remarkable contribution to the University was his leadership in the initial capital campaign. Beginning in mid-1898, Chamberlain personally solicited from friends and relations, industrialists and businessmen, and great philanthropists such as David Smith (created Lord Strathcona), builder of the Canadian Pacific Railway, and Andrew Carnegie, the Scot who became an American steel magnate. Within a short time, Chamberlain had raised a substantial £300,000 and persuaded Lord Calthorpe to donate 25 acres of his land in Edgbaston on which to build the university campus.

Less necessary to the construction of the University, but wholly characteristic of Chamberlain, was his insistence upon the erection of a university tower on the University grounds, modelled after the campanile at Siena, the Torre del Mangia on the Piazza del Campo, which he had once seen while on holiday in Italy. Fellow members of the University Council were not enthusiastic, primarily because the proposed tower had no obvious function apart from its support of a four-faced clock at a great height. Unkind critics thought it resembled an ornate chimneystack. Chamberlain, nevertheless, won the battle of the tower and it stands today as an honourable symbol of a great university.[26]

Of Chamberlain's mixed record on social and educational issues during the Boer War era, little more need be said. It appears that Chamberlain lost his reformist voice for a time. His crusading energy for economic and social advances for the many seemed stalled in the service of an imperial and military goal. Yet in the final years of his tumultuous career Chamberlain found an ingenious way to link the global goals of an imperial culture with a domestic reform agenda. In this, his last and most celebrated campaign, Chamberlain revealed all his superior political skills of organization and propaganda as well as his equally compelling tendency to disturb and to sow dissent. Engaging and energizing the electorate, Chamberlain was also divisive and polarizing, ultimately dividing the Unionists – just as he had divided the Liberals in the 1880s.

The beginning of Chamberlain's final campaign was misleadingly prosaic. He proposed a substantial revision of Britain's traditional schedule of tariffs. This was first announced publicly on 15 May 1903 with a speech to his Birmingham constituents, two months after his return from South Africa. Speaking in the town hall, Chamberlain made much of the 'new nation' that was emerging from the rubble of war in South Africa.[27] In spite of the great differences among the peoples of South Africa, Chamberlain believed that South Africa could nevertheless become a model for the empire as a whole – an empire that could 'stand together, one free nation, if necessary, against all the world'. Britain and the empire were at an important juncture in their history, Chamberlain declared. There was already in place an empire of sentiment; but it must be strengthened by the material ties of trade and commerce. In creating a 'community of interest', imperial union could be set on a firm foundation. The most important initial step was to establish a system of reciprocal preferential tariffs, by which both mother country and colonies offered mutual tariff advantages over foreign imports. Chamberlain denied that he was advocating a return to protectionism; but he also insisted that Britain would 'not be bound by any purely technical definition of free trade'.

Two weeks later, Chamberlain repeated his message in the House of Commons.[28] He admitted that a recently imposed corn duty to defray wartime expenses might be considered a tax on food – an important consideration for the working class. But, he argued (in a bow toward reformism), such a tax could be offset by higher wages and a revenue generated by reciprocal 'preferential arrangements' sufficient to fund social legislation. Specifically, 'old-age pensions or anything else which cost large sums of money, which have hitherto seemed to me to be out of reach of immediate practical politics, would become practicable if this policy were carried out'. Thus, the working class would benefit. Farmers, too, would have an advantage from a slight increase in tariffs on imported corn, which would protect the domestic agricultural market. Chamberlain additionally claimed that Britain had become the 'dumping ground of the world', and that it was time 'to defend our own trade against unjust competition'.

Chamberlain's unexpected and startling speeches created a sensation. At a stroke, he called into question the venerated free trade legislation hallowed by a half century of practice since the repeal of the Corn Laws in the 1840s. Any hint of a return to protectionism sent shock waves of disbelief throughout much of the country, especially in the Liberal Party. For the Liberals, rooted in their historic Cobdenism, free trade was more than an economic doctrine: it was the key to their political culture.[29] Free trade was a sacred idea, almost a law of commerce, certainly an unquestioned public good. In practical terms, an unhindered commercial exchange between nations was believed to promote peace and good will among nations.

Liberal leaders were quick to condemn Chamberlain's sacrilege. Lord Ripon declared Chamberlain's manifesto to be 'in the highest degree mischievous'. Spencer agreed, calling it 'most wicked'.[30] Campbell-Bannerman was harsher still, declaring that the speech was a 'reckless' and 'criminal escapade of Joe's'.[31] Harcourt wrote to his son that Chamberlain 'had irreparably damaged' his own ministry and that it could not survive 'his dynamite bomb'.[32] A more measured response was delivered by David Lloyd George, a rising Welsh radical nonconformist who had been repeatedly a thorn in Chamberlain's side during the Boer War. Speaking at Oxford a few weeks after Chamberlain's speech, Lloyd George predicted that Chamberlain's ascendancy in British politics, a career distinguished by a personal pursuit of power, 'was drawing to its close' should he attempt to lead the country 'into the morass of protection'.[33]

Chamberlain's outspoken position caused alarm not only among the Liberal opposition. Sir Almeric Fitzroy, Clerk of the Privy Council took note of Chamberlain's 'animated and provocative' speech in the House.[34] Some of Chamberlain's Unionist colleagues were equally agitated. George Wyndham, then Chief Secretary for Ireland, dashed off a message to Balfour as he listened to the speech in the House of Commons, condemning its 'verbal pugilism' as a disloyal act to the government.[35] Sir Alexander Acland-Hood, the conservative Chief Whip of the Unionist Party, was more critical. As he put it to Sandars: 'I hate the idea of the Tory party being dragged by Chamberlain to a disaster which will ruin us for a generation.'[36] C. R. Ritchie, who had replaced Hicks Beach as Chancellor of the Exchequer the year before, spoke in like mind to Balfour. Chamberlain, he wrote, 'seems to have set himself to the task of making it impossible for any one who does not share his views to remain a member of the Government'.[37]

For some, however, Chamberlain's speeches were a call to arms, a summons to a crusade. Fifty years later, Leo Amery could still recall the speech as 'the sudden awakening out of a nightmare', comparable to the theses that Luther had nailed to the church door centuries before.[38] No less enthusiastic was Henry Page Croft, a young conservative MP who was swept away by his veneration for Chamberlain as an icon for a new generation's passion for empire.[39] For these men, tariff reform was a way of reinvigorating political life after the uncertainties of the Boer War.

Clearly, Chamberlain had raised a storm of opposition among the most powerful and influential politicians in the country, including members of his own party. He had heightened the divisions between politicians and parties. He had attempted independently, publicly, and without ministerial sanction to bind Balfour's government to a sudden shift in policy. What had led him to take such controversial course of action? There is little agreement among historians. Political reasons were doubtless important in Chamberlain's mind. Some evidence exists for believing that Chamberlain had hoped for political advantage by diverting public attention – essentially 'changing the issue' – from the contentious Education Act of 1902 toward fiscal reform.[40] This could deflect nonconformist anger and keep the Liberals down in any future election.

Genuine policy goals may also have been at work. By promising enhanced revenues from a new tariff policy, social legislation could be funded, including the stalemated old-age pension scheme. Such a platform could also attract larger numbers of working-class voters, strengthening the Unionist Party. Alternatively, reciprocal tariff arrangements between the mother country and her colonies could be seen as part of a grand scheme to enhance Britain's standing in the world at large, elevate national efficiency, and instil a sense of patriotic renewal – all sorely needed after the Boer War.[41] These explanations of Chamberlain's initiative on tariff reform movement have varying degrees of validity. Chamberlain certainly advocated tariffs in the initial stages of the campaign as a source of funding for social programmes. And he explicitly and often advocated imperial union through a kind of *zollverein*. These explanations do not, however, wholly account for the 'seeming folly' of Chamberlain's pursuit of a destructive and dysfunctional policy, which 'perversely' gave every advantage to the political opposition, as Peter Fraser has suggested.[42] Nor do political and policy reasons fully explain his resignation from the cabinet, his furious campaign, and the growth of an obsession for tariff reform.[43]

However beneficial Chamberlain's scheme of tariff reform may have been, and however serious a challenge it presented to the free trade orthodoxy of the day, a careful reading of the important events preceding 1903, and an examination of the successive party struggles through 1906 reveals that Chamberlain's actions in attempting to implement tariff reform lies partly in his own need to maintain and pursue additional avenues of power.[44] Most simply put, Chamberlain – even at the pinnacle of power as a dominant member of the leading political party – was not yet fully satiated. Through his cultivation of domestic imperial sentiment and his use of coercive and manipulative practices, Chamberlain was determined at last to bring the diffuse and decentralized authority of the empire into his own hands. Tariff reform could, above all, create a partnership of colonies, dominions, and mother country tightly bound in a federated union, a unified empire over which Chamberlain himself would preside. To his way of thinking, it would be a short step from a position of such imperial power to attain authority in parliament and establish himself, if not as prime minister, as the unchallenged political leader in the country.[45]

To unravel the knot of Chamberlain's motives as they may have borne upon his behaviour during the tariff reform campaign, we must first trace in some detail the events prior to his famous speeches at Birmingham and the House of Commons in May 1903.[46] It becomes clear that Chamberlain's scheme evolved slowly over time as circumstances dictated. As we know, Chamberlain was initially opposed to tariffs. He had certainly been a staunch free trader during his earlier radical days. When President of the Board of Trade in Gladstone's second administration, he had denounced tariffs as inevitably leading to higher costs of living among working families.[47] But over time, Chamberlain came to doubt the efficacy of free trade as an economic doctrine in dealing with the complicated financial questions he encountered as President of the Board of Trade.[48] In addition, Chamberlain was impressed by the persistent opposition to free trade among some Birmingham businessmen who felt threatened by an unimpeded flow of cheaper foreign goods into Britain.

He may also have been influenced by the 'fair trade' and early imperial federation movements of the 1880s.[49] Nor could Chamberlain have been unaware of the development of protectionist policies in Europe and the United States since the 1870s, with Canada and Australia following on. Such global neo-mercantilism could place Britain at a severe economic disadvantage if it retained its policy of unilateral free trade. By 1900, British chambers of commerce were actively questioning traditional free trade doctrines and had begun to petition the foreign office expressing anxiety about increasing European tariffs, especially new German duties on imported steel.[50]

Chamberlain's term of office as Colonial Secretary was also important in altering his thinking on free trade. He encountered a far-flung world of economic complexity, in which the colonies could, and sometimes did, follow their own policies. The specific idea of colonial preferences, in fact, originated with the colonies. At the first conference of colonial premiers in London in 1887, the Cape Colony suggested such a tariff, as did a similar conference at Ottawa seven years later. But British governments, and Chamberlain particularly, were uninterested. After 1895, however, he began to view more favourably some sort of commercial arrangement that would fit within his larger scheme of an imperial customs union between the colonies and the mother country. Because it would essentially promote free trade within the empire, such a union need not be regarded as protectionist. Within the next few years, the notion of preferential tariffs slowly gained ground. In 1897 Canada unilaterally reduced tariffs on British imported goods by 12.5 per cent. Two years later, they were reduced a further 20 per cent. The Boer War diverted attention from tariffs for a time, but at the colonial conference of 1902 Canada made it known that it would not continue its unilateral policy of reducing tariffs in favour of Britain unless there was a reciprocal response. Strenuous negotiations at that conference resulted in an agreement that Chamberlain brought forward officially in cabinet.

Meanwhile the exigencies of wartime finance were also inclining Chamberlain toward a policy of reciprocal tariff agreements. Hicks Beach had been forced in his budget of 1901 to address a revenue shortfall by taxing consumers, including a levy on sugar. The following year, Hicks Beach reluctantly revived a registration duty on corn (grain) and flour to cover an additional deficit. From Hicks Beach's point of view, these were wartime measures only, to be repealed as soon as possible. But to Chamberlain, the corn duty provided a precedent and an ideal means of meeting Canadian demands for preferential treatment: by maintaining the duty against foreign grains and exempting Canada, reciprocal advantages could be secured.

At two cabinet meetings (in October and November 1902) Chamberlain proposed the admission of all colonial corn into Britain free of duty. The cabinet was generally favourable, but the free-trade Ritchie, Chancellor of the Exchequer, demurred and asked for a delay so that the impact of Corn Law exemption on the following year's budget could be gauged. This was agreed just prior to Chamberlain's post-war departure for South Africa. During Chamberlain's absence, Ritchie's views hardened. In line with his free trade propensities, he proposed instead abolishing the corn duty altogether. If his scheme were not accepted, Ritchie informed Balfour, he would resign.[51]

When Chamberlain returned from South Africa in mid-March 1903, he discovered a ministry divided over tariff policy. Within three days of his disembarking at Southampton, the cabinet began a series of meetings to resolve the conflict. By the end of the month, the cabinet had decided in favour of Ritchie's proposal – to abolish the corn duty – with the reluctant acquiescence of Chamberlain. Perhaps his lengthy absence had contributed to the wavering of the cabinet, and to Chamberlain's decision to back down. With the budget due within a few weeks, there was added pressure for a quick decision. But Chamberlain soon had second thoughts. Over the next several weeks, he became angry and dispirited over the cabinet's decision. Not only had he had been placed in an embarrassing position with regard to the Canadian government whose flag of tariff reform he bore: he also felt slighted and brushed aside.[52] Moreover, he had successfully concluded nearly eight years as a supremely confident and commanding Colonial Secretary during the most eventful era of British colonial history. He had helped conclude a difficult war, and had contributed significantly to the peace. He had toured the defeated territory healing the wounds of war. He was the most articulate spokesman of British imperial aims. He was in effect, the prime minister of the empire. But in his own government, he had been ignored.

The manifestations of Chamberlain's anger were numerous. His official correspondence with colonial officials in late March and April were painful exchanges and filled with accusations as he lashed out. His attitude in cabinet was no better. Sullen and negative in temper, he opposed measure after measure: Brodrick's army scheme in South Africa; Wyndham's Irish Land Bill; and the Bagdad railway project, which he had earlier enthusiastically supported.[53] At one time, he threatened resignation. On another occasion, he hoped for a general election 'so that the air might be cleared'.[54] Even Amery felt compelled to note Chamberlain's 'irritation', 'frustration', 'impotent rage', and the 'irascible' tone to his letters.[55] In this mood, Chamberlain decided that he could not accept the cabinet's decision. Instead, he prepared for an appeal to the country. He instructed his Birmingham agent, Charles Vince, to sound out his constituency on their views of a preferential tariff as a means of unifying the empire. He contacted the economist William Ashley (of Birmingham University), requesting that he write a book about tariff reform. And he began to write his bombshell speech given at Birmingham on 15 May 1903, the impact of which we have already noted.

To reinforce the substance of his tariff reform speeches, Chamberlain laid plans to take his opponents by storm. The first step was to create a cabinet of his own – men who could provide the expertise necessary for Chamberlain to draw upon. These advisors included Leo Maxse, editor of the *National Review* and the son of an earlier friend and adviser, Captain F. A. Maxse; J. L. Garvin, then a young journalist for the *Daily Telegraph*; Leo Amery, at that time leader writer and military correspondent of *The Times*; and W. A. S. Hewins, director of the London School of Economics. Quicker than expected, Chamberlain's house economists provided a valuable service when 14 economics professors, including the eminent William Marshall, signed a letter published in *The Times* on 5 August 1903 condemning Chamberlain's tariff proposals. With Chamberlain's encouragement, both Ashley and Hewins rebutted the professors, claiming they were not representative of the profession. The controversy which followed, with rival schools of economists squabbling over a proposed tariff policy, tended to neutralize the impact of both sides upon the public debate.[56]

This was no loss to Chamberlain's way of thinking. He had little interest in the details of tariff reform. Indeed, it seems that Chamberlain was so poorly versed on the subtleties of economic theory that even Hewins was taken aback. When Hewins attempted to supply Chamberlain with figures worked out by competent statisticians, he found that Chamberlain refused to accept the evidence. As late as 1906, Hewins complained that Chamberlain's speeches 'contained many inaccuracies of argument and statistics'. When proven wrong, Chamberlain simply insisted on using the faulty information, 'apparently on the singular ground that he had used them before'. It was, Hewins noted additionally, 'rather difficult to help him'.[57]

Chamberlain was, in short, never interested in establishing the accuracy of trade statistics. As he put to Amery: 'we must build up our own statistics with special view to the controversy in which we are engaged'.[58] The role of Hewins, Ashley, and others of his personal cabinet was primarily to defend tariff reform and to rebuff criticism at the theoretical level. This served to keep his opponents off balance. Chamberlain understood that the battle over tariff reform could not be won as an academic exercise. For him, tariff reform was increasingly a political struggle to be played out over the entire country – from the cabinet downward to parliament and ultimately to every voter. Political muscle was the requisite, not scholastic hair-splitting.[59]

Inspired by Chamberlain's determination and animated by smooth-running machinery staffed with loyalists, the movement for tariff reform spread rapidly during the summer months of 1903. To capture the national Liberal Unionist Association, Chamberlain won the approval of its executive committee meeting in June to begin extensive leafleting in support of tariff reform. As a complement to the national association, Chamberlain created a Tariff Committee from members of the local Birmingham Liberal Unionist Association. Made up of Chamberlain's friends, family, and associates – such as Collings, Vince, Powell Williams, and his son Neville – the new Committee soon began its own publications. The Birmingham Committee also contacted more than one hundred Chambers of Commerce to encourage discussion of the advantages of a preferential tariff. But the most formidable of all the organizations was the Tariff Reform League (TRL), created in July. Six hundred branches nationwide were eventually established, the largest of which had over a thousand members. Wealthy industrialists, Tory landlords, and most Unionist MPs were its eager subscribers.[60] Chamberlain's firmness of purpose and strength of leadership were clearly attractive not only in higher political circles but among the electorate at large: supporters from around the country flocked to his standard. William Primrose, for example, represented the prevailing enthusiasm for Chamberlain's campaign. Owner of the Centre Street Flour Mills in Tradston as well as president of his local Liberal Unionist Association, Primrose wrote to Chamberlain in his belief that 'a strong man should speak out ... in the best interests of our Country and Empire ... and ... you are the man for the work'.[61]

As the debate on tariff reform began to engage the attention of the country, the division of opinion within the cabinet widened. Balfour was placed in a particularly awkward position. With a cabinet nearly balanced between free trade and tariff reform forces (some Unionists were free traders), the prime minister worked hard to find a manageable majority. But pressure grew upon Balfour to declare openly for one side or another. His kinsman, Lord Hugh Cecil, a strong Unionist free trader, criticized Balfour for his anaemic response to the burgeoning tariff reform campaign. Balfour's 'dexterous series of questions and suggestions', Cecil claimed, were 'exquisitely calculated to smooth the way for Joe' and his 'relentless methods'. Without a firmer stand by Balfour, Unionist free traders 'have to face Joe at his best in the country with all his immense skill & ability, his unequalled prestige & his electioneering dexterity and unscrupulousness'. As Cecil admitted, none of them were 'within a mile of him'.[62]

To preserve the government, a compromise within the cabinet was necessary. But how to find a pivot between such irreconcilable opponents? The best chance for Balfour was to support a slight tariff revision, and then to nudge each side toward its acceptance. Should this fail, the most expendable minister could be replaced by someone more tractable. By everyone's reckoning, this would certainly be Ritchie. Chamberlain, whose strength in the countryside was already formidable, and whose value to the government was universally recognized, would be kept. This was Balfour's original thinking.

The key to a unified cabinet, however, was the Duke of Devonshire. Leader of the Liberal Unionists in the House of Lords and a moderate free trader, the wooden Duke had become a totemic presence in the government. His languor seemed to lend gravitas, and his land and lineage conveyed an aristocratic lustre to the Unionists. But the Duke was not a subtle thinker, and his grip upon complex matters such as tariff reform was imperfect.[63] His real value to the cabinet at this critical juncture was as free trade ballast within the cabinet should Ritchie and the other free trade ministers resign. His departure could fatally weaken the ministry. Thus Balfour worked hard to keep the Duke in harness. Chamberlain, too, from the standpoint of keeping up the strength of the Liberal Unionists in the cabinet, hoped for the Duke's retention. But Chamberlain's behaviour did little to further his aim. In a lengthy letter to the Duke in late August 1903, Chamberlain put forward a complicated and semi-statistical justification for his tariff reform programme.[64] The Duke, who admitted that he did not understand the complexities of the tariff, was unconvinced. Two days later, the Duke wrote Balfour that Chamberlain's position was increasingly protectionist, and that as the tariff movement went forward, Chamberlain would inevitably be driven 'further and further' in that direction.[65] This initiated an exchange of letters between Balfour and the Duke. Balfour admitted that Chamberlain's 'impulsiveness, combined with his extraordinary vigour and controversial skill' had alarmed more moderate cabinet members. He also blamed Chamberlain for threatening the party 'with serious disruption on the fiscal question'. But, he claimed, the 'Free Trade Three' of Ritchie, Hamilton, and Balfour of Burleigh also bore some responsibility for the impasse.[66]

If Balfour wished to retain Devonshire, he was also strongly inclined to clip Chamberlain's wings. Chamberlain's disconcerting summer campaign had begun to set its own course on tariff reform without regard to the cabinet. For his part, Chamberlain remained dissatisfied with his position in the cabinet, and aggravated with its rejection of the corn duty. Determined to break free from cabinet constraints and buoyed by his country campaign, he made an unusual proposal to Balfour in early September. He would resign from office and from the cabinet. This would allow Balfour to put forward a milder variant of tariff revision – for example, retaliatory tariffs against any dumping or unfair competition – without unnerving the cabinet as a whole. In the meantime, Chamberlain would support the government out of doors while continuing his campaign for preferential tariffs. If Chamberlain could swing public opinion behind him, he could later re-enter the cabinet and adopt a bolder approach to tariffs. Chamberlain advanced only one condition – that Austen must remain in the cabinet.[67]

For Balfour, there were a number of advantages to Chamberlain's proposal: the Duke would be mollified; antagonism in the cabinet would abate; and he could govern more easily. On 14 September, only an hour before the first autumn cabinet was to meet, Chamberlain and Balfour discussed Chamberlain's offer of resignation and agreed to its terms. No one else knew of their bargain. With Chamberlain's friendly offer of resignation in his pocket, Balfour's hands were untied. By forcing the resignation of Ritchie and his allies, he could reshuffle his contentious cabinet. During the tense cabinet meeting on the afternoon of 14 September, Balfour in effect completed a coup by asking for the resignations of the three irreconcilable free trad-ers.[68] In addition, Balfour indicated that although he would not rule out preferential tariffs, he did not believe them politically feasible at that time. He announced further that his preferred policy of tariff reform was for retaliation, or as he put it, the liberty of fiscal negotiation. These comments were Chamberlain's cue: from his seat in the cabinet he announced his own resignation.

Because the bargain with Balfour was not widely known, Chamberlain's resigna-tion at first was greeted with alarm by his supporters, who feared that his departure from the cabinet meant a loss of power and of influence. Rudyard Kipling, whose hero Chamberlain was, responded to the news of the resignation with sorrow and a bad poem, 'Things and the Man', which had taken its subtext from Genesis: 'And Joseph dreamed a dream, and he told it his brethren: and they hated him yet the more.'[69] But Chamberlain, as well as Balfour, had reasons to be pleased at the turn of events.[70] Balfour had accepted the principle of tariff reform, even if he and Chamberlain dif-fered on details. Austen, by taking Ritchie's place as Chancellor of the Exchequer, became in effect a delegate of his father. In addition, when the cabinet reshuffle sent Brodrick to the India Office, Balfour appointed Arnold Forster, a devoted follower of Chamberlain, to succeed Brodrick at the War Office. The Liberal Unionist Alfred Lyttelton replaced Chamberlain at the Colonial Office. With Balfour now a declared (however mildly declared) tariff reformer, the cabinet purged of its most fervent free traders, and the Duke co-opted, Chamberlain believed that he had consolidated cabinet support for his tariff campaign. He fully expected that his campaign would succeed and that he would likely return to office within a year or two, perhaps to ultimate power.[71]

Too soon, however, came an unravelling. The Duke resigned two weeks after Chamberlain and the free traders left office. He had remained in the cabinet after their resignations, puzzled and unsure of his role.[72] Under considerable pressure from the free trade lobby and conscience stricken by his survival in office, the Duke could no longer remain a firm supporter of the government. But it must be said that Chamberlain's behaviour hastened the Duke's resignation. Within a week of the fateful cabinet meeting of 14 September, Chamberlain wrote the Duke a letter full of reproach. Complaining that he had been 'bitterly hurt' by the Duke's persistent slights for almost two decades, Chamberlain pointed out he had 'never been called' to the Duke's counsels. The Duke, he wrote, was far more likely to engage in consultations with Balfour and Ritchie – men who were not even Liberal Unionists. Chamberlain also charged that the Duke was responsible for the ministerial turmoil. Before leaving for South Africa, the Duke had accepted a minimal corn duty; but while Chamberlain was abroad 'slaving [his] life out', the Duke and other members of the cabinet had thrown him over. It was, Chamberlain concluded, the Duke's 'indifference to a great policy' that had created the agitated 'present situation'.[73]

Doubtless Chamberlain received some personal satisfaction at the Duke's resignation. The Duke had resigned as a free trader; he could now be a fair target for personal censure. The political implications were less immediately clear, though hardly propitious for their continued dual leadership of the Liberal Unionist Party. The consequence of the rift between the two men was not long in coming. At a meeting of the Durham and North Riding Liberal Unionist Association at Newcastle on 20 October, a resolution was passed to reconsider the existing fiscal policy – a carefully worded tilt toward tariff reform. A letter from the Duke, read in opposition to the resolution, was voted down. Several prominent free traders then resigned from the Association. The Duke, realizing the example this action might set, urged upon Chamberlain the disbandment of the organization. Chamberlain refused and in the months that followed worked assiduously to capture the local Associations for tariff reform.[74] Liberal Unionism, as a recognizable and discrete political party allied to the Conservatives in the Unionist cause, was in danger of being split between Chamberlainite tariff reformers and the Devonshire-led free traders.

Spurred by this realization, Chamberlain intensified his campaign in the autumn of 1903. Backed by a substantial war chest, thanks to the Tariff Reform League, he was now ready to marshal his forces among the electorate at large. On the morning of 6 October 1903, Chamberlain and his wife left Birmingham by train for Glasgow, the citadel of free trade doctrine. Arriving during a torrential downpour, they were treated to a banquet by local dignitaries, and then set out for St Andrews Hall. Entering the hall promptly at 8 p.m., Chamberlain was, as *The Times* reported, wildly greeted by hats and handkerchiefs waving madly 'till the whole hall was aflutter with them'.[75] After the cheering subsided, rounds of 'For he's a jolly good fellow' broke out, followed by an organ playing the national anthem. For 15 minutes the crowd of 5,000 continued its tumultuous greeting. Finally Chamberlain – fortified by a box of throat lozenges supplied by Mary, and wearing a white orchid displayed prominently in the lapel of his frock coat – rose to speak.

Acknowledging the influence of Adam Smith, who had taught at the University of Glasgow, Chamberlain pointed out that Smith had never intended free trade to be a dogmatic principle. Smith had, he said, upheld the Navigation Laws, a form of mercantilism, in defence of the empire. Tariff revision merely followed Smith's logic. In times of declining trade, the state had its responsibilities in protecting commerce. There were, Chamberlain warned, ominous signs of decay. 'I see cracks and crevices in the walls of the great structure', he told the meeting. Exports were stagnating; industrial crisis would follow. With factories closing, workers would be unemployed. Protectionist countries such as Germany and the United States were already taking competitive advantage of the British economic malaise. Tariff reform was thus essential to the economic health and vigour of the nation and the empire.

No less important than its protective purpose, tariff reform would also foster commercial union among the colonies thus laying the foundations of an imperial confederation. Within that confederation, Britain's manufactured goods would have a guaranteed market: colonial produce would be favoured over foreign. Chamberlain also emphasized, as he had in previous speeches, the imperial ideal. Empire had 'ennobled our national life' and discouraged 'petty parochialism'. All that was 'best in our present life, best in this Britain of ours' was due to that fact that they were 'not only sons of Britain, but also ... sons of Empire'. Tariff reform strengthened the bonds of empire. 'We must', he asserted, 'either draw closer together or we shall drift apart.'

In addition to these lofty aims, Chamberlain for the first time set out a detailed and specific programme for tariff reform. He proposed 2 shillings a quarter duty on foreign corn and imported flour: no duty would be charged on imperial corn. Additionally, he proposed a 5 per cent duty on foreign meat and dairy produce, with the exception of bacon, considered a food of the very poor. A preference (unstated) would be assigned to colonial wines and possibly later, fruits. To offset these new taxes on food, Chamberlain proposed corresponding reductions on other foodstuffs such as tea, sugar, cocoa, and coffee. Finally, he proposed a 10 per cent reduction on the importation of foreign manufactures. With this speech, tariff reformers had a specific programme which they could defend.

After putting the case for colonial preferences in Glasgow, Chamberlain spoke the following day at Greenock where he again emphasized the dangers of a declining economy.[76] Once the centre of sugar refining, Greenock had suffered unfairly from foreign competition aided by government subsidies. 'Free imports have destroyed this industry', Chamberlain claimed. Some refineries had disappeared altogether, and their employees thrown out of work. He predicted more ominous consequences: 'Sugar has gone; silk has gone; iron is threatened; wool is threatened; cotton will go!' 'How long are you going to stand it?' he asked the crowd. After a fortnight's break, Chamberlain returned to the campaign trail, speaking at Newcastle, Tynemouth, and Liverpool in quick succession. In Liverpool he delivered three speeches, continuing his appeal to the special interests who, he claimed, would benefit from tariff reform. Tariff reform could best protect shipping – the lifeblood of Liverpool. In addition, the watchmakers of Prescot, the plate-glass industry of St Helens, and the wire works of Warrington, all harmed by foreign competition, would benefit.

The climax of these early speeches came at Birmingham on 4 November where Chamberlain spoke before a crowd of 10,000 at Bingley Hall.[77] The protectionist tone was again clearly evident. As in other speeches, he enumerated threatened industries – jewellery, brass, pearl buttons, bicycles. He also appealed to history to discount the Liberal contention that protection led inevitably to poverty, misery, and starvation. In a dramatic conclusion to this speech, he denied the Liberal claim that tariff reform would mean higher food prices for the workingman. He denounced the Liberal placards in the town which portrayed 'the big loaf' under free trade, and 'the small loaf' under protection. To challenge this claim, Chamberlain had asked a baker to make two loaves, one which would reflect the size under his tariff reform, and the other of that day's baking. Unwrapping a parcel on the platform, he pulled out both loaves and held them aloft, one in each hand. They were of virtually equal sizes. What could one say of those, Chamberlain asked, who support their cause 'by such dishonest representations'? The crowd roared with approval.

The remainder of Chamberlain's speaking tour, which carried him into January 1904, went equally well.[78] But he mentioned less frequently the putative social benefits of reform, emphasizing instead the twin themes of economic and imperial necessity. At Cardiff, for example, Chamberlain warned of foreign competition to the coalmining and tinplate industries, and at Newport he dwelt on the recent large imports of steel bars that year. Within a few weeks, he was at Leeds, proclaiming the ideal of empire. More than 'a beautiful dream', said Chamberlain, empire was the noblest aspiration that ever came to statesmen. Chamberlain's final speech in January was at the Guildhall in the City of London. Escorted by members of the Stock Exchange who marched in front of his carriage singing patriotic songs, Chamberlain received, as he had at previous meetings, a rousing welcome. In this speech, Chamberlain declared that riches alone were not enough to sustain a great country. If Britain wished to continue 'to be heard in Europe', it must not adhere to an 'insular spirit': it must remain imperial. Britain must explicitly use the power that it had 'to influence the civilization of the world'.

Chamberlain's messages of economic self-interest, patriotism, and imperial pride were powerful and effective. His determination to take action and to fight for his programme struck a responsive chord among the electorate. The extent of Chamberlain's successes obviously dismayed the Liberal opposition. In early December, R. B. Haldane told Fitzroy that he was 'greatly disquieted' at Chamberlain's progress. Two by-election victories for tariff reform in South London, at Dulwich and Lewisham, brought further evidence of Chamberlain's appeal. Fitzroy recorded ruefully that 'the clerks and small villa people' were apparently willing 'to take the risks' of Chamberlain's policy.[79] Fitzroy also reported that the Governor of the Bank of England thought that 'Chamberlainism' was gaining ground even in the City. Chamberlain's dynamism, eloquence, and popularity were carrying the day. Skipping from platform to platform, as Fitzroy put it, Chamberlain generated 'the new faith with the ardour of a neophyte and ... the authority of a seer'.[80] Campbell-Bannerman, the Liberal leader, was particularly alarmed at the popular reception Chamberlain had received in his countrywide speeches. To Harcourt he wrote that Chamberlain 'trusts to vulgar, ignorant applause of the "strong man", and to the selfish interests of particular trades'. To Earl Spencer,

Campbell-Bannerman complained that 'Joe has been mafficking about the country and rousing everybody's cupidity'. In essentially the same message to Bryce, the Liberal leader declared that Chamberlain always played up 'to the vulgarity and cupidity and other ignoble passions'. Chamberlain was, he believed, not beneath exploiting 'the foolishness of the fool and the vices of the vicious to overwhelm the sane and wise and sober'.[81]

Liberal denunciations of tariff reform were of course expected. But as the tariff reform campaign gained ground, there were noticeable abstentions among Unionists as well. The Balfour cabinet itself had been divided on the issue. After the cabinet resignations, a division among Unionist ranks in parliament opened, and then widened during the course of Chamberlain's autumn campaign. When the Duke of Devonshire accepted the presidency of the Free Food League, a Unionist organization founded as a counter to the Tariff Reform League, the split seemed irrevocable. Although the Free Food League was never more than a loosely structured parliamentary committee and lacked the resources and organization of its tariff reform rival, it formed the nucleus of more than 80 Unionist free traders in the House of Commons who opposed Chamberlain.[82] Hicks Beach perhaps put the object of the new organization best. It was not designed, he said, to break up the Unionist alliance, but rather 'to keep the Government together and prevent Balfour from committing himself to Joe'.[83]

Chamberlain thus faced growing opposition from both the Liberals and Unionist free traders. There was an additional danger to tariff reform – the moderates under Balfour. Chamberlain could rely on some support from this centrist group, but others were solidly behind the prime minister, whose position during the autumn campaign remained cautious. Perhaps the most committed Balfourites were the old-line Tories whose roots remained fixed in the land and who had always viewed Chamberlain's populist tendencies with suspicion. Aretas Akers-Douglas, for example, Balfour's Home Secretary, nursed a profound distaste for Chamberlain and his policy. He condemned Chamberlain as a 'wayward Radical' whom the Conservatives had 'with sickness in their hearts ... spent their lives trying to conciliate', and who now was thrusting tariff reform – 'this awkward baby' – into the arms of the party.[84]

Given the strong political opposition to himself and his fiscal policy emanating from so many sources, Chamberlain decided to tack lightly in December 1903. In that month, he established an (ostensibly) non-political tariff commission charged with the task of investigating the need for – as he put it – a 'scientific tariff' which would lay to rest any fears about the legitimate intent of tariff reform. Thus tariff reform could be cloaked in a mantle of impartiality. The Tariff Reform Commission was an impressively assembled body. Some of the most important businessmen in Britain agreed to serve, including Sir Alfred Hickman in iron and steel; Sir Andrew Jones, the Liverpool shipping magnate; and Sir Andrew Noble of Armstrong and Whitworth, munitions makers. Other members included landowner Henry Chaplin (known popularly as the 'Squire of Blankney'), representing agriculture; Sir Charles Tennant, Asquith's father-in-law (and a Liberal convert to tariff reform); and the well-known social investigator, Charles Booth.[85]

The organization of the Commission appeared to Chamberlain's opponents as presumptuous: it gave the appearance of being an official arm of government.[86] Chamberlain, of course, did not intend it to have independent powers of investigation. Treating it as a kind of private civil service, he drew upon the Commission's findings to substantiate his arguments during speeches in and out of parliament. From the first, Chamberlain kept a very tight grip on the Commission, insisting upon absolute loyalty. When Arthur Pearson, the newspaper publisher who chaired the Commission, intended to make public a weakened version of the tariff reform programme, Chamberlain replaced him with the more compliant Lord Ridley. To insure a more complete control of the Commission thereafter, Chamberlain arranged for weekly meetings of its executive committee and attended them as often as possible.[87]

Given Chamberlain's well-known reputation for ruthlessness and for an authoritarian managerial style, it is not surprising that his opponents doubted the neutrality of the Commission. The Commission simply appeared to be another agency for the unscrupulous manipulation of facts for Chamberlain's own purposes. After all, his own economic advisor had lamented his cavalier treatment of trading statistics as we have noted above. Nevertheless, the Commission had some stature in representing the genuine and growing concern about Britain's trading rivals, such as Germany and the United States. Questions were being asked in responsible places. Could Britain continue to dominate as it had in the past? Was Britain declining in real terms, as Chamberlain claimed? How could productivity be increased? Was the entrepreneurial spirit played out? A sense of unease was abroad in the land. A case could be made that tariff reform was a reasonable response to the issue.[88] Thus, a generalized anxiety about Britain's economic status in the world, heightened by Chamberlain's campaign, brought considerable success to the tariff reform movement in early 1904.[89] Indeed, by the end of that year, almost the whole of the Unionist press had declared for Chamberlain.[90] He had also gained complete control of the Liberal Unionist Party organization with the resignation of the Duke of Devonshire. At Chamberlain's 68th birthday celebration in July – to which only parliamentary Unionist supporters were invited – 200 MPs were in attendance.

As Chamberlain's project prospered, the Balfour government's legislative programme floundered. The political struggles over tariff reform had sapped the ministry's strength and diverted its attention. The government gave a growing impression of weakness and drift. Chamberlain realized that a rapidly declining Unionist governing impulse could mean disaster at the next general election. This sobering thought led him to open negotiations with the prime minister. If an agreement on tariff reform could be reached, a united front against the Liberals could be made and an electoral defeat avoided. Realizing that Balfour would be unlikely to accept a preferential tariff outright, Chamberlain devised a scheme that would allow Balfour to surrender with good grace. He proposed a colonial conference to discuss the implementation of a preferential tariff. If the conference were favourably inclined (as Chamberlain knew it would be), Balfour could bow to its recommendations.

Balfour, however, had been wary of Chamberlain's brand of tariff reform from the first. Craftily dodging the issue in his public pronouncements, he kept his options

open. At the Conservative Party conference in Sheffield in October 1903, for example – not long after Chamberlain's resignation from the cabinet – Balfour accepted
tariff reform only in principle. He expressly rejected preferential tariffs on the grounds
that the country would oppose any tax on food.[91] His next public pronouncement,
in Manchester in January 1904, made no advance on his Sheffield remarks. Balfour's
careful balancing act between Chamberlain's protectionism and the vociferous free
trade Unionist minority would, it seemed, continue.

While the prime minister mulled over the possibilities of a colonial conference,
Chamberlain began a second country campaign for tariff reform – this time among
the agriculturists in the rural districts. On 4 August 1904 he journeyed to Welbeck,
home of the dukes of Portland. The audience of 12,000, many of whom were agricultural labourers, arrived by wagonette, charabanc, trap, motorcar, and bicycle. Six
excursion trains had also been laid on.[92] Chamberlain spoke in the great riding school
on the estate, which stretched a hundred yards in length.[93] Although he could not
always be heard in this vast enclosure, his message was familiar. As he had during his
speeches in industrial centres, Chamberlain painted for the farm workers a gloomy
picture of declining productivity and unemployment. In the past 30 years, he said,
3 million acres of corn land had gone out of cultivation; animal stock had been
reduced by 2 million head; and the number of cultivators of the land had decreased
by 600,000. The lesson was obvious: the effect of free trade upon farm labourers had
been 'disastrous'. But, Chamberlain concluded, tariff reform was not only a matter of
pounds and pence, it was also a question of national pride and imperial responsibility. 'I address myself not merely to your pockets', he assured the crowd, 'but to your
patriotism' as well.

In mid-August, Austen Chamberlain, still a member of the cabinet and taking cues
from his father, began pressing Balfour for a general election at the earliest opportunity.[94] An election date would (the Chamberlains doubtless hoped) force Balfour
to make up his mind on tariff reform. Additionally, as Austen put it, an electoral
campaign was an opportunity for the Unionists to repair their 'timid, undecided,
vacillating' ideas on tariff reform and to adopt a 'constructive policy'. Austen further
suggested a campaign strategy based upon his father's Glasgow speech of the previous
October. If the Unionists should be returned to power on the basis of their campaign
promises, Austen recommended the summoning of a colonial conference to discuss
imperial trade, which would set the stage for parliamentary legislation based upon
conference recommendations. Balfour countered. He accepted the idea of a colonial
conference provided that he first received a mandate from the electorate before he
entered the conference. Then, following the conference, he would once again consult
the electorate about the conclusions of the conference. Not unnaturally, Chamberlain
père rejected this cumbersome 'two-elections' plan. The duel between them continued into the autumn with Chamberlain attempting to wrest from the prime minister
some definite word on preferential tariffs, and Balfour resisting.

These veiled exchanges exasperated Chamberlain and fuelled his determination
to replace Balfour as party leader. There are hints of this in communications to his
confederates. To Pike Pease he wrote in reference to Balfour and the prospects of

the party: 'The hesitation and timidity displayed up to the present time have done infinite and irreparable mischief.'[95] A few weeks later, he complained to Chaplin that Balfour 'gives no promise or sign of change. He will go his gait and we must go ours.'[96] To Lyttelton, he wrote a letter uncharacteristically indirect, though the thought behind it was clear enough. Admitting that he was 'anxious and uneasy' about the prime minister's intentions, he declared that Balfour must put tariff reform to the forefront of his endeavours. If, Chamberlain wrote, he were confronted with a final decision from Balfour 'such as recently I have had reason to fear', he could not accept it 'without some protest or declaration which would indicate a greater divergence than I have hitherto contemplated possible'.[97]

But Balfour would not be moved. At a dinner in Edinburgh given by the Scottish Conservative Club in early October 1904, Balfour reaffirmed his Sheffield declaration of 1903. In addition, he committed himself to the 'two-elections' plan. A few weeks later, at the conference of the National Union of Conservatives in Southampton – in spite of an overwhelmingly successful series of Chamberlainite tariff reform resolutions – Balfour held firm. Into the new year, unproductive public statements and fruitless correspondence magnified the differences between the two men. In an attempt to break the deadlock, a meeting was held in February 1905. The substance of their talk revolved around tariffs and the proposed colonial conference. Again, there was no resolution: the fundamental disagreement on preferential tariffs remained. As Balfour put it: 'The prejudice against a small tax on food … is a deep-rooted prejudice affecting the large mass of voters…'.[98] Chamberlain disagreed. Among the 'artisan population', he claimed, prejudice had largely disappeared: even in agricultural districts, 'where a proper house to house education' had been undertaken, the labourers were 'open to conversion'.[99]

By March 1905 relations between the two men had reached the breaking point. Fitzroy recorded in his diary the opinion of Jack Sandars, Balfour's private secretary, that Chamberlain's restless temperament and his tendency 'to force the hand of those who were in part association with him' would soon get the better of him and he would bring down the government. Sandars was also concerned about the effect of the conflict upon the Unionist Party: many were 'steeped in lukewarmness and discontent' and some were not seeking re-election 'from disgust'.[100]

Undeterred by the declining fortunes of his party and freed from any official ministerial connection, Chamberlain relentlessly pursued his independent policy. To the well-established machinery of the Tariff Reform League, the protectionist press and carefully orchestrated meetings, fresh tactics were put into use. A new and simplified slogan – 'Tariff Reform Means Work for All' – was widely publicized. To insure that individual voters would be reached, door-to-door canvassers were employed. A novel device was a recording of Chamberlain's voice for the gramophone, bringing the orator's voice to an even wider audience.[101] By the summer of 1905, Chamberlain's sharpened criticisms of Balfour's policy brought another strongly worded complaint from Lord Hugh Cecil to his cousin: 'The truth is that all along, Joe has been the aggressor', he wrote to Balfour. 'At present he is making war and we must do so too.'[102]

In July, Chamberlain unleashed one of his most vehement attacks. Speaking to a meeting of the Tariff Reform League at the Albert Hall, he warned that 'the obstructions that menace our trade are growing daily in their power for evil'.[103] He boasted to the cheering crowd: 'We have kindled a torch which not all the puny efforts of our opponents can extinguish.' Renewed cheers greeted his call to arms: 'We are a fighting force. We have a definite and a constructive policy.' Co-opting Balfour's policy of retaliation, Chamberlain redefined it as an all-round tariff on manufactured goods. Retaliation must be 'an effective engine to force a fair trade policy upon the nations with which we exchange our products'. Extending his military metaphor, Chamberlain further demanded: 'We want the big revolver when we meet men who are armed at all points ... We will load our revolver with a general tariff.' Such inflammatory language brought comments in kind from his opponents. Wyndham, in a letter to Balfour, spoke of the speech as 'highly contentious' and even 'militant'.[104] The Duke of Devonshire raised the subject in the House of Lords, seeking a resolution of condemnation.

By the time parliament rose in late summer 1905, political matters were unchanged, though a brief respite was at hand. Debate was suspended and the tariff reform campaign idled while Chamberlain went abroad for the waters at Aix-les-Bains and a tour through Switzerland and France. Upon his return, Chamberlain swung once more into action: the holiday had not weakened his resolve. Writing to Garvin, he revealed his intention to speak against 'the hesitation & weakness of the official position' in a forthcoming speech to his constituents.[105] He also began planning an autumn campaign.

But Balfour sprang an early November surprise. In a lengthy and unexpectedly revealing letter to Chamberlain, Balfour confided that he was 'very anxious to get out of office'.[106] Weary of politics after ten years of leading the House of Commons, Balfour had, he wrote, 'an unutterable desire for change' and a yearning for 'the comfort and repose of my own house!' To that end, he proposed to meet parliament in the new year, and then to resign almost immediately.

Chamberlain, whose combative instincts seemed to intensify when he scented weakness, replied to Balfour in public the following day at Birmingham.[107] He explicitly demanded an early general election. 'I wish an election', he told his audience, 'because the great Unionist party at the present ... is marking time, when it ought to be fighting the enemy ...'. An election campaign would provide an opportunity for the Unionists to 'shake off the apathy which has been born of timorous counsels and of half-hearted convictions'. They must fight, and fight soon under the banner of tariff reform to obtain 'the power of retaliation against those who treat us badly and ... the power of preference to those who treat us well'. Unstated by Chamberlain was the fact that an early election would also give him – the greatest campaigner of his day – a surpassing opportunity to remove recalcitrant free traders from the Unionist Party and replace them with his own followers. Equally important, it would at last provide a reasonable opportunity either to remove Balfour from office completely or to hold him in captivity, bound to the protectionist cause.

As a first step in implementing his heightened anti-Balfour scheme, Chamberlain hijacked the forthcoming Conservative Party Conference at Newcastle. Collaborating with Henry Chaplin, Chamberlain (who was not a member of the Conservative Party) concocted a resolution to be presented at the conference. It consisted of a number of selected extracts from Balfour's earlier speeches which, when combined, gave the impression that Balfour favoured Chamberlainite tariff reform. It was clearly designed to embarrass Balfour and undermine his authority with rank-and-file Conservatives attending the conference. The ruse worked to perfection: the resolution passed virtually unanimously.[108] A week later, Chamberlain fired again into the vacillating figure of the prime minister with deadly effect. At the annual conference of the Liberal Unionist Council in Bristol, Chamberlain praised the resolution passed at Newcastle for its 'strongly definite constructive policy'. Chamberlain's attempt to seize power had now become obvious. *The Times*, until now Chamberlain's supporter, raised a cautionary voice. Praising Balfour as a 'practicable' statesman who paid attention 'to the middle opinion of the party as a whole', *The Times* observed that 'Mr. Chamberlain' was too ready 'to go ahead on his own path' and 'staking far too much upon his personal opinion' in emphasizing tariff reform at the expense of 'all the other objects of Unionism …'.[109]

But Balfour, weary of the struggle and publicly humiliated, had little recourse. He had shown his weakness to Chamberlain and admitted his fatigue. Within two weeks, Balfour resigned. The long anticipated collapse of the once powerful Unionist government came to its abrupt and ignominious end. The political initiative now fell to the Liberals under prime minister Campbell-Bannerman, who swiftly formed a sturdy government. Among the members of the new ministry were rising Liberal stars such as Asquith (Chancellor of the Exchequer); Lloyd George (President of the Board of Trade); and Winston Churchill (Under-Secretary at the Colonial Office). Other ministers included Sir Edward Grey as Foreign Secretary and R. B. Haldane, Secretary of State for War. Morley, now finished with his monumental life of Gladstone, went to the India Office.

To bring the outstanding issues to the country, Campbell-Bannerman dissolved parliament early in 1906. Expectations among eager Liberals were high: they had last held office a full decade earlier. Their targets were self-evident: inadequate preparations for the South African War; the Education Act of 1902; Chamberlain and tariff reform; drift and dalliance instead of firm leadership from the Unionists. The Unionists could only manage a half-hearted defence.

Chamberlain was nevertheless determined to campaign as vigorously as ever. Tired of 'word-splitting' with Balfour,[110] he struck out on his own, conducting an independent campaign as the leader of a Tariff Reform party.[111] First in the field with an election address, he campaigned tirelessly against the Liberals, ignoring Balfour and the Unionist moderates. For him, such a tactic had the advantage of raising his voice above all other Unionists with the hope that he could emerge after the election – no matter what the outcome – as the leader of the largest faction within the Unionist alliance. During most of January, he spoke every other day, largely in the West Midlands. Beyond his Duchy, the Tariff Reform League was proving more effective than Conservative Party headquarters. The League's substantial election fund for Chamberlain's personal use, for example, was employed against Unionist free traders in the constituencies in order to strengthen tariff reform candidates within the Unionist Party.[112]

Chamberlain's success in Birmingham was complete after the polls closed: all seven Birmingham Unionists were returned. The Unionists as a whole, however, suffered disaster – greater by far than that of the Liberals at the Khaki Election of 1900. It was in fact the worst election defeat suffered by any party since 1832.[113] Of a total of 670 parliamentary seats, the new government won a thumping majority made up of 377 Liberals, 83 Irish, and 53 Labour – a combined total of 513. Only 157 Conservative and Liberal Unionist MPs were returned. Worse still, pre-election divisions among the Unionists remained. Chamberlain and his tariff reform supporters had become the largest group, followed by Balfour and the moderates with a small number of Unionist free traders lagging behind.[114]

If the Unionists were brought low by the election, Chamberlain at least had secured a desirable outcome. He now had the leverage necessary to take the next step in controlling what had become the minority party in the House of Commons. He turned his attention quickly to Balfour, who had lost his seat at Manchester, to reinforce what he saw as the lessons of the election. He strongly hinted that he himself should become interim leader of the Unionists, but only on the condition that such a move be sanctioned by a meeting of the party. Agreeing that Chamberlain should be leader pro tem, Balfour nevertheless refused to call a party meeting: he was wise enough to know that Chamberlain would, by some means or other, conspire to control any party gathering. Correspondence between the two quickly degenerated into an airing of their continuing differences over party policy.[115] Once again, they attempted to come to terms at Chamberlain's London house in Prince's Gardens on 2 February. But as in the past, there was no agreement. Mary Chamberlain, who was present, pronounced it 'a difficult situation'. Chamberlain termed the meeting 'most unsatisfactory' in a letter to Garvin.[116] Denouncing Balfour's continued policy 'of delay and mystification', Chamberlain declared his intention to organize a separate tariff reform group within the Conservative and Unionist Party.

Realizing that he held a weak hand without a seat in parliament and with fewer supporters in the Commons than Chamberlain, Balfour had little choice but to back down once more.[117] Balfour was fully aware of Chamberlain's uncompromising nature and knew that Chamberlain would be unwilling to alter his demands.[118] On 6 February, therefore, Balfour agreed to a party meeting. He also accepted Chamberlain's request for a committee to consider democratizing the party organization. In the next several days, a further flurry of letters and two additional meetings persuaded Balfour to support fiscal reform as a priority for the party. In addition, he agreed to a moderate general tariff and a small duty on corn as unobjectionable in principle.

These hectic days of hurried negotiation and general confusion in Unionist ranks were of considerable concern to party regulars. One of the party whips, Lord Balcarres, a protectionist but full of mistrust against the impertinent Chamberlain, thought the situation was 'extremely delicate' and blamed the 'devil of a row' on Chamberlain's 'frenzied haste'. Balcarres feared that Chamberlain, 'drunk with personal success' at the recent Birmingham elections, was planning to secede from Unionist ranks to form a new political party.[119] Chamberlain, however, proceeded apace to capture the Unionists from within. Worn down at last, Balfour capitulated, officially accepting the terms of 6 February. In an exchange of letters on 14 February 1906, St Valentine's Day, Balfour and Chamberlain sealed the bargain.[120]

The so-called Valentine Compact was viewed by nearly everyone as a victory for Chamberlain. Certainly Chamberlain himself thought so. At a private celebratory dinner party at Prince's Gardens on the evening of the 14th, Sir Herbert Maxwell found Chamberlain 'radiant'.[121] Chaplin, who was also present, declared Chamberlain's political triumph the greatest since Disraeli had captured the Conservative Party: 'no one but Joe could have done it', he exulted.[122] Published in the morning newspapers the next day, the letters forming the Compact brought jubilation to tariff reformers. Their festive mood spilled over at the party meeting that evening at Lansdowne House. Balfour seemed cowed and a captive of the Chamberlainites. Chamberlain was in triumphant mood, for he understood that the Valentine Compact could be used against party members who were unenthusiastic for tariff reform. Indeed, at the annual meeting of the Liberal Union Club in May, Chamberlain imposed a loyalty test of tariff reform upon every Unionist candidate for parliament. 'If a candidate refuses', he warned, 'let it be understood that he is not on this point in unison with the vast majority of his party.'[123]

The political conflict between Balfour and Chamberlain in 1905 and 1906 that we have examined reveals incontestably the strength of Chamberlain's drive for power. He was not merely interested in pushing hard for a favoured policy: he was also inflexibly determined to carry it forward without compromise; to persist unrelentingly in overturning every obstacle in his way; and to punish those who opposed him. These characteristics we have observed throughout the course of his career – a life of striving for power and control and the domination of others even when larger goals were jeopardized. In a largely neglected analysis of Chamberlain's behaviour during the leadership crisis, David Dutton has made a convincing case that Chamberlain plotted, in spite of his protestations otherwise, to displace Balfour as leader of the Unionists in the weeks following the election of 1906.[124] Indeed, the evidence is clear that Chamberlain had begun working against Balfour long before the election.

The Valentine Compact left Chamberlain as dominant in his party as he had ever been – and as ruthless. Fiscal reform and a general tariff had been recognized as part of the official party platform. Balfour had been contained. Rogue party members would be disciplined. Chamberlain's next task was to move quickly and thoroughly in restructuring the Unionist Party along more democratic (that is, Chamberlainite) lines. In addition to his labours for tariff reform and in drawing together the reins of power in the party, Chamberlain continued to push as far as possible his agenda in the new parliament.

But Chamberlain's plans were limited by the overwhelming Liberal parliamentary majority. Neophyte Liberal MPs treated him with disrespect and were unimpressed by his parliamentary performances. His speeches were less incisive; his voice was losing its once clarion quality.[125] Chamberlain himself complained of 'a coarser tone' in the new House: 'these fellows', he wrote to Chaplin, 'remind me of the behaviour of men in a second-rate County Council'.[126] The truth was that Chamberlain was aging. By the end of the parliamentary session, Chamberlain would complete 30 years in Parliament. Nearly 70, he was increasingly subject to bouts of ill health. Colds, influenza, and gout plagued him regularly. His remarkable stamina had been sapped.

He retained, nevertheless, the loyalty and support of his Birmingham base. In celebration of his long public service and in honour of his forthcoming 70th birthday, Birmingham city fathers planned a gala celebration in the summer of 1906.[127] Travelling by train from London to Highbury on Thursday, 5 July, Chamberlain and his family made ready for the festivities. The following day, commemorative medals were distributed to elementary school children. Faculty and students at the University of Birmingham sent congratulations to its founder. Factories and city shops were closed to allow workers to join in the celebrations. Meanwhile, spontaneous decorations complete with ribbons and bunting appeared along the streets of the city. The climax of the day was Chamberlain's appearance in an open motorcar being driven to the Council House for a civic luncheon. On Saturday, at a second luncheon, he was honoured by 200 Birmingham dignitaries, including MPs, aldermen and councillors, church leaders, and other officials, both clerical and lay. At mid-afternoon, he appeared at the head of an 80-car cavalcade on a 17-mile tour to each of the city's parks. Along the route, cheering thousands, some of whom had been brought in on special excursion trains from around the country, greeted Chamberlain.

Monday's activities were more partisan, for Chamberlain had decided to use the opportunity to send a clear political message to friend and foe alike. The main event was an evening rally, presided over by the chairman of the local Conservative Association to symbolize the solidarity of tariff-reforming Conservatives and Liberal Unionists. Thus was the Valentine Compact again impressed upon the public. In his speech that evening, Chamberlain engaged in a lengthy apologia for his political career.[128] Admitting that there might be the appearance that he had changed his principles and ideals over time, he justified any shift by quoting Gladstone that change was 'a sign of life. If you are alive you must change.' Only the dead never changed. In any case, the greatest change in recent political history, he maintained, was the adoption of a separatist Home Rule by the Liberals. That action had destroyed the Liberal Party: they had changed, not he. Birmingham, too, had remained staunch over the years. Birmingham had refused to weaken the heart of the empire by accepting a Liberal-style Home Rule, and it remained true to the principles of social reform. Chamberlain then attacked by name his enemies – the Duke of Devonshire, the old Whig elite, and all free traders. He castigated at length 'the Little Englander', who was 'utterly devoid of imagination', 'unpatriotic', 'foolish', and interested only in shortsighted material consequences of political actions. For the real statesmen at the beginning of the twentieth century, the task must be grander and nobler: it must be a closer sympathy for, and a better understanding of, the unity of empire. At the conclusion of his speech, Chamberlain left Bingley Hall to be met by 5,000 torch-bearers who accompanied his car to Cannon Hill Park where the torches, one by one, were thrown onto a mounting bonfire. From there, Chamberlain and Mary drove to Highbury, passing hundreds of celebratory Chinese lanterns. The celebration ended with a gigantic fireworks portrait of Chamberlain blazing over the night sky.

The following day, 10 July, he took the afternoon train to London in order to host a mens' dinner at the House of Commons, but, feeling fatigued, he invited them to Prince's Gardens. The next morning, he met with the Tariff Commission. Returning home, he again was tired and cancelled a trip to the House. After tea, he entered his library to read and work. That evening he was scheduled to attend, along with Mary, a dinner party at Lady Cunard's. As the time for departure approached and passed, and with the carriage waiting at the door, there was no sign of Chamberlain in the drawing room. Knocking on the bathroom door adjacent to the library, Mary discovered it was locked from the inside. Hearing Chamberlain faintly calling out, she immediately summoned a servant to fetch a crowbar. Before he arrived, the door latch slowly opened. Mary, rushing in, discovered her husband lying exhausted and almost helpless on the floor: he had crawled to the door, his right side paralyzed. He had suffered a massive stroke.

13

POWER LOST

To protect Chamberlain's political influence and guard his reputation, the family's immediate response was to conceal the extent of his illness. After issuing a public statement that he had been incapacitated by a severe attack of gout, Mary and the children drew a ring of silence around Chamberlain's condition.[1] But there was no doubt of its seriousness. His once clear and decisive speech was now thickened and indistinct. His right arm and leg were so badly paralyzed that he could scarcely move. For a month after the stroke, he lay in a darkened room at his home in Prince's Gardens. Very slowly, some slight mobility returned, but his progress was measured in a few hesitant steps. Only in mid-September was he well enough to travel to Birmingham where he continued rest and relaxation at Highbury, well out of the public eye.

Family members initially expected a full recovery, noting with hope every sign of improvement. In a letter to her mother two months after the stroke, Mary wrote that Joe was walking up and down stairs.[2] Austen also reported to Garvin that his father was 'going on very well', although he would undertake no public work that autumn. A few months later, in February 1907, Austen again informed Garvin that his father was improving 'but very slowly'.[3] To facilitate recuperation, Chamberlain and his wife headed for the warmth of southern France, renting a villa near St-Raphael from March until May 1907. While abroad, Chamberlain wrote reassuringly to Henry Chaplin that, though still lame, he hoped to return to the House of Commons at the next session.[4] As the months passed, however, it was obvious to all that his recovery would be only partial, never complete. An early indication of his own realization of this came in November 1907, when he admitted to Leopold Maxse that he was 'getting somewhat discouraged'.[5] Downcast by his illness, Chamberlain was also disheartened by fears that his active public life was finished. In more reflective mood, he was saddened, too, by the loss of many of his political comrades, most of whom were, as he wrote to Collings, 'all gone'.[6] Chamberlain's struggle to come to terms with his illness bore heavily on his family members. As Mary disclosed to Austen: 'it rends my heart when I stop to think how hard it is for him'.[7]

Chamberlain's illness and incapacity have led many historians to believe that his political career was effectively at an end. Lord Blake has written that Chamberlain's stroke left him 'an incoherent wreck of his former self'.[8] David Dutton character-ized Chamberlain after 1906 as 'a semi-paralysed spectator of the political scene'.[9] More recently, David Powell labelled Chamberlain 'an invalid recluse' following his stroke.[10] John Ramsden thinks that after his stroke, Chamberlain 'lingered on' until 1914.[11] Although recognizing some periods of remission, Michael Bentley neverthe-less writes that Chamberlain remained an 'incoherent paralytic' until his death.[12]

Not a few of Chamberlain's contemporaries had the same opinion. In the summer of 1907, Balcarres recorded that Chamberlain, in spite of optimistic reports from his family, was thought to be 'hopelessly incurable.'[13] Hewins, visiting him in February 1908, believed that his memory was good, his judgment sound, and his mental faculties as sharp as ever. His voice, however, the great instrument of his country campaigns, sounded as though 'some clumsy mechanical contrivance' had been fitted into his throat.[14] Hewins concluded that, in spite of Chamberlain's vigorous mind, he was 'in fact dying'.[15] Cecil Spring-Rice, who also saw him at Cannes in early 1908, was equally sorrowful: 'I almost wish I hadn't seen him', he wrote Lord Cranley, 'it is so sad to see that sort of power nearing its end.'[16]

These predictions were premature. Though his voice was effectively lost and his mobility severely restricted, Chamberlain was nevertheless determined to play an active role in party politics. He had lived for power and influence throughout his life. His unique stamina and strenuous administrative pace were slowed, but not extinguished. His attempts to dominate and control in the years following his stroke – even in a semi-paralytic state – gave testimony to the depth of his need for power. It is also clear that his political views were not softened by his illness.[17] By early 1908, he had begun to entertain guests and to receive visitors, both at Highbury and Prince's Gardens. Balfour, Hewins, Chaplin, Collings, and Amery among others came to his door. Utilizing Mary, his daughters, and professional secretaries, he con-tinued his communication with the outside world.

Most importantly in retaining his political contacts at large was the role that Chamberlain designated for his eldest son. Austen found himself more than ever a surrogate, a conduit through which the ideas, wishes, and demands of his stricken father would be carried forward. Austen was keenly aware of this responsibility. In a letter to his stepmother, he wrote: 'I feel that I stand as Father's son in a very special way for Tariff Reform; that men look to me to hold that citadel ...'.[18] Austen often found this arrangement uncomfortable. Lacking the drive and intensity of his father, he had no taste for the gruelling hours of work and endless attention to detail that Chamberlain had given to his own political ambitions. Moreover, Austen's political views were more moderate, less uncompromising than those of his father. Austen was, it seemed to his contemporaries, a gentleman – in clear contrast to his father. His education at Rugby and Trinity College, Cambridge, his privileged friendships, and his admiration for Balfour placed him firmly within the political establishment, a position that Joe never sought and never attained.[19]

Above all, there lay in Austen a flaw fatal to a politician – an inability to be ruthless. Well aware of these character traits, Austen once confessed to Walter Long: 'Through my father's illness I am necessarily forced more into the position of a protagonist.' It was a part, he admitted, 'which I am unfit for'.[20] Austen was thus continually placed in false positions. At a time when he might hope to play a significant role in politics based upon his own distinctive contributions, he was forced to bow to the continued domination of his father.[21] Even in the final months of his life, Chamberlain was controlling his son. When Chamberlain at last announced his retirement from his West Birmingham constituency in January 1914, he determined that Austen should take his place. At his father's 'urgent wish', Austen resigned his seat in East Worcestershire to stand for West Birmingham at the next general election. To Mary, Austen wrote of 'the pain' of his departure from his friends and colleagues in Worcestershire, a constituency he had served for 23 years. When Austen informed them of his future plans, 'the strain was so great that I came out after a short hour ... with a racking headache'. 'I feel', he confessed to Mary, 'as if at fifty I had got to begin life again ...'.[22]

Exerting his dominance over Austen as his faithful mouthpiece, Chamberlain could speak with authority for Unionist and tariff reform causes. Ever watchful for opportunities, he eagerly followed the political scene for a chance to influence events. His time came sooner than expected. Although the Liberals had been elected in 1906 with an overwhelming majority, Campbell-Bannerman's lacklustre leadership and a surprising failure of political will thwarted their legislative programme in the House of Commons. The Liberals were additionally stymied in the Lords, where the Unionist majority persistently blocked their agenda. In effect, the House of Lords was becoming an obstructionist tool of the Unionist Party. A debilitating economic depression in 1907–8 further dampened Liberal morale. With Chamberlain cheering them on, the Unionists claimed that the depression and growing unemployment was a result of rigidly held Liberal free trade doctrines. Only protectionism, they claimed, could revive the economy and put people back to work. The Unionist message was supported by the Colonial Conference of 1907 which advocated imperial preferences, the heart of Chamberlainite tariff reform. Balfour, perhaps influenced by the Conference and impressed by the continuing protectionist sentiment within the Unionist Party, accepted tariff reform as official party policy in November 1907. By then, Unionists had begun to enjoy some electoral successes, winning several by-elections, and taking control of the London County Council.[23]

The Unionists were further energized by the news that the Liberals were having difficulties in framing a budget for the fiscal year 1909–10. A large deficit was expected as a result of financing old-age pensions and increased military needs, especially naval construction. Where could the money be found? The new Liberal ministry under Asquith, who replaced the ailing Campbell-Bannerman in April 1908, decided upon increased taxes. It fell to David Lloyd George, now Chancellor of the Exchequer, to work up the details. Lloyd George's budget, presented to the House of Commons in April 1909, proved a shock to the Unionists. By increasing inheritance taxes, introducing a land valuation scheme, proposing a sharply progressive graduated income tax and a series of land taxes, the budget was overwhelmingly directed against the wealthier classes. Projecting substantial revenues – at £25,000,000 it was a 12 per cent increase over the previous year's estimate – the budget also allowed Lloyd

George to reap from it political advantages.[24] By raising taxes on the wealthy, especially the landed elite, Lloyd George could portray his proposals as an example of
'democratic' finance. This 'People's Budget' would force the privileged few to pay for
the needs of the many. Liberals could simultaneously increase their popularity among
working-class voters while sending a strong signal to the obstructionist House of
Lords. Equally important, progressive taxation would allow the Liberals to circum-
vent Chamberlainite populism by financing substantial social programmes, such as
old-age pensions, without resorting to tariff reform.[25]

Upon hearing the news of the budget 'with rueful admiration', as Amery puts
it,[26] Chamberlain, then at Cannes, left immediately for London. In opposing the
budget, Chamberlain and the Unionists had to tread carefully: otherwise it would
appear that they were acting against the people and defending the rich. The emerging Unionist strategy, devised in part by Chamberlain, therefore argued not on social
but on constitutional grounds. In other words, when the budget passed the Liberal
House of Commons, as it was certain to do, the House of Lords should reject it in
order to bring about a general election. The Unionists could then pose as upholders
of the democratic right of a referendum. This was the substance of Chamberlain's
advice widely given in the later months of 1909.[27] Wherever Unionist conferences
and rallies were held, Chamberlain was sure to send a message to be read, eschew-
ing compromise and enjoining those in attendance to fight hard against the Liberal
budget.[28] At a Unionist rally in Bingley Hall, Birmingham, in late September 1909,
for example, Balfour was the main speaker; but it was Chamberlain's letter that
drew the most attention. In that letter, he urged that the present controversy over
the budget be 'referred to the people' and if the Liberal government refused to do
so, Chamberlain hoped the House of Lords 'will see their way to force a general
election'.[29]

During the autumn of 1909, Highbury was again a centre of operations for
Unionist Party strategy as party leaders made their way to Birmingham. Balfour and
the Unionist peers were especially active in consulting with Chamberlain. Within a
few weeks, Chamberlain moved to London to be more accessible to the party. When
the Lords voted down the budget on 30 November, Asquith was forced to call an
election. During the campaign, Chamberlain remained in the thick of the fight and
his influence was evident until the polls closed in late January 1910. As the *National
Review* put it: 'Mr Chamberlain is the captain of the cause.'[30] In spite of his illness,
Chamberlain stood (as ever) unopposed for West Birmingham and engaged in as
vigorous a campaign as he could manage. He opened with a manifesto, later distributed as a pamphlet.[31] Portraying tariff reform as the only alternative to a confiscatory
Liberal budget, Chamberlain raised high the protectionist flag. The salience of tariff
reform in the campaign has since been confirmed by an analysis of election addresses
showing that 74 per cent of all Unionist candidates considered it as the primary issue
of the campaign.[32] Uniting under this slogan, the Unionists challenged the Liberals
with some success. At the close of the election, the Liberals had won 275 seats, with
the Unionists close behind at 273. But 82 Irish Nationalists and 40 Labour MPs in
alliance with the Liberals returned them to power.

Although Unionists had done surprisingly well, the election result was undoubt-edly disappointing for Chamberlain. Nevertheless, he reaffirmed symbolically his unswerving commitment to the tariff reform cause by personally taking the oath at the opening session of the new parliament. Supported by Austen, he was led into the chamber, took his seat on the opposition bench, and while seated, touched the pen which Austen used to sign the roll.[33] A few days later, Chamberlain was on his way to Cannes. While he was abroad – remaining in France until late May – the political battle went forward, though very largely against Chamberlain's hopes. The Budget became law and the Liberals then busily set to work curbing the power of the House of Lords. Their proposed Parliament Bill sought to prohibit the Lords from either amending or rejecting any future money bills. All other bills, even if the Lords vetoed them, automatically would become law within two years. As the proposals gained shape, the opposition in the House of Lords stiffened: they refused, as one historian has put it, to acquiesce in their own emasculation.[34] After a series of futile confer-ences to resolve the constitutional impasse, Asquith called another election, having first won a pledge from the new monarch, George V, to create enough Liberal peers to override continued obstruction in the Lords.

The Liberal's firm pursuit of their legislative agenda, as revealed by their determi-nation to call a second general election within a year, brought the Unionist leadership to an important decision. Even though there was evidence of a considerable sentiment for tariff reform in the country and an equally strong loyalty toward Chamberlain, the Unionists had lost two consecutive elections under the protectionist banner. The prospects of losing a third election were very real. An uncompromising tariff reform cry had gone as far as it could. To win, Unionists had to widen their appeal. On 29 November 1910, the day after the dissolution of parliament, Balfour publicly pledged at the Albert Hall that should the Unionists win the election, taxes on food would not be levied until a national referendum was held.

To the Chamberlains, Balfour's declaration was a stunning blow.[35] Balfour had sold the Chamberlainite pass. Attempting to regain lost ground, Austen publicly declared that Balfour's pledge was for the present election only, and would not be binding thereafter. The public disagreement between Balfour and Austen and the prospect of a Unionist split on the eve of an election campaign was an unhappy prospect. Garvin predicted ruin for the Unionists if, as he put it, the shadow of Joe's authority was 'to give a spurious influence to the essentially mediocre ... mind of his son'.[36] Unionist division did not materially affect the outcome of the election, however. The final result was a reprise of the January election: Liberals and Unionists were evenly divided – 272 seats each, with the Irish and Labour once again holding the balance.

Post-election consequences for the Unionists were quick to follow, and included more bad news for the Chamberlains. In February 1911, the Liberal government introduced its Parliament Bill. Chamberlain, who had once been the scourge of the Lords, now became their champion. He supported the hard-line 'Ditchers', a group of uncompromising peers who were unwilling to bend to Asquith's threat to pack the Lords with Liberal peers unless the Lords passed the Bill. Urging his son to 'fight to the end', Chamberlain hitched Austen to the Ditcher cart.[37] The final vote in August, however, found the Ditchers in a minority when the Parliament Bill passed the House of Lords.

Under pressure from the embittered Ditchers as well as from the more zealous tariff reformers, Balfour – weary of factional strife – decided to resign his post as Unionist leader in early November.[38] For Chamberlain, this presented a supreme opportunity for Austen, and vicariously for himself. Now was the chance for Austen at last to assume the reins of power, to lead the Unionists, and to stop the drift away from tariff reform. Summoning Austen home from a holiday in Lugano, Chamberlain made plain his ambitions to his son. But Austen, a Balfour loyalist, confessed to his father that he was 'sick' at the news of the resignation.[39] To Mary, too, Austen wrote of his reluctance to lead and how gladly he would serve as a 'second fiddle'.[40] Austen fully understood that, unlike his father, he lacked the will to power. After a week's half-hearted attempt at the leadership, Austen, along with Walter Long, stood down in favour of Andrew Bonar Law, a moderate tariff reformer. That Joe's hopes were blighted was an understatement: Amery claims it was 'a fearful blow'.[41] Indeed, at the news, Garvin thought he heard 'great heart strings snapping at last in Joe'.[42] Austen, above all, feared the impact of his withdrawal. His 'chief regret' at the loss of the leadership was that it 'would be a severe disappointment' to his father. He urged Mary to tell him 'that I am sorry to have grieved him'.[43] With the Chamberlain stars descending and the Liberals rapidly moving forward on the backs of three election wins in a row, Unionist fortunes deteriorated further. In attempting to find a winning platform, Bonar Law – following the lead of Balfour and the growing opinion within the party – jettisoned the notion of food taxes as detrimental to future Unionist successes at the polls. Bonar Law was also motivated by the need to consolidate Unionists against the Home Rule Bill for Ireland introduced by the Liberals in April 1912. Thus, the defence of Ulster trumped tariff reform as the dominant political issue.[44] Bonar Law had hoped to gain Chamberlain's acquiescence in this fundamental shift in the tariff reform programme, but the old man refused.

Thereafter, Chamberlain's advice and opinions were no longer solicited. Only a faithful few sought him out. His political resolve was finally broken. During his annual trek to Cannes in early 1913, he announced that he would not stand at the next general election. Successive attacks of gout made it increasingly difficult to craft the letters and directives which had once made up so much a part of his political life. His eyesight had begun to fail. Yet he had enough spark during the autumn of 1913 to condemn publicly the Home Rule policy of the Liberals and to confer with Edward Carson, leader of the Irish Unionists, at Highbury. He retained sufficient stamina to make a final appearance, pushed about in a bath chair, at an enormous garden party at Highbury on 6 June 1914.

Within two weeks, he left Highbury for the last time for a stay at Prince's Gardens London. One of his visitors, on 29 June 1914, was Leo Amery, who long remembered Chamberlain's parting words – to fight hard against the Home Rule Bill which had just been sent to the House of Lords after its passage in the Commons. The next day, Chamberlain suffered a slight heart attack. The following night, Mary heard her restless husband making a speech in his sleep. The morning after, Mary read to Joe from *The Times* as usual: the leading article commented on the murder of the Archduke Franz Ferdinand at Sarajevo. A second heart attack later in the day, more serious than the first, put him to bed. After several hours, he died peacefully that evening, on 2 July, surrounded by his family.[45] Although offered burial at Westminster Abbey, Chamberlain had been explicit in his wish for a final resting place in Birmingham. To that city his body was taken by train. On 6 July, after a simple service at the Church of the Messiah, where he had once taught Sunday School to young boys, a funeral cortege through the streets of Birmingham brought him to Key Hill Cemetery, where other members of his family lay.

Chamberlain's death was marked by national grieving. For several days, mourners paid homage to his life and career. The *Daily Mirror* brought out a 'Joseph Chamberlain Memorial Number'. In successive editions, *The Times* of London praised Chamberlain's vigour and 'energy of leadership'; his remarkable 'young man's capacity for growth'; and his 'directness of mind.' His courage, resourcefulness, and boldness were recalled. He represented in his own person, *The Times* noted, 'the spirit of civic betterment' in his 'keen and fruitful activity' in Birmingham. He was exemplary in his 'power of thought' and his vision as 'a builder-up all his life ... in turning a small into a great estate in successive spheres of activity'.[46] In parliament, public tributes to Chamberlain were no less laudatory. Bonar Law and Balfour gave expected eulogies. Asquith, too, praised 'that striking personality'.[47] More qualified, but still strong words of praise came from the Marquis of Crewe, the leader of the Liberals in the House of Lords. Acknowledging Chamberlain's contentiousness and his 'heavy' verbal blows in public and parliamentary debate, Crewe also called Chamberlain the greatest 'civic figure that has ever been engaged in British politics.'[48]

The power of Chamberlain's personality clearly comes through in the words of his colleagues, friends, and political opponents at the close of his life. The strength of his political dominance in the public sphere was uppermost in their minds. Their praise was largely the praise of a man, not a great politician, able legislator, or a notable statesman. They could not find the words to comment on his contributions to British politics. Historians, too, have found it difficult to evaluate Chamberlain's achievements. Indeed, he is difficult to classify. He cannot be easily compared to the great leaders of the nineteenth and early twentieth centuries. He was not a Peel, who could set aside party shibboleths for the common good. He did not inspire affection as did Disraeli. Nor was he a moral leader like Gladstone. Unlike Lloyd George, he did not successfully legislate for popular causes. Chamberlain's greatest cause – the British Empire – no longer exists. Tariff reform, at least in his lifetime, was a failed campaign. To modern eyes, then, Chamberlain's achievements seem distant and dim. He may best be remembered as the father of a more famous son, Neville, who pledged and lost 'peace for our time'.

If our analysis holds, a fundamental explanation for Chamberlain's inability to achieve his greatest political goals and his consequent lack of permanent historical stature lies in his need for control and dominance and his drive for power and authority. These characteristics can be a strength, serving useful political and social purposes in maintaining order and stability.[49] But it would seem that Chamberlain's need for power was greater than most. Too often, Chamberlain's tendency to dominate was dysfunctional, working against his larger goals. He often appeared unprincipled, greedily ambitious, and opportunistic, driving away potential sources of political support. Mistrust of Chamberlain's motives was rife on all sides of the political spectrum. Too often he changed his opinions, switched party allegiances, and alienated political colleagues.

It is not unusual, of course, for politicians to be inconsistent. But it is rare for them to launch sizable public campaigns in support of each shifting point of view. The comments of Bernard Coleridge, a Gladstonian Liberal, exasperated by Chamberlain's leadership of the tariff reform movement in the autumn of 1903, must stand for many. Denouncing Chamberlain in a public address, Coleridge asked rhetorically: 'Why should they trust him? Had he inflexible principles? They had changed more often than the moon ... He was once a Republican, now a Monarchist; once a Home Ruler, now a Unionist; once a Radical, now a Tory; Free Trader once, now Protectionist. And the worst was, he was always cocksure he was right!'[50] Many Conservatives, as we have seen, had the same strong reservations about Chamberlain. In his memoirs, Viscount Chelwood, a younger son of Lord Salisbury, summarized the opinions of 'the ordinary Conservative Party men' who were 'in considerable doubt' about following 'the lead of an old nonconformist Radical' like Chamberlain. The Conservative rank and file never forgot 'the bitterness' with which Chamberlain had attacked their leaders and 'his rather ill-considered reference to them as men "that toiled not, neither did they spin"'.[51]

If Chamberlain never won the support and loyalty of the majority of the politicians of his day, he was nevertheless widely recognized as a man of talent and dedication. He was a most extraordinary spokesman for his causes. He brought determination to politics and courage to his various campaigns. He understood the structures of political power and the importance of public opinion. He was an administrator of rare ability. His personal stamina buttressed his persistence in the pursuit of public policy. He was never less than bold when he staked out his positions. And there are real achievements to be found in his career. His accomplishments in Birmingham, where he promoted education and civic improvement, must rank high in any evaluation of his career. But there were greater achievements in the nation at large. If it is true that he polarized political parties, he also brought to a burgeoning democratic electorate important issues in a clear and incisive manner. Addressing massed assemblies year after year, he put forward for public debate some of the most critical issues of his day. Social and political reform, foreign policy, the nature of popular government were all touched upon to some degree by Chamberlain. His speeches – pithy, epigrammatic, and rousing – fairly leap from the printed page at the distance of more than a century. Denied the ultimate political prize he sought, he found adulation and approval from his natural constituency – the disadvantaged and disenfranchised of the nation. He was to them not 'pushful Joe', but 'our Joe'. Speaking directly to the people, he no doubt served his own needs as well: hearing the thunderous accolades of enthusiastic crowds was a tonic. The effect of a crowd upon Chamberlain was plainly visible to

Winston Churchill at Oldham during the election of 1900. As the two men stepped forward onto the platform, Churchill saw how 'the blood mantled' in Chamberlain's cheek, 'and his eye as it caught mine twinkled with pure excitement'. Chamberlain, he understood, 'loved the roar of the multitude'.[52]

In the roar of the multitude, Chamberlain discovered his most natural and abiding constituency. Harnessing public opinion as a vehicle for his own advancement, he served not only his own ends. His lifelong interest in the improvement of both urban and rural workingmen, whom he willingly met at workplaces and meeting halls and in country towns, was his most consistent political undertaking. His staunch advocacy on their behalf in parliament was a pioneering effort to expand the powers of the state to improve their working conditions and quality of life. As a radical, and as a member of both Liberal and Conservative governments, he kept alive the prospects of progressive legislation. Understanding the needs of a vast number of underprivileged members of the population and searching for solutions to meet them, Chamberlain was at his best. In this achievement alone, Chamberlain's career can be celebrated as a significant contribution to a broadening of opportunities for all the citizens of a fully modern democratic state.

NOTES

1 The Pursuit of Power

1   Chamberlain Papers, JC 24/3/5. From a typed memorandum by J. L. Garvin, who interviewed Morley in May 1923, shortly before Morley's death. Morley, then very old, was 'bent into half a hoop' and deaf but his mind was still sharp and acute. Morley knew Chamberlain well and initially shared with him a deep friendship and a common radical cause. Morley was editor of the influential *Fortnightly Review* from 1867 to 1882 and the *Pall Mall Gazette* from 1880 to 1883; served as a Liberal MP almost continuously from 1883 to 1908; and became Chief Secretary for Ireland under two administrations of William Gladstone. Although strongly anti-imperial, he became Chief Secretary for India in 1905.

2   *Moseley & King's Heath Journal*, IV, 38 (July 1895), a copy of which may be found in Chamberlain Papers, JC 34/2/2/4.

3   Chamberlain Papers, AC 4/11/16. This is a copy of a radio address given on the BBC in December 1948 by L. S. Amery.

4   Chamberlain Papers, JC 28 A1/18, JC to Mary Endicott, 6 May 1888.

5   See, for example, Denis Judd, *Radical Joe: A Life of Joseph Chamberlain* (Cardiff, paperback edn, 1993), xv and xvi; Duncan Watts, *Joseph Chamberlain and the Challenge of Radicalism* (London, 1992), [I] and 39–40; T. A. Jenkins, *The Liberal Ascendancy, 1830–1886* (New York, 1994), 184. Particularly damning was A. J. P. Taylor's assessment. Chamberlain, he wrote, 'had energy without principle' and was marked by such severely destructive political tendencies that 'he cannot be ranked much above the level of a Ramsay McDonald': *Essays in English History* (London, Penguin, 1976), 186–90.

6   Peter Marsh, *Joseph Chamberlain: Entrepreneur in Politics* (New Haven, 1994), Preface.

7   Philip Hills, 'Division and Cohesion in the Nineteenth-Century Middle Class: The Case of Ipswich 1830–1870', *Urban History Yearbook* (1987), 42–50. See also R. J. Morris, 'Voluntary Societies and British Urban Elites, 1780–1850: An Analysis', *Historical Journal*, 27/1 (1983), 95–118. Morris takes his examples from Leeds, Newcastle, and Edinburgh. See also Thomas Walter Laqueur, *Religion and Respectability: Sunday Schools and Working Class Culture, 1780–1850* (New Haven and London, 1976).

8   John Seed, 'Unitarianism, Political Economy and the Antinomies of Liberal Culture in Manchester, 1830–50', *Social History*, 7/1 (January 1982), 1–25. See also his 'Theologies of Power: Unitarianism and the Social Relations of Religious Discourse, 1800–50', in R. J. Morris (ed.), *Class, Power and Social Structure in British Nineteenth-Century Towns* (Leicester, 1986), 108–56. Seed's examples are drawn from Hull, Leeds, Newcastle, and Wakefield. Paul T. Phillips' *The Sectarian Spirit: Sectarianism, Society, and Politics in Victorian Cotton Towns* (Toronto, 1982) looks at Bolton, Preston, and Stockport. Koditschek, in discussing more broadly nonconformist congregations, believes that they

served as little republics in which the congregants could develop a 'capacity for command and self-government, so necessary for men who aspired to elite roles:' Theodore Koditschek, 'The Dynamics of Class Formation in Nineteenth-Century Bradford', in A. L. Beier, David Cannadine, and James M. Rosenheim (eds), *The First Modern Society: Essays in English History in Honour of Lawrence Stone* (Cambridge, 1989), 527.

9   Marsh *Chamberlain*, xi–xiii. Throughout his book, Marsh emphasizes the influence of Chamberlain's business career upon his political behaviour.

10 As F. M. L. Thompson points out, the role of the entrepreneur in economic growth is contested. Technical economic historians emphasize factor endowments and growth rates, whereas business and social historians tend to see entrepreneurs as having profound effects on the pace and direction of innovation and growth. Thompson believes that individual entrepreneurs were important in the motivation to take the risks involved in creating new enterprises: Thompson, *Gentrification and the Enterprise Culture: Britain 1780–1980* (Oxford, 2001), 6, 21. A sample of the scope and variety of entrepreneurial studies follows. Theoretical works include Edith Tilton Penrose, *The Theory of the Growth of the Firm* (Oxford, 1959); Mark Casson, *The Entrepreneur: An Economic Theory* (Totowa, N.J., 1982); and Robert F. Hebert and Albert N. Link, *The Entrepreneur: Mainstream Views and Radical Critiques* (New York, 1982). See also the important early article by George Herberton Evans, Jr., 'The Entrepreneur and Economic Theory: A Historical and Analytical Approach', *American Economic Review*, 39/13 (May 1949), 336–48. A useful summary is Charles Wilson, 'The Entrepreneur in the Industrial Revolution in Britain', *Explorations in Entrepreneurial History*, 7/3 (February 1955), 129–45. See also Sidney Pollard's *The Genesis of Modern Management: A Study of the Industrial Revolution in Great Britain* (London, 1965). Pollard's 'Reflections on Entrepreneurship and Culture in European Societies', *Transactions of the Royal Historical Society*, 5th ser., 40 (1990), 153–73 emphasizes the controlling and organizing functions of the entrepreneur.

11 Theodore Koditschek, 'Dynamics of Class Formation in Nineteenth Century Bradford', 511–48.

12 Theodore Koditschek, *Class Formation and Urban-Industrial Society: Bradford, 1750–1850* (Cambridge, 1990), 198.

13 Ibid., 196.

14 Francois Crouzet, *The First Industrialists: The Problem of Origins* (Cambridge, 1985), ch. 1, 'The Industrialist: A New Man'; D. C. Coleman and Peter Mathias (eds), *Enterprise and History: Essays in Honor of Charles Wilson* (Cambridge 1984), ch. 2, D. C. Coleman, 'Historians and Businessmen' and ch. 3, W. J. Reader, 'Businessmen and their Motives'.

15 Alfred Marshall, *Principles of Economics: An Introductory Volume,* 8th edn (London, 1938), 23.

16 The relevant sections are Schumpeter's *The Theory of Economic Development* (Cambridge, Mass, 1934), 62–94 – which may also be found in Peter Kilby, *Entrepreneurship and Economic Development* (New York, 1971), 43–70, especially 68–70.

17 David G. Winter, 'Power Motivation Revisited', and 'A Revised Scoring System for the Power Motive', in Charles P. Smith (ed.), *Motivation and Personality: Handbook of Thematic Content Analysis* (Cambridge, 1992), 301–10 and 311–24. Winter cites evidence that the power motive construct has proven valid across a wide variety of ethnic groups and cultures (305–6).

18 The classic work is David Winter, *The Power Motive* (New York, 1973): see also Winter's 'The Power Motive in Women – and Men', *Journal of Personality and Social Psychology*, 54/3 (1988), 510–19.

19 David C. McClelland and Robert I. Watson, Jr., 'Power Motivation and Risk-Taking Behavior', *Journal of Personality*, 41/1 (March 1973), 121–39.

20 Leonore Davidoff and Catherine Hall, *Family Fortunes: Men and Women of the English Middle Class, 1780–1850* (London, 1987).

21 As Tosh puts it: 'Authority, guidance and discipline continued to be viewed as central to the father's role. Masculinity, after all, was essentially about being master of one's own house, about exercising authority over children as well as wife and servants'; see John Tosh, *A Man's Place: Masculinity and the Middle-Class Home in Victorian England* (New Haven, 1999), 89; also 4, 77, 108.

2 An Entrepreneurial Heritage

1   Shoemakers were known as cordwainers, after the leather manufacturers of Cordova, Spain, whose high quality leather, known as cordovan, was often made into shoes. The sustained demand for footwear guaranteed by a steady rise in population made leather a flourishing business during much of the nineteenth century. See R. A. Church, 'The Shoe and Leather Industries', in Roy Church (ed.), *The Dynamics of Victorian Business: Problems and Perspectives to the 1870s* (London, 1980).

2   Peter Marsh, *Joseph Chamberlain: Entrepreneur in Politics* (New Haven, 1994), 6. For the details of Joseph's ancestors, family, and early life, see the initial chapters in Marsh's *Chamberlain*; Denis Judd, *Radical Joe: A Life of Joseph Chamberlain* (Cardiff, 1993); and Richard Jay's *Joseph Chamberlain: A Political Study* (Oxford, 1981). Also useful are the first four chapters of J. L. Garvin's *Life of Joseph Chamberlain* (London, 1932), vol. 1. Garvin's biography, the final three volumes of which were completed by Julian Amery (see Chapter 12, n. 52), remains valuable though clearly marked by a hero worship of its subject. Garvin's career in journalism brought him to the editorship of *The Outlook* (1905–6); *Pall Mall Gazette* (1912–15); and *The Observer* (1908–42).

3   R. J. Morris, 'The Middle Class and the Property Cycle during the Industrial Revolution', in T. C. Smout (ed.), *The Search for Wealth and Stability: Essays in Economic and Social History Presented to M. W. Flinn* (London, 1979), 91–113. For this and the following paragraph, see also Stana Nenadic, 'The Small Family Firm in Victorian Britain', *Business History*, 35/4 (October 1993), 86; Robert A. Pollak, 'A Transaction Cost Approach to Families and Households', *Journal of Economic Literature*, 23 (June 1985), 581–608; Yoram Ben-Porath, 'The F-Connection: Families, Friends, and Firms and the Organization of Exchange', *Population and Development Review*, 6/1 (March 1980), 1–30; Burton Benedict, 'Family Firms and Economic Development', *Southwestern Journal of Anthropology*, 24/1 (Spring 1968), 1–19.

4   Barbara M. D. Smith, 'The Galtons of Birmingham: Quaker Gun Merchants and Bankers, 1702–1831', *Business History* 9/2 (July 1967), 132–50.

5   David Cannadine, 'Joseph Gillott and his Family Firm: The Many Faces of Entrepreneurship', in Kristine Bruland and Patrick O'Brien (eds), *From Family Firms to Corporate Capitalism: Essays in Business and Industrial History in Honour of Peter Mathias* (Oxford, 1998), ch. 9. An even larger Birmingham pen maker was Gillott's friend and rival, Josiah Mason, who was later to play an important role in the establishment of Chamberlain's reputation as a civic benefactor.

6   See Marsh, *Chamberlain*, 24–8.

7   Packaging was not unimportant. Aldcroft reports that in the late nineteenth century German merchants successfully challenged English needle makers in the Brazilian market because the Brazilians disliked the black paper in which the English needles were wrapped, preferring the bright red paper of the Germans – even though English needles were of a higher quality. See D. H. Aldcroft, 'The Entrepreneur and the British Economy, 1870–1914', *Economic History Review*, 2nd ser., 17/1 (1964), 127.

8   Marsh, *Chamberlain*, 21.

9   Peter Marsh's designation: see the account of this episode in his *Chamberlain*, 44–8.

10 Ibid., 46.

11 As Hugh McLeod notes, belonging to the right church or chapel could not only pro-vide important connections but it also gave evidence of respectability and integrity for

businessmen on their way up. He cites the specific example of the young Chamberlain: Hugh McLeod, *Religion and Society in England, 1850–1914* (New York, 1996), 87–8.

12 J. A. Langford, *Modern Birmingham and Its Institutions* (Birmingham, 1873), I, 247; cited in Simon Gunn, *The Public Culture of the Victorian Middle Class: Ritual and Authority and the English Industrial City* (Manchester, 2000), 99.

13 For details of Chamberlain's drive for organization in his early Birmingham years, see Marsh, *Chamberlain*, ch. 2, and Garvin, *Life of Chamberlain*, vol. 1, ch. 4.

14 Chamberlain Papers, JC 1/1/1, 17 August 1857.

15 Ibid., JC 1/1/3, 2 August 1860.

16 Ibid., JC 1/1/8, 1 November 1860.

17 These quotations, from an unaddressed and undated memorandum, were clearly written after the death not of Harriet, but of his second wife in February 1875. See Chamberlain Papers, JC 1/5/1.

18 Chamberlain Papers, JC 5/58/3, 15 August 1867, JC to H. Peyton; quoted in Marsh, *Chamberlain*, 30.

19 This was not an uncommon assumption. Anthony Howe, in discussing the work of the Lancashire Public School Association during the 1840s and 1850s, notes that 'entrepreneurial interest' in education was predicated upon the need for improving human capital. Education could also inculcate moral principles in the belief that a moral worker was a better worker. See Howe, *The Cotton Masters, 1830–1860* (Oxford, 1984), 215–29.

20 A Unitarian and a partner in a firm associated with ironmongering, Collings later became the indispensable personal and political assistant to Chamberlain. A useful account of Collings' political career may be found in David Murray Aronson, 'Jesse Collings, Agrarian Radical, 1880–1892', (University of Massachusetts [Amherst] PhD Dissertation, 1975). See also Jesse Collings and Sir John L. Green, *The Life of the Right Hon. Jesse Collings* (London, 1920).

21 Forster was at that time Vice-President of the Committee on Council. Later he served in Gladstone's second ministry as Chief Secretary for Ireland (1880–2). He strongly opposed Chamberlain's radical policies as they had emerged by the 1880s.

22 Garvin, *Life of Chamberlain*, vol. 1, 109. Garvin's assessment of Chamberlain's leadership against the bill is characteristic: 'All his qualities as a man of action, and the defects of his qualities, now came out – swift and punctual in dispatch; prompt in decision; fibrous in tenacity; over-sanguine; full of venture; but full of resource; too blistering in attack and retort; but never fumbling or shrinking.'

23 To Dixon, he vowed: 'we will teach him his mistake' (Chamberlain Papers, JC 5/27/13, 3 March 1870). Most of this letter is reprinted in Garvin, *Life of Chamberlain*, vol. 1, 109–10. Garvin notes that Chamberlain 'fed on difficulties' (ibid., 147).

24 For Chamberlain's electoral efforts on behalf of the League, see Marsh, *Chamberlain*, 54–74.

25 A useful discussion of Chamberlain's role in local school board politics is A. F. Taylor, 'The History of the Birmingham School Board, 1870–1903' (MA Thesis, University of Birmingham, 1955).

26 Chamberlain Papers, JC 4/1/32–33, 19 February 1872.

27 As Margot Finn has persuasively argued in her richly detailed study, *After Chartism: Class and Nation in English Radical Politics, 1848–1874* (Cambridge, 1993). See also Eugenio F. Biagini and Alastair J. Reid, 'Currents of Radicalism, 1850–1914', and the introductory chapter to their edited volume, *Currents of Radicalism: Popular Radicalism, Organised Labour and Party Politics in Britain, 1850–1914* (Cambridge, 1991). For a specific example of a popular radical at work in the post-Chartist era, see *The Diaries of Samuel Bamford*, edited by Martin Hewitt and Robert Poole (New York, 2000).

British radicalism as a whole lacks its modern historian. Simon Maccoby's multivolume work is now more than half a century old. Recent useful works are: Paul Adelman,

Victorian Radicalism: The Middle-Class Experience, 1830–1914 (London, 1984); John Belchem, *Popular Radicalism in Nineteenth-Century Britain* (New York, 1996); and Rohan McWilliam, *Popular Politics in Nineteenth-Century England* (London, 1998). G. R. Searle's concise *The Liberal Party: Triumph and Disintegration, 1886–1929* (New York, 1992) has much to say about radicals and party politics. Searle's *Entrepreneurial Politics in Mid-Victorian Britain* (Oxford, 1993) emphasizes what he calls the role of 'entrepreneurial radicals' in politics.

28 As when Chamberlain asked Bunce to 'amplify and polish' a draft circular (Chamberlain Papers, JC 5/8/7, 26 March 1873).

29 See D. A. Hamer, *John Morley: Liberal Intellectual in Politics* (Oxford, 1968), especially ch. 2.

30 Chamberlain Papers, JC 5/54/13, 19 August 1873; and JC 5/54/15, 23 August 1873.

31 *Fortnightly Review*, new series 14 (September 1873), 292. As Marsh notes, so popular was Chamberlain's manifesto that this issue of the *Fortnightly* was reprinted (Marsh, *Chamberlain*, 65).

32 Indeed, Patricia Auspos believes that Chamberlain's control over the League was unique in the history of Victorian pressure groups. Its highly centralized and tightly managed organization, as well as Chamberlain's demand for uncompromising obedience and loyalty from the League's officers suggest to Auspos an authoritarian temperament and a personal drive for power. See her article 'Radicalism, Pressure Groups, and Party Politics: From the National Education League to the National Liberal Federation', *Journal of British Studies*, 20 (1980), 184–204. See also Peter Griffiths, 'Pressure Groups and Parties in Late Victorian England: The National Education League', *Midland History*, 3/3 (Spring 1976), 191–205.

33 Chamberlain Papers, JC 5/16/43, 10 February 1874. Further details about this election may be found in Peter T. Marsh, '"A Working Man's Representative": Joseph Chamberlain and the 1874 Election in Sheffield', ch. 3 in J. M. W. Bean (ed.), *The Political Culture of Modern Britain: Studies in Memory of Stephen Koss* (London, 1978).

3 The Radical Politician

1 In severing an active involvement with his company, Chamberlain was unusual among parliamentary businessmen, many of whom tended to regard parliament as a reward for their local economic successes and community standing rather than as a springboard for a notable public career. For examples, see H. L. Malchow, *Gentlemen Capitalists: The Social and Political World of the Victorian Businessman* (Stanford, Cal., 1992).

2 E. P. Hennock, *Fit and Proper Persons: Ideal and Reality in Nineteenth-Century Urban Government* (Montreal, 1973).

3 Linda Jones notes that the Birmingham civic gospel was at heart an entrepreneurial gospel, as the policies and rhetoric of the town council amply illustrated. See her 'Public Pursuit of Private Profit? Liberal Businessmen and Municipal Politics in Birmingham, 1865–1900' *Business History*, 25/3 (November 1983), 240–59.

4 Hennock, *Fit and Proper Persons*, 124.

5 *Birmingham Morning News* (14 January 1875),

6 See Derek Fraser, *Urban Politics in Victorian England: The Structure of Politics in Victorian Cities* (Leicester, 1976) which discusses primarily Leeds, Manchester, Liverpool, and Birmingham as well as Nottingham, Leicester, Sheffield, and other provincial towns. John Garrard, *Leadership and Power in Victorian Industrial Towns, 1830–80* (Manchester, 1983) emphasizes Rochdale, Bolton, and Salford.

7 See Marsh, ch. 4 for details of Chamberlain's carefully organized tactics.

8 Quoted in George A. Reigeluth, 'Municipal Reform in Birmingham, England: 1873–1876' (Johns Hopkins University, PhD Dissertation, 1981), 248.

9   Ibid., 96. Marsh succinctly describes the redevelopment scheme on pp. 92–8.
10   Gunn, *Public Culture of the Victorian Middle Class*, 46.
11   This was not uncommon in the Victorian era when, as John Garrard has pointed out, urban development schemes took the form of projects 'dear to the heart of businessmen interested in prestige and trade' (Garrard, *Leadership and Power In Victorian Industrial Towns*, 40).
12   Alan Hooper argues that Chamberlain was instrumental in establishing a new pattern of economic and political relations between workers and middle-class entrepreneurs. Not incompatible with conservative and corporative thinking, this alliance may help explain Chamberlain's later political career as a member of conservative Unionist governments. See Hooper's 'From Liberal-Radical to Conservative Corporatism: The Pursuit of "Radical Business" in "Tory Livery": Joseph Chamberlain, Birmingham, and British Politics, 1870–1930', in Richard Bellamy (ed.), *Victorian Liberalism: Nineteenth-century Political Thought and Practice* (London, 1990).
13   See Clive Behagg's revisionist view of Birmingham's labour history in his *Politics and Production in the Early Nineteenth Century* (London, 1990) where he takes issue with the social cohesion model. Behagg notes additionally that the famous Bull Ring Riots of 1839, often viewed as aberrant, were in fact characteristic of tensions between middle-class and working-class radicals in Birmingham. Michael Weaver agrees that the Riots should be seen as exemplifying tensions within the city, but he stresses 'intraclass' conflict between ruling elites on the town council. See his 'The Birmingham Bull Ring Riots of 1839: Variations on a Theme of Class Conflict', *Social Science Quarterly*, 78/1(March 1997), 137–48. The earlier view of Birmingham as a city of small workshops and social harmony has been put forward in various works by Asa Briggs, including his *Victorian Cities* (1968). See also Trygve R. Tholfsen, 'The Artisan and the Culture of Early Victorian Birmingham', *University of Birmingham Historical Journal*, 4/2 (1954), 146–66; and Dennis Smith, *Conflict and Compromise: Class Formation in English Society, 1830–1914: A Comparative Study of Birmingham and Sheffield* (London, 1982).
14   Chamberlain Papers, JC 5/54/36, 11 September 1874.
15   'The Next Page of the Liberal Programme', *Fortnightly Review*, no. 94, new series (1 October 1874), 405–29.
16   Chamberlain was quite willing to abandon any plank in his emerging radical platform if it proved unpopular. By early 1876, Chamberlain had revised his opinion on the abolition of the game laws because tenant farmers seemed to be divided on the issue. Radicals should nevertheless make a 'definite bid' to tenant farmers; and he recommended instead that they should 'plump for tenant right.' He was certain, as he put it to Morley, that 'if [only] we could get it into their dunder-heads that the new Radical Party mean a thorough measure of tenant right I believe they would swallow a good deal with it' (Chamberlain Papers, JC 5/54/74, 10 January 1876).
17   *Fortnightly Review*, 429.
18   As Marsh notes, each of Chamberlain's three wives complemented a major shift in his career. Harriet was an ideal wife for a businessman on the make; Florence supported his burgeoning radical political ambitions; and Mary, as we shall see, was an ornament to the greater social and political standing of his final years (Marsh, *Chamberlain*, 33).
19   Chamberlain's posthumous tribute to Florence may be found in Chamberlain Papers, JC 1/5/1.
20   Ibid., JC 5/20/29, 25 March 1875.
21   Ibid., JC 5/54/61, 7 December 1875.
22   Ibid., JC 5/54/119, 8 July 1876.
23   Ibid., JC 5/16/56, 9 July 1876.
24   Ibid., JC 5/54/141, 24 December 1876.
25   Garvin, *Chamberlain*, vol. 1, 210.

26 Marsh, *Chamberlain*, 91–2. Chamberlain declared in a letter to Collings many months after Florence's death that 'no one has a right to be happy in this brutal world' (Chamberlain Papers, JC 5/16/52, 5 May 1876).

27 Chamberlain Papers, JC 5/16/48, 13 February 1876.

28 In his restrained congratulatory letter, Dixon warned Chamberlain that he will have some difficulties to overcome in the House of Commons, 'as for instance your facility for invective, & your too low estimate of the position and character of your opponents' (Chamberlain Papers, JC 5/27/3, 28 June 1876). Chamberlain and Dixon were later reconciled.

29 Chamberlain also admitted, almost reluctantly, that Forster was 'immensely civil'. See Chamberlain Papers, JC 5/8/18, JC to Bunce, 28 July 1876.

30 Ibid., JC 5/16/58, JC to Collings, 27 July 1876.

31 The growth of nonconformity was reflected in the increase of nonconformist MPs. In 1868, 14% of Liberal MPs were nonconformists: by 1880, the year when Chamberlain entered Gladstone's cabinet, the numbers had risen to 24%. See D. W. Bebbington's *The Nonconformist Conscience: Chapel and Politics, 1870–1914* (London, 1982), especially ch. 1.

32 See Patricia Auspos, 'Radicalism, Pressure Groups, and Party Politics: From the National Education League to the National Liberal Federation', *Journal of British Studies*, 20 (1980), 184–204, especially 197–204. Older, but still useful sources are Francis Herrick, 'The Origins of the National Liberal Federation', *Journal of Modern History*, 17/2 (June 1945), 116–29; and Barry McGill, 'Francis Schnadhorst and Liberal Party Organization', *Journal of Modern History*, 34/1 (March 1962), 19–39.

33 Calculated from H. J. Hanham, *Elections and Party Management: Politics in the Time of Disraeli and Gladstone*, 2nd edn. (Hassocks, Sussex, 1978), Table III, 139. Hanham cites the NLF as an example of 'Birmingham imperialism' (137).

34 'The Caucus', *Fortnightly Review*, new series, vol. 30 (November 1878). The caucus system was not new to Birmingham and had grown out of the early political party registration societies organized in many urban areas following the Reform Bill of 1832. What distinguished Birmingham was the efficiency of its ward committees in drawing out Liberal voters, especially during municipal elections. See Fraser, *Urban Politics in Victorian England*, 192–4 and 281.

35 Marsh, *Chamberlain*, 120. As Gladstone noted in his diary, he was received with a 'triumphal reception', and his audience was 'most intelligent orderly [and] appreciative': H. C. G. Matthew (ed.), *The Gladstone Diaries* (Oxford, 1986), vol. 9, 31 May 1877, 223.

36 In the *National Review*, 22 (1 July 1877), 126.

37 Both quotations are from Chamberlain Papers, JC 5/54/221, JC to Morley, 29 September 1878.

38 Ibid., JC 5/54/223, JC to Morley, 1 October 1878.

39 Earlier historical works on the caucus denied that it was managed by an adroit manipulation of a tightly organized political machine. Tholfsen, for example, claims that its membership represented a propitious cooperation between beneficent middle-class liberals and grateful artisans and other members of the working class: Trygve R. Tholfsen, 'The Origins of the Birmingham Caucus', *Historical Journal*, 2/2 (1959), 161–84. Behagg, in *Politics and Production*, will have none of this. Marsh, too, is not taken in by Chamberlain's disclaimers. He notes that the NLF was essentially a vehicle for democratic centralism which allowed its middle-class activists who had the time and the talent to direct and manage its more numerous working-class membership. See Marsh, *Chamberlain*, 120.

40 As early as 1876, Chamberlain confided that he was no more Gladstonian than Dilke himself, but that Gladstone was 'our best card' and should Gladstone return to power, 'he would probably do much for us, & pave the way for more' (Dilke Papers, Add Mss 43885, JC to Dilke, 10 October 1876, fol. 49).

41 This complicated subject is most clearly and concisely treated – if from a Gladstonian perspective – in H. C. G. Matthew's authoritative *Gladstone, 1809–1898* (Oxford, 1997), 272–92.

42 *The Times*, 14 January 1878. Of Chamberlain's speech at the meeting, Morley had nothing but praise: 'one of the most vigorous and telling that you have yet made' (Chamberlain Papers, JC 5/54/201, Morley to JC, 14 January 1878). Morley's habit of flattering Chamberlain was well entrenched by then.

43 *The Times*, 1 May 1878 and 17 April 1879.

44 Chamberlain Papers, JC 5/16/81, JC to Collings, 2 April 1878.

45 The number is given by Garvin, *Life of Chamberlain*, vol. 1, 261, who takes it from Robert Spence Watson's *The National Liberal Foundation* (1907), 13.

4 Minister of the Crown

1 The most recent account of the Conservative election strategy may be found in Richard Shannon, *The Age of Disraeli, 1868–1881: The Rise of Tory Democracy* (London, 1992), ch. 14.

2 For a discussion of the making of Gladstone's cabinet, see H. C. G. Matthew (ed.), *The Gladstone Diaries* (Oxford, 1986), 364–73.

3 J. L. Garvin, *Life of Joseph Chamberlain* (London, 1932), vol. 1, letter dated 4 April 1880, 291–2. Dilke, according to his most recent biographer, thought Chamberlain's letter 'presumptuous', and realized Chamberlain's offer of an alliance was a ploy designed to benefit Chamberlain more than himself. See David Nicholls, *The Lost Prime Minister: A Life of Sir Charles Dilke* (London, 1995), 88–9.

4 Garvin, *Life of Chamberlain*, vol. 1, letter dated 16 April 1880, 294.

5 Ibid., letter dated 27 April 1880, JC to Collings, 298. Months before the election, Chamberlain revealed his frame of mind to Morley, promising 'a jolly row' unless the Liberal leadership paid more attention to radical demands (Chamberlain Papers, JC 5/54/243, 7 February 1879). Although Garvin defends Chamberlain's 'ingenuousness' in attaining cabinet office (289), he admits that it was 'a forced entry.'

6 Chamberlain Papers, JC 1/3/1, 4 May 1880.

7 See 'Memorandum of Events, 1880–92', Chamberlain Papers, JC 8/1/1, fol. 4. Written by Chamberlain himself, the 'Memorandum' was later edited by C. H. D. Howard as *A Political Memoir, 1880–92* (London, 1953).

8 H. C. G. Matthew (ed.), *The Gladstone Diaries* (Oxford, 1986), VI, Cabinet Minute, 3 May 1880, 513–14.

9 Garvin believes this bill was Chamberlain's 'chief mistake' at the Board of Trade (*Life of Chamberlain*, vol. 1, 415). See also Peter Marsh, *Joseph Chamberlain: Entrepreneur in Politics* (New Haven, 1994), 142–6 and 171–3 for Chamberlain's performance at the Board.

10 See Geoffrey Alderman, 'Joseph Chamberlain's Attempted Reform of the British Mercantile Marine', *Journal of Transport History*, New Series, 1/3 (February 1972), 169–84.

11 Plimsoll was a former Liberal MP for Derby and spokesman for the seamen. For his lengthy struggle for safer shipping before Chamberlain took up the issue, see Alderman's article 'Samuel Plimsoll and the Shipping Interest', *Maritime History*, 1 (1971), 73–95.

12 Dudley W.R. Bahlman (ed.), *The Diary of Sir Edward Walter Hamilton 1880–1885* (Oxford, 1972), 571.

13 Marsh observes that Chamberlain's mismanagement of the merchant shipping bill maximized the opposition to it (Marsh, *Chamberlain*, 171).

14 Garvin, *Life of Chamberlain*, vol. 1, 428.

15 Ibid., 425; Chamberlain Papers, JC 5/63/6, 1 March 1884. Schnadhorst reported his concern about involving the NLF with the shipping issue. Such action, he wrote Chamberlain, 'conflicts somewhat with the question of Reform'(ibid., JC 5/63/7, 11 March 1884).

16 As Garvin observes in his *Life of Chamberlain*, vol. 1, 429. The experience was perhaps all the more vexing because it was a public and very personal defeat.

17 See Matthew, *Gladstone*, 345–6 and 425–34; and *Gladstone Diaries*, X, Gladstone to Goschen, 1 June 1882, 272.

18 Chamberlain Papers, JC 8/1/1, 'Memorandum of Events', fol. 83.

19 Dilke Papers, Add. MSS 43866, ff 12–13, JC to Dilke, 20 January 1883 (cited in Nicholls, *The Lost Prime Minister*, 116).

20 *The Times*, 20 December 1882.

21 Ibid., 31 March 1883. Disraeli's death in 1881 had brought Lord Salisbury to the head of the Conservative Party.

22 Ibid., 2 July 1883.

23 Ibid., 27 November 1883.

24 Ibid., 5 December 1883.

25 Ibid., 18 December 1883.

26 Marsh, *Chamberlain*, 167–8.

27 Chamberlain Papers, JC 5/50/18, 18 December 1883. Henry Labouchere, the radical MP from Northampton (1880–1906), was a journalist, editor of *Truth*, and well-known purveyor of imagined influence. The most recent study of Labouchere is R. J. Hind, *Henry Labouchere and the Empire, 1880–1905* (London, 1972). Also useful is A. L. Thorold's biography of his uncle, *Life of Henry Labouchere* (New York, 1913).

28 James, not to be confused with the novelist, was the Liberal MP for Taunton and later for Bury. He broke with Gladstone on Home Rule. He was created Lord James of Hereford in 1895.

29 *Gladstone Diaries*, XI, Gladstone to Hartington, 22 October 1883.

30 The intricacies of franchise extensions and redistribution in 1884 have been addressed by Andrew Jones, *The Politics of Reform 1884* (Cambridge, 1972) and William A. Hayes, *The Background and Passage of the Third Reform Act* (New York, 1972). Hayes's preface gives a brief review of other relevant works, to which should be added Chapter 9 in Nicholls' *Lost Prime Minister*. See also Matthew, *Gladstone*, 425–33 and Marsh, *Chamberlain*, 165–76, *passim*.

31 These opinions, from a variety of contemporaries, may be found in Jones, *The Politics of Reform*, 32.

32 Nicholls, *Lost Prime Minister*, ch. 9, portrays Dilke's diplomatic skill in both forging redistribution and piloting it safely through the House.

33 Marsh, *Chamberlain*, 173–4.

34 *The Times*, 5 August 1884.

35 Ibid.

36 For these speeches, see *The Times*, 8 October 1884, 20 October 1884, and 21 October 1884.

37 Marsh, *Chamberlain*, 175. Garvin gives a measured response, suggesting that if Chamberlain was not directly at fault, he had at least incited the Birmingham caucus to action. He also condemns the riots as a 'ghastly blunder' because they created a backlash in the country to the benefit of the Conservatives (Garvin, *Life of Chamberlain*, vol. 1, 478). The Queen was more agitated. Labelling Chamberlain 'dangerous', she took particular umbrage at his tendency 'to stir up class against class in a very reckless manner': George Earle Buckle (ed.), *The Letters of Queen Victoria*, 2nd ser. (London, 1928), 3, Queen Victoria to Gladstone, 522–3.

38 *The Times*, 6 January 1885. It was widely understood that Chamberlain meant that the wealthy should be held to ransom. Garvin (*Life of Chamberlain*, vol. 1, 551), however, believed that Chamberlain meant something different. Arguing from the principle of equity, the wealthy ought in fairness to pay the expenses of the state in direct proportion to the advantages they themselves have gained from it. Put this way, 'ransom' might

justify the principle of a graduated income tax proposed by Chamberlain in his Ipswich speech.

39   *The Times*, 15 January 1885.

40   Ibid., 30 January 1885.

41   A. B. Cooke and J. R. Vincent (eds.), *Lord Carlingford's Journal: Reflections of a Cabinet Minister, 1885* (Oxford, 1971), 52. Chichester Fortesque, first Baron Carlingford, was then serving in the cabinet as President of the Council.

42   *Letters of Queen Victoria*, journal entry of 8 February 1885, 604. Hartington himself was probably more than annoyed. As one of Britain's largest landowners, he was not a disinterested party to radical taxation policies.

43   Bahlman, *Diary of Hamilton*, 773, 786. Hamilton also reported Lord Chancellor Selborne as indignant at Chamberlain's comments on plundering landlords (775). In the main, Hamilton thought that Chamberlain was overplaying his game.

44   See the two letters from Gladstone to Chamberlain in *Gladstone Diaries*, XI, dated 31 January 1885 and 5 February 1885, 286, 290.

45   Chamberlain's argument as summed up by Hamilton in Bahlman, *Diary of Hamilton*, 792.

46   Gladstone Papers, Add. MS 44126, Chamberlain to Gladstone, 7 February 1885, cited in Marsh, *Chamberlain*, 188.

47   See Eugenio F. Biagini, *Liberty, Retrenchment and Reform: Popular Liberalism in the Age of Gladstone* (Cambridge, 1992), ch. 7, 'The Charismatic Leader', where the author argues, in referencing Max Weber, that Gladstone's charisma forged the bonds between him and his crowds. Chamberlain, too, fit the charismatic mould. As Weber put it (in summary), the holder of charisma 'demands obedience and a following by virtue of his mission': see H. H. Gerth and C. Wright Mills (eds. and trans.), *From Max Weber: Essays in Sociology* (New York: paperback edn., 1958), 246.

48   See Norman and Jeanne MacKenzie (eds.), *The Diary of Beatrice Webb, 1873–1892: 'Glitter Around and Darkness Within'*, vol. 1 (Cambridge, Mass., 1982), 102. Chamberlain is a substantial topic in this volume, especially on pp. 101–19 covering the early months of 1884. See also Deborah Epstein Nord, *The Apprenticeship of Beatrice Webb* (Amherst, Mass., 1985), which portrays Beatrice's infatuation with Chamberlain as a crisis in her sexual identity. Barbara Caine's 'Beatrice Webb and the 'Woman Question'', *History Workshop*, 14 (Autumn 1982), 24–43 is a thoughtful reading of the diary from a feminist perspective.

49   *Diary of Beatrice Webb*, 103.

50   Ibid., 108. The meeting was reported in *The Times*, 31 January 1884. In it, Chamberlain reviewed his achievements as President of the Board of Trade, including the passage of the Patents Bill and the Bankruptcy Bill. He also appealed for support in his campaign to pass the merchant shipping bill.

51   Ibid., 333.

52   *Ibid.*, 266–7. Beatrice was writing in November 1888.

53   *Ibid.*, 267.

5 The Making of an Imperialist

1   One of Gladstone's 'six principles' of foreign policy. For a discussion of these and Gladstone's colonial and foreign policy during his second administration, see H. G. C. Matthew, *Gladstone, 1809–1898* (Oxford, 1997), ch. 6.

2   For this, and the quotations that follow, see Chamberlain Papers, JC 27/8, Chamberlain to W. T. Stead, 21 December 1877; JC 27/23, Chamberlain to Stead, 10 August 1878; JC 27/17, Chamberlain to Stead, 27 March 1878. Stead later became editor of the *Pall Mall Gazette* (1883–90) where he succeeded Morley. He founded the *Review of Reviews* in 1890.

3 As we have seen in Chapter 3.

4 For a summary of these reasons and for the argument that Gladstone was led in part by the need to establish order and stability in Egypt, see Travis L. Crosby, *The Two Mr. Gladstones: A Study in Psychology and History* (New Haven, 1997), 172–6. See also the useful accounts in Matthew, *Gladstone*, 382–94 and Richard Shannon, *Gladstone: Heroic Minister, 1865–1898* (London, 1999), 300–7.

5 Although not yet in the cabinet, Dilke's advice as under-secretary for foreign affairs was frequently sought by cabinet members during the Egyptian crisis.

6 Contemporary scholars have largely exonerated Arabi: see for example A. G. Hopkins, 'The Victorians and Africa: A Reconsideration of the Occupation of Egypt, 1882', *Journal of African History*, 27/2 (1986), 363–91, and M. E. Chamberlain, 'The Alexandria Massacre of 11 June 1882 and the British Occupation of Egypt', *Middle Eastern Studies*, 13 (1977), 14–39.

7 Chamberlain, 'Memorandum of Events', f. 68. See also Peter Marsh, *Joseph Chamberlain: Entrepreneur in Politics* (New Haven, 1994), 158–61.

8 A copy of Bright's letter is in 'Memorandum of Events' and is dated 4 January 1883, ff. 74–5. For Chamberlain's response, see ibid., f. 76; and Bright Papers, Add Mss 43387, 31 December 1882, ff. 184–8.

9 Chamberlain Papers, JC 5/7/21, 18 January 1884.

10 Ibid., JC 5/54/500, Chamberlain to Morley, 31 March 1883.

11 Escott Papers, Add Mss 58777, 3 December 1883, ff. 76–7. This letter refutes J. L. Garvin's denial of Chamberlain's jingoism during the Egyptian crisis: see his *Life of Chamberlain* (London, 1932), vol. 1, 446–55. Chamberlain's admission of jingoistic feelings also confirms Granville's recollection that in the thick of the Egyptian crisis Chamberlain was 'almost the greatest Jingo' during cabinet meetings: Edmond Fitzmaurice, *The Life of Granville George Leveson Gower, Second Earl of Granville, KG: 1815–1891* (London, 1905), vol. 2, 265.

12 See Ronald Robinson and John Gallagher, *Africa and the Victorians: The Climax of Imperialism* (Anchor Paperback edn, 1968), ch. 5.

13 D. A. Hamer, *John Morley: Liberal Intellectual in Politics* (Oxford, 1968), 141–4.

14 *The Times*, 16 January 1884. Morley had been elected MP for Newcastle at a by-election in 1883.

15 Chamberlain Papers, JC 5/54/611, Morley to Chamberlain, 14 February 1885.

16 Ibid., JC 5/54/607, Chamberlain to Morley, 11 February 1885; and JC 5/54/612, 15 February 1885. A few weeks earlier, Chamberlain, ill in bed with an abscessed jaw, was in an even more bellicose frame of mind about the deteriorating conditions in northern Africa. 'He wants to threaten and coerce and if necessary fight France', as one of his visitors recorded. From Lewis Harcourt's diary (Harcourt Papers, Bodleian Library, 735, leaves 71–2, 20 January 1885); partially quoted in A. G. Gardiner, *The Life of Sir William Harcourt* (London, 1923), vol. 1, 514.

17 Matthew, *Gladstone*, 401.

18 Chamberlain Papers, JC 5/50/22, Chamberlain to Labouchere, 28 December 1883.

19 Ibid., JC 5/7/23, Bright to Chamberlain, 27 January 1885.

20 Chamberlain, 'Memorandum of Events', ff. 78–9.

21 As he put it to Dilke in Chamberlain Papers, JC 5/24/396, 4 January 1885.

22 See the fragment of a letter to Dilke, possibly written in 1881, in Dilke Papers, Chamberlain to Dilke, Add Mss 43885, ff. 127–9.

23 Robinson and Gallagher, *Africa and the Victorians*, 282.

24 Richard Shannon's phrase in his *The Age of Salisbury, 1881–1902: Unionism and Empire* (London, 1996), 298. There is little doubt about the popularity of Seely's book: in its first two years, 80,000 copies were published. See Deborah Wormell, *Sir John Seely and the Uses of History* (Cambridge, 1980); and Marsh, *Chamberlain*, 176–77.

25 J. R. Seely, *The Expansion of England: Two Courses of Lectures* (Boston, 1883), 8.

26 Ibid., 11.

27 Ibid., 59.

28 See the concise and informative ch. 8 in Matthew's *Gladstone*.

29 Chamberlain, 'Memorandum of Events', ff. 13.

30 Ibid., f. 17.

31 Chamberlain's opinion of the Irish MP's had never been high: he once complained to Bunce that the Irish were 'a scurvy lot' (Chamberlain Papers, JC 5/8/25, 16 February 1877). His view was not exceptional among cabinet members. The mild mannered Kimberley, serving as Colonial Secretary (1880–82) and later as Indian Secretary (1882–85), denounced the 'vulgar ... Parnell & Co.' as 'scum': Angus Hawkins and John Powell (eds), *The Journal of John Wodehouse, First Earl of Kimberley for 1862–1902*, Camden Fifth Series, 9 (1997).

32 Chamberlain Papers, JC 5/54/381, JC to Morley, 18 October 1881.

33 See Chamberlain's hints to Morley in Chamberlain Papers, JC 5/54/381, 18 October 1881; and more explicitly in ibid., JC 5/54/385, 20 October 1881.

34 Ibid., JC 5/54/384, Morley to JC, 19 October 1881.

35 Ibid., JC 5/54/422, JC to Morley, 18 December 1881.

36 Ibid., JC 5/54/433, JC to Morley, 30 December 1881.

37 An excerpt of this speech may be found in Charles W. Boyd, *Mr. Chamberlain's Speeches* (Boston, 1914), vol. 1, 237–241.

38 Useful summaries of the making of the Treaty and its aftermath may be found in Matthew, *Gladstone*, 453–8; Marsh, *Chamberlain*, 152–5; and Garvin, *Life of Chamberlain*, vol. 1, 349–75. O'Shea was the husband of a more famous wife, Katherine O'Shea, the mistress of Parnell.

39 His enemies also wished Chamberlain to take the post, as Foster's adopted daughter reported, because 'they would like to watch him handle a red-hot poker'; see T. W. Moody and Richard Hawkins, with Margaret Moody (eds), *Florence Arnold-Forster's Irish Journal*, (Oxford, 1988), entry of 3 May 1882, 473–4.

40 The Irish leader Tim Healy (Home Rule MP for Wexford) reported after a meeting with Chamberlain on the very day that Forster resigned: 'I assumed from Chamberlain's conversation that he was to be Chief Secretary in lieu of Forster' (cited in Garvin, *Life of Chamberlain*, vol. 1, 359, quoting from Healy's memoirs).

41 See F. S. L. Lyons, *Charles Stewart Parnell* (New York, 1977), 216–26 for the negotiations between Chamberlain and Parnell.

42 Matthew, *Gladstone*, 458–9.

43 For this and the following quotations, see Chamberlain Papers, JC 8/3/1/24, Chamberlain to Duignan, 17 December 1884. Duignan – whom Chamberlain had courted in the early 1870s during his early radical campaign to capture the Liberal Party – had attempted in the early 1880s to persuade Chamberlain to give Irish Home Rule a sympathetic hearing. Duignan was known in Ireland as 'the man on a tricycle' because he used that mode of transportation in exploring Irish conditions in 1884.

44 The consequences of this misunderstanding were not apparent immediately, and were only discovered by Chamberlain four years later. Garvin's account of the fate of the Central Board remains informative (see Garvin, *Life of Chamberlain*, vol. 1, ch. 24). See also Lyons, *Parnell*, 268–74 and C. H. D. Howard, 'Joseph Chamberlain, Parnell and the Irish "central board" Scheme, 1884–5', *Irish Historical Review*, 8/32 (September 1953), 324–61.

45 Chamberlain Papers, JC 8/9/3/23, 13 April 1885. Spencer may have been motivated in part by his growing dislike of Chamberlain. In a startlingly terse sentence, he confessed to Granville: 'I begin to hate him': Earl Spencer, *The Red Earl: The Papers of the Fifth Earl Spencer, 1835–1910*, ed. Peter Gordon (Northampton, 1981), vol. 2, 18 June 1885, 308.

46 Chamberlain took this defeat in characteristic fashion. Reportedly in 'a fearful temper' at a dinner party several days after the cabinet decision on the Central Board, he informed Lewis Harcourt's stepmother that he no longer cared about the Liberals, only about his own party – 'which he says is to be the party of the future and that he has all the junior members of the cabinet with him' (Harcourt Papers, Bodleian Library, 735, leaf 120, 19 May 1885).

6 Fluctuating Schemes

1 Bernard Holland, *The Life of Spencer Compton, Eighth Duke of Devonshire* (London, 1911), vol. 2, 83–5.

2 H. C. G. Matthew (ed.), *The Gladstone Diaries* (Oxford, 1986), XI, Gladstone to JC, 11 September 1885.

3 As Lyons notes, Chamberlain nursed his resentment of Parnell until he had the opportunity to release it the following year 'with momentous effect': F. S. L. Lyons, *Charles Stewart Parnell* (New York, 1977), 290.

4 The authors were T. H. S. Escott, Frank Harris, Jesse Collings, John Morley, Francis Adams, and George Fottrell, with a brief preface by Chamberlain. Adams was secretary of the National Education League, Fottrell a Dublin lawyer, Harris (perhaps better known as the author of *My Live and Loves*) was a journalist who succeeded Escott as editor of the *Fortnightly* in 1886. See the reprint edition with D. A. Hamer's introduction: *The Radical Programme (1885)* (Brighton, 1971). T. A. Jenkins persuasively sets its publication date in September, 1885 – later than other historians: Jenkins, *Gladstone, Whiggery, and the Liberal Party, 1874–1886* (Oxford, 1988), 202, n. 18.

5 As Alan Simon has observed in his 'Joseph Chamberlain and the Unauthorized Programme' (D.Phil., Oxford, 1970).

6 See the account of the Hull meeting in *The Times*, 6 August 1885. Garvin reports that Chamberlain's reception was organized on an unprecedented scale in English politics. Visible everywhere were immense orange-coloured posters – 'of an American magnitude' – on which gigantic black type urged the people to meet 'Your coming Prime Minister': J. L. Garvin, *The Life of Joseph Chamberlain* (London, 1932), vol. 2, 59.

7 *The Times*, 9 September 1885.

8 Ibid., 16 September 1885.

9 Ibid.

10 Ibid., 19 September 1885.

11 Ibid., 21 September 1885.

12 Ibid., 15 October 1885.

13 Harcourt Papers, 716, leaves 151–53, JC to Harcourt, 20 September 1885. See also Dilke Papers, Add Mss 43887, f. 171–2, JC to Gladstone, 20 September 1885.

14 See Patrick Jackson, *The Last of the Whigs: A Political Biography of Lord Hartington, Later Eighth Duke of Devonshire (1833–1908)* (Cranbury, N.J., 1994), 193–5.

15 Chamberlain Papers, JC 5/38/151, JC to Harcourt, 9 October 1885; and Harcourt Papers, 716, JC to Harcourt, 9 October 1885, leaves 187–90. Harcourt was also the recipient of complaints about Chamberlain from Hartington, whose customary impassivity cracked toward the end of the campaign. 'Why is this bully to have all the talk to himself?' he asked of Harcourt from the ducal palace at Chatsworth (Harcourt Papers, 720, 4 December 1885, leaf 181). Hartington believed that Chamberlain's campaign was 'the most disloyal performance that could be conceived and I shall not forget it in a hurry' (Harcourt Papers, 720, Hartington to Harcourt, 6 December 1885, leaves 191–3).

16 See Chamberlain's preface in *The Radical Programme*, v–vi.

17 Harcourt Papers, 716, leaves 159–62, JC to Harcourt, 25 September 1885.

18 Chamberlain Papers, JC 5/56/34, JC to Lady Dorothy Neville, 7 October 1885.

19 Jay notes that Chamberlain's campaign – 'never before seen in British politics' – was essentially personal and resembled the style of a presidential candidate rather than that of a former minor cabinet member: Richard Jay, *Joseph Chamberlain: A Political Study* (Oxford, 1981), 111.

20 *The Times*, 21 November 1885, leader column.

21 See Chapter 4.

22 Patricia Lynch, *The Liberal Party in England 1885–1910: Radicalism and Community* (Oxford, 2003), esp. ch. 1.

23 Marsh, for example, believes that the radical land scheme 'tantalized' farm labourers and may help to account for the Liberal successes in the countryside: Peter Marsh, *Joseph Chamberlain: Entrepreneur in Politics* (New Haven, Conn., 1994), 213. Pelling, however, believes there is 'little contemporary evidence' that the slogan won votes for the Liberals: see Henry Pelling, *Social Geography of British Elections, 1885–1910* (London, 1967), 16.

24 Chamberlain Papers, JC 5/56/35, JC to Lady Dorothy Neville, 4 December 1885.

25 This argument is based upon John A. Archer, 'The Nineteenth Century Allotment: Half an Acre and a Row', *Economic History Review*, 50/1(1997), 21–36.

26 Although Alan Simon gives Chamberlain high marks for his attempt to ensure an adequate primary education for all British children, he believes that Chamberlain's free education platform was unequivocally an electoral failure in 1885. See his 'Joseph Chamberlain and Free Education in the Election of 1885', *History of Education*, 2 (1973), 56–78. See also Marsh, *Chamberlain*, 209.

27 See Alan Simon, 'Church Disestablishment as a Factor in the General Election of 1885', *Historical Journal*, 18/4 (1975), 791–820.

28 In a speech at York: see *The Times*, 21 October 1885.

29 Ibid., 24 October 1885.

30 Ibid., 9 November 1885.

31 Chamberlain Papers, JC 5/24/145, Dilke to JC, 19 November 1885; cited in Simon, 'Disestablishment in the 1885 Election', 813. Simon believes that Liberal success among agricultural labourers in the counties may be attributed to the traditional unpopularity of conservative country elites. The election of 1885 was the first in which they could express their views. Thus, rural voters were largely inoculated against the campaign of the Church. In urban areas, however, under the spur of an agitated clergy, Anglicans turned out in force against the radical Chamberlain (ibid., 816–19).

32 *Gladstone Diaries*, XI, Gladstone to JC, 6 November 1885, 423.

33 See particularly Jenkins, *Gladstone, Whiggery, and the Liberal Party*, ch. 6, 'The Crisis of 1885'. Kimberley believed the Liberals would have done very well in the election 'if Chamberlain had not frightened away many of our more moderate supporters': Hawkins, Angus and Powell, John (eds), *The Journal of John Wodehouse, First Earl of Kimberley for 1862–1902*, Camden 5th ser., 9 (1997), 14 December 1885, 361. C. H. D. Howard, on the other hand, makes a case that Chamberlain did moderate his message, especially near the end of the campaign. See Howard's 'Joseph Chamberlain and the "Unauthorized Programme"', *English Historical Review*, 65 (1950), 477–91.

34 Essential reading is H. C. G. Matthew, *Gladstone* (Oxford, 1997), ch. 9, 'Towards Home Rule'. See also Richard Shannon, *Gladstone: Heroic Minister, 1865–1898* (London, 1999), ch. 10.

35 Chamberlain Papers, JC 5/50/44, JC to Labouchere, 11 December 1885.

36 George John Shaw-Lefèvre (1831–1928) was a Liberal MP for many years for Reading and then Bradford. He served as cabinet minister in three Gladstone administrations, eventually breaking rank with Chamberlain over Home Rule. He was created 1st Baron Eversley in 1906.

37 Dilke Papers, Add Mss 43887, JC to Dilke, 16 December 1885, ff. 211–12.

38 Ibid.

39 Garvin, *Life of Chamberlain*, vol. 2, Dilke to JC, 17 December 1885, 140–1. Garvin follows this entire episode in some detail in ch. 29 – with an underlying tone of embarrassment.

40 Dilke Papers, Add Mss 43887, JC to Dilke, 17 December 1885, ff. 213–15.

41 *The Times*, 18 December 1885. Gladstone chose to accept Chamberlain's public assurances of support, though he may very well have had his private doubts. See Gladstone's letter to Chamberlain in *Gladstone Diaries*, XI, 18 December 1885, 452.

42 Harcourt Papers, 716, JC to Harcourt, 24 December 1885, leaf 213. Chamberlain was not far wrong in his assessment of Hartington's animus toward him, as we have noted.

43 Ibid., Harcourt to JC, 25 December 1885, leaf 216.

44 D. A. Hamer, *John Morley: Liberal Intellectual in Politics* (Oxford, 1968), ch. 10, 'Chamberlain's Radical Campaign, 1885', especially 157.

45 Chamberlain Papers, JC 5/54/628, Morley to JC, 19 September 1885.

46 Ibid., JC 5/54/669, JC to Morley, 24 December 1885.

47 Ibid., JC 5/54/675, Morley to JC, 28 December 1885.

48 In letters to Labouchere, Chamberlain declared his firm conclusion – based upon his personal observations among working men – that English opinion was 'set strongly against Home Rule'. For this reason, he was unwilling to grant any further concessions or support conciliatory policies for the Irish. See Chamberlain Papers, JC 5/50/44, 11 December 1885 and JC 5/50/51, 24 December 1885.

49 A. G. Gardiner, *The Life of William Harcourt* (New York, n.d.), vol. 1, 549.

50 There is general agreement on this among historians. Garvin writes that the friendly hand which Chamberlain extended to Parnell 'was bitten to the bone' (Garvin, *Chamberlain*, vol. 2, 12). F. S. L. Lyons thinks that Chamberlain 'felt himself humiliated as well as deceived': Lyons, *Ireland Since the Famine* (London, 1989), 184. Marsh observes that the Irish nationalist press followed Parnell's lead in printing 'crude insults' about the proposed tour of the radical leaders (Marsh, *Chamberlain*, 198–9).

51 See the account in *The Times*, 9 September 1885.

52 *United Ireland*, 19 September 1885.

53 The incident festered. Months later, Chamberlain had not forgotten about it. Especially galling was an editorial cartoon in the *United Ireland* which cast him in a distinctly unfavourable light. The Irish author and MP, Justin Huntly McCarthy, attempted to heal the breach by explaining to Chamberlain that his Warrington address had made 'a deep and painful impression' upon Irish nationalists because Chamberlain, the leader of the radicals, had suddenly proclaimed himself 'an advocate of the theory which of all others has always been most out of tune with radicalism, that might makes right' (Chamberlain Papers, JC 8/6/3k/4, 2 March 1886).

54 Morley himself brought the news to Chamberlain, who (in Morley's words) 'changed colour' for an instant, and then spoke 'in stiff murmurs against Mr. Gladstone': John Viscount Morley, *Recollections* (New York, 1917), vol. 1, 214.

55 Marsh, *Chamberlain*, 234.

56 Chamberlain Papers, JC 5/63/9, Schnadhorst to JC, 13 February 1886.

57 Richard Jay's exasperated comment on Chamberlain's 'tendency to extreme inconsistency in his comments' would surely have found sympathetic ears among Chamberlain's contemporaries: Gladstone himself complained of the difficulty of working with Chamberlain's 'fluctuating schemes'. See Jay, *Chamberlain*, 123–4.

58 For Chamberlain, an independent Ireland would not merely break historic imperial bonds. He had come to believe that Ireland's separation posed distinct dangers for England: Ireland could become a staging point for some other aggressive power – perhaps France or even America. This traditional argument against Irish independence was explicitly made to both Dilke and Labouchere: see Chamberlain Papers, JC 5/24/457, JC to Dilke, 26 December 1885; and Chamberlain Papers, JC 5/50/53, JC to Labouchere, 26 December 1885.

59 For a detailed discussion of the ambivalence of the radicals toward Ireland, see the early chapters in Thomas William Heyck's *The Dimensions of British Radicalism: The Case of Ireland, 1874–95* (Urbana, 1974).

60 Escott Papers, Add Mss 58777, JC to Escott, 30 December 1885, ff. 112–13.

61 *Fortnightly Review*, new ser., 39, February 1886.

62 As he put it to Bright, land was 'at the bottom of everything' (Bright Papers, Add Mss 43387, JC to Bright, 5 February 1886, ff. 200–1).

63 A useful summary of the intricacies of the land purchase scheme may be found in James Loughlin, *Gladstone, Home Rule and the Ulster Question, 1882–93* (Dublin, 1986), 80–94.

64 *Gladstone Diaries*, XI, Gladstone to JC, 15 March 1886, 510.

65 See the letter in Garvin, *Life of Chamberlain*, vol. 2, 187. Chamberlain's hint that Gladstone was proposing to bribe Irish landlords to accept Home Rule was nicely calculated to inflame opposition to the bill.

66 See Graham D. Goodlad, 'The Liberal Party and Gladstone's Land Purchase Bill of 1886', *Historical Journal*, 32/3 (1989), 627–41.

67 Thus Matthew's suggestion in his *Gladstone*, 500, that Gladstone had committed a tactical error in not including land and government within a single bill cannot be entertained: Gladstone had little choice.

68 Ibid., 500–3.

69 Chamberlain Papers, JC 5/50/79, JC to Labouchere, 21 April 1886.

70 Ibid., JC 5/50/80, JC to Labouchere, 22 April 1886.

71 Ibid., JC 5/50/88, JC to Labouchere, 2 May 1886.

72 Quotations are from Harcourt Papers, 716, JC to Harcourt, 27 March 1886, leaf 267; 21 April 1886, leaf 281; Chamberlain Papers, JC 5/38/157, JC to Harcourt, 22 April 1886; and (in a revealing later comment) 19 July 1886, leaf 328. Harcourt responded in sorrow: 'I am sorry you are so bloodthirsty' (Harcourt Papers, 716, Harcourt to JC, 25 April 1886, leaves 283–4).

73 Jackson, *Last of the Whigs*, 224.

74 See this important letter, dated 4 May 1886, in Garvin, *Life of Chamberlain*, vol. 2, 222. The following day, Chamberlain admitted candidly to Harcourt his frame of mind: 'I may frankly say that I do not want a compromise' (Garvin, *Life of Chamberlain*, vol. 2, 224). The day after his letter to Harcourt, he wrote in like manner to Dilke: 'I do not really expect the Government to give way, and indeed, I do not wish it. To satisfy others I have talked about conciliation, and have consented to make advances, but on the whole I would rather vote against the Bill than not, and the retention of the Irish members is only, with me, the flag that covers other objections.' Thus Chamberlain hoped 'to see the whole Bill recast and brought back to the National Council proposals': Gwynn and Tuckwell (eds.), *Life of Dilke*, 2, 222.

75 Jackson, *Last of the Whigs*, 236.

76 The account of this meeting may be found in Garvin, *Life of Chamberlain*, vol. 2, 189–91. Garvin presents it without comment. Balfour promptly reported to Salisbury the gist of the meeting. In reply, Salisbury made an invidious comparison. Chamberlain, he wrote, 'has not yet persuaded himself that he has any convictions, and therein lies Gladstone's infinite superiority': cited in L. P. Curtis, *Coercion and Conciliation in Ireland, 1880–1892* (Princeton, N.J., 1963), 99. See also Marsh, *Chamberlain*, 235.

77 Chamberlain Papers, JC 5/11/8, JC to Arthur Chamberlain, 15 May 1886.

78 Ibid., JC 5/11/3, Arthur Chamberlain to JC, 16 May 1886.

79 *The Times*, 22 April 1886.

80 Marsh, *Chamberlain*, 243.

81 Graham D. Goodlad, 'Gladstone and his Rivals: Popular Liberal Perceptions of the Party Leadership in the Political Crisis of 1885–1886', in Eugenio F. Biagini and Alastair J. Reid (eds), *Currents of Radicalism: Popular Radicalism, Organised Labour and Party Politics*

in Britain, 1850–1914 (Cambridge, 1991), ch. 8. Evidence especially from provincial newspapers suggests that Chamberlain was, in Goodlad's opinion, 'positively isolated' at this time (175).

82 This information was provided by James F. Stewart of the *Dundee Advertiser*, who had taken a survey of the five counties in which the *Advertiser* circulated. Because the letter was written to Harcourt, his information may be somewhat suspect; but it is consistent with the general impression that only a minority of Liberals shared Chamberlain's views on Home Rule. See Stewart's two letters in Harcourt Papers, Add 23, 6 April and 7 May 1886, leaves 122–3 and 129–32.

83 Stuart J. Reid (ed.), *Memoirs of Sir Wemyss Reid, 1842–1885* (London, 1905), 210–12.

84 See A. W. Roberts, 'Leeds Liberalism and Late-Victorian Politics', *Northern History*, 5 (1970), 131–56. Reid once characterized a series of Chamberlain's speeches as 'cowardly and crafty, mean and swaggering' (144). Reid was also a moving spirit behind the Hawarden Kite, which had been directly aimed at Chamberlain.

85 *The Times*, 6 May 1886.

86 Dilke Papers, Add Mss 43888, JC to Dilke, 20 May 1886, fol. 63.

87 Ibid., 7 May 1886, ff. 50–51.

88 Ibid., 20 May 1886, f. 64.

89 See A. B. Cooke and John Vincent, *The Governing Passion: Cabinet Government and Party Politics in Britain, 1885–86* (New York, 1974); and Bright Papers, Add Mss 43387, JC to Bright, 15 May 1886, fol. 203.

90 Bright Papers, Add Mss 43387, JC to Bright, 30 May 1886, fol. 205.

91 Chamberlain Papers, JC 5/7/27, Bright to JC 31 May 1886.

92 Ibid., JC 5/7/28, Bright to JC, 1 June 1886.

93 Ibid., JC 5/7/47, JC to Bright, 2 June 1886.

94 John Morley, *The Life of William Ewart Gladstone* (London, 1912), Shilling Edition, vol. 3, 254.

95 M. C. Hurst, 'Joseph Chamberlain, the Conservatives and the Succession to John Bright', *Historical Journal*, 7/1 (1964), 65n.7.

96 Roland Quinault, 'John Bright and Joseph Chamberlain', *Historical Journal*, 28/3 (1985), 642.

97 Jay, *Chamberlain*, 143.

98 Jackson, *Last of the Whigs*, 237.

99 Garvin, *Life of Chamberlain*, vol. 2, 242–7.

100 Ibid., 222, 224.

101 The radical Leonard Courtney, for example, no particular friend of Chamberlain, voted against Home Rule because he believed that the Irish were unfit to manage their own affairs. See G. P. Gooch, *Life of Lord Courtney* (London, 1920), 241; and Courtney's letter to Gladstone of 19 December 1885 on p. 237.

102 On the very day of Chamberlain's resignation from the cabinet in late March 1886, Harcourt had urged Gladstone to extend his hand to the younger man: 'I cannot too strongly express an opinion that you should see *him personally* as a matter of *feeling* as well as policy' (cited in Shannon, *Gladstone: 1865–1898*, 422). Earl Spencer, who disliked Chamberlain intensely, nevertheless had confided in Granville a few days earlier to the same effect. 'I am sure that part of the difficulty', he wrote, 'is that Chamberlain does not consider that Mr. Gladstone sufficiently values him': Peter Gordon (ed.), *The Red Earl: The Papers of the Fifth Earl Spencer, 1835–1910* (Northampton, 1981), 109. Kimberley concurred: 'our Chief's management … of his relations with Chamberlain was inexplicable to me, & certainly unfortunate. Why did he not take him more completely into his confidence about the Irish Bills?' (*Journal of Kimberley*, 29 September 1886, 371).

103 Marsh, while not ignoring Chamberlain's impatience, anger, and rebellious attitude, also notes Gladstone's growing resentment of the younger man's pretensions (Marsh,

Chamberlain, ch. 9, *passim*). Loughlin suggests that Chamberlain's criticisms of the Irish policy were based on equal parts personal antagonism of Gladstone and his dislike of the policy (Loughlin, *Gladstone, Home Rule and the Ulster Question*, 93).

104 Travis L. Crosby, *The Two Mr. Gladstones: A Study in Psychology and History* (New Haven, Conn., 1997), 204–8.

105 The most complete analysis of the conflict may be found in Peter T. Marsh, 'Tearing the Bonds: Chamberlain's Separation from the Gladstonian Liberals, 1885–6', in Bruce L. Kinzer (ed.), *The Gladstonian Turn of Mind: Essays Presented to J. B. Conacher* (Toronto, 1985), 123–53.

106 *The Times*, 3 July 1886.

107 Ibid. Perhaps Chamberlain's most antagonistic speech against Gladstone came late in the campaign when he was in Cardiff. Here he exhorted the meeting to resist the 'pretensions to infallibility' that some Liberals were employing in order to establish a 'dictatorship' upon the country (*The Times*, 7 July 1886).

7 In the Wilderness

1 Chamberlain Papers, JC 5/20/59, JC to Dale, 14 December 1886.

2 Ibid., JC 5/16/117, JC to Collings, 29 July 1886.

3 Ibid., JC 5/22/119, JC to Hartington, 16 July 1886.

4 Ibid., JC 5/22/123, JC to Hartington, 7 September 1886.

5 Ibid., JC 5/20/59, JC to Dale, 14 December 1886. Dale was a nonconformist minister and one of Chamberlain's closest Birmingham allies, as we noted in Chapter 3. Garvin argues that Chamberlain had 'a genuine longing' for Liberal reunification in the months following the defeat of Home Rule: J. L. Garvin, *Life of Joseph Chamberlain* (London, 1932), vol. 2, 265. It would appear, however, that his longing was for a reunified party without Gladstone.

6 For this speech, see *The Times*, 24 December 1886.

7 These quotations are from H. C. G. Matthew (ed.), *The Gladstone Diaries* (Oxford, 1986), vol. 11, Gladstone to Morley, 25 December 1886, 644; Gladstone to Harcourt, 27 December 1886, 645; and Gladstone to Labouchere, 29 December 1886, 647. Gladstone re-emphasized Chamberlain's weak negotiating position in a letter to Harcourt early in the new year. Gladstonians at the proposed conference would represent 195 parliamentary votes 'with firm ground under their feet': Chamberlain would represent only six or eight 'floating in the air': A. G. Gardiner, *The Life of Sir William Harcourt* (London, 1923), vol. 2, 7 January 1887, 26.

8 Harcourt Papers 702, Morley to Harcourt, 24 December 1886, leaves 92–4.

9 Earl Spencer, *The Red Earl: The Papers of the Fifth Earl Spencer, 1835–1910*, ed. Peter Gordon (Northampton, 1981), vol. 2, Spencer to Gladstone, 25 December 1886, 138.

10 Harcourt Papers 702, Harcourt to Morley, 9 December 1886, leaf 63.

11 Ibid., 24 December 1886, leaf 90. Michael Hurst sees Harcourt as the moving spirit of the Round Table Conference, at times lying 'like a hostess to get everyone to her party': see Hurst's *Joseph Chamberlain and Liberal Reunion: The Round Table Conference of 1887* (London, 1967), 176–7.

12 Harcourt Papers 702, 26 December 1886, leaf 106. Within a day or two of his letter to Morley, Harcourt received a communication from R. W. Dale, who encouraged Harcourt to follow up Chamberlain's conciliatory approach. It is difficult to believe that Dale acted on his own: Chamberlain's likely prompting suggests his strong desire to find a way out of an apparent political blind alley. Harcourt's reply to Dale clearly includes words of advice to be passed on to Chamberlain. Although he had no doubt, Harcourt wrote, of Chamberlain's sense of public duty in wishing to heal the Liberal division, he also counselled firmness of purpose. Chamberlain was often 'too sensitive to that rough treatment which is the inevitable lot of those who choose to play the football of public life'. Harcourt urged a 'tough

skin'. For this exchange of letters, see Harcourt Papers 215, Dale to Harcourt, 27 December 1886, leaves 125–32; and Harcourt to Dale, 29 December 1886, leaves 133–8.

13 Trevelyan was Chief Secretary for Ireland, 1882–4; Chancellor of the Duchy of Lancaster, 1884–5; and Chief Secretary for Scotland when he resigned with Chamberlain in March 1886 over Gladstone's Home Rule bill. He later returned to the Gladstonian fold, serving once again as Secretary for Scotland in 1892–5. His chequered career over Home Rule left an impression of weakness.

14 A respected legal mind, Herschell was Solicitor General in 1880–5 and Lord Chancellor in the Gladstone ministries of 1886 and 1892–5. He was regarded as a 'fairly neutral Gladstonian': Marsh, *Chamberlain*, 264.

15 Harcourt Papers 717, JC to Harcourt, 4 January 1887, leaf 17.

16 Chamberlain Papers, JC 5/22/130, JC to Hartington, 14 January 1887.

17 Gardiner, *Life of Harcourt*, vol. 2, Harcourt to Gladstone, 14 January 1887, 27–8.

18 Ibid., Appendix I, 603–8. The letter is quoted in full, and quotations are taken from that source.

19 Years later, in writing his biography of Gladstone, Morley had no firm answer to this question. He would only state publicly that the smooth waters of the Conference had been 'mysteriously ruffled': John Morley, *Recollections* (New York, 1917), vol. 3, 278.

20 Marsh, *Chamberlain*, 263–7.

21 As Garvin noted of Chamberlain at this time: 'Whenever his political position was in fact weakened, as sometimes happens to every active statesman, he attacked' (Garvin, *Life of Chamberlain*, vol. 2, 298).

22 Ibid., 290.

23 For this speech, see *The Times*, 31 January 1887. *The Times* hailed Chamberlain's speech as 'of peculiar significance', and proclaimed that the principle of unconditional surrender to the Irish leaders must now be abandoned (*The Times* leader page, 31 January 1887).

24 Gardiner, *Life of Harcourt*, vol. 2, Morley to Harcourt, 31 January 1887, 30–1.

25 *The Times*, 10 February 1887.

26 Chamberlain Papers, JC 5/38/178, JC to Harcourt, 10 February 1887. Gardiner considers this response to Morley's relatively mild personal comments another example of Chamberlain's 'amazingly thin skin' (Gardiner, *Life of Harcourt*, vol. 2, 32).

27 Harcourt Papers 735, Lewis Harcourt's Journal, 20 February 1887, leaf 269.

28 Garvin, *Chamberlain*, vol. 2, 292–3.

29 Gardiner, *Life of Harcourt*, vol. 2, 33.

30 Marsh, *Chamberlain*, 267.

31 *The Times*, 25 February 1887.

32 Harcourt Papers 717, Harcourt to JC, 25 February 1887, leaf 66.

33 Ibid.

34 Harcourt Papers 717, Harcourt to JC, 1 March 1887, leaves 111–12.

35 Chamberlain Papers, JC 5/38/181, JC to Harcourt, 26 February 1887.

36 Ibid., JC 5/38/184, JC to Harcourt, 1 March 1887.

37 Garvin notes the peculiar virulence between Chamberlain and Morley: 'lunging and stabbing at each other in nearly all their speeches', they exacerbated their political differences with personal rancor (Garvin, *Life of Chamberlain*, vol. 2, 310).

38 Chamberlain Papers, JC 5/54/711, Morley to JC, 21 September 1887.

39 See Marsh, *Chamberlain*, 269–73, for an account of Chamberlain's speaking tour among the Scots.

40 *The Times*, 14 April 1887.

41 Ibid., 15 April 1887.

42 Ibid., 16 April 1887. Chamberlain's Scottish tour did not always run smoothly. He was occasionally hissed and booed, and interruptions were not infrequent. At Edinburgh, the

protest was more elaborate. *The Times* reported that as the crowds gathered for Chamberlain's speech, a wagon with a full-length effigy of a statesman wearing a tall hat and eyeglass was driven through the neighbourhood of the Music Hall. The figure bore a placard with the words: 'Joseph's coat of many colours'. Additional signs included 'Welcome, renegade, welcome' and 'Traitor to the Liberal cause'.

43 Ibid.
44 Ibid., 12 October 1887.
45 Ibid., 13 October 1887.
46 Ibid., 14 October 1887.
47 Ibid., 15 October 1887.
48 Harcourt Papers 702, Morley to Harcourt, 15 October 1887, leaf 311.
49 Ibid., Harcourt to Morley, 27 October 1887, leaf 315.
50 As Loughlin has observed: see James Loughlin, *Gladstone, Home Rule and the Ulster Question, 1882–93* (Dublin, 1986), 236–7.
51 The letter, dated 27 October 1887, is cited in Garvin, *Life of Chamberlain*, vol. 2, 320–1. Garvin, though admitting Chamberlain's 'scathing invocations' in Ulster, does not comment further.
52 A tactic that Garvin identifies as an 'unhesitating tone of militant vigour' and 'a will of iron for combat' (*Life of Chamberlain*, vol. 2, 299).
53 For this letter, see Chamberlain Papers, JC 5/22/136, JC to Hartington, 16 August 1887.
54 Chamberlain may have been self-consciously following in the footsteps of Lord Randolph Churchill, who had launched a similar campaign in Ulster the year before. ('Ulster will fight; Ulster will be right' was Churchill's famous campaign slogan.) But Randolph's star was now dimming: his abrupt and ill-judged resignation from Salisbury's cabinet in December 1886, his financial difficulties, and the manifest signs of his syphilis and the decline of his health were diminishing his energy and reputation. See R. F. Foster's *Lord Randolph Churchill: A Political Life* (Oxford, 1988), 252–60.
55 For details of the Act, see L. P. Curtis, *Coercion and Conciliation in Ireland, 1880–1892* (Princeton, N.J., 1963), ch. 10.
56 The letters are printed in Garvin, *Life of Chamberlain*, vol. 2, 303–5.
57 Peter Davis has noted the 'significant influence' of Liberal Unionist pressure on the final shape of the bill. See his article, 'The Liberal Unionist Party and the Irish Policy of Lord Salisbury's Government, 1886–1892', *Historical Journal*, 18/1 (1975), 85–104.
58 F. S. L. Lyons, *Ireland Since the Famine* 2nd edn. (London, 1973), 178 and 188–8.
59 See his speech in *The Times*, 22 August 1887, to members of the Birmingham branches of the National Radical Union, gathered at Highbury for a garden party. He also defended at this meeting the Crimes Act as 'a very moderate measure' designed 'for the protection of our fellow subjects in Ireland'.
60 Chamberlain Papers, JC 5/22/135, JC to Hartington, 11 August 1887.
61 Peter Fraser, 'The Liberal Unionist Alliance: Chamberlain, Hartington, and the Conservatives, 1886–1904', *English Historical Review*, 77 (January 1962), 61.
62 Garvin, *Life of Chamberlain*, vol. 2, 317.
63 The details of Chamberlain's American mission are described in Chapter 8, 'The Puritan Maid'.
64 Marsh, *Chamberlain*, 281.
65 As Marsh persuasively argues: *Chamberlain*, 320.
66 Ibid., 300, 311.
67 For a brief description of this episode, see Marsh, *Chamberlain*, 314–16. Garvin believes the 'squabble' demonstrated a ruthless side to Chamberlain (Garvin, *Life of Chamberlain*, vol. 2, 436–39). Foster thought Chamberlain in his treatment of Churchill was implacable and 'flinty as ever' (Foster, *Lord Randolph Churchill*, 356–7).
68 Chamberlain Papers, JC 5/12/2, JC to Austen Chamberlain, 3 December 1888.

69 Ibid., JC 5/12/4, JC to Austen Chamberlain, 15 December 1888.

70 Ibid., JC 6/2/1/3, Powell Williams to JC, 28 March 1888.

71 Powell Williams had forewarned Chamberlain that the circumstances surrounding the by-election in April 1889 could place the Unionist alliance at 'a very dangerous juncture' (Chamberlain Papers, JC 6/2/1/3, Williams to JC, 28 March 1889).

72 Ibid., JC 6/2/1/2A, 20 April 1889.

73 For this lengthy and generally plausible letter, see Chamberlain Papers, JC 5/14/46, Churchill to JC, 22 April 1889.

74 Harcourt Papers 703, Harcourt to Morley, 20 April 1889, leaf 318.

75 Ibid., Morley to Harcourt, 22 April 1889, leaf 329.

76 Ibid., Harcourt to Morley, 24 April 1889, leaf 344–5.

77 Chamberlain Papers, JC 5/22/145, JC to Hartington, 14 October 1889.

78 Ibid., JC 6/2/5/7, 2 November 1889.

79 Ibid., JC 5/67/14, JC to Salisbury, 16 November 1891.

80 Selborne Papers 8, JC to Selborne, 25 January 1892, leaves 17–18. William Waldegrave Palmer was a Liberal Unionist MP from 1886–95. He bore the courtesy title of Viscount Wolmer from 1882 when his father became Earl of Selborne. He succeeded his father as the second Earl in 1895. During Chamberlain's term of office as Colonial Secretary under Salisbury and Balfour, Selborne was an important advisor and supporter. He became First Lord of the Admiralty (1900–5) and High Commissioner for South Africa (1905–10). In 1883, he married Lady Beatrix Maud Cecil, eldest daughter of Lord Salisbury.

81 Chamberlain Papers, JC 6/6/1C/3, JC to Balfour, 18 January 1892.

82 Ibid., JC 5/5/10A, 30 January 1892. Balfour wrote to Colonel Milward, chairman of the local Conservative Association.

83 E. D. Steele, *Lord Salisbury: A Political Biography* (London, 1999), 3. Steele believes that the beginnings of the welfare state can be traced to the social legislation enacted through the parliamentary leadership of Chamberlain and Salisbury.

84 As Bentley puts it, Salisbury feared 'the dithering of a nerveless elite': Michael Bentley, *Lord Salisbury's World: Conservative Environments in Late-Victorian Britain* (Cambridge, 2001), 154.

85 Marsh believes that Chamberlain was moving toward the right (Marsh, *Chamberlain*, 273); but the appearance of a philosophical or political shift may also be attributed to Chamberlain's willingness to find any suitable ideological port until more favourable winds could fill his sails.

86 Crucial to an understanding of the act is J. P. D. Dunbabin's 'The Politics of the Establishment of County Councils', *Historical Journal*, 6/2 (1963), 226–52. Chamberlain plays a central role in Dunbabin's account. See also Dunbabin's sequel, 'Expectations of the New County Councils, and their Realization', *Historical Journal*, 8/3(1965), 353–79.

87 With Chamberlain at one point in the negotiations predicting 'unbelievable mischief' if he failed to get his way (Dunbabin, 'Politics of the Establishment of County Councils', 245).

88 See F. S. L. Lyons, *Charles Stewart Parnell* (New York, 1977), 368–422 for a full account.

89 Marsh notes that Chamberlain, still angry at Parnell's snub of his offer to visit Ireland in 1885, pursued 'every opportunity' to blacken his reputation (Marsh, *Chamberlain*, 308).

90 Lyons, *Parnell*, 396.

91 *The Times*, 6 August 1888.

92 Ibid., 7 August 1888.

93 See Chapter 5, 'The Making of an Imperialist'.

94 *The Times*, 13 August 1888.

95 Lyons, *Parnell*, 399.

96 Garvin, *Life of Chamberlain*, vol. 2, 392.

97 Lyons, *Parnell*, 602.

98 Ibid., 151–2.
99 Ibid., ch. 15, 'The Crash'.
100 Ibid., ch. 10, 'The Galway "Mutiny"'.
101 For example, George Riddell, a friend and patron of David Lloyd George, claims in his diary that Lloyd George, when he was Chancellor of the Exchequer during Asquith's Liberal government, 'had discovered' Chamberlain had paid O'Shea £5,000 to initiate the divorce case. See Bentley Brinkerhoff Gilbert, *David Lloyd George: A Political Life*, vol. 1, *The Architect of Change, 1863–1912* (Columbus, Ohio), 476 n. 45. Gilbert cites Riddell's diary in the British Library, Add. MS 62970, TS, 10 Feb. 1912.
102 'Ranker fudge could not be conceived' (Garvin, *Life of Chamberlain*, vol. 2, 401). Garvin believes that the 'tragic pair' had underestimated the Captain's limits. He, driven 'to desperation', acted on his own against them (ibid., 402).
103 Lyons, *Parnell*, 458.
104 Curtis, *Coercion and Conciliation*, 309.
105 See Marsh, *Chamberlain*, 322–23.
106 Chamberlain Papers, JC 8/8/1/163, 5 February 1891.

8 The Puritan Maid

1 Cited in W. H. Armytage, *A. J. Mundella, 1825–1897: The Liberal Background to the Labour Movement* (London, 1951), 178. Born in Leicester of an Italian father and a Welsh mother, Mundella as a young man was influenced by both Chartist and Cobdenite ideals. He eventually made his fortune in the hosiery industry. Mundella's poor opinion of Chamberlain never mellowed. During the Home Rule crisis of 1886, he described Chamberlain as a man with 'no sense of gratitude of loyalty' who 'cannot *serve* or *wait*'; and who was 'implacable in his hatreds, and unceasing in his intrigues' (ibid., 252). Mundella served in both Gladstone's third and fourth ministries, succeeding Chamberlain as President of the Board of Trade.
2 G. P. Gooch, *Life of Lord Courtney* (London, 1920), 229. Courtney was a barrister and journalist, and professor of political economy at University College, London, before he entered parliament. He had married Catherine Potter in 1883. Kate, solicitous of Beatrice's welfare, warned her off Chamberlain, finding no trace in him of any other feeling than 'an intense personal ambition and a desire to dominate at whatever cost to other people's rights': Norman and Jeanne Mackenzie (eds.), *The Diary of Beatrice Webb*, vol. 1, *1873–1892: 'Glitter Around and Darkness Within'* (Cambridge, Mass., 1982), 135
3 Chamberlain Papers, JC 5/54/104, 28 June 1876.
4 Ibid., JC 5/ 54/111, 10 July 1876.
5 John Morley, *Recollections* (New York, 1917), vol. 1, 163.
6 Ibid., 147. More generally for Morley's estimation of Chamberlain's character, see 147–63.
7 Chamberlain Papers, JC 5/54/270, 23 August 1879.
8 Ibid., JC 5/16/52, 5 May 1876. D. A. Hamer's *John Morley: Liberal Intellectual in Politics* (Oxford, 1968) discusses in persuasive detail the initial symbiotic relationship between the two – as well as their ultimate parting as friends. Hamer points out that Morley's political ideas were influenced by his admiration for strong leaders and 'men of iron', such as Cromwell and Bismarck. Morley himself sometimes disparaged his own literary inclinations, craving a life of action. See especially ch. 4.
9 Ibid., ch. 9.
10 Chamberlain Papers, JC 5/54/539, 24 December 1883.
11 Ibid., JC 5/54/540, 25 December 1883.
12 Ibid., JC 5/54/588, 19 December 1884.
13 Jenkins has counted at least six occasions in the first 24 months of the ministry when they were prepared to resign together in opposition to cabinet measures: Roy Jenkins, *Victorian Scandal: A Biography of the Right Honourable Gentleman Sir Charles Dilke* (New York, 1965), 138.

14 Nicholls believes that Dilke's 'over-dependent and self-sacrificing relationship' with Chamberlain can be traced to the early death of his mother and the emotional distance of his father: David Nicholls, *The Lost Prime Minister: A Life of Sir Charles Dilke* (London, 1995), 11

15 Jenkins, *Victorian Scandal*, 134. Jenkins's comment is that Dilke's attitude toward Chamberlain as expressed in letters 'was sometimes almost that of an anxious lover rather than a political ally' (ibid.).

16 Ibid., 154.

17 Dilke Papers, Add Mss 43887, 5 January 1885, ff. 7–8.

18 Ibid., Add Mss 43887, 30 June 1885, fol. 158. Cited in Nicholls, *Lost Prime Minister*, 174.

19 The most recent account is Kali Israel, 'French Vices and British Liberties: Gender, Class and Narrative Competition in a Late Victorian Sex Scandal', *Social History*, 22/ 1 (January 1997), 1–26. Israel's concise discussion of the case and useful list of sources is somewhat marred by overly speculative theorizing. The same is true of her *Names and Stories: Emilia Dilke and Victorian Culture* (New York, 1999).

20 Nicholls, *Lost Prime Minister*, ch. 12. Nicholls thus takes issue with Roy Jenkins, who – although acknowledging that it was 'unlikely' that Chamberlain would want to destroy a valuable ally – nevertheless remains perturbed about Mrs Crawford's visit to Chamberlain. See Jenkins, *Victorian Scandal*, 354–9.

21 Chamberlain Papers, JC 28 A1/8, Chamberlain to Mary Endicott, 27 March 1888.

22 It may be that Morley's disagreements and Dilke's fall from grace in some way repelled Chamberlain. It has been suggested in the psychological literature that individuals high in power motivation need the reassurance supplied by ingratiating subordinates in order to feel worthy of respect. See Eugene M. Fodor and Dana L. Farrow, 'The Power Motive as an Influence on Use of Power', *Journal of Personality and Social Psychology*, 37/11 (1979), 2091–7.

23 Marsh characterizes Collings as Chamberlain's 'unquestioning friend' and 'loyal henchman': Peter Marsh, *Joseph Chamberlain: Entrepreneur in Politics* (New Haven, Conn., 1994), 91, 251. Garvin identifies the faithful Collings as 'Sancho' (this, of course, calls to mind, however inadvertently, the mad Don who tilted at windmills): J. L. Garvin, *Life of Chamberlain*, vol. 2, 336.

24 Chamberlain Papers, JC 28 A1/18, JC to Mary Endicott, 4 May 1888.

25 Ibid., JC 28 A1/15, JC to Mary Endicott, 25 April 1888.

26 See David Murray Aronson, 'Jesse Collings, Agrarian Radical, 1880–1892', (University of Massachusetts [Amherst] PhD Dissertation, 1975), for his political career.

27 By the end of the century, Highbury lost its anomalous urban/rural position as the dynamics of urban growth led to suburban villa development – made up of small houses and shops – which lapped at the base and ultimately surrounded the high ground on which the house rose massively. Today, much of Highbury's aspect is obscured by a modern office block directly across the roadway from its circular drive.

28 F. M. L. Thompson, *The Rise of Respectable Society: A Social History of Victorian Britain, 1830–1900* (Fontana Paperback, 1988), 165.

29 One appreciative gardening journalist eulogized Chamberlain, then Colonial Secretary, as an unofficial minister of horticulture. See Charles H. Curtis, 'Highbury Gardens, Birmingham', *The Gardener's Magazine*, 46 (18 April 1903), 253–6. Other sources on Highbury include Darby Stafford, 'The Colonial Secretary's Country Home'; James Adair, *The Weekly Scotsman*, 8 July 1899; and Frederick Dolman, 'Where Mr. Chamberlain Lives', *Cassell's Family Magazine*, all found in Chamberlain Papers, JC 4/11–12. See also Chamberlain Papers, C2/11/1–17; and Marsh, *Chamberlain*, esp. 139–41.

30 Highbury has not always pleased. As one might expect, Beatrice Potter had a strong distaste for the luxury of the house and sensed an underlying somberness. Her sister, Kate

Courtney, was similarly affected. She thought Highbury over colored, overheated, and the 'inmates' rather gloomy. See *Diary of Beatrice Webb*, 1, 105–6; and Carole Seymour Jones, *Beatrice Webb: Woman of Conflict* (London, 1992), 95.

31 *Diary of Beatrice Webb*, vol. 1, 175 and 170.

32 In later life, Beatrice worked for Unionist political causes and participated in philanthropic agencies, such as the Children's Country Holiday Fund Committee. During the First World War she served on the Food Economy and War Savings Committees. See Chamberlain Papers, BC 5/7/4.

33 Chamberlain Papers, AC 1/4/4a/1 (probably 1875).

34 Ibid., AC 1/4/4a/3 (probably 1875).

35 Ibid., AC 1/4/4a/5, 15 May 1875; AC 1/4/4a/7, 13 June 1875; AC 1/4/4a/8, 27 June 1875.

36 Ibid., JC 8/2/5/6, Austen Chamberlain to J. L. Garvin, 7 December 1932. Austen's half-sister Hilda had similar memories. Her father was 'deeply reserved', and 'never indulged in caresses' with his children. It seemed to her that they loved him, but only from afar (ibid., BC 5/10/1 and C 2/11/1).

37 Robert C. Self believes that Austen suffered from a 'near obsessive filial devotion' to his father which accounted for his mimetic behaviour: see Self's edition of *The Austen Chamberlain Diary: The Correspondence of Sir Austen Chamberlain with his Sisters Hilda and Ida, 1916–1937*, Camden 5th ser., 5 (Cambridge, 1995), 5. Austen's reaction upon reading Garvin's first volume of his father's life – which he meant as a compliment to the author – was also revealing. The more he read into the book, the smaller he felt until at last he 'became insignificance itself' (ibid., 420).

38 Chamberlain Papers, NC 1/6/9/2, 17 September 1891.

39 Ibid., NC 1/6/9/4, JC to Neville, 19 November 1891.

40 Ibid., NC 1/6/9/15, JC to Neville, 6 November 1891.

41 Ibid., NC 1/6/9/5, JC to Neville, 21 December 1891.

42 Ibid., NC 1/6/9/21, JC to Neville, 21 April 1894.

43 Cited in Robert Self, *Neville Chamberlain: A Biography* (Aldershot, Hants, 2006), 22: see also ch. 2, 'Formative Influences: From Highbury to Andros'. Additional useful sources are David Dilks, *Neville Chamberlain: Pioneering and Reform, 1869–1929*, vol. 1 (Cambridge, 1984), chs. 3–5 and Marsh, *Chamberlain*, 324–6.

44 As a schoolboy at Rugby, Neville complained to a friend with some asperity that he would never go into politics: 'You don't know what our home is like for days before my father makes one of his big speeches. Everybody has to be quiet and even at meals conversation is subdued' (Dilks, *Neville Chamberlain*, 24). Austen recalled long after his father's death the stressful preparations for speeches: see his memo to J. L. Garvin in Chamberlain Papers, JC 8/2/5/1, 13 March 1920. See also Diana Whitehill Laing, *Mistress of Herself* (Barre, Mass., 1965) for the impressions of the third Mrs. Chamberlain on her husband's work habits. Marsh argues plausibly that although Chamberlain was undoubtedly devoted to his children, his dominance and occasional distance from them may have retarded their emotional growth (Marsh, *Chamberlain*, 140–1).

45 Ralph Nevill (ed.), *The Reminiscences of Lady Dorothy Nevill*, (London, 1907), 193–6.

46 Chamberlain Papers, 'Extracts from Lady Dorothy Stanley's Diary, 1885–87', JC 8/2/2, 12 December 1885. These extracts were sent to Garvin in 1921 by Lady Dorothy who had recently discovered her diary, long forgotten, in a locked cupboard. As an example of those who thought Chamberlain subversive, Lady Dorothy quoted from an extended conversation with an unidentified member of Gladstone's ministry of 1880–85. The anonymous MP, who spoke with 'hatred', contrasted the self-seeking Chamberlain with Morley and Hartington, 'high minded men who will observe the traditions of the House', and who were additionally 'patriots and gentlemen' (ibid., 14 December 1885).

47 Ibid., 28 March 1886.

48 Ibid., 11 February 1887.

49 Bright Papers, Add Mss 43387, 8 September 1887.

50 Marsh's phrase: see his *Chamberlain*, 282.

51 Firsthand details of the trip may be found in Sir Willoughby Maycock, KCMG, *With Mr. Chamberlain in the United States and Canada, 1887–88* (London, 1914). The book is essentially a paean to Chamberlain. Whether riding out a monstrous storm in the Atlantic as a 'good sailor', or showing 'coolness and *sang froid*' at a hairbreadth escape on an ice-bound cattle track near a steep precipice over Niagara Falls, or reading with great rapidity all of *Ben Hur* (in only two hours), Chamberlain was the undoubted hero of the moment to Maycock.

52 Chamberlain Papers, JC 3/1/2, 18 November 1887, and JC 3/1/7, 8 December 1887.

53 Garvin, *Life of Chamberlain*, vol. 2, 329–30; and Marsh, *Chamberlain*, 299.

54 Chamberlain Papers, JC 3/14, Diary in America, 6 December 1887.

55 Ibid., AC 1/4/5/37, JC to Beatrice Chamberlain, 12 November 1887 (cited in Marsh, *Chamberlain*, 286).

56 Chamberlain Papers, JC 1/2/4, JC to Beatrice Chamberlain, 25 November 1887.

57 Ibid.

58 Ibid., JC 1/2/9, JC to Beatrice, 3 January 1888.

59 Ibid., JC 1/2/10, JC to Beatrice, 13 January 1888.

60 Dilke Papers, Add Mss 43888, JC to Dilke, 11 December 1887.

61 Chamberlain Papers, JC 1/2/10, JC writing from Washington to Beatrice, 13 January 1888.

62 Ibid., JC 1/2/13, JC to Beatrice, 3 February 1888.

63 Ibid., JC 1/2/15, JC to Beatrice, 17 February 1888.

64 In a letter to his brother: see Stephen Gwynn, *The Letters and Friendships of Sir Cecil Spring Rice: A Record* (London, 1930), 15 December 1887, 84. Spring Rice was a notable diplomat in his day. Educated at Eton and Balliol, he served in the British embassies in (among others) Germany, Russia, and twice in the United States, including the ambassadorship to Washington from 1913 to 1918.

65 Ibid., 10 February 1888, 85.

66 Chamberlain Papers, JC 1/2/6, JC to Beatrice, 9 December 1887.

67 In addition to political considerations for the delay of the marriage, apparent psychological disturbances were at play in Endicott's decision. At the time of Mary's informal betrothal, Endicott's father died. In a lengthy diary entry Endicott ruminated on these events. Each represented a loss, and these losses prompted a memory of the death of his mother 50 years earlier, when he was a child of 13. Upon her death, Endicott entered, as he recalled it, 'a new world unblest by her presence & her love. It seemed so cold and hard without interests or hopes. How my boyhood seemed to die out of me, and from that experience, I became another than I had been.' Now Mary, his daughter, 'in the first flush of the early passion of her noble womanhood', was soon to depart. Chamberlain's insistence upon an early marriage can only have exacerbated Endicott's sense of grieving. See William C. Endicott Sr. Papers, Massachusetts Historical Society, Boston, H. Bound volumes, Diaries 1888, Carton 17, 11 March 1888.

68 Written in tiny script and often in a scrawl across the page, Chamberlain's letters are difficult to read. Their contents have not been unknown to historians: Marsh has briefly analyzed them; and Garvin printed numerous excerpts. But Garvin, after noting that these letters were a revelation of Chamberlain 'such as he never put on paper before or after', pruned away the most revealing passages on the grounds that what 'was most personal is not for our knowledge' (Garvin, *Life of Chamberlain*, vol. 2, 346).

69 Chamberlain Papers, JC 28 1/1, JC to Mary Endicott, no date. The following citations are all from letters of Chamberlain to Mary Endicott.

70 Ibid., JC 28 A1/4, 3 and 6 March 1888.

71 Ibid., JC 28 A1/9, 31 March 1888.
72 Ibid., JC 28 A1/16, 29 April 1888.
73 Ibid., JC 28 A1/8, 26 March 1888.
74 Ibid., JC 28 A1/16, 28 April 1888.
75 Ibid., JC 28 A1/10, 8 April 1888.
76 Ibid., JC 28 A1/12, 14 April 1888.
77 Ibid., JC 28 A1/14, 21 and 24 April 1888.
78 Ibid., JC 28 A1/14, 24 April 1888.
79 Some examples follow. All are taken from Chamberlain's letters to Mary. He declared that 'if this goes on much longer I can never forgive those who have forced me to [such] a humiliation' (JC 28 A1/16, 28 April 1888). Their happiness 'hangs on a thread' and that if anything should go wrong, Mary's father would 'never forgive himself – but it will be too late' (JC 28 A1/19, 11 May 1888). 'I should not like to be in Mr. Endicott's position if anything happens during this long separation' (JC 28 A1/20, 14 May 1888).
80 Ibid., JC 28 A1/19, 9 May 1888 and JC 28 A1/21, 16 May 1888.
81 Ibid., JC 28 A1/35, 6 July 1888.
82 Ibid., JC 28 A1/16, 28 April 1888. The following day he still felt 'rather seedy and depressed' (ibid., 29 April 1888).
83 Ibid., JC 28 A1/17, 2 May 1888.
84 Ibid., JC 28 A1/21, 16 May 1888 and 17 May 1888; JC 28 A 1/23, 24 May 1888 and 25 May 1888; JC 28 A1/24, 27 May 1888 and 28 May 1888; JC 28 A1/30, 14 June 1888, 15 June 1888, 16 June 1888, and 18 June 1888; JC 28 A1/31, 23 June 1888 and 25 June 1888.
85 Ibid., JC 28 A1/33, 29 June 1888.
86 Ibid., 1 July 1888.
87 Ibid., JC 28 A1/24, 27 May 1888. See also JC 28 A1/14a, 24 April 1888 and JC 28 A1/28, 11 June 1888.
88 Ibid., AC 4/11/114, 4 June 1888.
89 Ibid., JC 28 A1/41, 27 July 1888.
90 Ibid., JC 28 A1/11, 10 April 1888.
91 Ibid., JC 28 A1/30, 18 June 1888.
92 Ibid., JC28 A1/20, 15 May 1888.
93 Ibid., JC 28 A1 22, 19 May 1888.
94 A nickname bestowed by Lord Salisbury, who once confessed that he liked 'looking at' Joe's pretty 'puritan maid': quoted from Andrew Roberts, *Salisbury: Victorian Titan* (London, 1999), 600.
95 Chamberlain Papers., JC28 A1/34, 2 July 1888.
96 Ibid., JC 28 A1/34a, 6 July 1888. Chamberlain concluded this letter in a slightly menacing tone: 'Women care most for their dogs when they are fierce to everyone but their mistress. I am your dog dear but I would not advise any one else to shake me the wrong way.'
97 Ibid., JC 28 A1/33, 29 June 1888.
98 Ibid., JC 28 A1/32, 25 June 1888.

9 Power Deferred

1 Many of the parliamentary rank and file, however, were uneasy at the prospect of Chamberlain as leader. See T. A. Jenkins, 'Hartington, Chamberlain and the Unionist Alliance, 1886–1895', *Parliamentary History*, 11/1 (1992), 129–30.
2 *National Review*, 18/108 (Feb 1892), 721–39.
3 *The Times*, 30 April 1892. Chamberlain was addressing the council of the Birmingham Liberal Unionist Association. Chamberlain was, as Marsh notes, the first British politician to raise the issue of state-sponsored old-age pensions: see Marsh, *Chamberlain*, 330.

4   Thus Chamberlain once again lifted this fractious comment from his Warrington address of 1885; and in so doing here made Bentham's moral calculus a crude political census. See Marsh, *Chamberlain*, 330.

5   Marsh, *Chamberlain*, 342–3.

6   Chamberlain Papers, JC 5/46/25, Sir Henry James to JC, 16 July 1892.

7   The most recent accounts of the election may be found in Andrew Roberts, *Salisbury: Victorian Titan* (London, 1999), 575–81, and E. D. Steele, *Lord Salisbury: A Political Biography* (London, 1999), 274–7.

8   *The Times*, 2 October 1891. Watson was a solicitor and social reformer who served as chair of the NLF from 1890–1902.

9   Ibid., 25 June 1892.

10 D. A. Hamer's suggestive book, *Liberal Politics in the Age of Gladstone and Rosebery: A Study in Leadership and Policy* (Oxford, 1972) has much to say on the topic of single issue versus programmatic politics. Relevant passages on Chamberlain may be found *passim*.

11 A useful summary is W. C. Mallalieu, 'Joseph Chamberlain and Workmen's Compensation', *Journal of Economic History*, 10 (May 1950), 45–57. See also E. P. Hennock, *British Social Reform and German Precedents: The Case of Social Insurance 1880–1914* (Oxford, 1987), especially chs. 2 and 3.

12 Origins of the old-age pensions act, including Chamberlain's contribution to the debate, may be found in Doreen Collins, 'The Introduction of Old Age Pensions in Great Britain', *Historical Journal*, 8/2 (1965), 246–59. See also John Macnicol, *The Politics of Retirement in Britain, 1878–1948* (Cambridge, 1998), pp. 65–75.

13 See H. C. G. Matthew's concise and thorough discussion of the Bill in *Gladstone, 1809–1898* (Oxford, 1997), 587–92.

14 In J. L. Garvin's words, the Commons had become 'a sizzling cauldron of partisanship': *The Life of Joseph Chamberlain* (London, 1932), vol. 2, 566.

15 Roberts, *Salisbury*, 587.

16 See Ch. 8 below.

17 See Marsh, *Chamberlain*, 324–6 and 361–2.

18 See Ian Cawood, 'Joseph Chamberlain, the Conservative Party and the Leamington Spa Candidature Dispute of 1895', *Historical Research*, 79/206 (November 2006), 554–77.

19 Garvin notes that Chamberlain, prompted by his 'pugnacious nature', was 'savage' in his response to the Tory threat (Garvin, *Life of Chamberlain*, vol. 2, 620).

20 Ibid., vol. 2, 628. Letters to Mary Chamberlain, dated 13 March and 20 March 1895.

21 Chamberlain Papers, JC 5/22/156, JC to Duke of Devonshire, 19 April 1895. As an indication of his willingness to work with the Tories, he admitted in a letter several months later that he had given up the idea of disestablishment 'as outside practical politics' (ibid., JC 5/22/157, JC to Devonshire, 15 December 1895).

22 Quoted in Marsh, *Chamberlain*, 364. Chaplin was a substantial Lincolnshire landowner and spokesman for the agricultural interests. He was Chancellor of the Duchy of Lancaster (outside the cabinet) in Salisbury's first ministry. He also had served in the cabinet as the first president of the new Board of Agriculture in Salisbury's second ministry, and was head of the Local Government Board in Salisbury's third ministry.

23 Salisbury to Wolmer in Selborne Papers 5, 13 April 1895, leaves 21–4.

24 Ibid., leaves 27–8, 20 April 1895.

25 See Peter Stansky, *Ambitions and Strategies: The Struggle for the Leadership of the Liberal Party in the 1890s* (Oxford, 1964), *passim*, but especially 130–80; and Hamer's *Liberal Politics in the Age of Gladstone and Rosebery*, ch. 8.

26 An interpretation put forward by John Cornford in his often cited 'The Transformation of Conservatism in the Late Nineteenth Century', *Victorian Studies*, 7 (September 1963), 35–66.

27 With the exception of the aberrant election of 1931: see Martin Pugh, 'Popular Conservatism in Britain: Continuity and Change, 1880–1987', *Journal of British Studies*, 27/3(July 1988), 254–82.

28 See Frans Coetzee, 'Villa Toryism Reconsidered: Conservatism and Suburban Sensibilities in Late-Victorian Croydon', *Parliamentary History* (1997), 29–47. Martin Pugh makes much of the Primrose League in his *The Tories and the People, 1880–1935* (London, 1985), believing that the organization helped conservatism take root in the lives of ordinary people. Not all historians agree about the efficacy of the League. R. F. Foster condemns it as a 'bizarre manifestation' of the English class system, with its 'sham titles and gimcrack rhetoric': 'Tory Democracy and Political Elitism: Provincial Conservatism and Parliamentary Tories in the early 1880s', in Art Cosgrove and J. I. McGuire (eds.), *Parliament & Community, Historical Studies*, 14 (Belfast, 1981).

29 See R. L. Greenall, 'Popular Conservatism in Salford, 1868–1886', *Northern History*, 9 (1974), 123–38. John A. Garrard's, 'Parties, Members and Voters after 1867: A Local Study', *Historical Journal*, 20 (1977), 145–63, also uses Salford as a case study. See also the work of Jon Lawrence: 'Popular Politics and the Limitations of Party: Wolverhampton, 1867–1900,' in Eugenio F. Biagini and Alastair J. Reid (eds.), *Currents of Radicalism: Popular Radicalism, Organized Labour and Party Politics in Britain, 1850–1914* (Cambridge, 1991), ch. 4; 'Class and Gender in the Making of Urban Toryism, 1880–1914', *English Historical Review*, 108/428 (July 1993), 629–52; and most recently *Speaking for the People: Language and Popular Politics in England, 1867–1914* (Cambridge, 1998).

30 Paul A. Readman, 'The 1895 General Election and Political Change in Late Victorian England', *Historical Journal*, 42/2 (1999), 467–93.

31 The following information on Birmingham may be found in Christopher Green's BA Dissertation, 'The Growth of Conservatism in Birmingham, 1873–1891' (Birmingham University, 1971); and in his 'Birmingham's Politics, 1873–1891: The Local Basis of Change', *Midland History*, 2/2 (1973), 84–98.

32 Ibid., 97–8.

33 Marsh, *Chamberlain*, 369.

34 Salisbury, in his revealing letter to Wolmer quoted above, acknowledged Chamberlain's valuable work for the Unionist Party: the conservative wing of the alliance had been 'amply paid by support in the constituencies, & still more in the House of Commons' (Selborne Papers 5, Salisbury to Wolmer, leaves 21–4, 13 April 1895).

35 Readman, 'The 1895 General Election', 477–9.

36 *The Times*, 8 July 1895. This constituency had become increasingly conservative over time, in part because of the personal influence of the Conservative Sir Henry Doulton, who employed 4,000 at his pottery works. See Henry Pelling, *Social Geography of British Elections, 1885–1910* (London, 1967), 50.

37 *The Times*, 17 July 1895.

38 Ibid., 20 July 1895. Perhaps especially gratifying to Chamberlain was the defeat of both Harcourt and Morley.

39 Ibid., 11 July 1895.

10 Power Gained

1 Michael Bentley, *Lord Salisbury's World: Conservative Environments in Late-Victorian Britain* (Cambridge, 2001), 290.

2 The conversation took place several weeks before the election of 1895: see Dudley W. R. Bahlman (ed.), *The Diary of Sir Edward Walter Hamilton 1880–1885* (Oxford, 1972), 16 April 1895, 296. To this diary entry, Hamilton added later in reference to Chamberlain: 'All he liked was having "his own regiment" under his command with which he could turn the fortunes of the day.'

3   Cawood argues that Chamberlain's choice of the Colonial Office also suited Salisbury in that it would distract Chamberlain from pursuing any further domestic reformist agendas: Ian Cawood, 'Joseph Chamberlain, the Conservative Party and the Leamington Spa Candidature Dispute of 1895', *Historical Research*, 79/206 (November 2006), 576–7.

4   Salisbury somehow misread his new Colonial Secretary. He believed that Chamberlain's interest in the colonies was 'entirely theoretic' and that he would leave 'the practical work' to Selborne. See Selborne Papers 5, Salisbury to Selborne, leaf 32, 30 June 1895.

5   Chamberlain Papers, NC 1/13/2/79, Beatrice Chamberlain to Neville, 4 December 1895.

6   Garvin, *Life of Chamberlain*, vol. 3, 11. The quotation is from Garvin's interview with Flora shaw (later Lady Lugard) who was then principal writer on colonial matters for *The Times*. Miss shaw also reported that Chamberlain's office subordinates referred to him as 'The Master'.

7   Ibid., ch. 48, passim. Garvin quotes Sir Harry Wilson, Chamberlain's principal private secretary from 1895–97 on the installation of modern lighting (ibid., 15). But as Marsh notes, the installation was a slow process, never reaching the third floor at Downing Street during Chamberlain's tenure of office (Marsh, *Chamberlain*, 417). Wilson was, no doubt, remembering the whirlwind effect that his chief often created – which could sometimes exaggerate his achievements.

8   *The New Penny Magazine*, vol. 3/38 (1897), in Chamberlain Papers, JC 34/2/25.

9   Robert V. Kubicek's evaluation in his *The Administration of Imperialism: Joseph Chamberlain at the Imperial Office* (Durham, N.C., 1969), however, gives Chamberlain mixed marks. Often disturbed by his 'impulsiveness' and his 'brusque methods and many schemes', the cabinet could not fully put their trust in his policies (175–6). Richard M. Kesner, *Economic Control and Colonial Development: Crown Colony Financial Management in the Age of Joseph Chamberlain* (Westport, Conn., 1981) is a useful complement to Kubicek's assessment of the operation of the Colonial Office. Kesner finds Chamberlain's energy, determination, and imperial vision admirable for its time. But, as he notes further, Chamberlain's personality was not 'well suited for laborious technical negotiations' (220).

10 For ideas on late nineteenth century imperial unity, see Peter Burroughs, 'Imperial Institutions and the Government of Empire' (ch. 9), and E. H. H. Green, 'The Political Economy of Empire, 1880–1914' (ch. 16), in Andrew Porter (ed.), *The Nineteenth Century*, vol. 3 of *The Oxford History of the British Empire* (Oxford, 1999).

11 As noted below in Chapter 5.

12 Chamberlain Papers, JC 5/20/44, JC to Dale, 10 March 1884.

13 See Garvin's account of the tour in his *Life of Chamberlain*, vol. 2, 452–6. Garvin notes that Chamberlain had hoped that the tour would relieve his gout; but the pain persisted, softened only by the occasional use of a cloth boot. Most of the time, he wore stiff boots – 'for discipline', as Garvin observes.

14 Ibid., JC 5/12/10, JC to Austen, 30 December 1889. Upon his return to Britain, he repeated essentially the same message to Hartington: see JC 5/22/147, JC to Hartington, 10 February 1890.

15 See Marsh, *Chamberlain*, 319.

16 See *The Times*, 25 March 1890.

17 Garvin believes that with this speech, Chamberlain became the leader of the 'New Imperialism' (Garvin, *Life of Chamberlain*, vol. 2, 456). But this seems premature: only from his platform as Colonial Secretary from 1895 onward could Chamberlain dominate the imperial discourse.

18 Dilke Papers, Add Mss 43889, JC to Dilke, 18 January 1892, ff. 82–3.

19 The literature on British imperial culture is vast. Many works touch upon common themes: the importance of manliness, courage, and patriotism; the spectacle of imperial targets with their exotic scenes and peoples; the dissemination of such spectacles, often through popular visual venues; and the uses of power both in capturing these spectacles

and in imperial conquests. First of note is the Manchester 'Studies in Imperialism' project. Representative among these is John M. MacKenzie (ed.), *Imperialism and Popular Culture* (Manchester, 1986), which depicts music halls, popular art, and juvenile fiction as important agents of imperial ideology. MacKenzie's (ed.) *Popular Imperialism and the Military* (Manchester, 1992) views military ritual and the martial spirit as a cultural grammar for stories of national service and sacrifice. Robert H. MacDonald's *The Language of Empire: Myths and Metaphors of Popular Imperialism, 1880–1918* (Manchester, 1994) analyses (among many other sources) the *Boy's Own Paper* and *Chums* as socializing influences upon young boys in the late nineteenth century with their illustrations of imperial power such as naval ships and cavalry charges. Other imperial approaches include Annie E. Coombes whose *Reinventing Africa: Museums, Material Culture, and Popular Imagination in Late Victorian and Edwardian England* (New Haven, 1994) discusses 'cultural vehicles', primarily the ethnographic collections in museums whose displays of weapons or ornaments or pottery suggest a reflected glory of those brave explorers who brought home these trophies at some risk to their own lives. Similarly, Timothy Mitchell's *Colonising Egypt* (Cambridge, 1988) examines the recreation of Cairo street scenes at the 1889 World Exhibition in Paris, which tended to validate the actions of imperializing nations in their organization of colonies as though they were exhibitions (the 'world-as-exhibition'). James R. Ryan, *Picturing Empire: Photography and the Visualization of the British Empire* (Chicago, 1997) believes that photos in the imperial era were 'culturally constructed "ways of seeing"' by which distant lands could be captured, made intelligible, and then explored. And, too, dramatic pictures of hunters posing with dead animals at their feet nicely symbolized the power of western technology over less advanced civilizations. Richard Phillips, *Mapping Men and Empire: A Geography of Adventure* (London, 1997) presents the notion that blank spaces on maps (say, in school textbooks) were often filled in imaginatively with 'geographies of adventure' in which imperial constructions (impenetrable jungles or burning deserts) excited the impressionable. Anne McClintock's *Imperial Leather: Race, Gender and Sexuality in the Colonial Contest* (New York, 1995) goes so far as to suggest that the fetish for order and cleanliness among middle-class Victorians, prompted by 'imperial advertising' especially of soap, led them into great unwashed areas of the world to cleanse and clothe the savage as a worthy civilizing mission. The imperial project was largely masculine in nature, but as Julia Bush reminds us, women had an important role to play: see her *Edwardian Ladies and Imperial Power* (London, 2000).

20   Excerpts from the speech, given on 23 March 1893, may be found in Charles W. Boyd, *Mr. Chamberlain's Speeches* (Boston, 1914), vol. 1, 341–53.

21   *The Times*, 1 April 1895.

22   Ibid., 16 July 1895.

23   R. E. Dumett put it somewhat differently: Chamberlain 'was the archetype of an aggressive, consolidationist business executive turned imperialist; his conception of the Empire resembled that of a multi-faceted corporate enterprise awaiting systematic management'. See Dumett's important article, 'Joseph Chamberlain, Imperial Finance and Railway Policy in British West Africa in the Late Nineteenth Century', *English Historical Review*, 90/355 (April 1975), 298. Dumett informs much of what follows on Chamberlain's West African project. This may be supplemented by Kesner, *Economic Control and Colonial Development*, ch. 4, 'The Imperial Government and the Development of Crown Colony Transportation Networks'. Kesner discusses the complicated procedure by which harbours, roads, and bridges, as well as railways were surveyed, funded, and put out for construction. Chamberlain's hand was much in evidence throughout.

24   For a case study in the economic circumstances and the impact of organized interest groups that lay behind Chamberlain's West African policy, see the valuable article by A. G. Hopkins, 'Economic Imperialism in West Africa: Lagos, 1880–92', *Economic History*

Review, 21/3 (December, 1968), 580–606. Chamberlain's policy was, as Hopkins notes, 'a major triumph for the economic imperialists of Victorian England' (606).

25 Chamberlain Papers, JC 37/3/2/23, 29 December 1898.

26 As Dumett observes in his 'Chamberlain, Imperial Finance, and Railway Policy', 308, Chamberlain's actions were indicative of his 'masterful self-confidence and aggressiveness which at times exasperated his cabinet colleagues as much as his political opponents'.

27 See Richard M. Kesner, 'Builders of Empire: The Role of the Crown Agents in Imperial Development, 1880–1914', *Journal of Imperial and Commonwealth History*, 5/3 (May 1977), 310–30.

28 Dumett's comment on this system of borrowing is succinct: it was 'somewhat devious' ('Chamberlain, Imperial Finance, and Railway Policy', 309). Dumett observes further that Chamberlain's extensive use of agents, 'this lateral agency', allowed him to launch construction and get short-term financing for West African railways 'outside close Treasury and parliamentary supervision' (310). Marsh notes that Chamberlain often played 'fast and loose' with conventional funding practices: Marsh, *Chamberlain*, 408–14.

29 Marsh credits Chamberlain's work on topical diseases as his 'most solid achievement' at the Colonial office (Marsh, *Chamberlain*, 414–17). See also Raymond E. Dumett, 'The Campaign Against Malaria and the Expansion of Scientific Medical and Sanitary Services in British West Africa, 1898–1919', *African Historical Studies*, 1/2 (1968), 153–97.

30 This could have the effect, of course, of artificially raising the price of imported sugar. See S. B. Saul, 'The Economic Significance of "Constructive Imperialism"', *Journal of Economic History*, 17/2 (June 1957), 173–92, which discusses at length Chamberlain's British West Indies colonial policy.

31 Chamberlain's attempt to establish a partnership of private and public enterprise in aid of the West Indies is evaluated in H. W. Will, 'Colonial Policy and Economic Development in the British West Indies, 1895–1903', *Economic History Review*, 23/1 (April 1970), 129–47.

32 For the historical background of the controversy, see R. A. Humphreys, 'Anglo-American Rivalries and the Venezuela Crisis of 1895', *Transactions of the Royal Historical Society*, 5th ser., 17 (1967), 131–64. See also J. A. S. Grenville's valuable *Lord Salisbury and Foreign Policy: The Close of the Nineteenth Century* (London, 1964), ch. 3.

33 Humphreys, 'Anglo-American Rivalries', 151.

34 Quoted in Grenville, *Lord Salisbury and Foreign Policy*, 63.

35 Chamberlain Papers, JC 7/5/1B/4, JC to Selborne, 20 December 1895.

36 Harcourt, attempting to play a calming role in the crisis, was perturbed by Chamberlain's attitude. 'The man whose obstinacy I fear most', he wrote to Morley, 'is Joe': A. G. Gardiner, *The Life of Sir William Harcourt* (London, 1923), vol. 2, 18 January 1896, 398. Chamberlain's views and temper were undoubtedly known to his family, and seem to have caused some stress with his American wife, Mary. Beatrice reported to Neville that Mary was so upset about the crisis 'that she won't talk of it to any outsider & says she hardly cares to do so even with us' (Chamberlain Papers, NC 1/13/2/82, 27 December 1895).

37 Chamberlain Papers, JC 11/30/28, Salisbury to JC, 23 December 1895; and Selborne Papers 5, Salisbury to Selborne, leaves 45–6, 23 April 1896.

38 See the informative and comprehensive volume edited by Prosser Gifford and William Roger Louis, *France and Britain in Africa: Imperial Rivalry and Colonial Rule* (New Haven, 1971), especially C. W. Newbury, 'The Tariff Factor in Anglo-French West African Partition', ch. 6,; and John D. Hargreaves, 'British and French Imperialism in West African, 1885–1898', ch. 7.

39 Dilke Papers, Add Mss 43889, Dilke to JC, ff. 124–5, 22 October 1894.

40 Ibid., JC to Dilke, f. 126, 25 October 1894.

41 A. S. Kanya-Forstner has termed Chamberlain's sharp reversal of policy a 'revolutionary transformation': see his 'Military Expansion in the Western Sudan – French and British Style', in Gifford and Louis, *France and Britain in Africa*, ch. 12, 410.

42 Lugard (created Baron Lugard of Abinger in 1928) had first made his name as a fearless, if impetuous, officer in the British East Africa Company in the late 1880s. Later he was an imperial publicist for the Uganda protectorate. As a young man, he had been commissioned directly out of Sandhurst for duty in Peshawar in the Northwest Frontier. Lugard ultimately made his name as a High Commissioner and Governor-General of Nigeria in the earliest years of the twentieth century. His biography by Dame Margery Perham, an Oxford don, African expert, and admirer of Lugard, remains compelling reading, as are her edited volumes of Lugard's diary. See Perham, *Lugard: The Years of Adventure, 1858* (London, 1956) and *Lugard: The Years of Authority, 1898–1945* (London, 1960).

43 See Lugard's account in Margery Perham and Mary Bull (eds.), *The Diaries of Lord Lugard* (London, 1963), vol. 4, 332–4. Better relations between the two followed: before his departure, Lugard was even invited to Princes' Gardens for tea. At a second interview, Lugard found Chamberlain less 'hectoring' (ibid., 347).

44 Chamberlain Papers, JC 9/4/2D/10, JC to Selborne, 29 September 1897.

45 Indeed, Goldie was no pushover. An adventurer, self-proclaimed atheist, and admirer of Ibsen, Goldie was out of place in Victorian society. After a bungled army career, he made his way to Africa through fortunate family connections, ultimately succeeding as the dominant imperial presence in one of Britain's most important colonies. For his life, see John E. Flint, *Sir George Goldie and the Making of Nigeria* (London, 1960). Goldie's negotiations with Chamberlain are thoroughly discussed in ch. 12.

46 Ibid., 277; letter dated 22 September 1897.

47 Chamberlain Papers, JC 9/4/2D/4, JC to Selborne, 12 September 1897. Chamberlain seemed at times to take affairs of state personally. He once explained his decision to adopt a more aggressive imperial policy thus: 'I was tired of having England kicked about all over the world.' Recounted by George W. Russell, *One Look Back* (New York, 1912), 238.

48 Flint, *Sir George Goldie*, 287–92. Flint has convincingly combed both Colonial Office and Foreign Office papers in reaching this conclusion.

49 Kanya-Forstner, 'Military Expansion in the Western Sudan', 413. Perhaps not surprisingly, defenders of Salisbury take a different line. Roberts believes that Salisbury's diplomacy avoided war in West Africa; and Steele maintains that Chamberlain's victory 'was really due to Salisbury'. See Andrew Roberts, *Salisbury: Victorian Titan* (London, 1999), 685, and E. D. Steele, *Lord Salisbury: A Political Biography* (London, 1999), 326.

50 Michael Crowder, *A Short History of Nigeria* (New York, 1962), 177.

51 Boniface I. Obichere, *West African States and European Expansion: The Dahomey-Niger Hinterland, 1885–1898* (New Haven, 1971), 217–19.

52 Marsh, *Chamberlain*, 431.

53 Garvin, *Life of Chamberlain*, vol. 3, 223.

54 Flint, *Sir George Goldie*, 294. But Flint also had a caveat. If France had imitated Chamberlain, and had met strength with strength, war would certainly have followed. Grenville agrees. Only by 'some miracle of good sense' had Chamberlain's 'reckless diplomacy' avoided a resort to arms. Grenville, *Lord Salisbury and Foreign Policy*, 123–4. J. D. Hargreaves also had reservations about Chamberlain's 'risky policy' in West Africa: see his 'The European Partition of West Africa' in J. F. A. Ajayi and Michael Crowder (eds.), *History of West Africa* (New York, 1973), vol. 2, 419.

55 Chamberlain Papers, JC 5/71/4, Bigge to JC, 30 October 1897.

56 Ibid., JC 7/2/1/5, Wilkinson to JC, 12 March 1898. Wilkinson was an influential author (*The Nation's Awakening*, 1896) and journalist with the *Morning Post*. Described by Paul M. Kennedy as a 'hyper-patriotic' intellectual, in *The Rise of the Anglo-German Antagonism*,

1860–1914 (London, 1980), 370, Wilkinson was appointed to the first professorship of military history at Oxford.

57 *The Times*, 4 November 1897. His partisan comments marred the speech to a degree, however. Slighting references to 'little Englanders' and their anti-imperial views were, even to Garvin, out of place in an academic setting (Garvin, *Life of Chamberlain*, vol. 3, 200).

58 *The Times*, 5 November 1897.

59 Ibid., 9 November 1897. In two other speeches during this busy Glasgow week, he spoke before the Imperial Union Club, where he was made an honorary member; and, briefly, at the Stock Exchange, where he raised the possibility of an 'Imperial union' (*The Times*, 6 November 1897).

60 The extent of British influence in China during the nineteenth century is well documented by Jurgen Osterhammel, 'Britain and China, 1842–1914' in Andrew Porter (ed.), *Oxford History of the British Empire*, vol. 3, *The Nineteenth Century*, (Oxford, 1999), ch. 8. See also Britten Dean, 'British Informal Empire: The Case of China', *Journal of Commonwealth and Comparative Politics*, 14/1 (March 1976), 64–81.

61 See the useful summary of European diplomatic and imperial aims toward China in L. K. Young, *British Policy in China, 1895–1902* (Oxford, 1970), chs. 1 and 3. France did not play a role in the scramble in north China, as did Britain, Germany, and Russia: it had, however, earlier won concessions and influence in the south (renamed French Cochin China) and in Cambodia and Laos.

62 Paul M. Kennedy discusses this sudden shift in German policy in his 'German World Policy and the Alliance Negotiations with England, 1897–1900', *Journal of Modern History*, 45/4 (December 1973), 605–625. Kennedy's argument here was incorporated into his larger work, *The Rise of the Anglo-German Antagonism, 1860–1914* (London, 1980).

63 Grenville, *Lord Salisbury and Foreign Policy*, ch. 6; and Steele, *Lord Salisbury*, 333–7.

64 A thorough discussion may be found in Pamela Atwell, *British Mandarins and Chinese Reformers: The British Administration of Weihaiwei (1898–1930) and the Territory's Return to Chinese Rule* (Hong Kong, 1985).

65 Roberts, *Salisbury*, 688–9.

66 Indeed, Weihaiwei's value as an imperial outpost was never realized. Its bleakness and the poverty of its surrounding province of Shantung are well documented (including photographs) in Atwell's *British Mandarins and Chinese Reformers*. As Ian Nish has pointed out, Weihaiwei was a second rate base which could be used only for emergency purposes: Ian H. Nish, *The Anglo-Japanese Alliance: The Diplomacy of Two Island Empires, 1894–1907*, 2nd edn. (London, 1985), 57. After lengthy negotiations, Weihaiwei was returned to China in 1930.

67 A somewhat different version may be found in Clarence B. Davis and Robert J. Gowen, 'The British at Weihaiwei: A Case Study in the Irrationality of Empire', *The Historian*, 63/1 (Fall 2000), 87–104. The authors, who tend to discount the impact of public opinion, believe that the cabinet as a whole resisted the acquisition of Weihaiwei.

68 This was reported to Salisbury by George Curzon, then parliamentary undersecretary at the Foreign Office, who attended the cabinet meeting during Salisbury's absence. Quoted in Grenville, *Lord Salisbury and Foreign Policy*, 144 n. 4; and Steele, *Lord Salisbury*, 333–34. Curzon was soon to become viceroy of India, beginning his career as one of the great imperial proconsuls.

69 See Chamberlain's letter to Salisbury, quoted in Garvin, *Life of Chamberlain*, vol. 3, 249.

70 Nish, *The Anglo-Japanese Alliance*, 63–6.

71 Chamberlain Papers, JC 5/5/70, JC to Balfour, 3 February 1898.

72 Young, *British Policy in China*, 91–99.

73 Chamberlain's proposals, if accepted, would as Marsh notes, 'place the whole foreign policy of Britain on a new footing' (Marsh, *Chamberlain*, 432).

74   For this German diplomatic initiative and Chamberlain's response, see Grenville, *Lord Salisbury and Foreign Policy*, ch. 7.

75   Chamberlain's initiative has been roundly condemned. Marsh thinks his unanticipated intrusion into foreign relations was both rash and irregular (Marsh, *Chamberlain*, 435–6). Grenville is equally harsh, calling it a fundamental miscalculation, and a 'clumsy overture' (Grenville, *Lord Salisbury and Foreign Policy*, 156–7).

76   Roberts, *Salisbury*, 690; and Grenville, *Lord Salisbury and Foreign Policy*, 159–62.

77   Known as 'the dying nations' speech: see *The Times*, 5 May 1898.

78   See *The Times*, 14 May 1898.

79   *Hansard*, 4th ser., vol. 58, 1347, 10 June 1898.

80   In a letter to Harcourt; see Gardiner, *Harcourt*, vol. 2, 457, letter dated 16 May 1898.

81   *Journal of Kimberley*, 19 May 1898, 460. Kimberley was then the leader of the small knot of Home Rule Liberals in the Lords.

82   Kimberley quotes the opinion of an unnamed Unionist colleague: '"Joe has behaved d—d badly."' (ibid.)

83   Garvin, *Life of Chamberlain*, vol. 3, 283.

84   Grenville, *Lord Salisbury and Foreign Policy*, 170.

85   The group included Goschen, First Lord of the Admiralty; Hamilton, Secretary of State for India; Henry Chaplin, President of the Local Government Board; Chamberlain; and Selborne, Chamberlain's parliamentary undersecretary. Lascelles, on leave in London, was also present. Accounts of the meeting are in Marsh, *Chamberlain*, 439; Grenville, *Lord Salisbury and Foreign Policy*, 173–4; and Garvin, *Life of Chamberlain*, vol. 3, 290–1.

86   A thorough background to the negotiations may be found in Philip R. Warhurst, *Anglo-Portuguese Relations in South-Central Africa, 1890–1900* (London, 1962), chs. 4 and 5.

87   Chamberlain wrote through an intermediary, the banker Alfred Rothschild. See Chamberlain Papers, JC 7/3/2D/19, JC to Alfred Rothschild, 28 July 1896.

88   Ibid., JC 7/3/2D/22, JC to Alfred Rothschild, 30 October 1896.

89   See Chamberlain's minute of the meeting in ibid., JC 7/3/2C/14, 6 July 1898. Warhurst notes the 'unfair bullying' of Portugal by the British (Warhurst, *Anglo-Portuguese Relations*, 152).

90   This was the first time, as Marsh notes, that the cabinet overruled Salisbury on a matter of foreign affairs in favour of Chamberlain (Marsh, *Chamberlain*, 440).

91   Chamberlain Papers, JC 5/5/77, JC to Balfour, 17 August 1898. See also Chamberlain's letter to Balfour of the previous day (ibid., JC 5/5/74, 16 August 1898).

92   Ibid., JC 5/5/32, Balfour to JC, 18 August 1898.

93   Grenville's *Lord Salisbury and Foreign Policy*, ch. 8 is indispensable for this complicated negotiation.

94   The most concise and thorough discussion of Fashoda is G. N. Sanderson, 'The Origins and Significance of the Anglo-French Confrontation at Fashoda, 1898', in Gifford and Louis, *France and Britain in Africa*, ch. 8, 285–331. See also Roberts, *Salisbury*, ch. 41; and Grenville, *Lord Salisbury and Foreign Policy*, ch. 10.

95   Steele, *Salisbury*, 327.

96   *The Times*, 16 November 1898.

97   Ibid., 17 November 1898.

98   Ibid., 18 November 1898

11 Joe's War

1   See John S. Galbraith's classic study of imperial border wars: 'The "Turbulent Frontier" as a Factor in British Expansion', *Comparative Studies in Society and History*, 2 (January 1960), 150–68.

2   As Christopher Saunders and Iain R. Smith note in their valuable and admirably concise 'Southern Africa, 1795–1910', ch. 26 in *The Oxford History of the British Empire*, vol.

3, *The Nineteenth Century*, ed. Andrew Porter (Oxford, 1999). I have relied heavily on Saunders and Smith in these introductory paragraphs. See also Smith's *The Origins of the South African War, 1899–1902* (London, 1996), ch. 1. An important earlier work is D. M. Schreuder, *The Scramble for Southern Africa, 1877–1895: The Politics of Partition Reappraised* (Cambridge, 1970). Useful, too, is Monica Wilson and Leonard Thompson (eds.), *The Oxford History of South Africa*, vol. 2 (Oxford, 1971), esp. chs. 1 and 5-7.

3 Chamberlain Papers, JC 10/6/3/1, Rhodes to JC, 9 July 1895.

4 The authoritative work on the Chartered Company is John S. Galbraith's *Crown and Charter: The Early Years of the British South Africa Company* (Berkeley, 1974). It is heavily critical of both the Company and of Rhodes.

5 Rhodes' imperial drive is explained psychologically in Robert I. Rotberg's provocative biography, *The Founder: Cecil Rhodes and the Pursuit of Power* (New York, 1988). In collaboration with Miles F. Shore, a psychoanalytic psychiatrist, Rotberg advances a theory of narcissism to explain Rhodes' grandiose schemes. See also Shore's article, 'Cecil Rhodes and the Ego Ideal', *Journal of Interdisciplinary History*, 10 (1979), 249–65. Though dated, J. G. Lockhart and C. M. Woodhouse, *Cecil Rhodes: The Colossus of Southern Africa* (New York, 1963) remains valuable for Rhodes' life.

6 The pioneers have been described as 'An invasion force of latter-day conquistadors in search of land and gold': Saunders and Smith, 'Southern Africa', 611.

7 See Kenneth E. Wilburn, Jr, 'Engines of Empire and Independence: Railways in South Africa, 1863–1916', and W. Travis Hanes III, 'Railway Politics and Imperialism in Central Africa, 1889–1953'. Both are in Clarence B. Davis and Kenneth E. Wilburn, Jr (eds.) with Ronald E. Robinson, *Railway Imperialism* (New York, 1991). For an analysis of Bechuanaland as the object of imperial ambitions, see Paul Maylan, *Rhodes, the Tswana, and the British: Colonialism, Collaboration, and Conflict in the Bechuanaland Protectorate, 1885–1899*, Contributions in Comparative Colonial Studies, 4 (Westport, Conn., 1980). Also useful is Anthony Sillery, *Founding a Protectorate: History of Bechuanaland, 1885–1895* (London, 1965).

8 Marsh, *Chamberlain*, 318.

9 This intriguing episode is told in detail by Neil Parsons, *King Khama, Emperor Joe, and the Great White Queen: Victorian Britain through African Eyes* (Chicago, 1998). For a shorter version, see Sillery, *Founding a Protectorate*, ch. 18, 'Visit of the Chiefs to England'.

10 See, for example, John Lambert, 'Chiefship in Early Colonial Natal, 1843–1879', *Journal of Southern African Studies*, 21/2 (June, 1995), 269–85.

11 Ripon Papers, Add. Mss. 43516, Ripon to Rosebery, ff. 224–5, 15 August 1895; cited in Stansky, *Ambitions and Strategies*, 236–7.

12 Rutherfoord Harris had gone to South Africa in 1882, became Rhodes's confidential agent, and member of the Cape House of Assembly, 1894–8. Grey, the 4th Earl, was a Liberal MP from 1880 to 1886, later a Liberal Unionist. He joined the board of the British South Africa Company in 1889 and served as administrator of Rhodesia between 1896 and 1897 (replacing Jameson). He was Governor-General of Canada from 1904 to 1911.

13 Marsh, *Chamberlain*, 376–7.

14 Although half a century old, Jean van der Poel's pioneering *The Jameson Raid* (Cape Town, 1951) remains authoritative and readable for the planning, execution, and consequences of the raid.

15 Rotberg, *The Founder*, 522.

16 Marsh, *Chamberlain*, 382–3.

17 Chamberlain Papers, JC 28/A/2/8/49, 31 December 1895.

18 Ibid., JC 28/A/2/9/1, JC to Mary Chamberlain, 1 January 1896.

19 Ibid., JC 28/A/2/9/2, JC to Mary Chamberlain, 2 January 1896.
20 In response to the belief that Chamberlain had turned over the Pitsani Strip for the express purpose of providing a 'jumping-off ground' for the Raid, Garvin declares, 'There never was a charge of its kind more iniquitously false': Garvin, *Life of Chamberlain* (London, 1932), vol. 3, 36. But later, he observes that it was beyond doubt that he understood that the new police force being formed at Pitsani 'might serve as first aid should intervention by the British Government at Johannesburg become necessary' (56). Still later, Garvin writes that although he was prepared to act in the event of an expected Johannesburg revolution, Chamberlain 'had not a shadow of complicity with the Raid' (125). Other sources for this paragraph include Peter Fraser, *Joseph Chamberlain: Radicalism and Empire, 1868–1914* (London, 1966), 171; Michael Bentley, *Politics without Democracy 1815–1914: Perception and Preoccupation in British Government*, 2nd edition (London, 1996), 214; Elizabeth Pakenham, *Jameson's Raid* (London, 1960) and the introduction to Pakenham's *Jameson's Raid: The Prelude to the Boer War* (London, 1982); Denis Judd, *Radical Joe*, 198–9. As Judd puts it here: 'Quite simply, it is beyond belief that Chamberlain, a newly-appointed minister with an outstandingly incisive and enquiring mind, with the need to dominate and control events, and with years of experience of political duplicity and sharp practice, could have remained perfectly unaware of the plans for the raid.' See also Marsh, *Chamberlain*, 372ff and Denis Judd and Keith Surridge, *The Boer War* (New York, 2003), 38. A useful historiographical essay is Melvin G. Holli's 'Joseph Chamberlain and the Jameson Raid: a Bibliographical Survey', *Journal of British Studies*, 3 (May 1964), 152–66.
21 Indeed, Britain's interest in establishing a firmer imperial presence in Bechuanaland was partly designed to create a buffer between the Transvaal and German South West Africa. See Jeffrey Butler's authoritative and concise chapter, 'The German Factor in Anglo-Transvaal Relations' in Prosser Gifford and Wm. Roger Louis (eds.), *Britain and Germany in Africa: Imperial Rivalry and Colonial Rule* (New Haven, 1967), 179–214.
22 Salisbury Papers, Chamberlain to Salisbury, 4 January 1896, cited (in slightly different versions) by Garvin, *Life of Chamberlain*, vol. 3, 95–6; and A. N. Porter, *The Origins of the South African War: Joseph Chamberlain and the Diplomacy of Imperialism, 1895–99* (New York, 1980), 86. Chamberlain's was, however, a curious, flailing response. It did not much matter which foe they defied, he wrote, but 'we ought to defy someone'. For the British press response to the Kruger Telegram, see Paul M. Kennedy, *The Rise of the Anglo-German Antagonism, 1860–1914* (London, 1980), 220.
23 See Porter, *Origins of the South African War*, 88–94, for a discussion of Chamberlain's motives.
24 See *The Times*, 1 January and 11 January 1896; *Daily Chronicle*, 1 January and 6 January 1896; *Evening News*, 1 January and 2 January 1896.
25 Chamberlain Papers, JC 30/4/45.
26 This, of course, had been true of the Company in its previous harsh dealings with indigenous African peoples in Rhodesia. But in the case of the Transvaal, with its network of modern communications, the Company's transgressions rapidly became front-page news around the world.
27 *The Times*, 22 January 1896. A few days later, Chamberlain elaborated on the theme of the inevitable difficulties and dangers of an active imperial policy. At a speech in Birmingham, he noted that these 'necessary incidents' of empire had to be dealt with resolutely and fairly (*The Times*, 27 January 1896).
28 In a memo to Balfour, Chamberlain wrote that a large committee of inquiry with the widest possible reference might last for at least a parliamentary session, perhaps two. Such a committee would, he predicted, 'get lost in a multiplicity of details and thus finally present a belated and inconclusive report': quoted in Jeffrey Butler, *The Liberal Party and the Jameson Raid* (Oxford, 1968), 74, from the Balfour Papers. Garvin quotes an additional

query to Balfour from that same memo: could we, Chamberlain asked, resist an inquiry 'without raising a suspicion that there is something behind?' (Garvin, *Life of Chamberlain*, vol. 3, 104, n. l). The answer was no.

29 After his release, Jameson returned to South Africa. He was elected to the Cape House of Assembly in 1900; four years later he became prime minister of the Cape Colony. He was knighted in 1911.

30 Five Liberals, including Harcourt, were balanced by five Unionists. There is some evidence that Chamberlain attempted to influence its membership (Butler, *The Jameson Raid and the Liberal Party*, 106). Rotberg calls Chamberlain's selection a 'strange surprise' (*The Founder*, 548). Robert Blake agrees: the selection was 'certainly odd' and thought suspicious at the time. See Blake, 'The Jameson Raid and "The Missing Telegrams"', in Hugh Lloyd-Jones, Valerie Pearl and Blair Worden, *History and Imagination: Essays in Honour of H. R. Trevor-Roper* (London, 1981), 338–9.

31 Chamberlain Papers, JC 27/128, JC to R. B. Brett, 1 February 1896. A second copy is at AC 1/4/4/1. Also published in Maurice V. Brett (ed.), *Journals and Letters of Reginald Viscount Esher* (London, 1934), vol. 1, 193–5. Chamberlain informed Sir Robert Meade, then permanent undersecretary at the Colonial Office, of his contact with Rhodes through Brett. Chamberlain also confided to Meade that Rhodes' recent actions in South Africa seemed 'a little too "proconsular" for the 19th century' (Chamberlain Papers, JC 37/3/3/12, JC to Meade, 1 February 1896).

32 Brett, *Journals and Letters of Esher*, vol. 1, 195–7.

33 See van der Poel, *Jameson Raid*, 158.

34 *Hansard*, 4th ser., vol. 37, 327–8 (13 February 1896), quoted in Marsh, *Chamberlain*, 389. In a letter to Harcourt later that year, Chamberlain persisted in this view. Rhodes was, he wrote, 'the one man who combines energy, wealth, ability and popularity. If he goes the whole population will be in a state of ferment and their attacks and demands upon the Home Government will be strenuous and persistent.' Chamberlain was also 'certain no Crown Administration would do better' (Harcourt Papers 717, JC to Harcourt, leaves 331–2, 19 November 1896). In a letter to Sir Robert Herbert, a former permanent head of the Colonial Office, Chamberlain reinforced his preference for the Company as the instrument of governing in South Africa: 'The Treasury would never give me the money that would be required to place the administration on a proper footing and at the same time to develop the estate' (Chamberlain Papers, JC 10/8/1/16, JC to Herbert, 10 June 1897).

35 A useful discussion of the tensions between 'the Rhodes group' and the Colonial Office prior to the inquiry may be found in van der Poel, *Jameson Raid*, ch. 6, 'Attempts at Exposure'.

36 The work of the Colonial Office staff in protecting their chief may be observed in Lord Selborne's comments on the telegrams. See his memo of 6 June 1896 in D. George Boyce (ed.), *The Crisis of British Power: The Imperial and Naval Papers of the Second Earl of Selborne, 1895–1910* (London, 1990), 37–40. Sir Robert Meade, in his memo, discounted the telegrams as either irrelevant or 'perfectly innocent'; but he also acknowledged that 'now and again' some sentences suggest reasons other than railway extension may account for the partitioning of parts of Bechuanaland (Chamberlain Papers, JC 10/1/90, 8 June 1896).

37 As a recent biographer has claimed, Salisbury very likely 'was involved in the successful Government cover-up of Chamberlain's role' in the Jameson Raid: Andrew Roberts, *Salisbury: Victorian Titan* (London, 1999), 635.

38 The telegrams have remained an intriguing source for Chamberlain's complicity in the raid, especially after the disappearance of several soon after they left Chamberlain's hands. Lord Blake believes that the culprit was Sir Robert Herbert, not only a former colonial officer with whom Chamberlain had been in contact (as we have seen in n. 28 above) but also a member of the board of the Eastern and South African Telegraph Company. See

Blake, 'The Jameson Raid and "The Missing Telegrams"'. Roberts, in his *Salisbury*, 637–8, accepts Blake's conjecture.

39 See Marsh, *Chamberlain*, 395.

40 Grey Papers, JC to Grey, 13 October 1896, cited in Marsh, *Chamberlain*, 395. A copy may be found in Chamberlain Papers, JC 10/6/1/7. A lengthy extract of this letter was also published by Ethel Drus in her pioneering work exploring Chamberlain's role in the raid. See Drus, 'A Report on the Papers of Joseph Chamberlain Relating to the Jameson Raid and the Inquiry', *Bulletin of the Institute of Historical Research*, 25 (1952), 33–62. Drus was the first historian to utilize the Chamberlain Papers since Garvin. Her conclusion was that Garvin attempted 'by the suppression and distortion of conflicting evidence' to defend Chamberlain's role in the uprising and the raid (62).

41 For Grey's role in the conspiracy and a succinct analysis of Chamberlain's complicity, see John S. Galbraith, 'The British South Africa Company and the Jameson Raid', *Journal of British Studies*, 10/1(1970), 145–61, especially 147–9.

42 Chamberlain Papers, JC 10/6/1/8, Grey to JC, 25 November 1896.

43 Grey to Chamberlain, 10 December 1896 in Drus, 'Report on the Papers of Joseph Chamberlain', 56. This much, perhaps surprisingly, was quoted in Garvin, *Life of Chamberlain*, vol. 3, 39. But Garvin did not print the sentence following: 'Altho' you declined to receive this information which you said you wd [sic] be obliged to use officially, if it were pressed upon you, the subsequent acts of the Govt. showed that you agreed with our view that it was desirable to give the B.S.A. Co. an opportunity of placing a force upon the frontier' (Drus, 'Report on the Papers of Joseph Chamberlain', 56). Garvin does print an additional sentence in Grey's letter: 'I most certainly can confirm you when you say that you did not know and could not know of any plan or intention of Mr. Rhodes which could possibly lead to such an invasion of the Transvaal in time of peace as was perpetrated by Dr. Jameson, for I did not know of any such plan of intention myself' (Garvin, *Chamberlain*, vol. 3, 39). The key phrase in this sentence is, of course, 'in time of peace'. Jameson was to invade only after the insurrection had begun. When he began his precipitous raid before a revolution was under way, it occurred technically in a time of peace. Thus Grey could claim ignorance of such a plan. This interpretation is confirmed by two concluding sentences in the letter not printed either by Drus or Garvin. 'Our whole object was to place Jameson in a position which wd. enable him to *assist* a Revolution at the right time. That he shd. attempt to *initiate* a Revolution by an invasion of the T[rans]vaal in time of peace never so much as entered into my imagination.' A copy of the complete letter may be found in Chamberlain Papers, JC 10/6/19, Grey to JC, 10 December 1896. Of equal importance in determining Chamberlain's complicity was a letter sent a year earlier from Grey to Chamberlain. In it, Grey – speaking for the BSAC – presses Chamberlain for an 'immediate' administration of the Bechuanaland Protectorate, not for commercial reasons but for 'political considerations alone' because the Company desires to place itself 'in a position to help British Interests in the Transvaal in the event of anything taking place there'. The letter is dated 17 November 1895 and may be found in the Earl Grey Papers GR 2/1/1, National Archives, Salisbury, Rhodesia (now Zimbabwe), as cited by Butler, *The Liberal Party and the Jameson Raid*, Appendix A, 295–6.

44 Apparently Chamberlain himself decided to sacrifice Fairfield: see Butler, *The Jameson Raid and the Liberal Party*, 128. Butler, especially ch. 6, is the general source for this paragraph.

45 Although both Bower and Newton were dismissed from the colonial service, Newton was later rehabilitated, eventually becoming High Commissioner in London for Southern Rhodesia. He was knighted upon retiring from the colonial service in 1919. Bower, on the other hand, who had been relegated to a modest posting as colonial secretary of Mauritius, never recovered his reputation. Ethel Drus believes that Bower, Newton, and Fairfield

were all 'victimized': 'The Question of Imperial Complicity in the Jameson Raid', *English Historical Review*, 68 (October 1953), 582–93. Drus bases her conclusions on the Bower papers, held in the South African Public Library at Cape Town, which were unsealed in 1946. Jean van der Poel's important work on the Jameson Raid was also based upon the Bower papers. Her poignant account of the later career of the self-sacrificing Bower may be found in *Jameson Raid*, 245–8.

In 1896, Robinson was created Baron Rosmead. In 1897, Chamberlain publicly accepted Robinson's claims of innocence. Most historians have long been convinced that Robinson was directly implicated in the larger scheme of supporting a revolution against the Transvaal government. Indeed, Robinson's report to Chamberlain two months before the Raid makes this incontestable. In the report, Robinson sets out his own role once the Johannesburg uprising had taken place. He would issue a proclamation calling on all parties to cease hostilities and submit to his arbitration. The British government would then issue a proclamation in support of this action: additionally, it would announce that a large military force had been placed on alert for possible action in South Africa. Robinson, proceeding to Pretoria, would begin the selection of a constituent assembly and devise a constitution. Robinson believed that it was important to act quickly to deter German intervention. See Chamberlain Papers, JC 10/2/4B/3, 4 November 1895.

46 Van der Poel, *Jameson Raid*, 207 and 223–4; for the inquiry generally, see ch. 7, 'The Lying in State at Westminster'.

47 Shaw was a fervent imperialist, a friend and supporter of Rhodes, and the first colonial correspondent for *The Times*. Later in life she married Lord Lugard. See Helen Callaway and Dorothy O. Helly, 'Crusader for Empire: Flora Shaw/Lady Lugard', 79–97 in Nupur Chaudhuri and Margaret Strobel (eds), *Western Women and Imperialism: Complicity and Resistance* (Bloomington, Ind., 1992); and Dorothy O. Helly and Helen Callaway, 'Journalism as Active Politics: Flora Shaw, *The Times* and South Africa', ch. 3 in Donal Lowry (ed.), *The South African War Reappraised* (Manchester, 2000).

48 As Marsh notes, Chamberlain's conversation with Shaw was 'worse than indiscreet': it made him 'an accessory to the plot' (Marsh, *Chamberlain*, 380–1).

49 Chamberlain Papers, JC 10/2/3/34, Shaw to JC, 21 May 1897.

50 Ibid., JC to Wilson, 23 May 1897. Also printed in Drus, 'A Report on the Papers of Joseph Chamberlain', 61.

51 Chamberlain Papers, JC 10/2/3/35, Wilson to JC, 24 May 1897. Again, printed in Drus, 'A Report from the Papers of Joseph Chamberlain', 61.

52 In spite of Kimberley's judgement – long after the fact – that Harcourt was 'completely the dupe of Chamberlain' during the inquiry: Angus Hawkins and John Powell (eds), *The Journal of John Wodehouse, First Earl of Kimberley for 1862–1902*, Camden 5th ser., 9 (1997), 464. Kimberley entered this comment in his journal on 12 December 1898 to account for Harcourt's recent resignation as leader of the Liberal Party. Kimberley believed that Harcourt's mismanagement of the inquiry more than anything else contributed to the party's discontent with Harcourt's leadership. The most recent biographer of Harcourt suggests an equivocal view of the matter. At first Harcourt may have believed in Chamberlain's innocence; but later – even if Chamberlain were guilty – he should be exonerated given the serious international implications that could follow if Chamberlain were found complicit in the Raid. See Patrick Jackson, *Harcourt and Son: A Political Biography of Sir William Harcourt, 1827–1904* (Madison, 2004), 274–8 and 282–7.

53 As Judd and Surridge succinctly put in their *Boer War*, it was 'a whitewash' (40).

54 Smith, *Origins of the South African War*, 140.

55 See Eric Stokes, 'Milnerism', *Historical Journal*, 5/1 (1962), 47–60.

56 Iain Smith has much to say in his *Origins of the South African War* about the Kruger government's willingness to engage in a modest reform programme in order to deflect British intransigence.

57 Chamberlain's low opinion of Kruger was widely known. As he expressed it to Harcourt, Kruger was 'an obstinate opinionated and above all intensely ignorant and narrow-minded man. He is not influenced by anything we say, but he is impressed by what we do' (Chamberlain Papers, JC 5/38/226, JC to Harcourt, 4 September 1897).

58 Cecil Headlam (ed.), *The Milner Papers: South Africa, 1897–1899* (London, 1931), vol. 1, Milner to Rhodes, 6 March 1898, 153–4.

59 Smith, *Origins of the South African War*, 213, and in general ch. 7 'Getting Things "Forrarder" in South Africa'.

60 See A. N. Porter, 'Sir Alfred Milner and the Press, 1897–1899', *Historical Journal*, 16/2 (1973), 323–39.

61 For this dispatch, sent to Chamberlain on 4 May 1899, see Headlam, *The Milner Papers*, 349–53. As Milner put it to Selborne in a letter written the same day, he hoped that his dispatches would be 'rubbed into the public mind' (348).

62 *The Times*, 27 June 1899. If to Chamberlain the speech was 'plain', to others it was provocative (Smith, *Origins of the South African War*, 303).

63 Chamberlain Papers, JC 10/4/2/41, Selborne to JC, 23 June 1899. As Selborne confided to Milner: 'I have implored him [i.e. Chamberlain] to give public opinion a lead and I think he will ...' (Boyce, *Crisis of British Power*, Selborne to Milner, 25 June 1899, 83–5). 'We must', Selborne added, 'eventually force the door at the other end, by peaceful pressure if possible, but if necessary by war.'

64 *Hansard*, 4th ser., vol. 75, 697–716, 28 July 1899.

65 *The Times*, 28 August 1899. Gardiner describes the tone of the speech as 'menacing': A. G. Gardiner, *The Life of Sir William Harcourt*, (London, 1923), vol. 2, 500.

66 Smith, *Origins of the South African War*, 360–1.

67 The policy debate on troop deployment may be found in Smith, *Origins of the South African War*, 'The Military Situation', 337–46.

68 Porter, *Origins of the South African War*, 70.

69 Andrew Porter, 'Lord Salisbury, Mr. Chamberlain and South Africa, 1895–9', *Journal of Imperial and Commonwealth History*, 1 (1972), 3–26.

70 J. A. S. Grenville, *Lord Salisbury and Foreign Policy: The Close of the Nineteenth Century* (London, 1964), 236.

71 Shula Marks and Stanley Trapido, 'Lord Milner and the South African State', *History Workshop*, 8 (Autumn, 1979), 50–80. See also ch. 4 by Marks and Trapido, 'Lord Miner and the South African State Reconsidered', in Michael Twaddle (ed.), *Imperialism, the State and the Third World* (London, 1992).

72 G. Blainey, 'Lost Causes of the Jameson Raid', *Economic History Review*, 18/2 (1965), 350–66.

73 I. P. Phimister carries Blainey's ideas forward by suggesting that disappointing financial returns in both the Transvaal and Zambesia threatened the solvency of the Chartered Company to such an extent that Rhodes was driven to act against the Transvaal government's restrictive practices imposed on deep mining. See his 'Rhodes, Rhodesia and the Rand', *Journal of Southern African Studies*, 1/1 (October, 1974), 74–90. Richard Mendelsohn largely agrees about the importance of the deep mining interests of Rhodes and others, but believes they were driven to action not because of economic necessity, but simply because replacing Kruger with 'a captive government' in the Transvaal would increase their profits even more: thus, 'the Jameson Raid was not the last throw of the despairing but, instead, a bold bid by the audacious'. In Mendelsohn's 'Blainey and the Jameson Raid: The Debate Renewed', *Journal of Southern African Studies*, 6/1 (October, 1979), 157–170. But Elaine N. Katz, writing more recently, believes that that the distinction that Blainey makes between outcrop and deep level mining, especially in costs of production, cannot be sustained, and that his thesis should be abandoned. Katz also believes that the negative impact of Kruger's economic policies relating to mining has often been exaggerated. See

her article 'Outcrop and Deep Level Mining in South African before the Anto-Boer War: Re-examining the Blainey Thesis', *Economic History Review*, 48/2 (1995), 304–28.

74 Porter casts doubt upon economic reasons as a dominant cause for the war, pointing out that there is no evidence that Chamberlain 'or other policy-makers' thought in those terms. He gives more credence to Chamberlain's 'narrowly political strategies' as causal. See Andrew Porter, 'The South African War (1899–1902): Context and Motive Reconsidered', *Journal of African History*, 31/1 (1990), 43–57, esp. 56–7.

75 Boyce, *Crisis of British Power*, memo of 30 March 1896, 34–7.

76 As Tamarkin puts it, Milner did not see himself 'as an obedient civil servant waiting for guidance and instructions from above': Mordechai Tamarkin, 'Milner, the Cape Afrikaners, and the Outbreak of the South African War: From a Point of Return to a Dead End', *Journal of Imperial and Commonwealth History*, 25/3 (September 1997), 392–414. See also John Benyon, 'Overlords of Empire? British "Proconsular Imperialism" in Comparative Perspective', *Journal of Imperial and Commonwealth History*, 19/2 (May 1991), 164–202, and Benyon's ch. 5 '"Intermediate" Imperialism and the Test of Empire: Milner's "Excentric" High Commission in South Africa' in Lowry, *The South African War Reappraised*.

77 To Harcourt, the imperial bond between Milner and Chamberlain was unsettling. In a letter to Chamberlain shortly before the war, he wrote: 'I regard you and the Kaiser William and Milner as by nature the pattern Jingoes of these times.' Viewing Milner especially 'with a good deal of disquietude', Harcourt observed additionally: 'There is nothing so irresistible to a new born Governor General fresh to the trade as the prospect of a sensational annexation and I see clearly enough that our dear Alfred has been bitten by this fly' (Harcourt Papers 717, Harcourt to JC, leaves 364–70, 29 August 1899).

78 Niall Ferguson believes that 'It can hardly be denied that Chamberlain and Milner provoked the Boer War': *Empire: The Rise and Demise of the British World Order and the Lessons for Global Power* (New York, 2003), 271. This was more true of Milner than of Chamberlain.

79 As Bill Nasson puts it in his lively and readable *The South African War, 1899–1902* (London, 1999), 42. Marsh is in agreement: see his *Chamberlain*, 470. The following account of the War is largely based upon Nasson.

80 Mordechai Tamarkin, 'The Cape Afrikaners and the British Empire from the Jameson Raid to the South African War', ch. 7 in Lowry, *The South African War Reappraised*.

81 W. K. Hancock, *Smuts: The Sanguine Years, 1870–1919* (Cambridge, 1962), 60.

82 Eric A. Walker, *W. P. Schreiner: A South African* (London, 1937), 162, 164.

83 Marsh, *Chamberlain*, 481.

84 Charles W. Boyd, *Mr. Chamberlain's Speeches* (Boston, 1914), vol. 2, 20–1. The speech was given on 19 October 1899.

85 Ibid., 26–7.

86 From a speech during a Unionist conference at Leicester: see *The Times*, 30 November 1899.

87 Boyd, *Chamberlain's Speeches*, vol. 2, 52–67.

88 *The Times*, 13 May 1900. Sir Henry Campbell-Bannerman, who served as Liberal MP for Stirling Burghs for forty years, became leader of the Liberal Party in 1898. In 1906 he became prime minister.

89 *The Times*, 30 June 1900.

90 Garvin, *Life of Chamberlain*, vol. 3, 588. The letter is dated 7 August 1900.

91 *Journal of Kimberley*, 25 July 1900, 477.

92 Cited in G. B. Pyrah, *Imperial Policy and South Africa, 1902–10* (Oxford, 1955), 23–4.

93 Roberts, *Salisbury*, 774–6.

94 Garvin's phrase (*Life of Chamberlain*, vol. 3, 600). Garvin notes further that Chamberlain campaigned 'with restless vigour, … threw amenity to the winds' and was 'remorseless' against his political opponents (594).

95   See the account in *The Times*, 24 September 1900.

96   Chamberlain Papers JC 30/4/110, Churchill to JC, 27 July 1900. Two months later, Churchill asked again for Chamberlain's help: 'I arrange words in all manner of ingenious combinations; I excite applause, but I do not shift votes!' Chamberlain's 'authority and experience' were desperately needed (JC 30/4/112, Churchill to JC, 16 September 1900). Churchill carried Oldham, then a marginal seat but increasingly Liberal, by some 200 votes. The account of Chamberlain's visit to Oldham may be found in Winston S. Churchill, *My Early Life: A Roving Commission* (New York, 1958 edn) 359.

97   *The Times*, 26 September 1900.

98   *The Times*, 28 September 1900.

99   *The Times*, 29 September 1900. Chamberlain here was referring to the so-called Bloemfontein letters discovered when British troops captured that city. See Marsh, *Chamberlain*, 493–4.

100   *The Times*, 25 October 1900.

101   Gardiner, *Life of Harcourt*, vol. 2, 524. Harcourt was a 'Little Englander', though he is difficult at times to classify. Judd, *Radical Joe*, 224, labels him a pro-Boer on the left wing of the Liberal Party. But John W. Auld does not include him in his analysis: see Auld's 'The Liberal Pro-Boers', *Journal of British Studies*, 14/2 (May 1975), 78–101. The truth seems to lie in between. On occasion, Harcourt cooperated with the centrist Campbell-Bannerman. The most consistent pro-Boers in parliament were, of course, the Irish Nationalists. Other well-known pro-Boers included John Morley, David Lloyd George, John Burns, and Henry Labouchere.

102   Herbert Gladstone Papers, Add Mss 45989, Asquith to Herbert Gladstone, 7 October 1900, f. 427; cited in H. C. G. Matthew, *The Liberal Imperialists: The Ideas and Politics of a Post-Gladstonian Elite* (Oxford, 1973). Matthew's book remains crucial to an understanding of the Liberal divisions in the 1890s.

103   *Journal of Kimberley*, 18 October 1900, 480. Kimberley also had unkind words for the Unionists as a whole: 'No such exhibition of party violence has ever taken place in my time.'

104   As Ramsden has pointed out, in a party led by the cool Salisbury and the detached and elegant Balfour, Chamberlain's 'sheer combativeness' had a strong appeal to Unionists as a whole: John Ramsden, *An Appetite for Power: A History of the Conservative Party since 1830* (London, paperback edn, 1999), 186.

105   Richard Price, however, believes that much of the working class was anti-imperialist: see his *An Imperial War and the British Working Class: Working Class Attitudes and Reactions to the Boer War, 1899–1902* (London, 1972). M. D. Blanch disagrees in 'British Society and the War', ch. 9 in Peter Warwick (ed.), *The South African War: The Anglo-Boer War 1899–1902* (Harlow, 1980). For pro-war pressure groups, see Andrew Thompson, 'Imperial Propaganda during the South African War', ch. 15 in Greg Cuthbertson, Albert Grundlingh, and Mary-Lynn Suttie (eds), *Writing a Wider War: Rethinking Gender, Race, and Identity in the South African War, 1899–1902* (Athens, Ohio, 2002).

106   Evidence may be found in Peter Harrington, 'Pictorial Journalism and the Boer War: The London Illustrated Weeklies', ch.14 in John Gooch (ed.), *The Boer War: Direction, Experience and Image* (London, 2000) and Jacqueline Beaumont, '*The Times* at War, 1899–1902', ch. 4 in Lowry, *The South African War Reappraised*.

107   See, for example, Greg Cuthbertson, 'Preaching Imperialism: Wesleyan Methodism and the War', ch. 8 in David E. Omissi and Andrew S. Thompson, *The Impact of the South African War* (Houndmills, Hants, 2002)

108   As Michael Bentley put it in *The Climax of Liberal Politics: British Liberalism in Theory and Practice, 1868–1918* (London, 1987), 107. See additionally chs 5 and 6 for Bentley's stimulating analysis of the dilemmas of the post-Gladstonian Liberal Party.

109   Cited in Pyrah, *Imperial Policy and South Africa*, 26.

110 See Nasson, *South African War*, chs 6 and 7.
111 Marsh, *Chamberlain*, 507–8.
112 The mere presence of such a system of chessboard fortresses spreading out over the landscape was intimidating and, as Nasson points out, created the 'stamp of imperial military authority' (*South African War*, 211).
113 Ibid., 222.
114 *The Times*, 15 June 1901.
115 *Hansard*, 4th ser., vol. 98, 1094–1191, 2 August 1901.
116 In his detailed account of British policies toward noncombatants, Spies notes that Chamberlain advocated some harsh methods, such as 'a sort of Sherman's march through Georgia' in the Orange Free State and the use of Boer civilians as hostages on British trains: S. B. Spies, *Methods of Barbarism? Roberts and Kitchener and Civilians in the Boer Republics, January 1900–May 1902* (Cape Town, 1977), 31 and 107. But in the main, Spies absolves Chamberlain from the establishment of concentration camps, blaming the 'military autocracy' of Roberts and Kitchener. Based upon a careful reading of Colonial Office and War Office papers, Surridge substantiates Spies' conclusion that the main responsibility in the progress of the war lay in the hands of the military leaders: Keith Terrance Surridge, *Managing the South African War, 1899–1902: Politicians and Generals* (Woodbridge, Suffolk, 1998).
117 See Stephen Koss (ed.), *The Anatomy of an Antiwar Movement: The Pro-Boers* (Chicago, 1973), esp. 10 and 11. Arthur Davey, *The British Pro-Boers, 1877–1902* (Cape Town, 1978) takes a longer look at sympathetic views in Britain toward Boer aspirations.
118 Henry Birchenough, 'Mr. Chamberlain as an Empire Builder', *The Nineteenth Century*, 51 (March 1902), 360–8. Birchenough was President of the British South Africa Company and Director of the Imperial Continental Gas Association and held directorships of other companies. He became a member of Chamberlain's Tariff Commission in 1904. He was also a frequent contributor of articles on political and economic subjects in journals such as *The Nineteenth Century*. He was created a baronet in 1920.
119 Julian Amery, *The Life of Joseph Chamberlain*, vol. 4, *1901–1903: At the Height of his Power* (London, 1951), 64 (see Chapter 12, n. 52). Even Marsh, no eulogist, admits that Chamberlain had reached 'a pinnacle of acclaim' (Marsh, *Chamberlain*, 512).
120 As Hicks Beach put it, Chamberlain's South African tour was 'something of a Royal position ... representing this country by himself': Lady Victoria Hicks Beach, *Life of Sir Michael Hicks Beach* (London, 1932), vol. 2, 182. See also the accounts in Marsh, *Chamberlain*, 543–57 and Amery, *Life of Chamberlain*, vol. 4, 283–385.
121 The details of Chamberlain's departure may be found in Amery, *Life of Chamberlain*, vol. 4, 284–8.
122 Marsh, *Chamberlain*, 544.
123 Hancock, *Smuts*, 192–3. Perhaps meetings such as this prompted the following remarks in a letter to Austen where he admitted the long hours, lack of sleep and the strain of 'all the time skating on thin ice & in deadly terror lest I should fall through' (Chamberlain Papers, AC 1/4/5/30a, 9 January 1903).
124 Extracts of which may be found in Chamberlain Papers, JC 37/3/7/3, ff. 151–66.
125 Ibid., ff. 159, 162, and 158.
126 See the account in *The Times*, 16 March 1903.

12 Tariff Reform

1 British deaths from battle and disease in the Crimean War have been most recently estimated at 22,000. Deaths from other combatants in that war were higher. French losses were 95,000; and Russian, nearly 475,000. See Winfried Baumgart, *The Crimean War 1853–1856* (London, 1999), 215–16.
2 Chapter 9 above.

3   In speeches at the Aston Manor by-election in March 1891 and at Portsmouth in April. See the accounts in J. L. Garvin, *The Life of Joseph Chamberlain* (London, 1932), vol. 2, 508–14 and *The Times*, 18 March 1891 and 3 April 1891. Garvin claims that this 'new line' of his social thinking was 'the most daring of his advances as a Unionist democrat' (508).

4   See the details of the plan in Chamberlain's article 'Old Age Pensions and Friendly Societies', *National Review*, 24 (January 1895), 592–615.

5   Henry Pelling, *Social Geography of British Elections, 1885–1910* (London, 1967), 182.

6   *The Times*, 1 October 1900. See also Marsh, *Chamberlain* (New Haven, Conn., 1994), 499–500; and Stephen Roberts, 'Politics and the Birmingham Working Class: The General Elections of 1900 and 1906 in East Birmingham', *West Midlands Studies*, 15 (1982), 12–21.

7   Chamberlain Papers, JC 11/18/13, JC to Hicks Beach, 20 September 1901.

8   Julian Amery, puzzled by the 'strangely passive' behaviour over old-age pensions, discusses Chamberlain's dilemma in his *The Life of Joseph Chamberlain*, vol. 4, *1901–1903: At the Height of his Power* (London, 1951), 391–400.

9   N. J. Richards, 'Religious Controversy and the School Boards, 1870–1902', *British Journal of Educational Studies* 18/2 (June 1970), 180–96.

10 The most concise account remains J. E. B. Munson, 'The Unionist Coalition and Education, 1895–1902', *Historical Journal*, 20/3 (September 1977), 607–45.

11 Ibid., JC 5/68/10, JC to George Titterton, 14 April 1896.

12 See Eric Eaglesham, 'Planning the Education Bill of 1902', *British Journal of Educational Studies*, 9/1 (November 1960), 3–24.

13 As he put it to Selborne, the education question was 'a very delicate one'. If a bill was passed granting rate aid to denominational schools, he feared that the whole of Birmingham could be lost to the Unionist Party (Chamberlain Papers, JC 11/32/19, JC to Selborne, 7 November 1901).

14 Pelling notes the 'Nonconformist explosion' at the by-election (*Social Geography of British Elections*, 291, 293).

15 Robert Smith, *Schools, Politics and Society: Elementary Education in Wales, 1870–1902* (Cardiff, 1999), 272.

16 John Satterfield Sandars, 'A. J. Balfour. (A Glimpse)', in Chamberlain Papers, JC 18/16/16.

17 Chamberlain Papers, AC 4/1/38, Austen to Mary Chamberlain, 28 August 1902.

18 Quoted in Amery, *Life of Chamberlain*, vol. 4, 4 August 1902, 495.

19 Chamberlain Papers, JC 11/11/10, 22 September 1902.

20 Ibid., JC 11/8/104, 5 October 1902. St John Brodrick was then Secretary for War.

21 A. G. Gardiner, *The Life of Sir William Harcourt* (London, 1923), 547–8.

22 Peter Gordon (ed.), *The Red Earl: The Papers of the Fifth Earl Spencer, 1835–1910* (Northampton, 1981), vol. 2, 46. Spencer replaced Kimberley, who had fallen ill in 1901 and never recovered: he died the following year.

23 *The Times*, 10 October 1902. See also Amery's account of the battle for the Bill in his *Life of Chamberlain*, vol. 4, 478–508.

24 As G. R. Searle has pointed out in *The Quest for National Efficiency: A Study in British Politics and Political Thought, 1899–1914* (London, paperback edn., 1990 (Berkeley, Cal., 1971]), especially 207–16.

25 Marsh, *Chamberlain*, 443–7, 460–2, and thereafter *passim*. See also Amery, *Life of Chamberlain*, vol. 4, 209–21. Eric Ives, Diane Drummond, and Leonard Schwarz, *The First Civic University: Birmingham 1880–1980* (Birmingham, 2000) is now the standard history of the University.

26 See A. P. D. Thompson, 'The Chamberlain Memorial Tower, University of Birmingham', *University of Birmingham Historical Journal*, 4/2 (1954), 167–79. The tower, at 99 meters in height and housing a 20-ton clockwork machine, was known as 'Big Joe'. It could be

seen from Highbury, several miles away. The view is now obscured by a modern office block, built directly across the road from Highbury.

27 See the account in *The Times*, 16 May 1903.

28 *Hansard*, 4th ser., vol. 123, 175–91, 28 May 1903.

29 See Anthony Howe's important book *Free Trade and Liberal England, 1846–1946* (Oxford, 1997). Especially relevant here are chs. 6 and 7.

30 Gordon, *The Red Earl*, vol. 2, Ripon to Spencer, 30 May 1903; and Spencer's reply, 31 May 1903, 310–11.

31 Cited in H. W. McCreedy, 'The Revolt of the Unionist Free Traders', *Parliamentary Affairs*, 16/2 (1962), 188.

32 Gardiner, *Life of Harcourt*, vol. 2, 554.

33 *The Times*, 15 June 1903.

34 Sir Almeric Fitzroy, *Memoirs* (New York, n.d.), vol. 1, entry of 29 May 1903, 133. Although a partisan of the Duke of Devonshire, Fitzroy is widely quoted by historians for his levelheaded observations.

35 Sandars Papers, c. 739, ff. 20–5, 28 May 1903.

36 Ibid., Acland-Hood to Sandars, ff. 32–5, 30 May 1903. Acland-Hood was first Baron St Audries from 1911.

37 Ibid., ff. 30–1, 30 May 1903.

38 Leo Amery, *My Political Life*, vol. 1, *England Before the Storm, 1896–1914* (London 1953), 236, and ch. 9 generally. Amery was one of the most loyal of all Chamberlain acolytes. He was MP for South Birmingham in the Commons for 35 years, holding numerous positions in Unionist ministries from 1911, including First Lord of the Admiralty, Colonial Secretary, and Secretary of State for India. His son, Julian, was Chamberlain's biographer.

39 Larry L. Witherell, *Rebel on the Right: Henry Page Croft and the Crisis of British Conservatism, 1903–1914* (Delaware, 1997), 27. Descended from ancient parliamentary forebears, Croft was in the family brewing and grain trade in Hertfordshire. In later life, he was a member of the Conservative Party's right wing.

40 Ruddock F. Mackay, *Balfour: Intellectual Statesman* (Oxford, 1985) reports conversations to this effect between Chamberlain and Jack Sandars (135).

41 Some sense of the disagreement among historians on Chamberlain's advocacy of tariff reform can be seen in the divergent views of Alan Sykes, *Tariff Reform in British Politics, 1903–1913* (Oxford, 1979), who emphasizes Chamberlain's interest in social welfare reforms; and Roland Quinault, 'Joseph Chamberlain: A Reassessment', in T. R. Gourvish and Alan O'Day (eds.), *Late Victorian Britain* (New York, 1988), who believes that Chamberlain was imperially motivated. See also E. H. H. Green, 'Radical Conservatism: The Electoral Genesis of Tariff Reform', *Historical Journal*, 28/3 (1985), 667–92. Green's ideas are more fully developed in his *The Crisis of Conservatism: The Politics, Economics, and Ideology of the British Conservative Party, 1880–1914* (London, 1995). Additional important sources are Peter Fraser, 'Unionism and Tariff Reform: The Crisis of 1906', *Historical Journal*, 5/2 (1962), 149–66; Andrew S. Thompson, 'Tariff Reform: An Imperial Strategy, 1903–1913', *Historical Journal*, 40 (1997), 1033–54; and Andrew Marrison, *British Business and Protection, 1903–1932* (Oxford, 1996).

42 Fraser, 'Unionism and Tariff Reform', 149.

43 Marsh, *Chamberlain*, 582.

44 As Michael Bentley observes, Chamberlain's motive for launching the tariff reform campaign 'still presents formidable interpretive problems', among them the fact that Chamberlain – having had his moment during the South African War – sought another avenue to sustain his political prominence: Bentley, *Politics without Democracy 1815– 1914: Perception and Preoccupation in British Government*, 2nd edn (London, 1996), 219.

45 Suggestive here are the theoretical works of Steven Lukes. See his *Power: A Radical View* (London, 1974); his *Essays in Social Theory* (New York, 1977), especially ch. 1, 'Power and

Structure'; and his 'Power and Authority', in Tom Bottomore and Robert Nisbet (eds), *A History of Sociological Analysis* (New York, 1978), ch. 16. See also Richard Sennett, *Authority* (New York, 1980); and David Beetham, *The Legitimation of Power* (Atlantic Highlands, N.J., 1991). See in addition A. J. Stockwell, 'Power, Authority and Freedom', in P. J. Marshall (ed.), *The Cambridge Illustrated History of the British Empire* (Cambridge, 1996), ch. 6.

46 For the evolution in Chamberlain's thinking on tariff reform, see particularly Marsh, *Chamberlain*, 420–6 and 530–5.

47 In a speech to his constituents in March 1883, a speech that, as Marsh notes, came back to haunt him (Marsh, *Chamberlain*, 146).

48 As reported by Austen, who remembered that his father often told him that his doubts concerning 'the old Free Trade gospel' had arisen during his tenure of President of the Board of Trade: Sir Austen Chamberlain, *Politics from Inside: An Epistolary Chronicle, 1906–1914* (London, 1936), 618–19.

49 Sydney H. Zebel, 'Joseph Chamberlain and the Genesis of Tariff Reform', *Journal of British Studies*, 7/1 (November 1967), 131–57.

50 See the important article by Frank Trentmann, 'The Transformation of Fiscal Reform: Reciprocity, Modernization, and the Fiscal Debate within the Business Community in Early Twentieth-century Britain', *Historical Journal*, 39/4 (1996), 1005–48. Trentmann emphasizes that the growing unease among businessmen at Britain's traditional policy of free trade was prior to and independent of Chamberlain's campaign for tariff reform. Indeed, Trentmann believes that Chamberlain's uncompromising positions on tariff reform very likely impeded its success by polarizing a potentially reasoned debate into extreme positions (1018–19). Martin Daunton agrees. By pushing the debate 'into two extreme positions of absolute free trade and imperial preference', Chamberlain excluded 'the less doctrinaire middle ground' of retaliation and a revenue tariff. Daunton further believes that Chamberlain, in arguing for a new fiscal balance to protect producers, was returning to the ideas of the Tory protectionists of the 1840s. See Daunton's *Trusting Leviathan: The Politics of Taxation in Britain, 1799–1914* (Cambridge, 2001), 314, 318.

51 Ritchie may have been motivated in part by his personal dislike of Chamberlain. Ritchie once spoke to Eddie Hamilton 'with a good deal of bitterness about Chamberlain' – 'an impossible man', said Ritchie. He 'could not stand "Joe's" ways: they were not straight': Dudley W. R. Bahlman (ed.), *The Diary of Sir Edward Walter Hamilton 1880–1885* (Oxford, 1972), 433–4.

52 52 This was certainly Balfour's impression. After Chamberlain's return from South Africa, Balfour noticed that he was 'by no means an agreeable colleague'. As Balfour explained it, in his curiously tentative way, to Devonshire: Chamberlain 'quite unconsciously to himself ... was perhaps influenced by the notion that his counsels had not all the weight, which his public position justified, in determining the legislative policy of his colleagues'. See Julian Amery, *The Life of Joseph Chamberlain*, vol. 5, *Joseph Chamberlain and the Tariff Reform Campaign* (London, 1969), letter of 27 August 1903, 175. A word here should be said about Amery's three volumes of his life of Chamberlain which finishes the work that Garvin had begun. Volume 4, published in 1951, continued Garvin's narrative format. But volumes 5 and 6 were delayed by Amery's active political life and were not published until nearly two decades later. This delay no doubt contributed to the altered shape and scope of the work. These final two volumes are primarily a collection of documents with attendant glosses and little analysis or narrative pace and are wholly concerned with Chamberlain's tariff reform movement. It would not be surprising that Julian carried the torch handed on by his father, Leo Amery, who had been a staunch tariff reformer. In any case, the reviews were unforgiving. Michael Hurst, for example, lambasted the final volumes as 'downright bad': *English Historical Review*, 86/4 (1971), 816–22. In addition, the substantial collection of documents in Amery's hands which formed the evidence

for volumes 5 and 6 were lost from view and did not resurface until 1998, several years after Julian Amery's death. They are now a part of the Special Collections section of the University of Birmingham Library. From a careful perusal of many of these documents, it can be stated that Amery's use of them, mostly letters, in volumes 5 and 6 were generally accurate and well chosen. Indeed, these letters carry the story of tariff reform surprisingly well. When possible, these original letters, drawn from the rediscovered Amery cache, have been used hereafter. Amery, of course, remains largely an apologist for Chamberlain just as Garvin was.

53 See Richard M. Francis, 'The British Withdrawal from the Bagdad Railway Project in April 1903', *Historical Journal*, 16/1(1973), 168–78. Lansdowne believed that '[b]ut for Joe's bile, the opposition would not be serious' (ibid., 172). The project was a commercial cooperation between English financiers and a German syndicate. Chamberlain's opposition may have been intended to signal a tough negotiating stance against any country which imposed tariffs against British goods.

54 Francis, 'Bagdad Railway Project', 172, n.17.

55 Amery, *Life of Chamberlain*, vol. 5, ch. 99, 'Plumbing the Depths', *passim*.

56 A. W. Coats, 'Political Economy and the Tariff Reform Campaign of 1903', *Journal of Law and Economics*, 11 (1968), 181–229.

57 W. A. S. Hewins, *The Apologia of an Imperialist: Forty Years of Empire Policy* (London, 1929), 163, 73.

58 Chamberlain Papers, JC 21/1/2, JC to Amery, 15 July 1903.

59 This was widely recognized. Recording the views of 'close observers', Fitzroy wrote that Chamberlain gave the impression of a man 'who is seeking arguments wherewith to prop conclusions which he has arrived at on *a priori* grounds, rather than one who has carefully worked out the data on which to build up his case'. This was, Fitzroy added, characteristic of Chamberlain, a man whose talents did not 'lie in the direction of patient investigation; indeed, his career is strewn with the debris of abandoned hypotheses': Fitzroy, *Memoirs*, vol. 1, 22 June 1903, 139.

60 Annual contributions to the League were substantial: in 1907 alone, more than £23,000 was raised. The most recent account of the TRL may be found in Thompson's 'Tariff Reform: An Imperial Strategy'. See also Marsh *Chamberlain*, 568; and Denis Judd, *Radical Joe: A Life of Joseph Chamberlain* (Cardiff, 1993), 247. Amery notes that the TRL was the newest version of a Chamberlain caucus (*Life of Chamberlain*, vol. 5, 307).

61 Chamberlain Papers, JC 18/18/107, Primrose to JC, 31 August 1903.

62 For Cecil's letters to Balfour, see Sandars Papers, c. 740, ff. 27–35, 15 July 1903; and c. 740, f. 44, 19 July 1903. Cecil was the youngest son of Lord Salisbury and thus Balfour's cousin. Conservative MP for Greenwich, 1895–1906, Cecil was addressed by Balfour in the familial Cecil patois as 'Linky'. One of the few men in public life to treat Chamberlain openly with aristocratic disdain, Cecil once called the Birmingham boss – during a debate in the House of Commons – 'an alien immigrant' in the Conservative Party: Richard A. Rempel, 'Lord Hugh Cecil's Parliamentary Career, 1900–1914: Promise Unfulfilled', *Journal of British Studies* 11/2 (May 1972), 104–30, quoting from *Hansard,* 7 June 1905). More information about Lord Hugh's free trade views and his later career may be found in Kenneth Rose, *The Later Cecils* (New York, 1975), ch. 8, 'Lord Hugh Cecil, Baron Quickswood (1869–1956)'.

63 Sandars charged him with forgetfulness, apathy, and a lack of interest in parliamentary business. Like Melborne, Devonshire often slept in cabinet meetings (Chamberlain Papers, JC 18/16/17, 'The Duke of Devonshire'). Indeed, cartoons of the day portrayed Devonshire in the House of Lords leaning back on the front bench, hands in his pockets, top hat in place, eyes closed, quietly dozing.

64 Amery, *Life of Chamberlain*, vol. 5, JC to Devonshire, 15 August 1903, 372–4.

65 Ibid., Devonshire to Balfour, 27 August 1903, 374.

66 Ibid., Balfour to Devonshire, 27 August 1903, 376–8; and 29 August 1903, 381–2.

67 See Chamberlain's letter, marked 'Secret', to Balfour in Amery, *Life of Chamberlain*, vol. 5, 9 September 1903, 291–2. Chamberlain informed neither his wife nor Austen of his plans.

68 Fitzroy's information was that they 'were practically drummed out' (*Memoirs*, vol. 1, entry of 19 September 1903, 149).

69 Briefly discussed in David Gilmour, *The Long Recessional: The Imperial Life of Rudyard Kipling* (New York, 2002), 193. The refrain was 'Once on a time there was a Man'.

70 Thus it seems erroneous to conclude, as does Alfred Gollin, that 'All the immediate and solid benefits of the arrangement lay upon Balfour's side': see Gollin, *Balfour's Burden: Arthur Balfour and Imperial Preference* (London, 1965), 127. Indeed, in the intermediate term, the game went Chamberlain's way.

71 That Chamberlain's resignation was a tactic based at least in part upon his ambitions for higher office is suggested by his letter to Parker Smith within a week of his resignation. The cabinet, he wrote, was now 'purged of bigoted Free Trade members'; those who remained were 'heartily' with him 'as to principle'. He hoped that the government would remain in power long enough 'to give us time for our educational work': Chamberlain Papers, JC 30/4/218, JC to Parker Smith, 21 September 1903; letter printed only in part in Amery, *Life of Chamberlain*, vol. 6, 458–9. Chamberlain's communication was a response to Parker Smith's letter of the previous day in which Smith expressed (elliptically) the hope that Balfour's government would soon fall, opening the way 'for the man' who will be in no other position 'but the first'(Chamberlain Papers, JC 30/4/210, Parker Smith to JC, 20 September 1903). Parts of this letter were published in two separate volumes of Amery's *Life of Chamberlain*: see vol. 5, 436, and vol. 6, 458. Smith is described as Chamberlain's 'Scottish lieutenant' by Marsh, *Chamberlain*, 627.

72 As he confessed to one of his free trade supporters, Lord James: 'I have made a mess of this business' (Amery, *Life of Chamberlain*, vol. 5, 5 October 1903, 447).

73 In a letter dated 21 September 1903: see Amery, *Life of Chamberlain*, vol. 5, 431–2. Privately, Chamberlain was more contemptuous of the Duke. In a letter to Lansdowne, Chamberlain complained that he thought he had the support of the Duke on tariff reform. But apparently 'he was asleep when the matter was discussed' (Chamberlain Papers, JC 18/17/15, 19 September 1903). The 5th Marquess of Lansdowne had served as secretary of state for war from 1895–1900 and was secretary of state for foreign affairs from 1900 to 1905.

74 See Fraser, 'The Liberal Unionist Alliance', 73–5.

75 For an account of the meeting, see *The Times*, 7 October 1903. *The Times,* in praising Chamberlain's speech as 'a great triumph', believed that he had struck 'the first blow in the big fight which he promised the country; and the power and effect of that blow it would be difficult to exaggerate'.

76 Ibid., 8 October 1903.

77 Ibid., 5 November 1903. By now a firm supporter of tariff reform, *The Times* this day vigorously applauded Chamberlain's message: 'His fundamental proposition – that our exports to protectionist countries are declining, that our trade with neutral countries is stationary, and that only the growth of our exports to our own Colonies and dependencies saves us from serious industrial depression – can no longer be denied …'.

78 For these speeches, see Amery, *Life of Chamberlain*, vol. 6, ch. 110, 'Stumping the Country'.

79 See Fitzroy, *Memoirs*, vol. 2, 19 November 1903, 168; 3 December 1903, 172; 16 December 1903, 174–5. Richard Burdon Haldane was the Liberal MP for East Lothian from 1885 to 1911, when he was created viscount. He was Secretary for War in the Liberal administration of 1905 to 1912. Considered a Liberal Imperialist.

80 Ibid., 27 December 1903, 177.

81 See Gardiner's *Life of Harcourt*, vol. 2, 27 November 1903, 559; and Gordon, *The Red Earl*, vol. 2, 26 December 1903, 320. The letter to Brice is quoted in Amery, *Life of Chamberlain*, vol. 6, 31 December 1903, 541. James Bryce, a professor of law and constitutional expert, was then Liberal MP for South Aberdeen. He had been Chancellor of the Duchy of Lancaster in 1892–94 and President of the Board of Trade the year following. He served as Chief Secretary for Ireland, 1905–06.

82 McCreedy, 'Revolt of the Unionist Free Traders', describes an abortive attempt by the Free Fooders to ally themselves to the largely free-trade Liberals. Richard A. Rempel's *Unionists Divided: Arthur Balfour, Joseph Chamberlain and the Unionist Free Traders* (Newton Abbot, 1972) remains the standard account for the history of the Unionist free traders.

83 Lady Victoria Hicks Beach, *Life of Sir Michael Hicks Beach* (London, 1932), vol. 2, letter to his wife, 10 June 1903, 192–93. The cabinet crisis in September 1903 confirmed Hicks Beach's opinion. To his son, he wrote that the ministry was 'now at heart a Protectionist Government without the courage for a Protectionist policy – and we Unionist Free-traders will have to support it on its present lines, to try and prevent it from going bodily over to Chamberlain' (ibid., 9 October 1903, 195).

84 See Eric Alexander, 3rd Viscount Chilston, *Chief Whip: The Political Life and Times of Aretas Akers-Douglas, 1st Viscount Chilston* (London, 1961), 330.

85 See Marsh, *Chamberlain*, 591–3, for the organization of the Commission. Marrison's lengthy work, *British Business and Protection, 1903–1932*, is essentially the history of the Commission and an examination of the case that could be made for protection. He is not unsympathetic to Chamberlain's efforts.

86 As Marsh puts it, Chamberlain acted as would a prime minister in nominating a royal commission (*Chamberlain*, 592). Chamberlain's manoeuvre gave rise to a howl of outrage from Harcourt: 'Joe's Commission … was the most revolting thing I ever knew or dreamed of' (in a letter to his son: see Gardiner, *Life of Harcourt*, vol. 2, 561).

87 Marsh, *Chamberlain*, 608, 612, 614. Marrison, however, takes a more benign view of Chamberlain's relationship with the Commission, claiming that he 'tended to leave the Commission alone'; that his requests for Commission material 'were fairly objective'; and that 'his use of Commission material for his own ends cannot be counted as interference in any significant sense' (*British Business and Protection, 1903–1932*, 138.)

88 Indeed, Andrew Marrison has argued that tariff reform had at least the potential to raise growth rates. See his 'Businessmen, Industries and Tariff Reform in Great Britain, 1903–1930', *Business History*, 25/2 (July 1983), 148–78, and an elaboration of his argument in *British Business and Protection, 1903–1932*. Peter Cain, on the other hand, believes that tariff preferences would likely have inoculated Britain against the need for economic change 'with drastic long-term consequences' and could also have provoked 'damaging' retaliation against British exports to countries outside the empire. See Cain's 'Political Economy in Edwardian England: The Tariff Reform Controversy', in Alan O'Day (ed.), *The Edwardian Age: Conflict and Stability, 1900–1914* (Hamden, Conn., 1979), 51. The question of tariff reform must be placed within the context of an ongoing debate, principally among economic historians, on whether or not there was an economic decline in Britain at the turn of the century. Works which address this issue with specific references to Chamberlain include Barry Supple, 'Fear of Failing: Economic History and the Decline of Britain', *Economic History Review*, 47/3 (1994), 441–58; P. J. Cain and A. G. Hopkins, *British Imperialism: Innovation and Expansion, 1688–1914* (London, paperback edn, 1994), ch. 7, 'Challenging Cosmopolitanism: The Tariff Problem and Imperial Unity, 1880–1914'; and David Cannadine, 'Apocalypse When? British Politicians and British "Decline" in the Twentieth Century', in Peter Clarke and Clive Trebilcock (eds), *Understanding Decline: Perceptions and Realities of British Economic Performance* (Cambridge, 1997), 261–84.

89 Sykes, however, believes that Chamberlain's campaign had 'collapsed' in early 1904 and by the spring, Chamberlain was 'in trouble': *Tariff Reform in British Politics*, 76, 77, 84. Sykes does admit that Chamberlain nevertheless kept up the pressure both on Balfour and on Unionist free traders in the constituencies.

90 John Ramsden, *An Appetite for Power: A History of the Conservative Party since 1830* (London, paperback edn, 1999), 202.

91 Arthur Pearson, not surprisingly as a Chamberlainite, found the speech 'inspirationless and flabby' (Amery, *Life of Chamberlain*, vol. 5, Pearson to Chamberlain, 1 October 1903, 443). Pearson also reported that the majority of the delegates at the conference favoured Chamberlain: 'You have a unique reputation when you speak. The bold uncompromising attitude is the one that will receive support. The people want a strong man' (Chamberlain Papers, JC 18/18/104, 2 October 1903).

92 *The Times*, 5 August 1903.

93 Also in attendance was the elderly Duke of Rutland, who as Lord John Manners had been Disraeli's colleague in the famous protectionist controversies of the 1840s and 1850s. Portland, who chaired the meeting, recorded with interest that Chamberlain's only notes were on a small piece of paper twisted around his fingers, to which he rarely referred: see the Duke of Portland, *Men, Women, and Things* (London, 1937), 183–6.

94 The idea was first put forward by Austen in a meeting with Balfour, the substance of which was recorded in a letter (written at Highbury). See Amery, *Life of Chamberlain*, vol. 6, 24 August 1904, 615–17.

95 Ibid., 8 September 1904, 625.

96 Ibid., 27 September 1904, 626.

97 Ibid., 24 September 1904, 629.

98 Ibid., Balfour to JC, 18 February 1905, 657.

99 Ibid., JC to Balfour, 24 February 1905, 659.

100 Fitzroy, *Memoirs*, vol. 1, 18 March 1905, 245 and 31 January 1905, 232. Fitzroy, of course, agreed with Sandars. Chamberlain, he wrote, had 'no conception of obligation in any fine sense of the phrase, and … his masterfulness and lack of restraint are sure to prejudice, if not to ruin, any cause' in which he was engaged (18 March 1905, 246).

101 Denis Judd, *Balfour and the British Empire: A Study in Imperial Evolution* (London, 1968), 125.

102 Letter dated 5 June 1905, cited in Sykes, *Tariff Reform in British Politics*, quoting from the Balfour Papers.

103 *The Times*, 8 July 1905.

104 Amery, *Life of Chamberlain*, vol. 6, 8 July 1905, 727–8.

105 Ibid., 23 October 1905, 733.

106 Ibid., 2 November 1905, 737–40.

107 *The Times*, 4 November 1905.

108 Amery describes the plot in his *Life of Chamberlain*, vol. 6, 752–3.

109 *The Times*, 22 November 1905.

110 Chamberlain Papers, JC 30/4/296, JC to Pearson, 21 December 1905; also in Amery, *Life of Chamberlain*, vol. 6, 772.

111 As Amery notes, ibid.

112 Marsh, *Chamberlain*, 626–7.

113 The most thorough account of the election is A. K. Russell, *Liberal Landslide: The General Election of 1906* (Newton Abbot, 1973).

114 Most historians (including Amery) have followed the post-election calculations of *The Times*: Chamberlainites, 109; Balfour supporters, 32; Free Fooders, 11; and uncertain, 5. But Neal Blewett suggests the following: Chamberlainites, 79; Balfour supporters, 49; Free Fooders, 31. See Blewett's 'Free Fooders, Balfourites, Whole Hoggers: Factionalism within the Unionist Party, 1906–10', *Historical Journal*, 11/1 (1968), 96–7.

115 Letters between the two politicians in late January 1906 make engrossing reading as each attempted – Balfour with subtlety and Chamberlain more bluntly – to sway the other. See the correspondence in Amery, *Life of Chamberlain*, vol. 6, 800–5.

116 Ibid., Mary to her mother, 6 February 1906, 817; Chamberlain's letter to Garvin, 5 February 1906, 813–16. Balfour gave his own view of the meeting to his brother, Gerald. Both Joe and Austen were 'nasty' at the dinner table, Balfour claimed, to the point that Mrs Chamberlain was nearly in tears. Gerald's opinion was that Joe's behaviour was 'the action of a madman' who had become 'a monomaniac' ready to sacrifice everything to achieve tariff reform, even if it meant shattering the Conservative Party. Quoted in Judd, *Balfour and the British Empire*, 136, from the Balfour Papers at Whittingehame, Betty Balfour (Gerald's wife) to Alice Balfour (Arthur's sister), 4 February 1906.

117 Balfour's apologists have usually attributed to him a deliberate and calculated motive of delay in capitulating to Chamberlain's demands. Some historians have suggested that Balfour was cannily giving ground so that he may gain his own ends later. Judd claims that Balfour's ability to maintain the party leadership can be attributed in part to his 'verbal juggling' (*Balfour and the British Empire*, 137). Kenneth Young praised Balfour a 'master of tactics' and a 'skillful tactician' during these negotiations. See Young's *Arthur James Balfour: The Happy Life of the Politician, Prime Minister, Statesman, and Philosopher, 1848–1930* (London, 1963), 262, 259. But the evidence suggests otherwise – that Chamberlain drove Balfour into a corner.

118 If he had forgotten, Lansdowne was on hand to remind him. Reporting to Balfour the proceedings of a recent Liberal Unionist Executive Committee meeting, Lansdowne recounted Chamberlain's 'bitterness' at the Unionist free traders and his determination to repudiate them (Amery, *Life of Chamberlain*, vol. 6, 4 February 1906, 811–12). Although Lansdowne was a Liberal Unionist, he was closer to Balfour than to Chamberlain. Perhaps the old school tie still bound them: Balfour had fagged for Lansdowne at Eton.

119 John Vincent (ed.), *The Crawford Papers: The Journals of David Lindsay, twenty-seventh Earl of Crawford and tenth Earl of Balcarres, 1871–1940, during the years 1892 to 1940* (Manchester, 1984), diary entries from 26 January 1906 to 15 February 1906, pp 88–92. Balcarres, known familiarly as 'Bal' was MP for the Chorley constituency of North Lancashire from 1895, serving as a party whip from 1903 until he became Chief Whip in 1911. Two years later, upon the death of his father, he succeeded to the titles of 17th Earl of Crawford and 10th Earl of Balcarres and was elevated to the House of Lords. He was well placed to know at first hand important political news and much personal gossip. A born and bred Tory.

120 The letters may be found in Amery, *Life of Chamberlain*, and vol. 6, 846–7.

121 Chamberlain Papers, JC 18/18/93, manuscript memoir of Maxwell, f. 10.

122 Ibid., JC 37/3/7/4, 17 February 1906, f. 4; quoted in Amery, *Life of Chamberlain*, vol. 6, 848.

123 Amery, *Life of Chamberlain*, vol. 6, 850.

124 David Dutton, 'Unionist Politics and the Aftermath of the General Election of 1906: A Reassessment', *Historical Journal*, 22/4 (1979), 861–76.

125 Marsh, *Chamberlain*, 639.

126 Amery, *Life of Chamberlain*, vol. 6, 20 February, 857.

127 For details, see Marsh, *Chamberlain*, 642–7; and Amery, *Life of Chamberlain*, vol. 6, 896–907.

128 *The Times*, 10 July 1906.

13 Power Lost

1 Several years after Chamberlain's stroke, Leo Amery confided to his wife that a recent conversation with Mary Chamberlain revealed that Mary had 'deliberately minimized things for fear of any collapse of the movement': John Barnes and David Nicholson (eds), *The*

Leo Amery Diaries, vol. 1, *1896–1929* (London, 1980), Amery to Mrs Amery, 19 October 1911, 82.

2   Julian Amery, *The Life of Joseph Chamberlain*, vol. 6 (London, 1969), 910.

3   Chamberlain Papers, JC 30/4/392, 25 September 1906; and Amery, *Life of Chamberlain*, vol. 6, 912.

4   Amery, *Life of Chamberlain*, vol. 6, 919. Because Chamberlain could no longer write, Mary often served as his amanuensis.

5   Chamberlain Papers, JC 30/4/397, 22 November 1907.

6   Ibid., JC 30/4/405, JC to Collings, 26 April 1908. The most recent was the death of the Duke of Devonshire, who had died a month earlier in a hotel only a few hundred yards from Chamberlain's villa in Cannes.

7   Chamberlain Papers, AC 4/2/5, 8 March 1907.

8   Robert Blake, *The Conservative Party from Peel to Churchill* (New York, 1970), 189.

9   David Dutton, *'His Majesty's Loyal Opposition': The Unionist Party in Opposition, 1905–1915* (Liverpool, 1992), 262.

10   David Powell, *The Edwardian Crisis: Britain 1901–14* (London, 1996), 49.

11   John Ramsden, *An Appetite for Power: A History of the Conservative Party since 1830* (London, paperback edn, 1999), 206.

12   Michael Bentley, *Politics without Democracy 1815–1914: Perception and Preoccupation in British Government*, 2nd edn (London, 1996), 249.

13   John Vincent (ed.), *The Crawford Papers: The Journals of David Lindsay, twenty-seventh Earl of Crawford and tenth Earl of Balcarres, 1871–1940, during the years 1892 to 1940* (Manchester, 1984), 9 June 1907, 102. Eighteen months later, Balcarres had a further dejected comment on the fallen leader: 'It would be a misfortune for Joe himself were he to return to public life – for his power is gone' (ibid., 29 November 1908, 119).

14   Amery, *Life of Chamberlain*, vol. 6, 924, quoting from Hewins, *Apologia of an Imperialist*, vol. 2, 12 February 1908, 220–222.

15   Amery, *Life of Chamberlain*, vol. 6, 931, again quoting Hewins, *Apologia of an Imperialist*, vol. 1, 225.

16   Stephen Gwynn, *The Letters and Friendships of Sir Cecil Spring Rice: A Record* (London, 1930), vol. 2, 24 March 1908, 114.

17   As Marsh puts it: 'The stroke rigidified his politics along with his body': Peter Marsh, *Joseph Chamberlain: Entrepreneur in Politics* (New Haven, Conn., 1994), 648).

18   Austen Chamberlain, *Politics from Inside: An Epistolary Chronicle 1906–1914* (London, 1936), 376. Comprised almost wholly of Austen's letters to Mary Chamberlain, *Politics from Inside* contains frequent references to Chamberlain, revealing an emotional ambivalence (as Marsh, *Chamberlain*, 659, notes it) that son felt toward father. Austen's relationship with Mary, to whom this book is dedicated and whose picture forms the frontispiece, was affectionate and relaxed. Mary, too, seems to have been fond of Austen. After her first meeting in December 1888, Mary wrote her mother that she was charmed with Austen, who was not only 'tall and very good-looking' but also had 'a most attractive manner': D. H. Elletson, *The Chamberlains* (London, 1966), 85.

19   See Standish Meacham's perceptive review of David Dutton's *Austen Chamberlain: Gentleman in Politics* (Bolton, 1985): 'Lives in Politics', *Journal of Modern History*, 62 (March 1990), 94–96.

20   Sir Charles Petrie, *Walter Long and his Times* (London, 1936), AC to Long, 20 November 1907, 130.

21   David Dutton's *Austen Chamberlain: Gentleman in Politics* (Bolton, 1985) sets out in its early chapters the effect upon Austen's serving as 'Joe's standard bearer'.

22   Chamberlain, *Politics from Inside*, 29 January 1914, 602–03.

23   For the political battles and constitutional conflicts alluded to here, see G. R. Searle, *A New England? Peace and War 1886–1918* (Oxford, 2004), 358–434. The opening

chapters of Dutton's *'His Majesty's Loyal Opposition'* discuss Unionist tactics. Neal Blewett, 'Free Fooders, Balfourites, Whole Hoggers: Factionalism within the Unionist Party, 1906–10', *Historical Journal*, 11/1 (1968), speaks to the success of the Chamberlainite 'whole hogger' protectionist movement within the Unionist Party.

24 Bentley Brinkerhoff Gilbert, 'David Lloyd George: Land, the Budget, and Social Reform', *American Historical Review*, 81/5 (December 1976), 1058–66.

25 Murray has made it clear that the People's Budget was formed to a fair degree in reaction to the continuing strength of tariff reform sentiment in the post-1906 era. 'To a very considerable extent', he writes, 'it was the campaign mounted by the Tariff Reformers ... that impelled the Liberal Government to focus more on social reform and the maintenance of its support among the working classes.' See Bruce K. Murray, *The People's Budget 1909/10: Lloyd George and Liberal Politics* (Oxford, 1980), 5–6.

26 Amery, *Life of Chamberlain*, vol. 6, 935.

27 John Grigg, Lloyd George's biographer, notes that though disabled by his stroke, Chamberlain 'was still active and alert', and determined to use all his influence and authority to bring about the budget's rejection by the House of Lords. See Grigg, *Lloyd George: The People's Champion, 1902–1911* (Berkeley, 1978), 196.

28 See Marsh, *Chamberlain*, for his discussion of these 'aggressive tactics' (652).

29 *The Times*, 23 September 1909. In this day's edition of *The Times*, a leader column observed that although Chamberlain 'was not visible to the bodily eyes of the meeting, every one there must have been conscious of his influence'. An arrangement had been made for a number of 'electrophone transmitters' to be placed in front of the platform so that Chamberlain, nearby at Highbury, could hear Balfour's speech at first hand.

30 Quoted in Neal Blewett, *The Peers, the Parties and the People: The General Elections of 1910* (London, 1972), 121.

31 See *The Times*, 30 December 1909.

32 Blewett, 'Free Fooders, Balfourites, Whole Hoggers', 122.

33 Amery, *Life of Chamberlain*, vol. 6, 948.

34 G. R. Searle, *The Liberal Party: Triumph and Disintegration, 1886–1929* (New York, 1992), 86.

35 Dutton, *Austen Chamberlain*, 75. 'Poor Joe! Poor Austen!' was Mary's comment to her mother (Amery, *Life of Chamberlain*, vol. 6, 2 December 1910, 959).

36 Dutton, *Austen Chamberlain*, 76.

37 Amery, *Life of Chamberlain*, vol. 6, AC to Garvin, 14 July 1911, 968. As Dutton puts it, Austen was 'egged on by his father' to join the Ditchers (Dutton, *Austen Chamberlain*, 85). The 'Ditchers', who were willing to 'die in the last ditch' rather than compromise, were also known as 'Diehards'. For an analysis of their principal organizer, see Gregory D. Phillips, 'Lord Willoughby de Broke and the Politics of Radical Toryism, 1909–1914', *Journal of British Studies*, 20/1 (Fall 1980), 205–24. Phillips's longer work, *The Diehards: Aristocratic Society and Politics in Edwardian England* (Cambridge, Mass., 1979) emphasizes the importance of tariff reform to the Ditchers.

38 For details, see Alan Sykes, *Tariff Reform in British Politics, 1903–1913* (Oxford, 1979), ch. 11, 'Balfour's Resignation', and Peter Fraser, 'The Unionist Debacle of 1911 and Balfour's Retirement', *Journal of Modern History*, 35/4 (December 1963), 354–65.

39 Amery, *Life of Chamberlain*, vol. 6, AC to JC, 4 November 1911, 973.

40 Ibid., 5 November 1911, 974.

41 Amery, *Life of Chamberlain*, vol. 6, 975.

42 Ibid.

43 Chamberlain, *Politics from Inside*, 381–2,

44 See R. J. Q. Adams, *Bonar Law* (London, 1999), ch. 5, 'Unfinished Business', for Bonar Law's decisive shift against tariff reform.

45 For his last days, see Amery, *Life of Chamberlain*, vol. 6, 988–9.

46 See *The Times*, 4 July, 6 July, 7 July 1914.

47 Quoted in Judd, *Radical Joe*, 271.

48 *The Times*, 7 July 1914.

49 Bernard Trainor has shown how Victorian middle-class industrialists, serving as political and social leaders in urban areas during a 'quasi-democratic age', promoted accommodation between the classes. See his *Black Country Elites: The Exercise of Authority in an Industrialized Area, 1830–1900* (Oxford, 1993).

50 Bernard John Seymour Coleridge, 2nd Baron Coleridge, a Gladstonian Liberal, enjoyed a distinguished career at the bar, and was MP for the Attercliffe division of Sheffield from 1885 to 1894 when he succeeded to the peerage at the death of his father. Coleridge was quoted by his friend, Francis Alston Channing, also a Gladstonian Liberal and MP for Northamptonshire: see Channing's *Memories of Midland Politics, 1885–1910* (London, 1918), 290.

51 See Robert Cecil, Viscount Cecil of Chelwood, *All the Way* (London, 1949), 88–9.

52 Winston Churchill, *My Early Life: A Roving Commission* (New York, 1958 edn.), 359.

BIBLIOGRAPHY

Manuscript collections

Bodleian Library

Harcourt Papers
Sandars Papers
Selborne Papers

British Library

Bright Papers
Dilke Papers
Escott Papers

Cadbury Research Library, Special Collections, University of Birmingham
Chamberlain Papers

Secondary sources

Adams, R. J. Q., *Bonar Law* (London, 1999).

Adelman, Paul, *Victorian Radicalism: The Middle-Class Experience, 1830–1914* (London, 1984).

Aldcroft, D. H., 'The Entrepreneur and the British Economy, 1870–1914', *Economic History Review*, 2nd ser., 17/1 (1964), 113–34.

Alderman, Geoffrey, 'Samuel Plimsoll and the Shipping Interest', *Maritime History*, 1 (1971), 73–95.

——, 'Joseph Chamberlain's Attempted Reform of the British Mercantile Marine', *Journal of Transport History*, new ser., 1/3 (February 1972), 169–84.

Alexander, Eric, 3rd Viscount Chilston, *Chief Whip: The Political Life and Times of Aretas Akers-Douglas, 1st Viscount Chilston* (London, 1961).

Amery, Julian, *The Life of Joseph Chamberlain*, vol. 4, *1901–1903: At the Height of his Power* (London, 1951).

——, *The Life of Joseph Chamberlain*, vols. 5 and 6, *Joseph Chamberlain and the Tariff Reform Campaign* (London, 1969).

Amery, Leo, *My Political Life*, vol. 1, *England Before the Storm, 1896–1914* (London 1953).

Archer, John A., 'The Nineteenth Century Allotment: Half an Acre and a Cow', *Economic History Review*, 50/1(1997), 21–36.

Armytage, W. H., *A. J. Mundella, 1825–1897: The Liberal Background to the Labour Movement* (London, 1951).

Aronson, David Murray, 'Jesse Collings, Agrarian Radical, 1880–1892' (University of Massachusetts [Amherst] PhD Dissertation, 1975).

Atwell, Pamela, *British Mandarins and Chinese Reformers: The British Administration of Weihaiwei (1898–1930) and the Territory's Return to Chinese Rule* (Hong Kong, 1985).

Auld, John W., 'The Liberal Pro-Boers', *Journal of British Studies*, 14/2 (May, 1975), 78–101.

Auspos, Patricia, 'Radicalism, Pressure Groups, and Party Politics: From the National Education League to the National Liberal Federation', *Journal of British Studies*, 20 (1980), 184–204.

Bahlman, Dudley W. R. (ed.), *The Diary of Sir Edward Walter Hamilton 1880–1885* (Oxford, 1972).

Bamford, Samuel, *The Diaries of Samuel Bamford*, ed. Martin Hewitt and Robert Poole (New York, 2000).

Barnes, John and Nicholson, David (eds.), *The Leo Amery Diaries*, vol. 1, *1896–1929* (London, 1980).

Baumgart, Winfried, *The Crimean War 1853–1856* (London, 1999).

Beaumont, Jacqueline, '*The Times* at War, 1899–1902', in Donal Lowry (ed.), *The South African War Reappraised* (Manchester, 2000).

Bebbington, D. W., *The Nonconformist Conscience: Chapel and Politics, 1870–1914* (London, 1982).

Beetham, David, *The Legitimation of Power* (Atlantic Highlands, N.J., 1991).

Behagg, Clive, *Politics and Production in the Early Nineteenth Century* (London, 1990).

Belchem, John, *Popular Radicalism in Nineteenth-Century Britain* (New York, 1996).

Benedict, Burton, 'Family Firms and Economic Development', *Southwestern Journal of Anthropology*, 24/1 (Spring 1968), 1–19.

Ben-Porath, Yoram, 'The F-Connection: Families, Friends, and Firms and the Organization of of Exchange', *Population and Development Review*, 6/1 (March 1980), 1–30.

Bentley, Michael, *The Climax of Liberal Politics: British Liberalism in Theory and Practice, 1868–1918* (London, 1987).

——, *Politics without Democracy 1815–1914: Perception and Preoccupation in British Government*, 2nd edn (London, 1996).

——, *Lord Salisbury's World: Conservative Environments in Late-Victorian Britain* (Cambridge, 2001).

Benyon, John, 'Overlords of Empire? British "Proconsular Imperialism" in Comparative Perspective', *Journal of Imperial and Commonwealth History*, 19/2 (May 1991), 164–202.

——, '"Intermediate" Imperialism and the Test of Empire: Milner's "Excentric" High Commission in South Africa', in Donal Lowry (ed.), *The South African War Reappraised* (Manchester, 2000).

Biagini, Eugenio F., *Liberty, Retrenchment and Reform: Popular Liberalism in the Age of Gladstone* (Cambridge, 1992).

Biagini, Eugenio F., and Reid, Alastair J., (eds.), *Currents of Radicalism: Popular Radicalism, Organised Labour and Party Politics in Britain, 1850–1914* (Cambridge, 1991).

Birchenough, Henry, 'Mr. Chamberlain as an Empire Builder', *The Nineteenth Century*, 51 (March 1902), 360–8. .

Blainey, G., 'Lost Causes of the Jameson Raid', *Economic History Review*, 18/2 (1965), 350–66.

Blake, Robert, *The Conservative Party from Peel to Churchill* (New York, 1970).

——, 'The Jameson Raid and "The Missing Telegrams"', in Hugh Lloyd-Jones, Valerie Pearl and Blair Worden, *History and Imagination: Essays in Honour of H. R. Trevor-Roper* (London, 1981).

Blanch, M. D., 'British Society and the War', in Peter Warwick (ed.), *The South African War: The Anglo-Boer War 1899–1902* (Harlow, 1980).

Blewett, Neal, 'Free Fooders, Balfourites, Whole Hoggers: Factionalism within the Unionist Party, 1906–10', *Historical Journal*, 11/1 (1968), 95–124.

——, *The Peers, the Parties and the People: The General Elections of 1910* (London, 1972).

Boyce, D. George (ed.), *The Crisis of British Power: The Imperial and Naval Papers of the Second Earl of Selborne, 1895–1910* (London, 1990).

Boyd, Charles W., *Mr. Chamberlain's Speeches*, 2 vols (Boston, 1914).

Brett, Maurice V. (ed.), *Journals and Letters of Reginald Viscount Esher* (London, 1934).

Briggs, Asa, *Victorian Cities* (London, 1968).

Buckle, George Earle (ed.), *The Letters of Queen Victoria*, 2nd ser. (London, 1928).

Burroughs, Peter, 'Imperial Institutions and the Government of Empire', in *The Oxford History of the British Empire*, vol. 3, *The Nineteenth Century*, ed. Andrew Porter (Oxford, 1999).

Bush, Julia, *Edwardian Ladies and Imperial Power* (London, 2000).

Butler, Jeffrey, 'The German Factor in Anglo-Transvaal Relations' in Prosser Gifford and Wm. Roger Louis (eds.), *Britain and Germany in Africa: Imperial Rivalry and Colonial Rule* (New Haven, 1967).

——, *The Liberal Party and the Jameson Raid* (Oxford 1968).

Cain, P. J. and Hopkins, A. G., *British Imperialism: Innovation and Expansion, 1688–1914* (London, paperback edn, 1994).

Cain, Peter, 'Political Economy in Edwardian England: The Tariff Reform Controversy', in Alan O'Day (ed.), *The Edwardian Age: Conflict and Stability, 1900–1914* (Hamden, Conn., 1979).

Caine, Barbara, 'Beatrice Webb and the "Woman Question"', *History Workshop*, 14 (Autumn 1982), 24–43.

Callaway, Helen and Helly, Dorothy O., 'Crusader for Empire: Flora Shaw/Lady Lugard', in Nupur Chaudhuri and Margaret Strobel (eds.), *Western Women and Imperialism: Complicity and Resistance* (Bloomington, Ind., 1992).

Cannadine, David, 'Apocalypse When? British Politicians and British "Decline" in the Twentieth Century', in Peter Clarke and Clive Trebilcock (eds.), *Understanding Decline: Perceptions and Realities of British Economic Performance* (Cambridge, 1997).

——, 'Joseph Gillott and his Family Firm: The Many Faces of Entrepreneurship', in Kristine Bruland and Patrick O'Brien (eds), *From Family Firms to Corporate Capitalism: Essays in Business and Industrial History in Honour of Peter Mathias* (Oxford, 1998).

Casson, Mark, *The Entrepreneur: An Economic Theory* (Totowa, N.J., 1982).

Cawood, Ian, 'Joseph Chamberlain, the Conservative Party and the Leamington Spa Candidature Dispute of 1895', *Historical Research*, 79/206 (November 2006), 554–77.

Cecil, Robert, Viscount Cecil of Chelwood, *All the Way* (London, 1949).

Chamberlain, Austen, *Politics from Inside: An Epistolary Chronicle, 1906–1914* (London, 1936), 618–19.

Chamberlain, Joseph, 'Old Age Pensions and Friendly Societies', *National Review*, 24 (January 1895), 592–615.

Chamberlain, Joseph, and others, *The Radical Programme (1885)*, with T.H.S. Escott, *The Future of the Radical Party*, ed. and intro. D.A. Hamer (Brighton, 1971).

Chamberlain, M. E., 'The Alexandria Massacre of 11 June 1882 and the British Occupation of Egypt', *Middle Eastern Studies*, 13 (1977), 14–39.

Channing, Francis Alston, *Memories of Midland Politics, 1885–1910* (London, 1918).

Church, R. A., 'The Shoe and Leather Industries', in Roy Church (ed.), *The Dynamics of Victorian Business: Problems and Perspectives to the 1870s* (London, 1980).

Churchill, Winston S., *My Early Life: A Roving Commission* (New York, 1958 edn.).

Coats, A. W., 'Political Economy and the Tariff Reform Campaign of 1903', *Journal of Law and Economics*, 11 (1968), 181–229.

Coetzee, Frans, 'Villa Toryism Reconsidered: Conservatism and Suburban Sensibilities in Late-Victorian Croydon', *Parliamentary History* (1997), 29–47.

Coleman, D. C., 'Historians and Businessmen', in D. C. Coleman and Peter Mathias (eds.), *Enterprise and History: Essays in Honor of Charles Wilson* (Cambridge, 1984).

Collings, Jesse and Green, Sir John L., *The Life of the Right Hon. Jesse Collings* (London, 1920).

Collins, Doreen, 'The Introduction of Old Age Pensions in Great Britain', *Historical Journal*, 8/2 (1965), 246–59.

Cooke, A. B. and Vincent, J. R. (eds.), *Lord Carlingford's Journal: Reflections of a Cabinet Minister, 1885* (Oxford, 1971).

Cooke, A. B. and Vincent, John, *The Governing Passion: Cabinet Government and Party Politics in Britain, 1885–86* (New York, 1974).

Coombes, Annie E., *Reinventing Africa: Museums, Material Culture, and Popular Imagination in Late Victorian and Edwardian England* (New Haven, 1994).

Cornford, John, 'The Transformation of Conservatism in the Late Nineteenth Century', *Victorian Studies*, 7 (September 1963), 35–66.

Crosby, Travis L., *The Two Mr. Gladstones: A Study in Psychology and History* (New Haven, Conn., 1997).

Crouzet, Francois, *The First Industrialists: The Problem of Origins* (Cambridge, 1985) .

Crowder, Michael, *A Short History of Nigeria* (New York, 1962).

Curtis, Charles H., 'Highbury Gardens, Birmingham', *The Gardener's Magazine*, 46 (18 April 1903), 253–6.

Curtis, L. P., *Coercion and Conciliation in Ireland, 1880–1892* (Princeton, N.J., 1963).

Cuthbertson, Greg, 'Preaching Imperialism: Wesleyan Methodism and the War', in David E. Omissi and Andrew S. Thompson, *The Impact of the South African War* (Houndmills, Hants, 2002).

Daunton, Martin, *Trusting Leviathan: The Politics of Taxation in Britain, 1799–1914* (Cambridge, 2001).

Davey, Arthur, *The British Pro-Boers, 1877–1902* (Cape Town, 1978).

Davidoff, Leonore and Hall, Catherine, *Family Fortunes: Men and Women of the English Middle Class, 1780–1850* (London, 1987).

Davies, Peter, 'The Liberal Unionist Party and the Irish Policy of Lord Salisbury's Government, 1886–1892', *Historical Journal*, 18/1 (1975), 85–104.

Davis, Clarence B. and Gowen, Robert J., 'The British at Weihaiwei: A Case Study in the Irrationality of Empire', *The Historian*, 63/1 (Fall 2000), 87–104.

Dean, Britten, 'British Informal Empire: The Case of China', *Journal of Commonwealth and Comparative Politics*, 14/1 (March 1976).

Dilks, David, *Neville Chamberlain: Pioneering and Reform, 1869–1929* (Cambridge, 1984), vol. 1 .

Drus, Ethel, 'A Report on the Papers of Joseph Chamberlain Relating to the Jameson Raid and the Inquiry', *Bulletin of the Institute of Historical Research*, 25 (1952), 33–62.

——, 'The Question of Imperial Complicity in the Jameson Raid', *English Historical Review*, 68 (October 1953).

Dumett, Raymond E., 'The Campaign Against Malaria and the Expansion of Scientific Medical and Sanitary Services in British West Africa, 1898–1919', *African Historical Studies*, 1/2 (1968), 153–97.

——, 'Joseph Chamberlain, Imperial Finance and Railway Policy in British West Africa in the Late Nineteenth Century', *English Historical Review*, 90/355 (April 1975), 287–321.

Dunbabin, J. P. D., 'The Politics of the Establishment of County Councils', *Historical Journal*, 6/2 (1963), 226–52.

——, 'Expectations of the New County Councils, and their Realization', *Historical Journal*, 8/3(1965), 353–79.

Dutton, David, 'Unionist Politics and the Aftermath of the General Election of 1906: A Reassessment', *Historical Journal*, 22/4 (1979), 861–76.

——, *Austen Chamberlain – Gentleman in Politics* (Bolton, 1985).

——, 'His Majesty's Loyal Opposition': The Unionist Party in Opposition, 1905–1915 (Liverpool, 1992).

Eaglesham, Eric, 'Planning the Education Bill of 1902', British Journal of Educational Studies, 9/1 (November 1960), 3–24.

Elletson, D. H., The Chamberlains (London, 1966).

Evans, George Herberton, Jr., 'The Entrepreneur and Economic Theory: A Historical and Analytical Approach', American Economic Review, 39/13 (May 1949), 336–48.

Ferguson, Niall, Empire: The Rise and Demise of the British World Order and the Lessons for Global Power (New York, 2003).

Finn, Margot, After Chartism: Class and Nation in English Radical Politics, 1848–1874 (Cambridge, 1993).

Fitzmaurice, Edmond, The Life of Granville George Leveson Gower, Second Earl of Granville, KG: 1815–1891 (London, 1905).

Fitzroy, Sir Almeric, Memoirs (New York, n.d.).

Flint, John E., Sir George Goldie and the Making of Nigeria (London, 1960).

Fodor, Eugene M. and Farrow, Dana L., 'The Power Motive as an Influence on Use of Power', Journal of Personality and Social Psychology, 37/11 (1979), 2091–7.

Foster, R. F., 'Tory Democracy and Political Elitism: Provincial Conservatism and Parliamentary Tories in the early 1880s', in Art Cosgrove and J. I. McGuire (eds.), Parliament and Community, Historical Studies, 14 (Belfast, 1981).

——, Lord Randolph Churchill: A Political Life (Oxford, 1988), 252–60.

Francis, Richard M., 'The British Withdrawal from the Bagdad Railway Project in April 1903', Historical Journal, 16/1(1973), 168–78.

Fraser, Derek, Urban Politics in Victorian England: The Structure of Politics in Victorian Cities (Leicester, 1976).

Fraser, Peter, 'The Liberal Unionist Alliance: Chamberlain, Hartington, and the Conservatives, 1886–1904', English Historical Review, 77 (January 1962), 53–78.

——, 'Unionism and Tariff Reform: the Crisis of 1906', Historical Journal, 5/2 (1962), 149–66.

——, 'The Unionist Debacle of 1911 and Balfour's Retirement', Journal of Modern History, 35/4 (December 1963), 354–65.

——, Joseph Chamberlain: Radicalism and Empire, 1868–1914 (London, 1966).

Galbraith, John S., 'The "Turbulent Frontier" as a Factor in British Expansion', Comparative Studies in Society and History, 2 (January 1960), 150–68.

——, 'The British South Africa Company and the Jameson Raid', Journal of British Studies, 10/1 (1970), 145–61.

——, Crown and Charter: The Early Years of the British South Africa Company (Berkeley, Cal., 1974).

Gardiner, A. G., The Life of Sir William Harcourt, 2 vols (London, 1923).

Garrard, John A., 'Parties, Members and Voters after 1867: A Local Study', Historical Journal, 20 (1977), 145–63.

——, Leadership and Power in Victorian Industrial Towns, 1830–80 (Manchester, 1983).

Garvin, J. L., The Life of Joseph Chamberlain (London, 1932).

Gerth, H. H. and Mills, C. Wright (eds. and trans.), From Max Weber: Essays in Sociology (New York, 1958).

Gifford, Prosser and Louis, Wm Roger, France and Britain in Africa: Imperial Rivalry and Colonial Rule (New Haven, 1971).

Gilbert, Bentley Brinkerhoff, 'David Lloyd George: Land, the Budget, and Social Reform', American Historical Review, 81/5 (December 1976), 1058–66.

——, David Lloyd George: A Political Life, vol. 1, The Architect of Change, 1863–1912 (Columbus, Ohio, 1987).

Gilmour, David, The Long Recessional: The Imperial Life of Rudyard Kipling (New York, 2002).

Gollin, Alfred, *Balfour's Burden: Arthur Balfour and Imperial Preference* (London, 1965).

Gooch, G. P., *Life of Lord Courtney* (London, 1920).

Goodlad, Graham D., 'The Liberal Party and Gladstone's Land Purchase Bill of 1886', *Historical Journal*, 32/3 (1989), 627–41.

——, 'Gladstone and his Rivals: Popular Liberal Perceptions of the Party Leadership in the Political Crisis of 1885–1886', in Eugenio F. Biagini and Alastair J. Reid (eds), *Currents of Radicalism: Popular Radicalism, Organised Labour and Party Politics in Britain, 1850–1914* (Cambridge, 1991).

Gordon, Peter (ed.), *The Red Earl: The Papers of the Fifth Earl Spencer, 1835–1910* (Northampton, 1981).

Green, Christopher, 'The Growth of Conservatism in Birmingham, 1873–1891' (BA Dissertation, Birmingham University, 1971).

——, 'Birmingham's Politics, 1873–1891: The Local Basis of Change', *Midland History*, 2/2 (1973), 84–98.

Green, E. H. H., 'Radical Conservatism: The Electoral Genesis of Tariff Reform', *Historical Journal*, 28/3 (1985), 667–92.

——, *The Crisis of Conservatism: The Politics, Economics, and Ideology of the British Conservative Party, 1880–1914* (London, 1995).

——, 'The Political Economy of Empire, 1880–1914', in *The Oxford History of the British Empire*, vol. 3, *The Nineteenth Century*, ed. Andrew Porter (Oxford, 1999).

Greenall, R. L., 'Popular Conservatism in Salford, 1868–1886', *Northern History*, 9 (1974), 123–38.

Grenville, J. A. S., *Lord Salisbury and Foreign Policy: The Close of the Nineteenth Century* (London, 1964).

Griffiths, Peter, 'Pressure Groups and Parties in Late Victorian England: The National Education League', *Midland History*, 3/3 (Spring 1976), 191–205.

Grigg, John, *Lloyd George: The People's Champion, 1902–1911* (Berkeley, 1978).

Gunn, Simon, *The Public Culture of the Victorian Middle Class: Ritual and Authority and the English Industrial City* (Manchester, 2000).

Gwynn, Stephen, *The Letters and Friendships of Sir Cecil Spring Rice: A Record* (London, 1930).

Hamer, D. A., *John Morley: Liberal Intellectual in Politics* (Oxford, 1968).

——, *Liberal Politics in the Age of Gladstone and Rosebery: A Study in Leadership and Policy* (Oxford, 1972).

Hancock, W. K,. *Smuts: The Sanguine Years, 1870–1919* (Cambridge, 1962).

Hanes, W. Travis, III, 'Railway Politics and Imperialism in Central Africa, 1889–1953', in Clarence B. Davis and Kenneth E. Wilburn, Jr (eds.), with Ronald E. Robinson, *Railway Imperialism* (New York, 1991).

Hanham, H. J., *Elections and Party Management: Politics in the Time of Disraeli and Gladstone*, 2nd edn (Hassocks, Sussex, 1978).

Hargreaves, John D., 'British and French Imperialism in West African, 1885–1898', in Prosser Gifford and Wm. Roger Louis, *France and Britain in Africa: Imperial Rivalry and Colonial Rule* (New Haven, 1971).

——, 'The European Partition of West Africa', in J. F. A. Ajayi and Michael Crowder (eds), *History of West Africa* (New York, 1973).

Harrington, Peter, 'Pictorial Journalism and the Boer War: The London Illustrated Weeklies', in John Gooch (ed.), *The Boer War: Direction, Experience and Image* (London, 2000).

Hawkins, Angus and Powell, John (eds.), *The Journal of John Wodehouse, First Earl of Kimberley for 1862–1902*, Camden 5th ser., 9 (1997).

Hayes, William A., *The Background and Passage of the Third Reform Act* (New York, 1972).

Headlam, Cecil (ed.), *The Milner Papers: South Africa, 1897–1899* (London, 1931).

Hebert, Robert F. and Link, Albert N., *The Entrepreneur: Mainstream Views and Radical Critiques* (New York, 1982) .

Helly, Dorothy O. and Callaway, Helen, 'Journalism as Active Politics: Flora Shaw, *The Times and South Africa*', in Donal Lowry (ed.), *The South African War Reappraised* (Manchester, 2000).

Hennock, E. P., *Fit and Proper Persons: Ideal and Reality in Nineteenth-Century Urban Government* (Montreal, 1973).

——, *British Social Reform and German Precedents: The Case of Social Insurance 1880–1914* (Oxford, 1987).

Herrick, Francis, 'The Origins of the National Liberal Federation', *Journal of Modern History*, 17/2 (June 1945), 116–29.

Hewins, W. A. S., *The Apologia of an Imperialist: Forty Years of Empire Policy* (London, 1929).

Heyck, Thomas William, *The Dimensions of British Radicalism: The Case of Ireland, 1874–95* (Urbana, 1974).

Hicks Beach, Lady Victoria, *Life of Sir Michael Hicks Beach* (London, 1932).

Hills, Philip, 'Division and Cohesion in the Nineteenth-Century Middle Class: The Case of Ipswich 1830–1870', *Urban History Yearbook* (1987), 42–50.

Hind, R. J., *Henry Labouchere and the Empire, 1880–1905* (London, 1972).

Holland, Bernard, *The Life of Spencer Compton, Eighth Duke of Devonshire*, 2 vols (London, 1911).

Holli, Melvin G., 'Joseph Chamberlain and the Jameson Raid: a Bibliographical Survey', *Journal of British Studies*, 3 (May 1964), 152–66.

Hooper, Alan, 'From Liberal-Radical to Conservative Corporatism: The Pursuit of "Radical Business" in "Tory Livery": Joseph Chamberlain, Birmingham, and British Politics, 1870–1930', in Richard Bellamy (ed.), *Victorian Liberalism: Nineteenth-century Political Thought and Practice* (London, 1990).

Hopkins, A. G., 'Economic Imperialism in West Africa: Lagos, 1880–92', *Economic History Review*, 21/3 (December 1968), 580–606.

——, 'The Victorians and Africa: A Reconsideration of the Occupation of Egypt, 1882', *Journal of African History*, 27/2 (1986), 363–91.

Howard, C. H. D., 'Joseph Chamberlain and the "Unauthorized Programme"', *English Historical Review*, 65 (1950), 477–91.

——, 'Joseph Chamberlain, Parnell and the Irish "Central Board" Scheme, 1884–5', *Irish Historical Review*, 8/32 (September 1953), 324–61.

——, *A Political Memoir, 1880–92* (London, 1953).

Howe, Anthony, *Free Trade and Liberal England, 1846–1946* (Oxford, 1997).

——, *The Cotton Masters, 1830–1860* (Oxford, 1984).

Humphreys, R. A., 'Anglo-American Rivalries and the Venezuela Crisis of 1895', *Transactions of the Royal Historical Society*, 5th ser., 17 (1967), 131–64.

Hurst, M. C., 'Joseph Chamberlain, the Conservatives and the Succession to John Bright', *Historical Journal*, 7/1 (1964), 64–93.

Hurst, Michael, *Joseph Chamberlain and Liberal Reunion: The Round Table Conference of 1887* (London, 1967).

——, 'Reviews of Books', *English Historical Review*, 86/4 (1971), 816–22.

Israel, Kali, 'French Vices and British Liberties: Gender, Class and Narrative Competition in a Late Victorian Sex Scandal', *Social History*, 22/1 (January 1997), 1–26.

——, *Names and Stories: Emilia Dilke and Victorian Culture* (New York, 1999).

Ives, Eric, Drummond, Diane, and Schwarz, Leonard, *The First Civic University: Birmingham 1880–1980* (Birmingham, 2000).

Jackson, Patrick, *The Last of the Whigs: A Political Biography of Lord Hartington, Later Eighth Duke of Devonshire (1833–1908)* (Cranbury, N.J., 1994).

——, *Harcourt and Son: A Political Biography of Sir William Harcourt, 1827–1904* (Madison, 2004).

Jay, Richard, *Joseph Chamberlain: A Political Study* (Oxford, 1981).

Jenkins, Roy, *Victorian Scandal: A Biography of the Right Honourable Gentleman Sir Charles Dilke* (New York, 1965).

Jenkins, T. A., *Gladstone, Whiggery, and the Liberal Party, 1874–1886* (Oxford, 1988).

——, 'Hartington, Chamberlain and the Unionist Alliance, 1886–1895', *Parliamentary History*, 11/1 (1992), 129–30.

——, *The Liberal Ascendancy, 1830–1886* (New York, 1994).

Jones, Andrew, *The Politics of Reform 1884* (Cambridge, 1972).

Jones, Carole Seymour, *Beatrice Webb: Woman of Conflict* (London, 1992).

Jones, Linda, 'Public Pursuit of Private Profit? Liberal Businessmen and Municipal Politics in Birmingham, 1865–1900' *Business History*, 25/3 (November 1983), 240–59.

Judd, Denis, *Balfour and the British Empire: A Study in Imperial Evolution* (London, 1968).

——, *Radical Joe: A Life of Joseph Chamberlain* (Cardiff, 1993).

Judd, Denis and Surridge, Keith, *The Boer War* (New York, 2003).

Kanya-Forstner, A. S., 'Military Expansion in the Western Sudan – French and British Style', in Prosser Gifford and Wm Roger Louis, *France and Britain in Africa: Imperial Rivalry and Colonial Rule* (New Haven, 1971).

Katz, Elaine N., 'Outcrop and Deep Level Mining in South African before the Anto-Boer War: Re-examining the Blainey Thesis', *Economic History Review*, 48/2 (1995), 304–28.

Kennedy, Paul M., 'German World Policy and the Alliance Negotiations with England, 1897–1900', *Journal of Modern History*, 45/4 (December 1973), 605–625.

——, *The Rise of the Anglo-German Antagonism, 1860–1914* (London, 1980).

Kesner, Richard M., 'Builders of Empire: The Role of the Crown Agents in Imperial Development, 1880–1914', *Journal of Imperial and Commonwealth History*, 5/3 (May 1977), 310–30.

——, *Economic Control and Colonial Development: Crown Colony Financial Management in the Age of Joseph Chamberlain* (Westport, Conn., 1981).

Kilby, Peter, *Entrepreneurship and Economic Development* (New York, 1971).

Koditschek, Theodore, 'The Dynamics of Class Formation in Nineteenth-Century Bradford', in A. L. Beier, David Cannadine, and James M. Rosenheim (eds), *The First Modern Society: Essays in English History in Honour of Lawrence Stone* (Cambridge, 1989).

——, *Class Formation and Urban-Industrial Society: Bradford, 1750–1850* (Cambridge, 1990).

Koss, Stephen (ed.), *The Anatomy of an Antiwar Movement: The Pro-Boers* (Chicago, 1973).

Kubicek, Robert V., *The Administration of Imperialism: Joseph Chamberlain at the Imperial Office* (Durham, N.C., 1969).

Laing, Diana Whitehill, *Mistress of Herself* (Barre, Mass., 1965).

Lambert, John, 'Chiefship in Early Colonial Natal, 1843–1879', *Journal of Southern African Studies*, 21/2 (June 1995), 269–85.

Langford, J. A., *Modern Birmingham and Its Institutions* (Birmingham, 1873).

Laqueur, Thomas Walter, *Religion and Respectability: Sunday Schools and Working Class Culture, 1780–1850* (New Haven and London, 1976).

Lawrence, Jon, 'Popular Politics and the Limitations of Party: Wolverhampton, 1867–1900', in Eugenio F. Biagini and Alastair J. Reid (eds), *Currents of Radicalism: Popular Radicalism, Organized Labour and Party Politics in Britain, 1850–1914* (Cambridge, 1991).

——, 'Class and Gender in the Making of Urban Toryism, 1880–1914', *English Historical Review*, 108/428 (July 1993), 629–52.

——, *Speaking for the People: Language and Popular Politics in England, 1867–1914* (Cambridge, 1998).

Lockhart, J. G. and Woodhouse, C. M., *Cecil Rhodes: The Colossus of Southern Africa* (New York, 1963).

Loughlin, James, *Gladstone, Home Rule and the Ulster Question, 1882–93* (Dublin, 1986).

Lukes, Steven, *Power: A Radical View* (London, 1974).

——, *Essays in Social Theory* (New York, 1977).

——, 'Power and Authority', in Tom Bottomore and Robert Nisbet (eds), *A History of Sociological Analysis* (New York, 1978).

Lynch, Patricia, *The Liberal Party in England 1885–1910: Radicalism and Community* (Oxford, 2003).

Lyons, F. S. L., *Ireland Since the Famine*, 2nd edn (London, 1973).

——, *Charles Stewart Parnell* (New York, 1977).

McClelland, David C. and Watson, Robert I., Jr, 'Power Motivation and Risk-Taking Behavior', *Journal of Personality*, 41/1(March, 1973), 121–39.

McClintock, Anne, *Imperial Leather: Race, Gender and Sexuality in the Colonial Contest* (New York, 1995).

McCreedy, H. W., 'The Revolt of the Unionist Free Traders', *Parliamentary Affairs*, 16/2 (1962), 188–206.

MacDonald, Robert H., *The Language of Empire: Myths and Metaphors of Popular Imperialism, 1880–1918* (Manchester, 1994).

McGill, Barry, 'Francis Schnadhorst and Liberal Party Organization', *Journal of Modern History*, 34/1 (March 1962), 19–39.

Mackay, Ruddock F., *Balfour: Intellectual Statesman* (Oxford, 1985).

MacKenzie, John M. (ed.), *Imperialism and Popular Culture* (Manchester, 1986).

—— (ed.), *Popular Imperialism and the Military* (Manchester, 1992).

MacKenzie, Norman and MacKenzie, Jeanne (eds.), *The Diary of Beatrice Webb*, vol. 1, *1873–1892: 'Glitter Around and Darkness Within'* (Cambridge, Mass., 1982).

McLeod, Hugh, *Religion and Society in England, 1850–1914* (New York, 1996).

Macnicol, John, *The Politics of Retirement in Britain, 1878–1948* (Cambridge, 1998).

McWilliam, Rohan, *Popular Politics in Nineteenth-Century England* (London, 1998).

Malchow, H. L., *Gentlemen Capitalists: The Social and Political World of the Victorian Businessman* (Stanford, Cal., 1992).

Mallalieu, W. C., 'Joseph Chamberlain and Workmen's Compensation', *Journal of Economic History*, 10 (May 1950), 45–57.

Marks, Shula and Trapido, Stanley, 'Lord Milner and the South African State', *History Workshop*, 8 (Autumn, 1979), 50–80.

——, 'Lord Miner and the South African State Reconsidered', in Michael Twaddle (ed.), *Imperialism, the State and the Third World* (London, 1992).

Marrison, Andrew, 'Businessmen, Industries and Tariff Reform in Great Britain, 1903–1930', *Business History*, 25/2 (July 1983), 148–78.

——, *British Business and Protection, 1903–1932* (Oxford, 1996).

Marsh, Peter T., '"A Working Man's Representative": Joseph Chamberlain and the 1874 Election in Sheffield', in J. M. W. Bean (ed.), *The Political Culture of Modern Britain: Studies in Memory of Stephen Koss* (London, 1978).

——, 'Tearing the Bonds: Chamberlain's Separation from the Gladstonian Liberals, 1885–6', in Bruce L. Kinzer (ed.), *The Gladstonian Turn of Mind: Essays Presented to J. B. Conacher* (Toronto, 1985).

——, *Joseph Chamberlain: Entrepreneur in Politics* (New Haven, Conn., 1994).

Marshall, Alfred, *Principles of Economics: An Introductory Volume*, 8th edn. (London, 1938).

Matthew, H. C. G., *The Liberal Imperialists: The Ideas and Politics of a Post-Gladstonian Elite* (Oxford, 1973).

—— (ed.), *The Gladstone Diaries* (Oxford, 1986).

——, *Gladstone, 1809–1898* (Oxford, 1997).

Maycock, Sir Willoughby, KCMG, *With Mr. Chamberlain in the United States and Canada, 1887–88* (London, 1914).

Maylan, Paul, *Rhodes, the Tswana, and the British: Colonialism, Collaboration, and Conflict in the Bechuanaland Protectorate, 1885–1899*, Contributions in Comparative Colonial Studies, 4 (Westport, Conn., 1980).

Meacham, Standish, 'Lives in Politics', *Journal of Modern History*, 62 (March 1990), 89–100.

Mendelsohn, Richard, 'Blainey and the Jameson Raid: The Debate Renewed', *Journal of Southern African Studies*, 6/1 (October 1979), 157–170.

Mitchell, Timothy, *Colonising Egypt* (Cambridge, 1988).

Moody, T. W. and Hawkins, Richard, with Margaret Moody (eds.), *Florence Arnold-Forster's Irish Journal*, (Oxford, 1988).

Morley, John, *The Life of William Ewart Gladstone* (London, 1912), Shilling Edition.

Morley, John, 1st Viscount Morley of Blackburn, *Recollections* (New York, 1917).

Morris, R. J., 'The Middle Class and the Property Cycle during the Industrial Revolution', in T. C. Smout (ed.), *The Search for Wealth and Stability: Essays in Economic and Social History Presented to M. W. Flinn* (London, 1979), 91–113.

——, 'Voluntary Societies and British Urban Elites, 1780–1850: An Analysis', *Historical Journal*, 27/1 (1983), 95–118.

Munson, J. E. B., 'The Unionist Coalition and Education, 1895–1902', *Historical Journal*, 20/3 (September 1977), 607–45.

Murray, Bruce K., *The People's Budget 1909/10: Lloyd George and Liberal Politics* (Oxford, 1980).

Nasson, Bill, *The South African War, 1899–1902* (London, 1999),.

Nenadic, Stana, 'The Small Family Firm in Victorian Britain', *Business History*, 35/4 (October 1993), 86.

Nevill, Ralph (ed.), *The Reminiscences of Lady Dorothy Nevill* (London, 1907).

Newbury, C. W., 'The Tariff Factor in Anglo-French West African Partition', in Prosser Gifford and Wm. Roger Louis, *France and Britain in Africa: Imperial Rivalry and Colonial Rule* (New Haven, 1971).

Nicholls, David, *The Lost Prime Minister: A Life of Sir Charles Dilke* (London, 1995).

Nord, Deborah Epstein, *The Apprenticeship of Beatrice Webb* (Amherst, Mass., 1985).

Obichere, Boniface I., *West African States and European Expansion: The Dahomey-Niger Hinterland, 1885–1898* (New Haven, 1971).

Osterhammel, Jurgen, 'Britain and China, 1842–1914', in *The Oxford History of the British Empire*, vol. 3, *The Nineteenth Century*, ed. Andrew Porter (Oxford, 1999).

Pakenham, Elizabeth, *Jameson's Raid* (London, 1960).

——, *Jameson's Raid: The Prelude to the Boer War* (London, 1982).

Parsons, Neil, *King Khama, Emperor Joe, and the Great White Queen: Victorian Britain through African Eyes* (Chicago, 1998).

Pelling, Henry, *Social Geography of British Elections, 1885–1910* (London, 1967).

Penrose, Edith Tilton, *The Theory of the Growth of the Firm* (Oxford, 1959).

Perham, Margery, *Lugard: The Years of Adventure, 1858* (London, 1956).

Perham, Margery, and Bull, Mary (eds.), *The Diaries of Lord Lugard* (London, 1963).

Petrie, Sir Charles, *Walter Long and his Times* (London, 1936).

Phillips, Gregory D., *The Diehards: Aristocratic Society and Politics in Edwardian England* (Cambridge, Mass., 1979).

——, 'Lord Willoughby de Broke and the Politics of Radical Toryism, 1909–1914', *Journal of British Studies*, 20/1 (Fall 1980), 205–24.

Phillips, Paul T., *The Sectarian Spirit: Sectarianism, Society, and Politics in Victorian Cotton Towns* (Toronto, 1982).

Phillips, Richard, *Mapping Men and Empire: A Geography of Adventure* (London, 1997).

Phimister, I. P., 'Rhodes, Rhodesia and the Rand', *Journal of Southern African Studies*, 1/1 (October 1974), 74–90.

Pollak, Robert A., 'A Transaction Cost Approach to Families and Households', *Journal of Economic Literature*, 23 (June 1985), 581–608.

Pollard, Sidney, *The Genesis of Modern Management: A Study of the Industrial Revolution in Great Britain* (London, 1965).

——, 'Reflections on Entrepreneurship and Culture in European Societies', *Transactions of the Royal Historical Society*, 5th ser., 40 (1990), 153–73.

Porter, A. N., *The Origins of the South African War: Joseph Chamberlain and the Diplomacy of Imperialism, 1895–99* (New York, 1980).

Porter, Andrew, 'Lord Salisbury, Mr. Chamberlain and South Africa, 1895–9', *Journal of Imperial and Commonwealth History*, 1 (1972), 3–26.

——, 'Sir Alfred Milner and the Press, 1897–1899', *Historical Journal*, 16/2 (1973), 323–39.

——, 'The South African War (1899–1902): Context and Motive Reconsidered', *Journal of African History*, 31/1 (1990), 43–57.

Powell, David, *The Edwardian Crisis: Britain 1901–14* (London, 1996).

Price, Richard, *An Imperial War and the British Working Class: Working Class Attitudes and Reactions to the Boer War, 1899–1902* (London, 1972).

Pugh, Martin, *The Tories and the People, 1880–1935* (London, 1985).

——, 'Popular Conservatism in Britain: Continuity and Change, 1880–1987', *Journal of British Studies*, 27/3(July 1988), 254–82.

Pyrah, G. B., *Imperial Policy and South Africa, 1902–10* (Oxford, 1955), 23–4.

Quinault, Roland, 'John Bright and Joseph Chamberlain', *Historical Journal*, 28/3 (1985), 623-46.

——, 'Joseph Chamberlain: A Reassessment', in T. R. Gourvish and Alan O'Day (eds.), *Late Victorian Britain* (New York, 1988).

Ramsden, John, *An Appetite for Power: A History of the Conservative Party since 1830* (London, paperback edn., 1999), 186.

Reader, W. J., 'Businessmen and their Motives', in D. C. Coleman and Peter Mathias (eds.), *Enterprise and History: Essays in Honor of Charles Wilson* (Cambridge, 1984).

Readman, Paul A., 'The 1895 General Election and Political Change in Late Victorian England', *Historical Journal*, 42/2 (1999), 467–93.

Reid, Stuart J. (ed.), *Memoirs of Sir Wemyss Reid, 1842–1885* (London, 1905).

Reigeluth, George A., 'Municipal Reform in Birmingham, England: 1873–1876' (Johns Hopkins University, PhD Dissertation, 1981).

Rempel, Richard A., *Unionists Divided: Arthur Balfour, Joseph Chamberlain and the Unionist Free Traders* (Newton Abbot, 1972).

——, 'Lord Hugh Cecil's Parliamentary Career, 1900–1914: Promise Unfulfilled', *Journal of British Studies* 11/2 (May 1972), 104–30.

Richards, N. J., 'Religious Controversy and the School Boards, 1870–1902', *British Journal of Educational Studies* 18/2 (June 1970), 180–96.

Roberts, A. W., 'Leeds Liberalism and Late-Victorian Politics', *Northern History*, 5 (1970), 131–56.

Roberts, Andrew, *Salisbury: Victorian Titan* (London, 1999).

Robinson, Ronald and Gallagher, John, *Africa and the Victorians: The Climax of Imperialism* (New York, 1968).

Rose, Kenneth, *The Later Cecils* (New York, 1975).

Rotberg, Robert I., *The Founder: Cecil Rhodes and the Pursuit of Power* (New York, 1988).

Russell, A. K., *Liberal Landslide: The General Election of 1906* (Newton Abbot, 1973).

Russell, George W., *One Look Back* (New York, 1912).

Ryan, James R., *Picturing Empire: Photography and the Visualization of the British Empire* (Chicago, 1997).

Sanderson, G. N., 'The Origins and Significance of the Anglo-French Confrontation at Fashoda, 1898', in Prosser Gifford and Wm. Roger Louis, *France and Britain in Africa: Imperial Rivalry and Colonial Rule* (New Haven, 1971).

Saul, S. B., 'The Economic Significance of "Constructive Imperialism"', *Journal of Economic History*, 17/2 (June 1957), 173–92.

Saunders, Christopher and Smith, Iain R., 'Southern Africa, 1795–1910', in *The Oxford History of the British Empire*, vol. 3, *The Nineteenth Century*, ed. Andrew Porter (Oxford, 1999).

Schreuder, D. M., *The Scramble for Southern Africa, 1877–1895: The Politics of Partition Reappraised* (Cambridge, 1970).

Schumpeter, Joseph A., *The Theory of Economic Development* (Cambridge, Mass., 1934).

Searle, G. R., *The Quest for National Efficiency: A Study in British Politics and Political Thought, 1899–1914* (London, paperback edn., 1990 [Berkeley, Cal., 1971]).

——, *The Liberal Party: Triumph and Disintegration, 1886–1929* (New York, 1992).

——, *Entrepreneurial Politics in Mid-Victorian Britain* (Oxford, 1993).

——, *A New England? Peace and War 1886–1918* (Oxford, 2004).

Seed, John, 'Unitarianism, Political Economy and the Antinomies of Liberal Culture in Manchester, 1830–50', *Social History*, 7/1 (January 1982), 1–25.

——, 'Theologies of Power: Unitarianism and the Social Relations of Religious Discourse, 1800–50', in R. J. Morris (ed.), *Class, Power and Social Structure in British Nineteenth-Century Towns* (Leicester, 1986), 108–56.

Seely, J. R., *The Expansion of England: Two Courses of Lectures* (Boston, 1883).

Self, Robert C., *The Austen Chamberlain Diary: The Correspondence of Sir Austen Chamberlain with his Sisters Hilda and Ida, 1916–1937*, Camden 5th ser., 5 (Cambridge, 1995).

——, *Neville Chamberlain: A Biography* (Aldershot, Hants, 2006).

Sennett, Richard, *Authority* (New York, 1980).

Shannon, Richard, *Gladstone: Heroic Minister, 1865–1898* (London, 1999).

——, *The Age of Disraeli, 1868–1881: The Rise of Tory Democracy* (London, 1992).

——, *The Age of Salisbury, 1881–1902: Unionism and Empire* (London, 1996).

Shore, Miles F., 'Cecil Rhodes and the Ego Ideal', *Journal of Interdisciplinary History*, 10 (1979), 249–65.

Sillery, Anthony, *Founding a Protectorate: History of Bechuanaland, 1885–1895* (London, 1965).

Simon, Alan, 'Joseph Chamberlain and the Unauthorized Programme' (D.Phil., Oxford, 1970).

——, 'Joseph Chamberlain and Free Education in the Election of 1885', *History of Education*, 2 (1973), 56–78.

——, 'Church Disestablishment as a Factor in the General Election of 1885', *Historical Journal*, 18/4 (1975), 791–820.

Smith, Barbara M. D., 'The Galtons of Birmingham: Quaker Gun Merchants and Bankers, 1702–1831', *Business History*, 9/2 (July 1967), 132–50.

Smith, Dennis, *Conflict and Compromise: Class Formation in English Society, 1830–1914: A Comparative Study of Birmingham and Sheffield* (London, 1982).

Smith, Iain R., *The Origins of the South African War, 1899–1902* (London, 1996).

Smith, Robert, *Schools, Politics and Society: Elementary Education in Wales, 1870–1902* (Cardiff, 1999).

Spencer, John Poyntz, Earl, *The Red Earl: The Papers of the Fifth Earl Spencer, 1835–1910*, 2 vols, ed. Peter Gordon (Northampton, 1981).

Spies, S. B., *Methods of Barbarism? Roberts and Kitchener and Civilians in the Boer Republics, January 1900–May 1902* (Cape Town, 1977).

Stansky, Peter, *Ambitions and Strategies: The Struggle for the Leadership of the Liberal Party in the 1890s* (Oxford, 1964).

Steele, E. D., *Lord Salisbury: A Political Biography* (London, 1999).

Stockwell, A. J., 'Power, Authority and Freedom', in P. J. Marshall (ed.), *The Cambridge Illustrated History of the British Empire* (Cambridge, 1996).

Stokes, Eric, 'Milnerism', *Historical Journal*, 5/1 (1962), 47–60.

Supple, Barry, 'Fear of Failing: Economic History and the Decline of Britain', *Economic History Review*, 47/3 (1994), 441–58.

Surridge, Keith Terrance, *Managing the South African War, 1899–1902: Politicians and Generals* (Woodbridge, Suffolk, 1998).

Sykes, Alan, *Tariff Reform in British Politics, 1903–1913* (Oxford, 1979).

Tamarkin, Mordechai, 'Milner, the Cape Afrikaners, and the Outbreak of the South African War: From a Point of Return to a Dead End', *Journal of Imperial and Commonwealth History*, 25/3 (September 1997), 392–414.

——, 'The Cape Afrikaners and the British Empire from the Jameson Raid to the South African War', in Donal Lowry (ed.), *The South African War Reappraised* (Manchester, 2000).

Taylor, A. F., 'The History of the Birmingham School Board, 1870–1903' (MA Thesis, University of Birmingham, 1955).

Taylor, A. J. P., *Essays in English History* (London, 1976).

Tholfsen, Trygve R., 'The Artisan and the Culture of Early Victorian Birmingham', *University of Birmingham Historical Journal*, 4/2 (1954), 146–66 .

——, 'The Origins of the Birmingham Caucus', *Historical Journal*, 2/2 (1959), 161–84.

Thompson, A. P. D., 'The Chamberlain Memorial Tower, University of Birmingham', *University of Birmingham Historical Journal*, 4/2 (1954), 167–79.

Thompson, Andrew S., 'Tariff Reform: An Imperial Strategy, 1903–1913', *Historical Journal*, 40 (1997), 1033–54.

——, 'Imperial Propaganda during the South African War', in Greg Cuthbertson, Albert Grundlingh, and Mary-Lynn Suttie (eds.), *Writing a Wider War: Rethinking Gender, Race, and Identity in the South African War, 1899–1902* (Athens, Ohio, 2002).

Thompson, F. M. L., *The Rise of Respectable Society: A Social History of Victorian Britain, 1830–1900* (Fontana Paperback, 1988).

——, *Gentrification and the Enterprise Culture: Britain 1780–1980* (Oxford, 2001).

Thorold, A. L., *Life of Henry Labouchere* (New York, 1913).

Tosh, John, *A Man's Place: Masculinity and the Middle-Class Home in Victorian England* (New Haven, 1999).

Trainor, Bernard, *Black Country Elites: The Exercise of Authority in an Industrialized Area, 1830–1900* (Oxford, 1993).

Trentmann, Frank, 'The Transformation of Fiscal Reform: Reciprocity, Modernization, and the Fiscal Debate within the Business Community in Early Twentieth-century Britain', *Historical Journal*, 39/4 (1996), 1005–48.

van der Poel, Jean, *The Jameson Raid* (Cape Town, 1951).

Vincent, John (ed.), *The Crawford Papers: The Journals of David Lindsay, twenty-seventh Earl of Crawford and tenth Earl of Balcarres, 1871–1940, during the years 1892 to 1940* (Manchester, 1984).

Walker, Eric A., *W. P. Schreiner: A South African* (London, 1937).

Warhurst, Philip R., *Anglo-Portuguese Relations in South-Central Africa, 1890–1900* (London, 1962).

Watts, Duncan, *Joseph Chamberlain and the Challenge of Radicalism* (London, 1992).

Weaver, Michael, 'The Birmingham Bull Ring Riots of 1839: Variations on a Theme of Class Conflict', *Social Science Quarterly*, 78/1(March 1997), 137–48.

Wilburn, Kenneth E., Jr, 'Engines of Empire and Independence: Railways in South Africa, 1863–1916', in Clarence B. Davis and Kenneth E. Wilburn, Jr (eds.), with Ronald E. Robinson, *Railway Imperialism* (New York, 1991).

Will, H. W., 'Colonial Policy and Economic Development in the British West Indies, 1895–1903', *Economic History Review*, 23/1 (April 1970), 129–47.

Wilson, Charles, 'The Entrepreneur in the Industrial Revolution in Britain', *Explorations in Entrepreneurial History*, 7/3 (February 1955), 129–45.

Wilson, Monica and Thompson, Leonard (eds.), *The Oxford History of South Africa*, vol. 2 (Oxford, 1971).

Winter, David G., *The Power Motive* (New York, 1973).

——, 'The Power Motive in Women – and Men', *Journal of Personality and Social Psychology*, 54/3 (1988), 510–19.

——, 'A Revised Scoring System for the Power Motive', in Charles P. Smith (ed.), *Motivation and Personality: Handbook of Thematic Content Analysis* (Cambridge, 1992), 311–24.

——, 'Power Motivation Revisited', in Charles P. Smith (ed.), *Motivation and Personality: Handbook of Thematic Content Analysis* (Cambridge, 1992), 301–10.

Witherell, Larry L., *Rebel on the Right: Henry Page Croft and the Crisis of British Conservatism, 1903–1914* (Delaware, 1997).

Wormell, Deborah, *Sir John Seely and the Uses of History* (Cambridge, 1980).

Young, Kenneth, *Arthur James Balfour: The Happy Life of the Politician, Prime Minister, Statesman, and Philosopher, 1848–1930* (London, 1963).

Young, L. K., *British Policy in China, 1895–1902* (Oxford, 1970).

Zebel, Sydney H., 'Joseph Chamberlain and the Genesis of Tariff Reform', *Journal of British Studies*, 7/1 (November 1967), 131–57.

INDEX